How to Write
for the World of Work

How to Write for the World of Work

THOMAS E. PEARSALL
University of Minnesota

DONALD H. CUNNINGHAM
Morehead State University

Holt, Rinehart and Winston
New York   Chicago   San Francisco   Atlanta   Dallas
Montreal   Toronto   London   Sydney

Library of Congress Cataloging in Publication Data

Pearsall, Thomas E
  How to write for the world of work.

Bibliography: p.
Includes index.
  1. Technical writing. 2. Commercial correspondence.
3. Business report writing. I. Cunningham, Donald H.,
joint author. II. Title.
HF5721.P39   651.7′5   77-24498

ISBN 0–03–040371–5

8 9 0 1 2 032 9 8 7 6 5 4 3 2 1

To Anne and Pat

Preface

This is a book about writing for the world of work. We believe that effective correspondence and reports are the basic tools upon which every business depends. No matter how effective their technology may be, businesses that do not communicate successfully within and without their walls, that do not maintain accurate written records, will slip into ineffectuality and failure. We believe also that writing for the world of work is as important and challenging as any other kind of writing. We echo the sentiments of the noted Shakespearean scholar and teacher, G. B. Harrison, who wrote

> The most effective elementary training I ever received was not from masters at school but in composing daily orders and instructions as staff captain in charge of the administration of seventy-two miscellaneous military units. It is far easier to discuss Hamlet's complexes than to write orders which ensure that five working parties from five different units arrive at the right place at the right time equipped with the proper tools for the job. One soon learns that the most seemingly simple statement can bear two meanings and that when instructions are misunderstood the fault usually lies with the original order.[1]

To another professor, John A. Walter of the University of Texas, we owe the expression of the theme uppermost in our minds while we wrote this book. Professor Walter said, "Scientists and engineers are concerned, when they write, with presenting information to a specific body of readers for a specific purpose."[2] We believe *all* occupational writers have these basic concerns. Our version of the statement—*occupational writing presents specific information to a specific audience for a specific purpose*—is stated frequently throughout this book. Whether we are talking about correspondence or written and oral reports, we are talking about the basic three elements of communication: message . . . audience . . . purpose.

Perhaps it is only fair, then, that we tell you here in the preface what our message, audience, and purpose are.

---

[1]*Profession of English* (New York: Harcourt, Brace and World, 1962): 149.

[2]"Confessions of a Teacher of Technical Writing," *The Technical Writing Teacher* 1, no. 1 (1973):3–9.

Message

Our message, our specific information, is about occupational writing. We break it into its two major components—correspondence and reports. In reports, we also cover oral reports. We break these components down into their day-to-day tasks, such as employment letters, customer relations letters, periodic reports, and proposals. We tell you as carefully and precisely as we can how to accomplish each of these tasks. We use real examples, many produced exactly as they originally appeared in some occupational writing situation. Some we have modified slightly to make them more generally applicable. We have designed this book to have the feel of the real world.

Audience

For what audience have we designed this book? We have written for the student in pre-professional training and for the established professional. We have visualized such persons for ourselves. They are practical and industrious, willing to work when shown what needs to be done. They already know or will quickly see the need for good communication in any occupation. But being of a practical turn of mind, they want to learn good communication practice in a realistic way—a way longer on real-life communication situations than on theory. If you feel we have described you accurately, then you are our audience.

Purpose

Our intent is to lead you from the simpler forms of correspondence on to the challenging complexity of analytical reports—to reports like proposals that combine information-giving with analysis and both with persuasion. By going through this sequence, you should end up with more than the information needed to go about any particular writing task. You should have a grasp of basic principles. You should be able to see, for example, that the principles of persuasion involved in a letter of application are related to the same skills in a sales letter or in a proposal. When you see that, then you'll know how to plan a persuasive strategy, whatever the communication situation. With a genuine competence in the basic skills, you'll have the confidence and ability to face a communication situation not covered in this book. When you can, then we will have fulfilled our purpose. If we have analyzed our audience correctly, it is your purpose, too.

● ● ●

We wish to thank the following, who read the manuscript and made constructive comments: William G. Clark, Margot A. Haberhorn, John S. Harris, Frances Blosser Maguire, L. Dan Richards, Arlo Stoltenberg, Hilbert B. Williams.

T.E.P.
D.H.C.

Contents

How to Write
for the World of Work

INTRODUCTION

Writing for the World of Work

Occupational writing is writing that links people together in the world of work. It links businessperson to businessperson, management to labor, business to government, engineer to technician, buyer to seller. Occupational writing provides the records that industry and government need to function year by year. Basically, occupational writing consists of correspondence and reports. A look at our table of contents will suggest the variety: request and response letters . . . customer relations letters . . . informational reports . . . proposals. Because reports must frequently be made orally, we have included a section on this method of presentation as well. Communication is important in the world of work; no one escapes the necessity for taking part in it. Certainly, few educated people escape without producing a share of the writing done at their place of work.

Your previous writing courses may have dealt with personal or literary writing. You'll find occupational writing considerably different. Read a few lines of John Donne's "The Bait":

> Come live with me, and be my love,
> And we will some new pleasures prove,
> Of golden sands, and crystal brooks,
> With silken lines, and silver hooks.

Donne is making a personal artistic statement with skill and beauty that are quite beyond most of us.

Look now at a piece of occupational writing:

> The CSAH 15 intersection is a standard diamond interchange. CSAH 15 will be constructed to provide four traffic lanes (two in each direction), crossing over I–94 on a single bridge. Washington County has already constructed two lanes of CSAH 15 and has acquired the right of way for the additional two lanes in anticipation of the construction of I–94.

The technician who wrote that paragraph was making an impersonal statement to convey a specific piece of information. The style is not particularly artistic, but it is competent. The paragraph is easily understood by its intended audience. To make sure it would be understood, the writer has included a graphic that we have reproduced in Figure 1. The paragraph represents a style and a method of writing within the grasp of most of us.

Occupational writing is a craft, not an art form. Like carpentry and knitting, it can be learned even by those of us who have no particular artistic skill. As a craft, occupational writing has several characteristics: a heavy reliance on formulas, a wide use of graphics, and an intense awareness of purpose and audience. By way of introducing you further to occupational writing, we explore briefly these three characteristics.

FORMULAS

As you read the chapters that follow, you will frequently find formulas to follow in writing a certain kind of letter or report. For example, when you are writing a sales letter, you'll be told to remember AIDA—*attention, interest, desire, action*. That is, your sales letter must first gain the attention of the reader. Next, it should arouse the reader's interest in the product, then his or her desire for it. Finally, the letter must move the reader to action.

These formulas may seem arbitrary; in fact, they follow function quite closely. That is, over the years, the use or function of a letter or report has indicated that certain information is always needed and that a certain organization will best display that information. For example, a proposal is a proposition for providing some product or service for a price. What are some of the things the buyers of the product or service will want to know? They will want to know exactly what the seller is to furnish, how much it will cost, and when it will be delivered. They will want information about the people furnishing the product or service—such things as experience, education, and proof of reliability. The function of proposals, therefore, has caused them to be organized in ways that make such information easily accessible to the reader. The readers of proposals look for headings such as *Cost, Schedule of Delivery, Personnel,* and so forth. They expect to find specifically needed information in expected locations, and formula writing assures that they do.

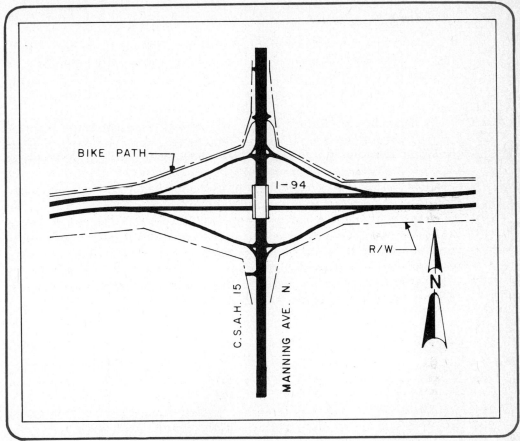

Figure 1 Illustration of diamond interchange. (*Draft Environmental Impact Statement for Interstate 94,* Minnesota Department of Highways, 1976, p. 68)

Formulas also release you from the anxiety of wondering how to organize a letter or report. You'll know how because you'll have a formula for it. You'll have to find the needed information and write it plainly and clearly, but you'll have a map to follow.

Finally, speed is essential in the world of work. Business can't wait while the writer waits for inspiration. Letters must be answered promptly. Reports must be written while their information is still useful. Formulas help make this kind of speed possible.

None of this is to say our or anyone else's formulas are sacred and inflexible. All formulas change and improve over the years, and no formula may be exactly right for the task you have in hand. But formulas will usually be a comfort to the beginning writer. Before changing them too much, you should remember their utility for the reader who will be looking for specific information in an expected location.

GRAPHICS

Occupational writers rely on graphics of all sorts to help them deliver their message. They see no particular value in saying something in words if an illustration or graph will make the concept clearer. Also, tables displaying needed statistical information will usually save the writer words and the reader time.

The illustration reproduced in Figure 1 makes it clear that the highway intersection portrayed is a *diamond* interchange. And even the proverbial thousand words wouldn't describe your authors as well as Figure 2 does (that's Cunningham with the beard).

Figure 3 clarifies where local tax dollars come from and go to in a way that would be difficult to do in prose.

The table in Figure 4 makes the total information it displays far more accessible than would an essay giving the same information. And putting your information in tables frees you to interpret the material important to your purpose. For example, in Figure 4 you might point out that in the years from 1950 to 1971, the income generated by medical and health services expanded to almost eight times its original volume.

Figure 2 Your authors.

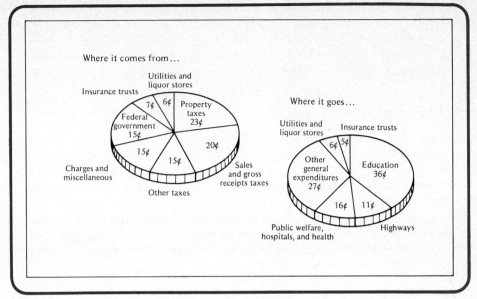

Figure 3 The state and local government dollar, 1970. (U.S. Bureau of the Census)

NATIONAL INCOME ORIGINATING IN DISTRIBUTION AND SERVICE INDUSTRIES: 1950 TO 1971

In millions of dollars. Prior to 1960, excludes Alaska and Hawaii. Data represent net value added at factor costs.

INDUSTRY	1950	1955	1960	1965	1968	1969	1970	1971
Wholesale and retail trade	**40,943**	**52,270**	**64,396**	**84,302**	**106,069**	**114,811**	**121,188**	**130,780**
Wholesale trade	13,307	17,841	23,126	30,341	38,394	41,872	44,715	47,426
Retail trade	27,636	34,429	41,270	53,961	67,675	72,939	76,473	83,354
Services	**21,768**	**31,131**	**44,480**	**64,076**	**85,721**	**94,706**	**102,661**	**110,589**
Hotels and other lodging places	1,388	1,717	2,111	2,788	3,744	4,051	4,204	4,531
Personal services	3,021	3,661	4,608	5,993	7,265	7,384	7,417	7,471
Miscellaneous business services	1,684	3,011	5,093	8,413	11,490	12,980	13,888	14,241
Automobile repair, services, and garages	864	1,172	1,762	2,450	3,106	3,449	3,621	3,913
Miscellaneous repair services	665	873	1,105	1,501	1,866	2,092	2,121	2,236
Motion pictures	866	979	894	1,205	1,535	1,465	1,551	1,564
Amusement and recreation services, except motion pictures	788	1,121	1,661	2,221	2,783	2,863	3,239	3,515
Medical and other health services	4,412	7,097	10,731	16,256	23,250	26,604	29,775	33,490
Legal services	1,344	1,926	2,636	4,069	5,114	5,631	6,426	7,411
Educational services	1,109	1,524	2,449	4,191	5,975	6,648	7,292	8,049
Nonprofit membership organizations	1,803	2,675	3,870	5,306	6,955	7,762	8,411	9,063
Miscellaneous professional services	1,252	2,324	3,761	5,719	8,009	9,092	9,886	10,146
Private households	2,572	3,051	3,799	3,964	4,629	4,685	4,830	4,959

Source: U.S. Bureau of Economic Analysis, *The National Income and Product Accounts of the United States, 1929-1965* and *Survey of Current Business*, July 1972.

Figure 4 U.S. Government income table.

Because we consider graphics to be so important to occupational writing, we have not segregated a discussion of them in a single chapter. Instead, we have discussed and illustrated them wherever they are important to the kind of writing being considered. And we urge you always to be alert to the possibility of using an illustration to carry part of your message.

MESSAGE, AUDIENCE, AND PURPOSE

The unifying theme of this book is that occupational writing presents specific information to a specific audience for a specific purpose. To put it another way: an occasion for a piece of occupational writing always exists. The occasion includes the message to be transmitted, the receiver of the message, and the purpose for the transmission.

Occupational writing is usually generated by a specific piece of information that has to be transmitted: *Your bicycle has been repaired; please pick it up. . . . We missed your payment for last month's statement. . . . Congratulations on your new job. . . . We attended the convention in Seattle. . . . This is how you build the 86204 Heat Exchanger. . . . Your insurance costs are rising.* Occupational writing is not generated for the joy of personal expression, although you may enjoy doing it. In the world of work, you write when you have something to say.

When you prepare to send your message, you must think of your audience. Messages are not merely sent—they are sent to someone. You must always be concerned with these questions: "Who will read my report?" "Why will they read it?" "What will they want from it?" "What do they already know about the subject?" "What is left to tell them?" Writers of sales letters try to fix in their minds the typical buyer of the product being sold. If you are writing a letter of application, you should know something about the employer. How else can you emphasize the skills the employer needs?

Suppose you have a new product, a heat exchanger for getting more heat from an open fireplace into the house. You would explain the heat exchanger one way to the bankers from whom you plan to borrow the money needed to manufacture the product. They need to know only enough technical details to be sure the product will work. Mostly, bankers will want convincing evidence that there is a market for your product. You would explain the heat exchanger another way to the people who will manufacture it for you. They need step-by-step instructions about the manufacturing process. You will explain your heat exchanger still another way to the people to whom you intend to sell it. They will want to know what the heat exchanger will do for them in their homes. How much, for example, could it save them in fuel bills?

As you have perhaps noticed, purpose is usually closely meshed with the audience chosen to receive the message. You write a certain way for bankers so that the bankers can get the information they need. But you go to bankers in the first place because your purpose is to get a loan.

It is not always quite that simple. Sometimes writers don't recognize the multiple purposes that should govern their work. Suppose, for example, you are writing to give someone bad news, perhaps that his automobile insurance rates are going up. If your purpose were only to announce the new rates, you could send out a printed table showing the increase. But you will have another purpose as well. Your additional purpose will include keeping the policyholder with the company. To do this you must maintain good will. Therefore, you must do more than merely announce the rate hike. You will have to justify the hike—to show how conditions beyond your company's control have forced it. You would probably take the time to mention the good service your company has given in the past and plans to give in the future. None of this justification and explanation would be necessary if your purpose were only to announce the rate hike.

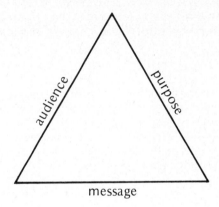

Message . . . audience . . . purpose . . . the basic triangle of occupational communication. We will remind you of it often in these pages, because the bringing together of these three elements is really what this book is all about.

SUGGESTIONS FOR APPLYING YOUR KNOWLEDGE

Any textbook can supply only a limited number of examples to illustrate its subject matter. Yet, for most of us, an ounce of example is worth a pound of theory. Therefore, we urge you to begin gathering examples of occupational writing that will help you to grasp the concepts in this book. Examples will bring the use of formulas and graphics to life. Examine them to see how they have been written to meet a specific purpose for a specific audience. Not all the examples you find will be equally good, so they'll provide you with ample material for discussion as well as instruction. There are many potential sources of examples.

Government Publications

Thousands of publications pour out from the federal government every year on a vast number of subjects. *Selected U.S. Government Publications*, probably available in your library, lists many of the more useful ones. Many are quite reasonably priced. For example, 65 cents buys *Simple Home Repairs*, which tells how to fix leaking faucets, faulty electric plugs, and so forth. This booklet furnishes numerous examples of process and mechanism descriptions. An example of an informational report is *Social Security Inequities Against Women*, which costs 55 cents. Your library probably has a collection of government publications you can use at no cost at all.

Your state university almost certainly has an extension service. This service prints fact sheets, pamphlets, and booklets on a wide variety of subjects such as choosing insecticides, detecting oak wilt, choosing a television set, and planning a meeting. Other state agencies, such as the highway department, also publish informational pamphlets of many kinds.

Magazines and Professional Journals

Your library should have a good collection of magazines and professional journals. These publications represent an enormous reservoir of examples. The advertisements in professional and trade journals, for example, are often fine examples of high-level persuasion and also process and mechanism description. A magazine like *Consumer Reports* contains numerous examples of analytical essays written to compare and contrast various kinds of consumer goods.

Company Sources

Companies of any significant size must publish a good deal of material. They can often provide you with examples of handbooks, sales literature, proposals, and so forth. They have printed forms for such things as accident and trip reports. And, of course, business and government agencies depend for their very existence on the kinds of correspondence we describe in this book. If you have legitimate access to such correspondence, it will provide you with both good and, unfortunately, bad examples for evaluation and discussion.

A Note About the "Suggestions"

We have not supplied the traditional exercises at the ends of our chapters. We believe that only the classroom instructor, perhaps in collaboration with the students, can design the exact exercises needed to fit the needs of any particular class. This belief stems directly from our basic principle that successful communication brings specific information to a specific audience for a specific purpose. Therefore, we have provided not exercises but "Suggestions for Applying Your Knowledge," addressed to both student and instructor. In these sections we suggest a wide range of possible methods and sources that can be used to construct the out-of-class and in-class exercises needed.

UNIT ONE
Correspondence

CHAPTER 1
Basic Principles of Correspondence

The professionalism we wish to emphasize in this book is illustrated well in correspondence. There *is* a difference between school and the world of work: school is more forgiving. A teacher may give a grade of C or even B to a letter that is good except for three misspelled words. In business, the letter may be totally unsatisfactory. It may lose you the job you seek or the order you want. It may convince someone you are irresponsible. The letters that get the order or the job or that explain the details of a transaction so well that no further questions are needed are successful professional efforts. Letters that do not accomplish these goals are unsuccessful, no matter how close they come.

To help you reach these goals, in this chapter we explain some basic correspondence strategies and give you some common formats for letters and memorandums.

BASIC STRATEGIES

Chapters 2 through 5 analyze letters that we have classified as inquiry and response letters, employment letters, customer relations letters, and persuasive letters. Another way of viewing letters is as good-news letters and bad-news letters. Most letters, we're happy to say, are good-news letters, even those you would not ordinarily think of as such. Every letter that moves business forward, even if it's only a routine notice that a shipment is on the way, is a good-news letter. Any letter that slows business—for example, a letter denying a request or postponing an expected shipment—is bad news. The basic strategies we outline here for these two types of letters will be followed closely in all the letters discussed in this unit.

Good News

When you get good news, what do you want first—the good news or the details behind the good news? If someone writes to say that you have landed a job you were after, the first thing you really want to know is, "You have the job." You'll be delighted to read in the rest of the letter why you got the job and on what date you report to work. So point number one in good-news letters is *announce the big news first:*

```
We're delighted to tell you that we want you to come
to work for us.
```

```
Your bicycle is repaired and is ready for pickup.
```

```
Congratulations on your promotion to head of
merchandising.
```

And we really do mean that the big news comes first. Don't delay it with trivialities.

After the reader has been pleasantly moved by the big news, provide the details. Dates, prices, explanations, analyses—whatever is needed—become the second part of your letter.

For the third part of your letter, do something that salespeople call "reselling the customer." Recently, we bought an appliance to seal plastic bags air and water tight. As the salesperson was wrapping our package, she said: "You are really going to be delighted by this. It's so easy to use. And the money you save by freezing leftovers in these bags will pay for the appliance in a couple of months." She had already made her sale. What she was doing was reselling the customer. She wanted us to go away happy, convinced that we hadn't thrown away our money on a useless gadget. You end your good-news letter in a similar manner:

```
We know you'll be happy working for Julia Alm. She's
a fine person.
```

```
For your one-stop convenience, we carry a full line
of bicycle supplies.
```

```
You'll make a great supervisor.
```

The letter writers and the appliance salesperson have identical goals—*to achieve good will*. We have numerous short-term goals in our correspondence—to order, to request, to sell, to move to action. But our long-range goal must always be to create and maintain good will. The good-news strategy helps to do precisely that. So remember:

1. Report the good news first.
2. Supply the necessary details.
3. Resell the customer.

Bad News

A small number of letters bring bad news. Examples are the letter denying a request for an adjustment or the collection letter for an overdue bill. For these letters a different strategy makes sense. Rather than announcing your big news first, delay it a bit and open with a buffer statement of some sort. Buffer statements should not be self-serving soft soap, but genuine attempts to express regret or to seek common ground. If you write, "We share your concern for the problem you have raised," you should mean it.

After your buffer statement provide details and analysis that support the bad news that is coming. After the analysis is complete , announce the bad news:

A complete refund of your money does not seem justified.

Third, you present an alternative if you possibly can:

We will be happy, however, to discuss a partial refund with you.

Finally, you close in a friendly way:

Thank you for drawing this problem to our attention.

You hope to persuade your reader that your bad news is unavoidable. At the same time you want to retain good will. Obviously, to do this your analysis has to be detailed and persuasive, and it must precede the bad news. So remember the order:

1. Buffer statement
2. Explanation and analysis
3. Bad news
4. Alternative
5. Friendly close

You Attitude

Whether you are the bearer of good news or bad, remember to maintain a "you attitude." Consider your reader's needs and viewpoint at all times. This is easier said than done. All of us view the world through our own eyes, shaded by our own concerns. Another problem is the nature of letter writing. Unlike face-to-face communication, in letter writing there is no face across from you when you send your message. You lack the immediate feedback of a raised eyebrow, yawn, scowl, or smile. The writer of the successful letter must be sensitive in the extreme.

If you know the people you are writing to, try to anticipate their reactions. Think about what pleases them and what annoys them. If you don't know them, you probably won't go too far wrong by asking yourself how you would react in a similar situation. Statements that would make you feel abused or annoyed are likely to do the same for someone else.

You can also follow the example of the writers of successful sales letters who construct in their imaginations a person typical of the people who are to receive the sales message. Are you selling a resort vacation designed for youthful men and women? You imagine someone young, middle income, responsive to cool breezes, warm sun, comfortable clothes, and good food—someone distrustful of too much artificiality but not totally immune to it. With this reader firmly in mind, you then pitch your sales message at *someone*, not into empty space.

Remember that all of us respond most favorably when we are convinced our own interests are being served. Every company is in business to turn a profit, yet to stay in business they must provide a service or product that people need or desire. In correspondence, you emphasize the service, the product, the need or the desire, and not the profit. You don't say things like

```
Pay your bill because we need the money.
```

Rather you say,

```
Prompt payment of bills protects your good credit
rating.
```

Less obviously, we are often misled by our own skill and hard work into making statements of no concern to our readers. Consider this approach:

```
We have created with considerable expense and time a
new fire detector for use in private homes.
```

All wrong. The readers don't care about your time and expense. Also, while the readers may live in "private homes," they won't relate to such a nonspecific term. Compare this approach:

```
You'll sleep more easily tonight and every night when
you and your family are protected from smoke and
flame by our new battery-operated fire detector.
```

In the second example you are dealing directly with your readers' concerns, not yours. Always in correspondence ask yourself what your readers' needs and problems are. Use that knowledge to give your message from the readers' point of view, not yours. Face the reality that people will seldom do something merely for your benefit; they will usually act when convinced that the action benefits them.

FORMATS

Business letters must be neat and follow consistent formats. They must be typed. Sloppiness and inconsistency will be taken as indicators of carelessness and a lack of professionalism on your part. Look now at Figures 1-1 to 1-4. In each we have demonstrated an acceptable format and indicated the conventional spacing and punctuation. Choose a format you like and follow it. We comment here in the text about a few major points concerning the letter and its parts.

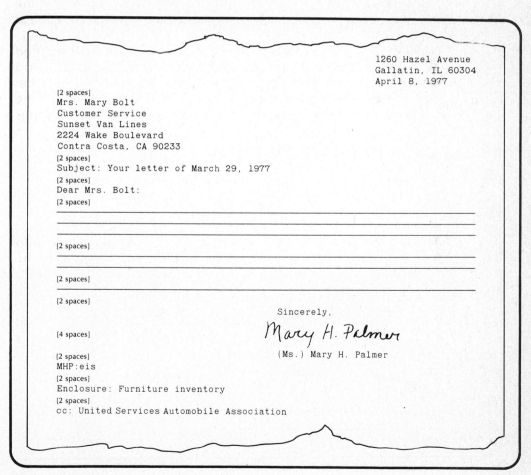

Figure 1-1 Block format.

```
                                          1492 Columbus Avenue
                                          Belmont, OH 45420
                                          October 4, 1977
[2 spaces]
Public Documents
Distribution Center
Pueblo, CO 81009
[2 spaces]
Re: Shipment of Index of National Park System
[2 spaces]
Gentlemen:
[2 spaces]
         _____
         _____
         _____
[2 spaces]
         _____
         _____
         _____
[2 spaces]
         _____
         _____
[2 spaces]
                              Sincerely,

[4 spaces]                    Robert G. Cortez

                              Robert G. Cortez
[2 spaces]
Enclosures (2)
[2 spaces]
cc: Superintendent of Documents
```

Figure 1-2 Modified block format.

5200 Yadkin Road
Fayetteville, VA 22212
26 February 1977

Mr. James W. Whittaker, General Manager
Recreational Equipment, Inc.
1225-11th Avenue
Seattle, WA 98122

Dear Mr. Whittaker:
[2 spaces]
_____
_____

[2 spaces]
_____
_____
_____

[2 spaces]
_____
_____

[2 spaces]
Sincerely,

Gerard B. Hewlett   [4 spaces]

Gerard B. Hewlett
[2 spaces]
cc: Anne K. Chimato

Figure 1-3 Full block format.

```
[person receiving letter]
Miss Janice C. Huer                    -2-                    April 8, 1977
[2 spaces]
_____
_____
_____

[2 spaces]
_____
_____

[2 spaces]
Sincerely,

John R. Gilmore                           [4 spaces]

John R. Gilmore
Highway Department Technician
[2 spaces]
JRG:hrw
```

Figure 1-4 Continuation page.

Stationery

Go to the campus bookstore or a stationery store and choose a good quality white bond paper of about 20-lb. weight—a paper that looks good and feels good in your hand. Don't buy cheap, lightweight paper. It's a false economy.

Typewriter

Type with a clean typewriter in good repair. Dirty type produces fuzzy, broken letters. Choose a standard typeface such as pica or elite. For business correspondence, don't choose a face such as italic. It will be considered unprofessional. If you can't type well enough to produce a clean, evenly printed letter, hire someone to type important letters, such as letters of application, for you. Better still, learn to type well. It will be a skill that will be useful all your life.

Margins

Letters should never look crowded or off-balance on the page. Leave generous margins, at least one inch on either side and one and one-half inches on top and bottom. For a short letter, come down farther on the page so that your letter doesn't hang at the top like a balloon on a string.

Heading

The heading includes your complete address but not your name. Do not abbreviate words like *street* or *avenue*. You may abbreviate the state, using the Postal Service's new two-letter abbreviations (see the list below). The date is part of the heading. It may be written April 9, 1977 or 9 April 1977. Do not write numbers as *9th* or *3rd*. Use the number by itself.

Alabama	AL	Montana	MT
Alaska	AK	Nebraska	NE
Arizona	AZ	Nevada	NV
Arkansas	AR	New Hampshire	NH
California	CA	New Jersey	NJ
Colorado	CO	New Mexico	NM
Connecticut	CT	New York	NY
Delaware	DE	North Carolina	NC
District of Columbia	DC	North Dakota	ND
Florida	FL	Ohio	OH
Georgia	GA	Oklahoma	OK
Guam	GU	Oregon	OR
Hawaii	HI	Pennsylvania	PA
Idaho	ID	Puerto Rico	PR
Illinois	IL	Rhode Island	RI
Indiana	IN	South Carolina	SC
Iowa	IA	South Dakota	SD
Kansas	KS	Tennessee	TN
Kentucky	KY	Texas	TX
Louisiana	LA	Utah	UT
Maine	ME	Vermont	VT
Maryland	MD	Virginia	VA
Massachusetts	MA	Virgin Islands	VI
Michigan	MI	Washington	WA
Minnesota	MN	West Virginia	WV
Mississippi	MS	Wisconsin	WI
Missouri	MO	Wyoming	WY

Inside Address

Set up the inside address as you do your own address in the heading. Do include your correspondent's name, however, and any titles. The titles *Mr.*, *Mrs.*, *Ms.*, and *Dr.* are abbreviated. Most other titles are written out in full, such as *Professor* and *Sergeant*.

Subject Line

A subject or reference line is more and more frequently used in business correspondence. Usually placed above the salutation—see Figures 1-1 and 1-2—it is preceded by either the term *Subject* or *Re* followed by a colon. Using a subject line allows your correspondents or their secretaries to locate previous correspondence on the same subject. It also saves your readers from trite, trivial openers like "With reference to your letter of June 27, 1977."

Salutation

We are still slaves to convention in the salutation and use *Dear* _____. Most people accept the *Dear* as a convention. They don't take it seriously, and yet they would probably notice and even resent its absence. If at all possible, use a name in the salutation: *Dear Ms. Jones, Dear Dr. White, Dear Professor Souther,* and so forth. If names are not known to you, *Gentlemen,* without the *Dear,* is acceptable for most business correspondence. Less frequently, if you are writing to one person whose name you don't know, you may use *Dear Sir* or *Dear Madam.* Use a colon after the salutation.

It seems inappropriate to many people that general business salutations continue to be male, such as "Gentlemen" and "Dear Sir." After all, many of the people handling company correspondence are women. No universally accepted substitute has been found as yet. Some people have begun to address the department directly, as in "Dear Credit Department" or "Dear Consumer Complaints." Other people simply forget the "Dear" and use "Good Day" as their opener. Others use "Ladies and Gentlemen" or "To Whom It May Concern." Use your imagination, and you can probably avoid sexism and still maintain a courteous, businesslike manner.

In routine correspondence it may not matter very much which of these alternatives you use. But in important correspondence do everything you reasonably can to get an exact name to address. By the way, there is no reason why you can't use a first name for people with whom you are normally on a first-name basis.

Body

In the body, single-space the paragraphs and double space between them. In very short letters of several lines, you may double-space everything. In the modified block format, indent the paragraphs five spaces. In the other formats, do not. Keep sentences and paragraphs short. Average 14–17 words a sentence and don't let paragraphs run more than four or five lines. Generous use of white space in a letter invites readers in. Cramped, crowded spacing shuts them out.

Complimentary Close

Use a conventional close such as *Sincerely* or *Sincerely yours* for people you don't particularly know. For people with whom you have some friendship, you may close with *Warm regards, With best wishes,* and so forth. Capitalize only the first word in the close. Follow the close with a comma.

Signature Block

Type your name four spaces below the complimentary close. (Women without honorific titles such as *Dr.* or *Professor* should indicate the mode of address they prefer in parentheses to the left of their typed name—*Ms., Mrs.,* or *Miss.* A married woman should use her own first name, not her husband's.) Below the typed name, put your business title if you have one. Sign your name legibly above your typed name.

Special Notations

Three special notations—identification, enclosure, and carbon copy—are frequently made below the signature block. Their order and spacing are indicated in Figures 1-1 to 1-4.

Identification   When a typist rather than the writer types a letter, an identification line is used. Usually the writer's initials are upper-case letters while the typist's are lower-case, as in

```
AJB:whm
```

Enclosure   The enclosure line tells the reader that something is enclosed with the letter. The format of the line and the amount of information given varies. Typical lines might be

```
Enclosure
Enclosures (3)
Encl: Medical examination form
```

Carbon copy   Business courtesy and ethics dictate that you inform anyone you write when someone else is receiving a copy of the letter. The notification requires a simple notation such as the following:

```
cc: Ms. Janet Kimberly
```

Continuation Page

The format for one or more continuation pages is shown in Figure 1-4. Use plain white bond for page 2 and beyond; do not use letterhead stationery. Plan your spacing so that at least two or three lines of the body are carried over to the continuation page.

Envelope

The envelope format is shown in Figure 1-5. Letters sent to business people will sometimes quite legitimately be opened by their coworkers, for example, when the person addressed is ill or on vacation. The assumption is that the letter concerns company business, and business goes on regardless of who is present to conduct it. *Therefore,* if you are writing a personal or

confidential letter to a person at a business address, mark it with the words
<u>PERSONAL</u> or <u>CONFIDENTIAL</u> directly under the address on the envelope.

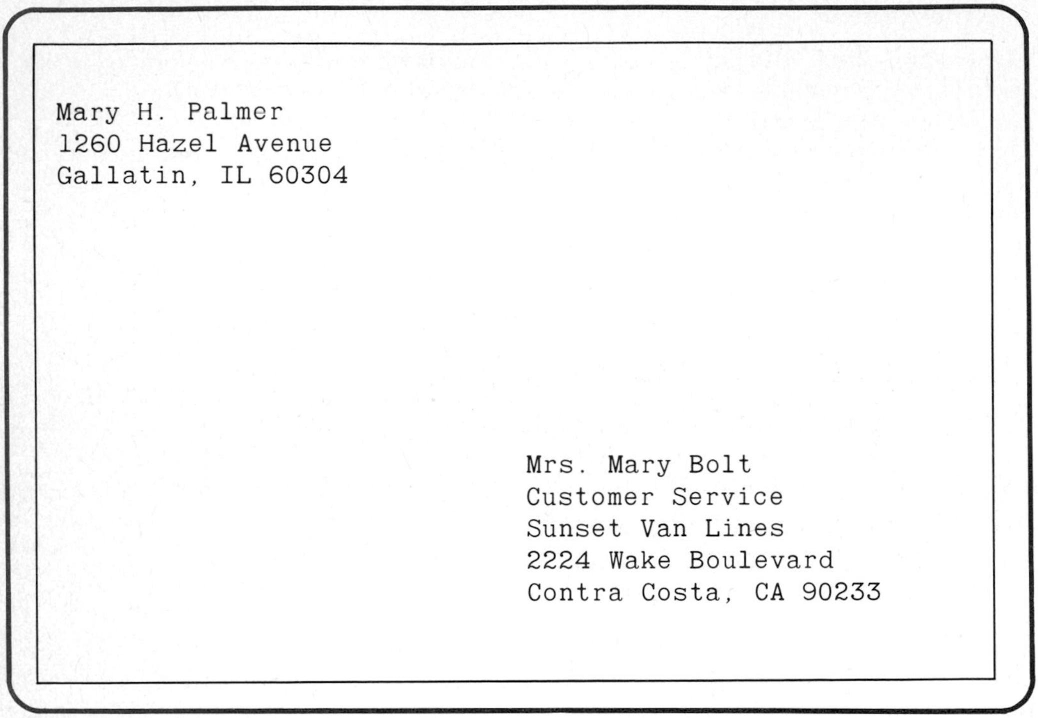

```
Mary H. Palmer
1260 Hazel Avenue
Gallatin, IL 60304




                        Mrs. Mary Bolt
                        Customer Service
                        Sunset Van Lines
                        2224 Wake Boulevard
                        Contra Costa, CA 90233
```

Figure 1-5   Envelope.

MEMORANDUMS

Letters are external business correspondence that carry messages outside
of an organization. Memorandums—usually called memos—are internal
business correspondence. They carry messages inside an organization.
They go from office to office, branch to branch, supervisor to subordinate,
and so forth. Like letters, memos have many uses. For example, you may
use them to confirm a conversation, clarify a previous message, request
information, supply information, congratulate someone, announce
changes in policy, report meetings, and transmit documents.

Most organizations have preprinted memo forms that differ from the
forms used for letters. Generally, these forms contain the organization's
name, but not address, and guide words for *To, From, Subject,* and *Date.*
See Figures 1-6 and 1-7. Because of the preprinted format, memos don't
require a salutation or signature. Frequently, though, people write their

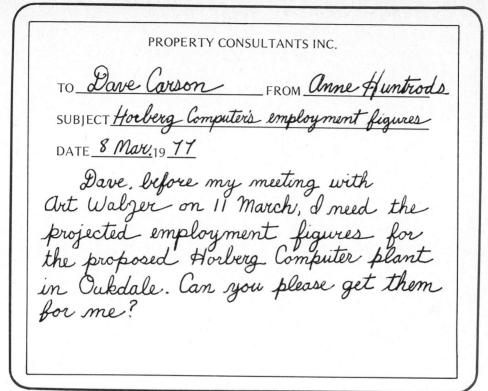

PROPERTY CONSULTANTS INC.

TO *Dave Carson* FROM *Anne Huntrods*

SUBJECT *Horberg Computer's employment figures*

DATE *8 Mar.* 19 *77*

Dave, before my meeting with Art Walzer on 11 March, I need the projected employment figures for the proposed Horberg Computer plant in Oakdale. Can you please get them for me?

Figure 1-6 Handwritten memo of inquiry.

initials next to their names on the *From* line. To speed correspondence and to avoid taking a secretary's time, many organizations allow short memos to be handwritten—a good reason for developing a legible handwriting.

Few fundamental differences exist between writing the body of a memo and any other piece of correspondence. You must be as clear and well organized as you would be in a letter. Maintain the "you attitude." Use "good news" and "bad news" strategies.

Because of the frequent contacts that people in the same organization often have, however, memos can be somewhat different from letters. Often, the person receiving the memo knows all about a situation except for the point being raised in the memo. Consequently, no long explanations are necessary. The memo's writer can come immediately to the point. Often, too, friendships that exist within an organization allow for more informality than you might use in external correspondence. Do not allow either of these points, however, to mislead you into thinking memos need not be both complete and courteous. Missing information or a tone too brisk and abrupt can be as annoying in a memo as in a letter. Figures 1-6 and 1-7 show you two typical memos.

PROPERTY CONSULTANTS INC.

TO ___Anne Huntrods___ FROM ___Dave Carson___

SUBJECT ___Horberg Computer employment figures___

DATE ___10 Mar___ 19___77___

    With staged development beginning in 1977 or 1978, Horberg Computer Company estimates employment at the Oakdale site will be approximately 600 in 1979, 8,500 in 1990, and 20,000 by 1998.

    My source for this info is the Horberg Computer Company Site Environmental Assessment submitted to the state Environmental Quality Board, 20 April 1975.

Figure 1-7 Typed memo of reply.

SUGGESTIONS FOR APPLYING YOUR KNOWLEDGE

For each kind of letter discussed in Chapters 2 through 5 we suggest specific applications at the ends of those chapters. For the moment, we suggest that you prepare for your study of correspondence by gathering examples of business letters. Most members of the class have probably received various kinds of selling letters. Many students generate correspondence with department stores, book clubs, and similar institutions. Some students already work and have legitimate access to business correspondence.

The staff members of your school send and receive an enormous amount of correspondence. People such as the dean, bursar, placement officer, maintenance superintendent, and admissions officer do much of their business by mail, so much so that they often use form letters. Some members of the class can go to these school officials and ask permission to reproduce some samples of their correspondence for classroom use. The names of people involved should be removed, of course, when letters are reproduced.

Look around you and gather as many examples of real letters and memos as you can. They will be invaluable in your study of occupational letter writing.

When you have the letters and memos in class, you can use them as the basis for discussion. What is your honest opinion of them? Do they work? Is their information complete? Is their tone right? Have they used a good-news or bad-news approach? Have their writers sufficiently considered audience and purpose as well as the information they intended to convey?

CHAPTER 2

Inquiry and Response Letters

Much of the routine correspondence you'll write will ask someone to do something for you: provide information, perform a service, send materials and equipment. These are inquiry and request and order letters. In addition, you are likely to write letters that respond to such letters. Although these letters are routine, you'll need to know how to write them well, because the quality of these letters reflects your and your organization's ability to communicate clearly.

INQUIRY AND REQUEST LETTERS

Even though inquiry and request letters arise from almost any situation and deal with almost any subject, their function is always the same—they begin a correspondence cycle by asking one or more questions or making one or more requests. If successful, they obtain a favorable response from the persons to whom you send them.

Writing inquiry and request letters may at first appear to be easy. But many things can go wrong. Your question might be worded so vaguely that your readers will have to guess at what you want. You might ask so bluntly for something that requires a special favor that your readers will be offended. You might even forget to include your complete return address.

There are two keys to writing a successful inquiry or request letter. First is the ability to ask questions and to phrase requests so clearly (yet politely) that you receive the exact information or services you want; second is the ability to determine whether your question or request is reasonably routine or involves a special favor from your reader.

Make Your Inquiry or Request Clear

If questions or requests are vague or general, readers will have little way of knowing exactly what is wanted. The result is likely to be an incomplete or unnecessary response, causing extra letters to be sent back and forth. Look how vague this request is:

```
Dear Sir:

Would you please send me information about your new
fuel pump.
```

What kind of information? Assuming that the recipient can figure out which new fuel pump the inquirer would like to know about, he or she might state the price, assure that it will fit any engine, and explain how soon it can be delivered. But what if the inquirer already knows those things but needs to know where and how the fuel pump can be mounted? Result: a second exchange of letters.

Making the inquiry or request specific reduces the risk of the recipient's arriving at the wrong idea of what is needed.

```
Dear Sir:

      Can your new adjustable pressure electric fuel pump
   type AK306J be used with the Continental O-470R engine,
   and can it be mounted in any position?
```

This illustrates another way to clarify: by using questions rather than statements to make inquiries. The question mark underscores the question and implies that an answer is expected.

A third way to clarify more complicated inquiries is to tabulate the information needed. Such a series of questions might read like this:

```
Dear Sir:

Please give me the following information about your
new adjustable pressure electric fuel pump type
AK306J:

   1. Can it be mounted anywhere and in any position?

   2. Does it come with mounting bracket?

   3. Does it operate independently of the engine?
```

4. How many pounds of pressure does it adjust to?

5. Is the flow adequate for a Continental 0-470R engine?

Tabulating questions or requests encourages specific phrasing that will provide easy reference for the recipient.

Decide Whether Your Inquiry or Request Is Routine or Special

Inquiry and request letters are of two kinds, and you need to know which kind you're writing. If your inquiry or request will benefit the reader as much as it will you, your letter will be easy to write, because the reader will be predisposed to respond favorably to it. An example of such a letter would be a request for a catalog or other information that was evoked by a salesperson or a sales document— a sales letter, an advertisement, or a news release. If your inquiry or request has been solicited, your letter can be brief and to the point. You won't need to persuade your readers to respond; they'll be ready to apply. Adopt the strategy of the good news– bad news concept described in Chapter 1. A routine request that will benefit the receiver is good news. A special request that will cause the receiver work and perhaps be of no benefit to him or her is bad news.

Making a routine request Your major objective in making a solicited inquiry or request is to state it so that you get exactly what you want. Don't forget to be courteous as well—even with the most routine inquiry or request. Politeness should be so natural that you practice it almost unconsciously. It's as easy as saying "please." The easiest way to show appreciation is to use "Thank you" as your complimentary close. We can't urge you enough to be courteous. A warm note is always pleasant to receive—and rewarding to include.

Here are two typical routine inquiry and request letters that are clear and polite.

Dear Sir:

Does your new spring line of men's golf pullovers come in size 48?

Your advertisement in today's <u>Mayfield</u> <u>Bugle</u> listed men's golf pullovers in XL size, but I'm not sure whether size 48 is XL or larger.

Thank you,

Because the inquiry is routine and might benefit the reader as much as the inquirer (if he carries size 48 or the equivalent, there's a potential sale), the

question should open the letter. It's a good-news letter. The second paragraph may help the reader answer the question by explaining the reason
for the question and by identifying precisely what merchandise is involved.
  Here's the second letter:

Dear Sir:

     Please send me your current automotive parts and
     accessories catalog. I'm especially interested in
     overhaul kits and remanufactured block assemblies.

                              Thank you,

The request for the catalog, of course, is good news. So the request opens
the letter. Is the second sentence necessary? Perhaps. Any information
that might help the reader give the information or material needed should
be included. In this case, the reader may have additional catalogs or
brochures on overhaul kits and remanufactured block assemblies.

  Making a special request   Just because you want something is no
guarantee that your readers will feel obliged to give it to you. If you initiate
the inquiry or request, or if you will primarily benefit from its fulfillment,
then you're asking a special favor of your readers. Such a situation calls for
you not only to state your inquiry or request clearly and politely, but also
to persuade your readers to comply with it. The best ways to encourage
your readers to respond favorably are to help them understand your need
and your rationale for sending the letter to them. Going beyond the inquiry or request itself lets readers know you're aware that you're asking a
favor.
  Here's a sample:

Dear Mr. Bradley:

     I am a second-year industrial technology student at
     Northern Technical Institute and am writing a paper
     for one of my courses on the hiring and recruiting
     practices of large industrial firms like yours.

     I have done considerable library work on the subject,
     but I want to augment my reading with information
     collected from the six largest industrial firms in the
     tristate area. The results of my study will be shared
     with the other members of my class. I should also be
     very happy to send a copy of my completed report to you,
     should you desire one.

Would you spend a few minutes to answer the following questions about the way your firm recruits employees?

1. What priorities are placed on candidates' academic performance, experience, and on-campus or in-plant interviews?

2. What is expected of candidates' behavior and dress when they report for an interview?

3. How much importance is placed on recommendations from faculty, school officials, and previous employers?

4. Do you give any standard or in-house tests to candidates? If so, how much weight is given to their scores?

My paper is due April 10, so I would like very much to receive your response by early March. I certainly appreciate your taking the time to read my letter, and am very hopeful of receiving a reply from you.

Thank you,

Because the letter is asking a special favor of the reader, the writer holds up the questions until he identifies himself, establishes his need, and explains why he's written to the reader. He also offers some potential benefit to the reader by offering to share the results with him. He then itemizes the questions for easy reference and closes by explaining when he'd like to have the information. The writer prepares the reader for the inquiry because he realizes he is asking questions that are normally not asked and that might even be for information not normally given.

We think the above letter is structured appropriately. By introducing himself and explaining why he is writing, the writer buffers the request. But he doesn't bury the question or request so deep in the letter that it comes at the very end. Even a bothersome question or request should not be delayed until the end of the letter. There needs to be room at the end of the letter to build good will of some kind.

The strategy when making an unsolicited inquiry or request is as follows:

1. Introduce yourself and explain why you are addressing your inquiry or request to that particular reader.
2. State your inquiry or request.

3. If appropriate, explain when you need the information or service.
4. Close by expressing your appreciation, but do not use a trite expression like "Thanking you in advance."

ORDER LETTERS

You'll write order letters when you wish to place written purchase orders but don't have your own forms or those of companies you're ordering from. As with inquiry letters, order letters range from the simple to the complicated. First, you won't need to persuade readers to respond. Order letters are good-news letters. Readers are prepared to respond to all orders. Just start by making your orders as clear and exact as possible. Then supply the necessary details of payment and shipment.

The things to remember about an order letter are these:

- Tell exactly what you want: article name, catalog or stock number, price, color, style, size, and so forth.
- If you're ordering more than one item, list them in tabular form and double-space between each item.
- Tell how you intend to pay: by check, money order, credit card, or by charging to your account if you have one established with the seller; in advance or after delivery; all at once or in installments; and so on.
- If you wish to have the order delivered a certain way by a certain time, tell how and when you want it sent.
- Be courteous. Your order will probably be filled, regardless of how impolitely it's placed, but saying "please send" is a more polite and businesslike than "I want" or "I need."

Orders can be placed like this:

```
Dear Sir:

    Please add my name to the list of subscribers to
Nursing Notes. Enclosed is my personal check for $10 to
pay the year's rate.

    If possible, please start my subscription with the
current issue (December, 1977) because it contains
several articles on nursing of the aged that are of
interest to me.

                    Thank you,
                _____
```

```
Dear Sir:

        Please ship via United Parcel Service the following
three items:

        Rear Tire Carrier       Stock # 19-3096Y   $15.98
        (15", 4-lug wheel)

        Cab Step for Truck      Stock # 15-1303B    11.50
        (Deluxe Step, 19"
        wide to fit 1975
        Chevrolet)

        Pick-up Camper          Stock # 75-2921T    29.98
        Stabilizers
        (1-pr.)                                     _____
                                       Total  $57.46

        If this order is too large for UPS, send by truck
express. Make no substitutions and cancel the order
if not deliverable within a month.

        Please charge this order to my BankAmericard
(#2240 000 120 820). My card expires April, 1979.

                        Thank you,
```

Before you mail the order, check a second time to ensure that you have included all necessary information. Incomplete or incorrect information means another letter or the wrong product. And that's a bother to both you and your reader.

RESPONSE LETTERS

"Every inquiry is an opportunity to make a friend," according to an old business adage. So it goes with receiving inquiries, requests, and orders. If you show a sincere interest in your readers and their needs, your response builds good will. Your courteous and prompt response demonstrates your willingness to help.

To write a good response letter, you must know exactly what the reader wants, what you can and should say in response, and how to organize what you say. Since your letter is always at least the second letter in a correspondence cycle, your response must be shaped by the letter it is answering. Let's look at the circumstances in which you might write a response letter and what the characteristics of your response should be.

The "Yes" Answer

When you can fill an order or send requested items routinely, it's fine to use a standardized acknowledgment that thanks readers for their orders and requests and indicates what's being sent to them. It can be enclosed with an invoice and shipped with the order, attached to the requested items, or can be sent separately. Such acknowledgment forms are illustrated below:

```
            THANK YOU FOR YOUR ORDER


The green sheet enclosed is an invoice showing the
items shipped along with date and method of shipment.

If the shipment is not correct, please return your
order with your request for adjustment.

We appreciate your order. We hope you will let us
be of service to you again in the future.

            PERRY'S ELECTRONICS
            1010 Hill Avenue
            Cincinnati, OH 45223


            ──────────


It is a pleasure to send you the enclosed material in
response to your recent request.

            TRS Homes, Inc.
            400 West Aldeah Street
            Sharkeytown, IL 62001
```

Such standardized acknowledgments are a good way to respond to many routine orders and requests. Nobody will feel his or her order or request has been handled indifferently; after all, the items are on their way. But it might appear brusque simply to send something without some accompanying message.

Of course, you must be able to determine when more than a standardized acknowledgment is required. If, for instance, you have information your readers want and you can give, you should take a different course of action—you should write a letter that explains amply what they want to know. Because you're providing the information the reader wants, your letter carries good news. Here's the way Mr. Bradley answered the letter on pages 28–29 asking him about the way his firm recruits employees.

Dear Mr. Kenney:

Because our drivers operate $40,000 vehicles carrying highly flammable cargo and are our company's most visible representatives, we take great care in hiring them. A specific job description helps us greatly in judging whether an applicant will make a good driver. It also gives applicants a clear idea of what their job will be. If the applicant is hired, it also guides our supervisors in providing the new driver with adequate training.

We obtain as much pertinent information as we can about applicants. Our application form (which I have enclosed) and personal interview allow us to gain a fairly comprehensive picture of the applicant. Personal appearance, physical characteristics, ability to write routine reports, friendliness, education, and experience are the aspects we evaluate. A physical examination is important because of the strength and endurance required for loading and driving operations.

We have found that it costs about $1,000 to find and train a new driver. But we have also found that the money is well spent, for good drivers keep our operating costs down and our business up.

I'm sure you've conducted a thorough search of the subject in your library, but just in case you have overlooked a source, may I recommend that you look through The Fleet Owner, which frequently publishes information about hiring and training good truck drivers.

Sincerely,

R P Bradley

R. P. Bradley
Vice President of Personnel
Acme Trucking Company

Enclosure (1)

In the above letter the writer has done a good job. He gives the information requested and indicates where the reader can get additional information. He doesn't restate the original request or acknowledge receipt of the original letter. The reader will remember his request; the response makes it obvious the request was received. Because the writer complies with the reader's request, the response is good news. Therefore, the writer doesn't delay giving the reader what he wants to know.

The "No" Answer

If you aren't able to provide readers with what they have asked for, your answer is essentially "no"—for your letter carries bad news. And bad news should be communicated indirectly so your readers can sense it before they see it. Such strategy helps them prepare for it. Actually, most bad news isn't all that shattering, but if there's any good news at all, it should come first. Let's see how the writer of the following letter handles a request she can't comply with.

Dear Ms. Matthews:

I have referred your letter to Ms. Jayne Miles, Director of Nursing Services at Appleby Memorial Hospital, because Appleby Memorial is the hospital in this area that specializes in long-range geriatric nursing.

You might also write to Dr. Priscilla Cox, University of Missouri School of Medicine, Columbia, Missouri 60521, who has done much research on the subject of hospital staff stereotypes of elderly patients. In addition, you might look into the series of annotated bibliographies published by the Gerontology Branch of the Public Health Service, Department of Health, Education, and Welfare, Washington, D.C. 20201.

I wish I could provide you with the information you request, but our hospital does not receive many elderly patients. I'm sure that Ms. Miles and Dr. Cox will be most happy to respond to your requests.

Sincerely,

Patsy Dickson

Patsy Dickson
Assistant Director, Nursing Services

The writer softens her "no" answer by explaining that she has passed the inquiry on to someone who might be able to help, and by suggesting other likely sources. Then she explains why she can't comply with the request. Although the reader may have hoped for the information immediately, she should appreciate the efforts of the writer.

SUGGESTIONS FOR APPLYING YOUR KNOWLEDGE

Several situations call for writing inquiry, request, and order letters and writing responses to such letters. Here are some things you might try:

1. Select an advertisement that invites you to send away for a free catalog, brochure, booklet, or sample. Write the letter requesting the material. Include with your letter a photocopy of the advertisement so your instructor can better evaluate your letter.
2. Select an advertisement in a nationally circulated magazine and write a letter asking for more information about the product or service advertised. Include a photocopy of the advertisement so your instructor can better evaluate your letter.
3. If you are writing a research paper for one of your courses, supplement material you've found locally by writing to several companies for additional information. Get your instructor's opinion of your letters before you mail them.
4. Exchange inquiry and request letters you have written with those of other students in your occupational writing course and write responses to their letters. Include a photocopy of the letter you are answering so your instructor can better evaluate your letter.
5. Collect several order forms and write a brief report explaining what features they have in common and what special features they have that help customers prepare their orders. Include the order forms as appendixes to your report.
6. Working with the printed order form of a catalog or advertisement, make out an order. Then, disregarding the printed order form, write an order letter.
7. Collect several acknowledgment forms that serve as letters of transmittal for orders and requests that can be routinely filled. Write a brief report explaining what features they have in common and what special features they have that attempt to personalize the acknowledgment. Include the acknowledgment forms as appendixes to your report.

CHAPTER 3
Employment Letters and Interviews

Every step of seeking employment is highly competitive in matters both large and small. A letter from an ex-student to one of the authors illustrates this point rather painfully. He told us that in one instance he and his staff were choosing between two recent graduates who seemed equal in every professional way. The decision was finally made by taking the person who prepared the *neatest* application. Seeking employment will thrust you into many such competitive communication situations, both written and oral. Your first contact with a potential employer may be by means of a letter of application and a resume of your education and experience. If your letter and resume succeed, you will likely be interviewed. You may also need to write requests for letters of recommendation and several follow-up letters such as letters of acceptance and refusal. To help you successfully reach your goal of a job, we discuss all these communication situations in this chapter.

PREPARATION

Before the letter writing begins, you must prepare yourself. The first step should be to inventory your own interests, education, experience, and abilities. Many personnel directors recommend writing an auto-biography—sit down and write an account of the significant things in your life. What did you do in high school? What do you remember of your course work there? Which courses did you enjoy? Which courses could you barely tolerate? Where did you get your highest grades? Your lowest? Answer the same questions for your vocational or college education.

What did you do for extracurricular activities? Have you any long-standing hobbies such as photography or needlepoint? Have you been active in political, social, or religious groups? Do you enjoy athletics, singing, or dramatics?

What has been your work experience? What was your first job? Your last? What have been your duties and responsibilities? What sort of work have you really enjoyed? Have you been in the military? What training and jobs did you have there?

The autobiography, at least in its first draft, is for your own use. It can be roughly written as long as it is complete, and it should be as honest and private as you want it to be. However, some employers now ask for a brief autobiography as part of the application. You can draw on your rough biography for this, but now you must write as well as you can. The rewrite will be a public document; omit anything that is purely your private business.

The autobiography is a useful document for at least two reasons. First, it helps you get in touch with your own identity. Look at the things you have succeeded in and enjoyed the most. Which did you enjoy the most, shop or English? Do you prefer math to social science or the other way around? Do you relate best to people or things? What would you rather do, read a book or go to a large noisy party? Never mind which you think you *should* like. Which do you *really* like? Have you ever sold merchandise in a store? Did you enjoy it? Is money extremely important to you or not? Do you stick to jobs? Do you see new ways to get an old job done? Are you willing to take a chance on people or jobs? Do you find the most satisfaction in stability or change? Do you work well independently?

Be honest in your answers and analysis. It's your life. You would not want to spend it doing something you don't enjoy. And it's likely you'll be more successful at work you truly enjoy and have the capabilities for. The good sales representative might make a terrible horticulturist and vice versa.

A second use of the autobiography is to remind yourself of all the education and experience you have had that will make you attractive to a potential employer. While you're analyzing yourself, be alert for evidence of those qualities employers value: loyalty, willingness to shoulder responsibility, ability to stick to a task until it is done, initiative, enough sense of proportion to realize that things don't always go perfectly. You can use this information during job interviews, occasions when you are expected to be able to talk about your abilities and goals.

You'll be able to draw upon the autobiography for information used in writing letters of application and your resume and for filling in employers' application blanks—the written communication of the job hunt.

WRITTEN COMMUNICATION

Look for a moment at Figures 3-1 and 3-2. Figure 3-1 is a company application blank. Many employers will ask you to complete such a form before they consider you for work. If you do have to complete such a form, print your answers as neatly as possible in ink. Better yet, type in your answers. Figure 3-1 is doubly useful, because from it you can learn what employers want to know about you. So study it with some care. Notice that for the most part it covers the same areas we have urged you to cover in your autobiography. Sometimes you must complete the application blank at the employer's office. So be sure to have all the needed information with you—from your social security number to specific details of education and experience.

Resume

Figure 3-2 (pages 43–44) is a sample resume (pronounced *rez-uh-may* and sometimes given its original French accent marks—résumé). Many formats are acceptable for resumes. We recommend a fairly simple one-page format as being most suitable for young people without extensive experience. If you need samples of longer forms, check your library's card catalog under *business correspondence* for books on the subject.

You can use the resume in combination with a letter of application to attract the attention of potential employers. You can mail them a copy of your resume and a personal letter of application or simply bring the resume to an interview that has been arranged in some other way.

Whatever form you choose for your resume, keep it as brief as is consistent with good coverage of your education and experience. Use phrases and dependent clauses rather than complete sentences. Both Figures 3-1 and 3-2 suggest the full range of possibilities for appropriate headings you can use. Don't crowd things on the page. Leave lots of white space. If you have to, don't be afraid to go to a second page. However, personnel directors will be attracted more by a well-organized brief summary than they will be by a long detailed discussion of everything you have ever done. They are busy people.

Have your resume professionally typed and then reproduced in as many copies as you anticipate needing. Use a process such as photocopying or lithography, neither of which is too expensive. Check the yellow pages of your telephone directory under *photocopying* or *printing* for shops to do the work for you.

Letters of Application

The letter of application is your way of introducing yourself to an employer. When accompanied by your resume, it should present a picture that is complete enough so that prospective employers can decide whether or not they want to find out even more about you. Your desire, of

FMC Corporation An equal opportunity employer

Application for employment | salaried personnel

It is the policy of FMC Corporation
to provide equal opportunity
for all qualified persons
and not to discriminate
against any employee or applicant
for employment because of race,
creed, color, sex or national origin
and to insure that employees
are treated during employment
without regard to their race,
creed, color, sex or national origin.
In any state whose laws
prohibit discrimination
on account of age,
do not answer any question
regarding your age.

Date

Return completed
application to

NORTHERN ORDNANCE DIVISION
4800 Marshall Street Northeast
Minneapolis, Minnesota 55421

Telephone 560-9201
Area Code (612)

Identification

(print) First name	Middle name		Last name			Social security number	
Local address Street and number		City	State	Zip		Telephone	
Permanent address Street and number		City	State	Zip		Telephone	
Name of person to be notified in case of emergency						Telephone	
Address Street and number			City		State		Zip
Are you a U S citizen? If no, what type visa do you hold? ☐ Yes ☐ No							

U S military service

Branch of U S service	Date entered		Date discharged		Rank at discharge	Type of discharge
	Month	Year	Month	Year		
Nature of duties and any special training and honors received						
Have you ever received a military disability pension?		If so, give nature of disability				
Present draft, reserve or military status						

References

If applying for professional or technical position, include at least one professional reference familiar with your work performance		
Name (not a relative or employer)	Complete mailing address	Occupation

Figure 3-1   Application blank. (Reprinted by permission of FMC Corporation)

Education and training

Education

Name of school	Location	Dates attended From	Dates attended To	Years credit	Year grad.	Degree	Course or major subject
High school							
Business or trade school							
College or university							
Graduate study							
Other							

Note: A copy of your college transcript should accompany this application if you graduated from college within last 5 years

High school and undergraduate record

	High school	College (undergraduate)
Scholastic standing (estimate if not known)	Average grade, standing in class, etc.	Average grade, gradepoint, standing, etc.
Scholastic honors		
Significant extracurricular activities if attended within last 5 years		Significant courses in major subject if attended within last 5 years
		Expenses earned (percent and how earned)

Graduate study

Field of graduate study	Scholarships, fellowships, assistantships, etc.	Name of major professor
Courses in specialized fields	Research problems	

Special training or qualifications

Languages spoken fluently	Languages read fluently	Factory or shop machines operated
Office machines operated		
Typing speed _____ wpm	Shorthand speed _____ wpm	

Describe any other special training or skills which are in any way related to the kind of work you want to do

Figure 3-1 Application blank *(continued)*.

Work experience If additional space is needed, attach separate sheets

Present or last employment

Name of present or last employer		Type of business		Address		
Starting date	Leaving date	Starting pay	Final pay	Reason for leaving		May we contact?
Month	Year	Month	Year			
Job title (present or last)		Name of supervisor		Supervisor's job title		
Description of work and responsibilities						

Previous employment

Name of next previous employer		Type of business		Address		
Starting date	Leaving date	Starting pay	Final pay	Reason for leaving		May we contact?
Month	Year	Month	Year			
Job title (last)		Name of supervisor		Supervisor's job title		
Description of work and responsibilities						

Name of next previous employer		Type of business		Address		
Starting date	Leaving date	Starting pay	Final pay	Reason for leaving		May we contact?
Month	Year	Month	Year			
Job title (last)		Name of supervisor		Supervisor's job title		
Description of work and responsibilities						

Additional experience

State what you did in any periods not already covered, including part-time or self employment

Dates	

Unless otherwise indicated, state any prior work experience with FMC Corporation, its divisions or subsidiaries

Figure 3-1 Application blank *(continued).*

Activities

Professional organizations, including offices (Omit union organizations and organizations which would indicate race, creed, color or national origin)

Hobbies and leisure interests

Publica-tions

Title (include patents)

Journal reference or patent number

Work preferences

Kind of work most wanted

Other kinds of work in which interested

Location preferences or limitations

Approx. salary range expected

Date available to start work

Previous address

List home address in U.S for last 5 years

Dates   Street and number   City   State   Zip

Remarks

Have you ever been convicted of, or entered a plea of guilty to, a felony or misdemeanor other than parking or minor traffic violation?

☐ Yes   ☐ No   If yes, explain fully

List serious operations, accidents, illnesses, disabilities, and limitations (if none, so state)

Have you ever received workman's compensation for an industrial illness/injury?   ☐ Yes   ☐ No   If yes, explain

Signature

Are you aware of any reason why you might not be able to obtain a fiduciary bond or government security clearance, if required?

☐ Yes   ☐ No

It is understood and agreed that any misstatement made by me in this application will be sufficient cause for discharge from the company's service if I have been employed. It is also understood that this employment is subject to satisfactory physical examination by the company physician at the time of employment and thereafter at any time required by the company.

Date _____

Signature of applicant _____

Form 609—June 73

Figure 3-1 Application blank *(continued).*

course, is that the letter result in an interview. In a very real sense, therefore, the letter of application is a selling letter.

Letters of application should be neat, correct, and well written. Type them, or have them typed, on good bond paper of about 20-lb. weight. You may be short of cash when you're job hunting, but letters and resumes are not the places to be cheap. They represent you, and they should represent you well. Ill-typed, fuzzy letters littered with blotches or misspelled words will convince people that you are sloppy and careless.

Read the letter in Figure 3-3. Notice that the salutation uses a name and

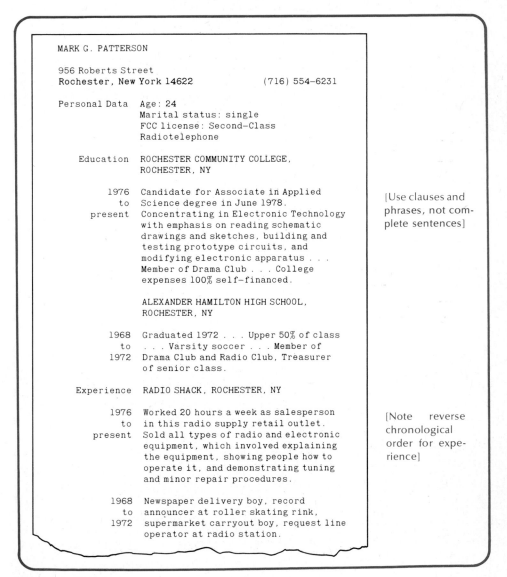

Figure 3-2 Resume.

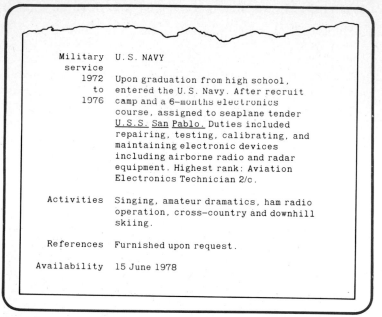

```
Military    U.S. NAVY
service
    1972    Upon graduation from high school,
      to    entered the U.S. Navy. After recruit
    1976    camp and a 6-months electronics
            course, assigned to seaplane tender
            U.S.S. San Pablo. Duties included
            repairing, testing, calibrating, and
            maintaining electronic devices
            including airborne radio and radar
            equipment. Highest rank: Aviation
            Electronics Technician 2/c.

Activities  Singing, amateur dramatics, ham radio
            operation, cross-country and downhill
            skiing.

References  Furnished upon request.

Availability  15 June 1978
```

Figure 3-2   Resume *(continued)*.

not "Dear Sir." Its introduction straightforwardly tells the employer how the writer learned about the job. It names the job and makes it clear that the writer seeks it. Avoid tricky openers. One of us recently received a letter that began, "If you don't want to hire a well-educated, fine, industrious instructor, stop right here." Unfortunately for the writer, his reader took him at his word and stopped. Courtesy, tact, and solid information will take you farther than trickery.

In the middle of the letter in Figure 3-3, the writer does several things. First, he makes it clear that he knows something about the company, thus letting the personnel director know that he has been doing his homework. Where can you get such information? For large companies and government agencies your best source is the *College Placement Annual,* a directory of employers that also includes the names of personnel directors and good advice on how to conduct a job hunt. Other sources are *Standard Statistics* and *Standard Corporation Reports.* For smaller companies you may want to write a letter of inquiry first asking for company brochures and other promotional literature. Often your school placement office will have information. Don't overlook newspaper ads. Finding out such information should be part of your preparation for the job hunt. Having it shows your professionalism.

Going along to the late-middle part of the illustrated letter, the writer digs into his autobiography and comes up with facts that should interest the employer. Normally, these will concern past work and educational

956 Roberts Street
Rochester, NY 14622
24 March 1978

Ms. Joan B. Mills
Employment Manager
Warren Radio Company
252 Foss Avenue
Bedford, MA 01730

Dear Ms. Mills:

The placement director at Rochester Community College has drawn my attention to your need for an FCC licensed Communication Technician. I have a second-class radiotelephone license and will be available for work in June of this year.

I have had considerable theoretical training and practical experience in your company's field of designing, manufacturing, and selling electronic instruments and testing and measuring systems. As a Navy Aviation Electronics Technician 2/c, I had over three years of practical experience doing first- and second-echelon maintenance of radio and radar equipment. My experience includes working with most of the sophisticated electronic testing equipment that the Navy furnishes its electronic maintenance units.

At Rochester Community College, I have majored in Electronic Technology, with courses in electronic circuit theory, tests and measurement, and microwaves.

Please see my enclosed resume that gives the details of my education and experience.

May I drive over to Bedford to talk with you? I can arrange my schedule to be available for an interview on any weekday afternoon.

Sincerely,

Mark G. Patterson

Mark G. Patterson

Enclosure: Resume

[Identify position sought and the way you heard of it]

[Show knowledge of employer and give details of education and experience]

[Refer to resume]

[Request interview]

Figure 3-3 Letter of application.

experience. But don't overlook the value of referring to extracurricular activities if they tie in to the job you seek. This portion of the letter may repeat information that is also in the resume, but try to include additional information as well. Knowing something about the employer guides you in choosing appropriate facts. Stick to the facts. Don't express opinions about yourself. Let employers form their own opinions. If you have the right facts and choose them well, the opinions will be favorable.

In the closing part of the letter, the writer refers the reader to his resume for additional information. Finally, he attempts to set up an interview— almost always the object of a letter of application. Make the interview as easy and convenient for the employer as possible.

Never send out duplicated letters of application. You may have one standard letter that you modify only slightly from employer to employer, but each letter must be freshly typed.

Other Letters

Several other letters are either necessary or desirable during the job hunt: requests for recommendation, interview follow-up letters, job-offer acknowledgments, status inquiries, job refusals, and job acceptances. Our sample letters in Figures 3-4 to 3-9 illustrate how to proceed in each of these matters. Only a few additional points are necessary here.

Always be as courteous as possible in business correspondence and especially in employment letters. Don't overlook the value of the letter following up an interview, even if all you do is thank the interviewers for their time and courtesy. The letter will be appreciated, and your name will become that much more familiar to the employer. Other excellent letters to write express appreciation to people who have provided references for you or helped in other ways (see pages 59–60). Such people deserve your thanks, and they'll be more inclined to help another time if their first experience with you has been a pleasant one.

956 Roberts Street
Rochester, NY 14622
20 February 1978

Lieutenant David L. Gomez
Box 4822
Headquarters USNE
FPO New York 09555

Dear Lieutenant Gomez:

During 1974 and 1975, I worked as an electronics
technician in your maintenance unit aboard the U.S.S.
San Pablo. I remember the assignment as a happy one and
know that I learned a good deal about electronics in
those two years.

In June of this year, I'll graduate from Rochester
Community College with an A.A.S. degree in Electronic
Technology. I'll be seeking employment soon. Would you
be kind enough to allow me to give your name as a
reference?

I intend to start sending out my resumes on 15 March and
hope that I'll hear from you before that time. I'll be
happy to send you a copy of my resume to bring you up to
date on my activities.

Thank you for all your past kindnesses to me.

Best regards,

Mark G. Patterson

Mark G. Patterson

[Recall the as-
sociation]

[Explain   need
for recommen-
dation and
request it]

[Set a date and
offer resume]

Figure 3-4   Request for recommendation.

956 Roberts Street
Rochester, NY 14622
16 April 1978

Ms. Joan B. Mills
Employment Manager
Warren Radio Company
252 Foss Avenue
Bedford, MA 01730

Dear Ms. Mills:

Thank you for the opportunity to interview with your
company. I particularly enjoyed the chance to tour your
Bedford plant and to talk to your chief technical
representative, Mr. Brunson.

[Thank for
interview]

Mr. Brunson's suggestion that I might qualify for a job
as a field technical representative of Warren Radio
surprised me. I had thought I was interviewing for a job
in your plant. I didn't realize the importance of my
sales and instructional work with Radio Shack.

[Give or request
additional
information]

After thinking over whether or not I would like to
travel regularly, I have decided that I would like such
an opportunity. Therefore, please tell Mr. Brunson that
I am definitely interested.

Sincerely,

Mark G. Patterson

Mark G. Patterson

Figure 3-5 Interview follow-up.

956 Roberts Street
Rochester, NY 14622
20 April 1978

Mr. Robert B. Small
Employment Manager
Power Electronics
5643 Parker Avenue
Rochester, NY 14608

Dear Mr. Small:

Thank you for offering me a position as communication
technician with Power Electronics.

[Acknowledge offer]

I am considering several other possibilities as well. I
will, however, decide by 5 May and send you a definite
answer at that time.

[Give reason for delay and request or give a deadline]

Thank you for your consideration.

Sincerely,

Mark G. Patterson

Mark G. Patterson

Figure 3-6 Job offer acknowledgment.

956 Roberts Street
Rochester, NY 14622
27 April 1978

Ms. Joan B. Mills
Employment Manager
Warren Radio Company
252 Foss Avenue
Bedford, MA 01730

Dear Ms. Mills:

I enjoyed my pleasant interview with you and Mr. Brunson on 13 April. At that time you indicated that I would have some word about my employment with you in a week or two.

[Recall the association]

At the present time I have been offered another position, and the company would like an answer from me by 5 May.

[State reason for need]

I am still nevertheless interested in the position you outlined for me. Would it be possible for you to give me a definite answer before 5 May? I will appreciate your help in this matter.

[Request information]

Sincerely,

Mark G. Patterson

Mark G. Patterson

Figure 3-7 Status inquiry.

956 Roberts Street
Rochester, NY 14622
5 May 1978

Mr. Robert B. Small
Employment Manager
Power Electronics
5643 Parker Avenue
Rochester, NY 14608

Dear Mr. Small:

Thank you for your offer of a position with Power
Electronics. However, I have decided to accept another
offer.

Thank you very much for your time and patience with me.
I enjoyed talking to you and the other employees at
Power, particularly Mr. Walker.

Sincerely,

Mark G. Patterson

Mark G. Patterson

[Acknowledge and decline offer]

[State your appreciation]

Figure 3-8 Job refusal.

956 Roberts Street
Rochester, NY 14622
5 May 1976

Ms. Joan B. Mills
Employment Manager
Warren Radio Company
252 Foss Avenue
Bedford, MA 01730

Dear Ms. Mills:

I was happy to hear that Warren Radio wants me as a tech rep for the company. I see it as a splendid opportunity and accept your offer.

[Acknowledge and accept offer]

I will be in Bedford as requested by 20 June to start my six weeks of training.

[Confirm reporting date]

Thank you again.

Sincerely,

Mark G. Patterson

Mark G. Patterson

Figure 3-9 Job acceptance.

INTERVIEWS

If your letters of application succeed, the next stage of the job hunt is usually the interview. Interviews frighten a great many job hunters, probably more than they should. Interviewers really aren't out to trap people. Their job is to evaluate people, to find people that their employers need, and also to help people find out what they are best suited for. They know how to assess your qualities. They ask questions to determine if you are a responsible person. They want to see if you are friendly and good humored, someone who will work well with other people. They examine your vocational and professional skills. You will find most professionally trained interviewers helpful and friendly.

You have certain responsibilities for the interview as well. You have to prepare for the interview beforehand. Here again your autobiography is good preparation. Look through it and select those items from your background that demonstrate those characteristics employers look for, such as loyalty and stick-to-itiveness. Also, you will look through it for jobs, education, and extracurricular activities that relate to the job sought. If you did your homework for the letter of application, you'll already know something about the employer. If you haven't, find out what you can before the interview.

How should you dress for the interview? Like it or not, first impressions are important. Studies show interviewers are more favorably inclined toward neatly dressed, well-groomed people. For men this means shined shoes, sport coat, slacks, shirt, and tie For some positions, particularly office work, a suit is probably even better. It doesn't matter that you may wear work clothes on the job sought. Dress well for the interview. For women, a dress suitable for office use is the best attire. An attractive pantsuit would be an alternative. Women should avoid jeans and being braless. The latter, particularly, offends many interviewers both male and female. Avoid extremes of all sorts: for men, hair too long, beard too bushy are extremes. Excessive makeup or perfume, many jangling bracelets, or flashy, dressy clothes are extremes for women.

It should go without saying that you have to be clean. Dirty fingernails have lost as many jobs for people as low grades. Don't chew gum during the interview. Don't smoke even if invited to.

O.K., you're suitably dressed. You arrive at the place of the interview at least ten minutes early. You meet the interviewer and shake his or her hand firmly but comfortably—avoid bone crunchers or limp-as-a-fish shakes. You get the interviewer's name straight and sit down erectly but comfortably. How will the interview go from that point forward?

Interviews usually last about thirty minutes. After introductions are over, interviewers usually spend a few minutes setting you at ease. They do not want you to be tense. The best interviews are relaxed and friendly, even a bit casual. Neither party should dominate. After some casual talk, perhaps about sports or current events, the interviewer may then shift into telling you something about the employer. If so, listen closely and be prepared to come in at natural pauses with intelligent questions. But don't interrupt the interviewer when he or she is going full steam. If your question can demonstrate previous knowledge about the employer, so much the better.

Sometimes this talk about the employer comes later in the interview. In any event, questions and answers about you are the heart of the interview. Sometimes, even testing may be a part of the interview. The questions may be deliberately rather vague to see if you can develop ideas on your own, or they may be quite specific and penetrating. Here are some samples:

- Why do you want to work for us?
- Tell me something about yourself.
- What sort of summer work have you had?
- What were your responsibilities in your last job?
- Why did you leave your last job?
- Do you enjoy sales (office), (experimental), (manual), (troubleshooting), (etc.) work?
- Can you take criticism?
- Why have you chosen your vocation?
- What subjects did you enjoy most in school?
- How have you paid for your education?
- What are your strong (weak) points?
- If you were rich enough not to have to work, how would you spend your life?

Like athletic events, no two interviews are exactly alike. But certain situations and questions do repeat. Good answers prepared for the questions listed here would go a long way to get you ready for any interview. And you can practice. Get together with friends and interview each other. Learn how to talk about yourself and your accomplishments and how to articulate your desires. Learn how to be assertive·about yourself but stop short of being aggressive.

Sometime in the interview the interviewer will discuss with you the job or jobs the employer has to offer. Here you should be able to display your professional knowledge about jobs for which you are suited. You should be fairly firm about your vocational goals but flexible enough to discuss a related job if it looks good. But avoid the appearance of being willing to take any job at all.

When the interviewer discusses salary and job benefits such as hospitalization insurance, pensions, and vacations, then you are free to ask questions about these items. But don't ask about them until the interviewer brings them up.

You will rarely be offered a job at a first interview. Sometimes this may be done at a second interview. Normally, however, the job offer will come at some later time. Don't try to extend interviews. When the interviewer closes up your folder and indicates that the interview is over, for better or for worse it is. Stand up, shake hands once again, thank the interviewer, and leave.

What characteristics should you display to have a successful interview? According to many interviewers, the following rank high on the list:

- Be neat and well groomed.
- Be natural, friendly, relaxed, but not sloppy or overly casual.
- Be more interested in the work involved on the job and in its potential than in salary and benefits.
- And this last may be most important: Have definite vocational goals. Know what you're good at and what you want to do. Be ready to articulate these goals.

SUGGESTIONS FOR APPLYING YOUR KNOWLEDGE

The employment situation with its correspondence and interviews is one place where your practice can approach or even be the real thing. The facts you have to work with are the real facts of your own life along with information you can gather about real employers you might want to work for.

Begin by writing a rough-draft autobiography of your life. Keep it as reference material for the other assignments you may write, such as letters of application and resumes.

With the help of your school placement officer make up a list of potential employers for people with your skills. Look up companies in places like *The College Placement Annual*, *Standard Statistics*, and *Standard Corporation Reports*. Most states have an agency with the job of keeping track of employment opportunities for state citizens. Check the *Readers' Guide to Periodical Literature* for articles about large companies and agencies. Work up some letters of inquiry to potential employers asking for promotional literature and application blanks. And don't overlook friends who work in places where you might want to work. They can tell you a good deal about working conditions, chances for advancement, company policies, needed skills, and so forth. In other words, you can obtain a good deal of information from many sources about employers. Gather as much as you can.

All the communications of the job-hunting situation are potential assignments: letters of application, autobiographies, resumes, interview follow-up letters, and so forth. All should be typed and thoroughly professional looking.

Get into the interviewing aspects of job hunting as well. For a start, divide the class into pairs. Have each person interview the other, developing the information about the interviewee we have mentioned in this chapter as being important—favorite courses, job experience, hobbies, etc. This interview relaxes people and gets them talking freely about themselves. A good follow-up to this interview is to have the interviewer write a letter of application for the interviewee. Some people have difficulty drawing attention to their own strong points but can do it easily for others.

Conduct mock interviews before the entire class. You can even role-play in these interviews. One person can play an ill-prepared, unsuccessful interviewee, another a well-prepared, successful one. If your school has the proper equipment, videotape interviews for later study.

People who have participated in real interviews should tell the class about their experiences. Outside of class you can practice interviews with friends. Get so familiar with the process that you are totally at ease with it.

CHAPTER 4

Customer Relations Letters

Every letter you write should build good will for you and your organization. Good-news letters are automatic good-will carriers. As such, they are fairly easy to write. However, bad-news letters—complaint letters, adjustment letters that say no, and collection letters—are potential destroyers of good will. But the long-range goal of bad-news letters should be to build or to reestablish good will.

In this chapter we'll look first at two types of letters that build good will easily, because they pleasantly move readers—the congratulatory letter and the thank-you letter. Then we'll look at letters that are more difficult to write graciously—the complaint letter, the adjustment letter, and the collection letter.

CONGRATULATORY LETTERS

If you remember how good you felt when you were praised or congratulated on some occasion, you'll see the nature of congratulatory letters. They are sincere gestures of friendliness and good will that are easy and a joy to write. Readymade congratulations printed on cards are available, of course, but a personal letter, no matter how brief, means something extra to the recipient.

Letters of congratulation may be written to individuals or organizations (even competitors!) on many occasions:

- receiving an honor or distinction
- being promoted
- undertaking a new venture

As special-occasion letters they should be timely—written as soon as possible after you've learned of the news or written to coincide with other recognitions merited by the event. As genuine good-will letters, they should be informal and friendly but to the point, concerned only with creating good feelings between the writer and the recipient.

Two basic features of a congratulatory letter are shown in the following:

Dear Patrolman Greer:

Congratulations on receiving the Esteem and Valor Award for 1975. Our city is extremely fortunate to have officers like you.

The very nature of police work calls for dedication to duty, and your work with the Special Emergency Team sets an excellent example for other members in the department.

Sincerely yours,

Always be sure to mention specifically the occasion for congratulations. If you feel like adding something more that expresses your feelings about the significance of the recipient's behavior that merited the award, feel free to do so. It shows that your congratulations are sincere.

Everybody is happy to learn when a friend is promoted. To express your pleasure and share in the happiness, you should write a congratulatory letter.

Dear Paula,

The good word that you were promoted to office manager was in the Business News section of this morning's <u>Tribune</u>. Weymeyer Brothers certainly picked the right person for the job. Congratulations.

You've earned this advancement, Paula, and you have my best wishes for continuing success.

Cordially,

In addition to referring to the promotion and to expressing congratulations, you may want to mention how you learned of the promotion.

Congratulations may also be extended to organizations—whether they are potential customers or competitors. Perhaps the most awkward letter to write is to a competitor. But since you probably know each other and work together in civic and joint-business projects, it would appear ungracious if you didn't extend your best wishes when the competitor undertakes a new venture that's not *too* threatening to you. Be flattering and noncompetitive in your remarks. Of course, a little good-natured humor is appropriate.

```
Dear Curt,

     Your new store in South Bonifield is certainly a
beautiful piece of architecture that blends well with
the character of the neighborhood.

     You have our best wishes for a reasonable amount
of success in your new location.

                    Cordially,
```

THANK-YOU LETTERS

Good will is a two-way street. So anytime persons do something for you, you should show your appreciation. Not every act of kindness and thoughtfulness requires a letter, of course. But when persons have gone out of their way to do something special for you, you should write them a cordial letter of appreciation. It doesn't matter if you've already thanked them in person; you should still write a thank-you letter. Write the letter within a day or so after you realize their help or consideration.

Since readers enjoy receiving thank-you letters, you should use the good-news strategy. Start the letter with an expression of your appreciation. Here, for example, is a letter written to R. P. Bradley, whose letter on page 33 answered Jack Kenney's unsolicited request letter. Jack just naturally felt like telling Mr. Bradley how grateful he was for the letter.

```
Dear Mr. Bradley:

     Thank you for explaining your company's
procedures in hiring new employees. It was kind of you
to get the information to me so soon.

     You gave me new insight into the importance of
selecting employees. I had no idea how carefully new
```

drivers had to be considered. Your information helps make a big point about careful recruiting.

And thanks for the lead on <u>The Fleet Owner</u>. Our library doesn't subscribe to it, but a trucking firm in my home town receives it, and I've been able to read the last few issues.

You'll be receiving a copy of my report in about two weeks.

                    Thanks again,

                    Jack Kenney

                    Jack Kenney

Notice how Jack develops the letter briefly to point out exactly what was helpful. This kind of specific detail is effective two ways. First, it prevents the thank-you letter from being an extremely short—almost embarrassingly brief—one-line thank you. Second, it provides "feedback" to the reader that Jack understands the significance of what he received.

Congratulatory letters that you receive are also occasions for thank-you letters. After all, when persons have been thoughtful enough to write and congratulate you, you owe them a note of thanks in acknowledgment.

Dear Frank,

Thanks much for your good wishes. I know now what you meant last year when you told our management association that managers "manage" information as much as they do people.

I'm planning to attend the Western Management Association Convention in Springfield March 5 and 6. How about lunch on me at The Purple Mousetrap?

                    Cordially,

And, of course, those who provided references for you or were in some way helpful in your successful application for a job should receive your written appreciation.

COMPLAINT LETTERS

"The best-laid plans of mice and men . . ."

How often have you heard this modern rephrasing of that famous line from Robert Burns' "To a Mouse"? Occasionally things don't go the way they are supposed to: the raincoat we ordered comes in the wrong size, the new gutter joint leaks, the new air conditioner makes an odd and alarming noise, the delivery of potatoes is short by ten 25-lb. bags. When these things happen, we tend to be disappointed at best—irritated, perhaps even extremely angry at worst.

But it does little good to moan about the inconvenience we've suffered or to allow our blood pressure to start pounding. What we must do is register our complaint with those we feel are at fault.

Once you remind yourself that a letter of complaint—like all the letters you write—should present facts clearly, fully, and courteously, you are well on your way to being able to write a successful one. The more objective and businesslike your complaint is, the easier it is for your reader to answer.

In writing a complaint letter:

- Identify the transaction, with references to contracts, invoices, dates, etc.
- Explain as clearly as possible what is wrong.
- Explain what you want the reader to do to satisfy you.

These three features are shown in the following letter, written by the architect of a building project to the general contractor.

Dear Mr. Roberts:

Three convection ovens furnished by Cookcraft Metals Company for the McKenzie Cafeteria project are not giving satisfactory service. The ovens were installed July 19, and it has been necessary for the supplier to make a number of service calls in the two months that the ovens have been in operation.

Two of the ovens (#5336190 and #5336187) do not heat properly, apparently because of malfunctioning thermostats. The other oven (#5336188) is not operating as of this date. It appears to have been used at some time before this installation.

Would you please have your subcontractor either replace these ovens or take some measure to ensure that the cause for underheating is eliminated.

And would you please investigate whether oven number 5336188 has been used before this installation.

Sincerely,

Christopher Offutt

Christopher Offutt, FAIA

CO/jo

cc: Cookcraft Metals Company

Four points. Four paragraphs. The opening paragraph refers to the pertinent project and the involved parties. The second paragraph explains clearly what is wrong. Serial numbers of the ovens are given so there will be no misunderstanding about which ovens are malfunctioning. The third and fourth paragraphs explain what two actions will satisfy the writer.

ADJUSTMENT LETTERS

Some of the worst letters we have ever seen were adjustment letters—those written in answer to complaint letters. When they are bad, they are really bad—with ready-made phrases that might apply to almost any situation, but work well for none . . . with decisions based on vague, unexplained "policy" . . . with buck-passing and red-tape entanglements . . . with countercharges that the complaint is unreasonable. Bad adjustment letters lose customers forever. It's as simple as that.

So what do you do when you're faced with a complaint about some work or merchandise that you've provided? Here are some guidelines.

1. *Take every complaint seriously.* Regardless of whether or not you can allow the adjustments the complainants want, you must make them feel their complaints are important to you. This means you do three things: (1) handle complaints quickly, (2) have as liberal an adjustment policy as sound business practices will allow, and (3) shape your response to match the specific complaint.

When people make complaints, they feel they are justified in doing so. You must study the situation carefully, make your decision with "all deliberate speed," and work toward maintaining good will regardless of your decision.

When persons make complaints, they usually are justified. You should try to give them what they want. James Cash Penney, that enterprising businessman with the prophetic name, built a national chain of department stores on one simple rule—"The customer is always right." We're not suggesting that you give in to obviously unreasonable complaints, because there will be times when you have to say no. But maintain a fairly lenient adjustment policy.

When persons make a complaint, they expect some specific word that tells them that *their* complaint has been read and investigated, and that the decision has been based on the merits of their specific circumstances. If the complaint is about a jar of mayonnaise that is spoiled, or a chafing dish that melted, or a paint job that flaked within two months, mention the mayonnaise, or the chafing dish, or the paint job. Form letters are out.

2. *When you can grant full adjustment, do so—and announce it early in your letter.* When circumstances call for full adjustment, grant it and explain why the mistake occurred. Granting full adjustment is good news to the reader, so begin your letter by explaining what adjustment you're making. After all, it's the most important news you can give readers. And do it cordially. A gruff adjustment letter might as well be a negative reply, for the reader will feel the begrudging tone.

Follow up your opening paragraph by a second one that explains what caused the foul-up and what you intend to do to reduce the chances that it will happen again. Your explanation will lengthen your letter, but it is length well invested. Your readers will feel that you really care about the mistake and that you really looked into the matter to see what happened and why.

An experience one of us had a few years ago will illustrate the difference a cordial adjustment letter can make. The difficulty was over the payment of our subscription to a magazine. We had paid the bill for a three-year subscription by check, but we kept receiving collection letters. After the second collection letter, we sent the company a brief note explaining we had paid our bill and enclosed a copy of the canceled check. For the next three months we continued to get requests for payment. Finally, after we received the *seventh* monthly plea for payment, a rather nasty note, we were mad. We wrote a moderately restrained letter to the manager of the company's customer service department explaining the situation to him, again enclosing a copy of our canceled check. Here's the letter we received:

```
     We are sorry to learn of the problem you've had
with your subscription.


     We're happy to inform you that we have taken
action to stop the bills which were sent after your
payment was received. It may be that one more bill which
we were unable to prevent will reach you; please
disregard it.
```

> We hope you will enjoy the coming issues of the
> magazine.
>
> Cordially,
>
> *Henry Dysart*
>
> Henry Dysart
Manager Customer Service

HD/pl
cc: Ms. Jean Binkley
    Mr. Chris Harrell

Well, we were relieved that we at least got the billing stopped. But other than that, we weren't very satisfied. After all, the company had threatened to sue us over the alleged nonpayment. Their response that they were "sorry to learn of the problem" didn't put us in much of a mood to "enjoy the coming issues of the magazine."

A letter that arrived three days later made us a lot happier:

> You are right. You paid your subscription bill
> exactly when you said you did. We are wrong and we
> apologize.
>
> Please let me explain what happened. The reason
> that a bill was sent repeatedly to you is that the
> payment got caught in the new data processing machine
> recently installed to give customers faster and more
> accurate service, and it kept getting marked unpaid.
> Yours was one of several payments recycled this way. We
> now have the system straightened out, and you should
> not be receiving any more bills.
>
> At least no bill until three years from now, when
> your three-year subscription is up. We want you to have
> the past seven monthly issues at no cost to you. I hope
> this will help compensate for the trouble we've caused
> you.
>
> Sincerely,
>
> *Jean Binkley*
>
> Jean Binkley
Vice President of Sales

JB/fr
cc: Mr. Henry Dysart
    Mr. Chris Harrell

What do you think of that? Can you figure out why we received that second letter? Look at the signatures of the two letters and the names in the distribution lists. Jean Binkley was undoubtedly Henry Dysart's boss, and she didn't like the answer Mr. Dysart gave us. Notice how she disarmed us by admitting the mistake and apologizing for it. It's difficult not to forgive in a situation like that. The second paragraph was especially welcome in that we now knew what had caused the problem and what the company was doing to prevent its happening again. And check that sweetener at the end. It melted us. Talk about reestablishing good will! We still subscribe.

Such concern can earn you a special place in the heart of complaining customers who are right.

3. *When you must refuse adjustment, prepare the reader for the bad news and work toward reestablishing good will.* When circumstances do not allow for granting an adjustment, your letter carries bad news. You need to buffer the negative decision by at least a sentence or two and to end by attempting to reestablish good will.

Never open with the bad news. Such a beginning is like a slap in the face. Delay your negative decision at least to the second paragraph to give your reader a chance to sense the refusal before actually seeing it in writing. But don't put the refusal at the very end of the letter, where there's no room left to work toward reestablishing good will.

The opening buffer is important. Try to begin by making a statement your reader can agree with. This establishes a common ground from which you can move into your refusal. Some authorities on business writing suggest that you should open by thanking the reader for calling attention to the trouble. But that's being slightly dishonest. You don't appreciate receiving a complaint. So you can't agree with that statement, nor is your reader likely to believe you.

After the opening buffer, state your refusal and explain why you cannot grant the adjustment. Give your answer so the reader cannot misunderstand your decision or the reasoning behind your refusal.

After your refusal, reestablish good will by offering to help the reader solve the problem. This ending will swing your letter away from the psychological low point of the refusal and tell the reader you're anxious to help in some other way.

The following letter shows how to explain a refusal.

Dear Mrs. Rhodes:

> Our service representative has examined your dryer and discovered that the motor was clogged with lint, which caused it to overheat and cut off. The cutoff is a protective feature of your dryer to keep the motor from burning out.

However, he also found that the motor has been overheated so much that it is damaged to the point that it should be replaced. In his investigation he discovered that the lint filter was so clogged with lint that it was not functioning properly. Instead of being trapped in the filter, the lint packed into the motor, causing it to overheat. He also reported that on a previous service call to your home he had found the lint filter full. At that time he showed you the instruction in your operating manual where it says to clean the filter after each drying load to prevent lint from getting into the motor.

Since the replacement guarantee for the motor includes only defects by the manufacturer and improper installation by us, we feel that in this circumstance we cannot replace the motor free, as you request.

However, we are anxious to help you get your dryer working again. Should you want our service representative to install a new motor, please let us know. Because the installation would be a continuation service call, your cost would be only $50 for the motor and $10 for the installation.

Sincerely,

Willoughby Johnson

Willoughby Johnson
Service Manager

4. *When you grant partial adjustment, prepare the reader for the mixed good news–bad news and work toward reestablishing good will.* A liberal adjustment policy sometimes allows you to make a good-will gesture of partial adjustment rather than a flat refusal. Because you are not granting full adjustment, your letter carries bad news. It is thus a variation of the basic refusal letter. You must review the situation that caused the complaint so your reader understands why you cannot grant full adjustment and, at the same time, is satisfied with the partial adjustment.

Granting partial adjustment is a lot like walking a tightrope. If you sound the least bit unsure about your reasons for not granting full adjustment, or if you sound unduly charitable, you may fail to achieve the good will your partial adjustment intends. You have to know your reader. Explaining that you're allowing partial adjustment to a "preferred customer" satisfies some, irritates others. If preferred-customer status is the main grounds for partial adjustment, it's probably best not to say so. The reader knows this and would probably not like to be reminded that it is the preferred-customer status rather than the legitimacy of the complaint that has caused the settlement.

So the partial adjustment letter can be tricky to write. Let's go back to the letter above in which Willoughby Johnson had to refuse Mrs. Rhodes' request that her dryer motor be replaced free. Assume that because of the Rhodes family's long and steady patronage, Mr. Johnson believes that a good-will partial adjustment is in order. How might he write the letter?

The letter would probably be much the same as the refusal letter until the third paragraph where the decision is announced. After the second paragraph the letter might go like this:

> Since the motor damage was caused by excessive lint, not from a manufacturing defect or improper installation, we feel that we cannot replace the motor under the terms of the replacement guarantee.
>
> However, we can install a new motor at less than retail price. You may have a new motor for the wholesale price of $30. And since we would also consider the installation a continuation service call, you would pay only the wholesale price and $10 for installation.
>
> If you would drop us a card or call us within the next few days, we can send our service representative within 24 hours to replace the motor.
>
> Sincerely,
>
> *Willoughby Johnson*
>
> Willoughby Johnson
> Service Manager

COLLECTION LETTERS

Writing collection letters is an unpleasant but necessary task. Fortunately, of the many customers to whom credit is extended, perhaps less than 10 percent ever need reminding of their indebtedness. But for those few who do not pay promptly, you should design a series of letters that ask for payment with increasing insistence. Once the bill is overdue, probably four letters will do: an initial friendly reminder; a second friendly reminder; a tactful, insistent reminder; and a final demand. These letters can be spaced about three or four weeks apart.

The first letter should be regarded as a standardized (but friendly) reminder of debt. A "please remember us" note will do. Simply state the debt, tactfully remind, and ask for payment.

```
        Have you forgotten something?

        On February 8 you bought a 36-inch Carthage
Cooktop Unit for $209.95. Perhaps you've overlooked
this bill, so we'd like to bring it to your attention.

        Will you please help us clear the charge?
```

If your reminder is ignored, send a second letter that tactfully, but clearly, asks for the money. Here are the ideas you wish to convey in whatever letters are necessary after the initial reminder:

- that you want your money;
- that you want it as quickly as possible;
- that you're willing to listen to extenuating circumstances, but you need to know what they are;
- that you wish to accomplish this with as little hassle as possible to yourself and your customer;
- that you *expect* to be paid.

Setting up this series of expectations is important.

In your second letter be polite, assume your readers intend to pay, give them a chance to explain their predicament if they can't pay immediately—maybe even offer a partial payment plan. But in this second letter be more forceful.

```
        We have a problem.

        Your charge of $209.95 for a 36-inch Carthage
Cooktop Unit on February 8 has not been paid.

        If there is some reason why you are unable to pay
the bill, won't you come in and talk it over with us?

        If not, please send us your check so we can clear
our books and bring your account up to date.
```

This second letter reminds readers once again of the amount and date of their debt. The invitation to discuss the nonpayment is of utmost importance. Readers may have some temporary problem that prevents their meeting the bill, they may be dissatisfied with their purchase, or they may be waiting for a correction to be made in what they believe is an erroneous billing. Perhaps they have not received the merchandise if it's something you shipped them. Of course, they should have told you their reasons for not paying, but for some reason have not done so. This second letter is a good time to ask them about it. Assure your readers that you are reasonable and willing to cooperate, if they will only tell you what the problem is. Like the first reminder, the second one closes by stating the action you want your readers to take.

Persistence is important. If your second reminder is also ignored, send a third letter that is still polite and tactful, but that shows readers the seriousness of their failure to pay. This third letter can express surprise that they haven't paid you or contacted you.

> Because you have paid your bills promptly in the past, we are surprised that you have not paid your February 8 charge of $209.95 for the 36-inch Carthage Cooktop Unit.
>
> The bill is now more than three months overdue.
>
> Good credit is an asset that is very important to you. Good customers are a very important asset to us, too, and we would like very much to have you continue doing business with us.
>
> So won't you please send us a check at once?

If your third reminder is also ignored, send a last letter that is still polite and tactful, but that shows readers the urgent need to settle the claim. Don't worry about being too forceful. The only conciliatory note is to ask once again for payment to avoid possible legal action by you. But don't rant and rave. It will do no good.

> Your bill of $209.95 due us for purchase of a 36-inch Carthage Cooking Unit on February 8 is now more than four months overdue.
>
> Since you have not responded to our three earlier notices to settle your account and to our invitation to explain to us your reason for not paying the bill, we must assume that you do not intend to pay it.
>
> Therefore, if we do not hear from you by June 15, we will turn this claim over to our attorney.
>
> Won't you act now and save yourself the additional expense and annoyance of a lawyer's fee and court costs?

A word of caution is necessary, though, about writing letters that threaten legal suit. Customers have a legal right not to be plagued for bills they don't owe. If your billing is inaccurate, whether caused by machine or human, they can take legal action against you. While there's no federal law that specifically covers this kind of action, some states do have such laws. Besides, persons who feel they are being harassed for an unowed bill can legally charge you with harassment. So make sure that the debt you're attempting to collect really exists.

If you threaten legal action, make sure you take it. The word gets around quickly to deadbeats if you don't follow through on your threat.

SUGGESTIONS FOR APPLYING YOUR KNOWLEDGE

1. To someone you know, write a congratulatory letter that would be appropriate for one of the following occasions: receiving a promotion, winning an award, or celebrating an anniversary or other milestone.
2. Write a thank-you letter to someone who has done something helpful for you.
3. Write a complaint letter that would be appropriate for one of the following situations: receipt of damaged merchandise, receipt of wrong merchandise, receipt of merchandise or service of unsatisfactory quality, or receipt of incorrect billing.
4. Exchange the complaint letters you have written with your fellow students in your occupational writing course and write three different adjustment letters in response to their complaint letters: one that grants full adjustment, one that refuses adjustment, and one that grants partial adjustment. Include a photocopy of the letter you are responding to so your instructor can better evaluate your letters.
5. Collect several examples of collection letters and write a brief report explaining what phrases and approaches they have in common. Make note of any that attempt a humorous or casual approach to the collection and analyze their effectiveness or lack of effectiveness. Include the sample letters as appendixes to your report.
6. Study a series of collection letters and write a report explaining under what circumstances each letter is to be mailed and what approaches each letter takes. Include the sample letters as appendixes to your report.
7. Assume someone owes you $100 and the debt is overdue. Write a series of four collection letters designed to be mailed out at 30-day intervals.

CHAPTER 5

Persuasive Letters

When you think of persuasive letters, you perhaps think in terms of selling people merchandise. They are used for that, naturally. But there are many other things to sell besides material goods. You may be selling ideas or services or asking for political or charitable contributions. You may be selling yourself. The letter of application (see pages 38–46) is a specialized form of sales letter. The proposal, which we take up in Chapter 13, can be either a persuasive report or letter. Persuasive letters can be used to keep you in touch with customers. At Christmastime regular customers of a department store may receive a letter like this one:

```
     Christmas isn't too far away, and we'd like to
help you select some gifts for your family. Right now
our selections are at their peak. You'll see a great
variety of things in almost every price range you
desire.

     Please come by. It will be good to see you again.
```

Gentle and understated, this letter reminds the reader that Christmas is coming. It does not sell anything directly. But it is likely to draw the reader into the store in the near future.

You receive many such sales messages in the mail, perhaps almost daily.

You see ads in newspapers and magazines day after day. Some you read thoroughly; some you start to read and then stop; others you ignore completely. In part your attention is attracted by those letters and ads that speak to your particular interests—tools, cars, education, travel, clothes, whatever. In part your attention is attracted and held by the power of the message. And behind the power is, of course, the skill of the writer. In this chapter we let you in on a few secrets of the direct-mail writer's trade—the art of writing persuasive letters.

The basic secret lies in the direct-mail writer's organizational formula AIDA, an acronym for *attention, interest, desire, action*. That is, you get the reader's *attention*, you awaken *interest and desire* in the reader, and you ask for *action*. Here's how you do it.

ATTENTION

Remember that your letter is uninvited. Most people will open your letter and at least glance at it. But your opening sentence has to give them a good reason to continue reading. If not, they're likely to throw your letter away immediately.

What reasons do people have to continue reading? Most ad and direct-mail writers recognize at least three—promoting self-interest, gaining new information, and satisfying curiosity. To put it another way, there must be some reward for readers if they are to continue reading.

Self-Interest

Self-interest is perhaps the strongest of the three appeals. People respond strongly to openings that promise them such things as health, comfort, leisure, popularity, good looks, status, money, education, love, social success, admiration, or sensory pleasure. People respond to appeals that promise them ways to avoid work, worry, discomfort, and embarrassment.

Ads are quite instructive in how to begin a letter. The headline in an ad and the opening sentence of a letter serve the same attention-getting purpose. One of the most successful ads in history began with the question, "Do you make these mistakes in English?" This is primarily a self-interest opening, although it also arouses curiosity. The appeal to the readers is the avoidance of embarrassment through the avoidance of mistakes in English. The readers are promised a reward. By reading on, they will learn about some *specific* mistakes. The key word in promising such a reward is *these*. The headline would not be nearly as powerful if phrased, "Do you make mistakes in English?" No specific information or reward is implied in this statement. The reader, not given a clear reason to continue, is likely to stop.

Dale Carnegie's famous phrase, "How to win friends and influence people," appearing on his book and in ads sold the book and the Carnegie course to millions of people. The reward is obvious. Most of us desire both friendship and influence. Dale Carnegie is going to tell us *how to* gain both. He promises specific information, and we read on.

Another successful opener has been, "To people who want to write—but can't get started." Here the appeal is to a selected audience. A specific, common writing problem—getting started—is pinpointed. A way of solving the problem is implied. Readers interested in writing but who don't know how to begin are hooked.

New Information

In other openers the reward is new information: "Now, General Electric refrigerators have a roll-out freezer." Other examples:

Announcing a new broiler-toaster

Now—a watch that never needs winding

Now a beer bottle you can open with your bare hands

The appeal in such openers is similar to that of a newspaper headline. It gives readers a little piece of the story and whets their appetites for more.

Curiosity

Openers that arouse curiosity are the third most used, and often curiosity is wedded to self-interest. The classic, "Do you make these mistakes in English?" combines both curiosity and self-interest, as does "How a fool stunt made me a star salesman."

"Revolutionary! It completely revises our outmoded ideas . . ." combines curiosity with a news approach. What is the revolutionary "It" that changes outmoded ideas?

Key Words and Questions

Certain key words show up in openers again and again—words such as *how, who, what, when, which, where,* and *why. Announcing, new,* and *now* are common. When you're stuck for an opener, write one of these words and see what you can build onto it to hook your reader's interest in your subject.

Questions are another frequently used approach. An ad for a weight-reducing diet drink asked, "Is this the day you do something about your weight?" Millions of Americans are slightly overweight. This opener appeals to most of them. It assumes that they want to do something about their weight—they just need a little push in the right direction.

Be as specific as you can in your questions. Which of these openers would be the best for a Navy recruiting message?

Do you want a job in the Navy?

Which of these 45 jobs do you want?

Right, the second, much more specific question is the best. And, in fact, it was the opener used.

GAINING INTEREST AND DESIRE

How do you keep people reading after you have gained their attention? How do you build a desire in them for what you are selling? First of all, you must get your readers into the picture. If your opener doesn't do it, you must do it immediately thereafter. If you don't, you'll lose your readers to a so-what attitude.

Place your readers in the picture by showing how the product or service relates to them. The ad that began, "Do you make these mistakes in English?" continued as follows:

Sherwin Cody's remarkable invention has enabled more than 100,000 people to correct their mistakes in English. Only 15 minutes a day is required to improve your speech and writing.

If you think you make mistakes in English, you are now interested. You are in the picture. It takes only 15 minutes a day.

Involve your reader. The weight-reducing ad that began, "Is this the day you do something about your weight?" included charts that showed desirable weights for different heights. Few people can resist checking such charts to see how close their weight is to the desired level. If their weight is more than desirable—as is likely—they are immediately interested.

To build desire you take advantage of the reader's attention and interest by making specific claims for your product or service. You must be quite specific here. If you are vague, you will lose credibility and lose the interest already gained. If physical facts such as size, weight, color, or ingredients are needed, you must supply them. Don't forget the functional characteristics of your product or service. What does it do? How well does it do it? What is its use? What problems does it solve? Most important, how will it benefit the reader? Mail order catalog writers are masters at compressing a good deal of specific detail into a small space. Notice how AIDA can be compressed into just a few lines if need be:

Sheepskin Boot Socks

When you're wearing rubber boots, waders or rubberized footwear, here's the best way to keep your feet warm and snug. Cut 6" high from long wool sheepskin, these boot socks will take up extra moisture in rubber boots. For men only in sizes 6 through 13. No half sizes. Indicate shoe size when ordering.[1]

[1] Gokeys' Sportsman Catalog, St. Paul, Minnesota; reprinted by permission.

In a sales message like this one you are seeing a specific application of the you-attitude. Successful ad and direct-mail writers always have a specific reader in mind. They visualize him or her before them as they begin their sales message. What sort of person would buy sheepskin boot socks? We visualize him as a middle-aged man, ruddy of complexion from being outdoors, hair touched with gray. As he reads the message, he is sitting comfortably in an easychair, a favorite hunting dog nearby. He likes natural materials next to his skin. He prefers soft wool to polyester. He is a fisherman who has often experienced cold and damp feet. When he was young that was OK, but now he'd like a bit more comfort. This message will speak to him. A romanticized image? Probably so. But that image would put us in the proper frame of mind to write a sales message to a fisherman who probably romanticizes *his* image of himself.

Look at another successful sales message; like the first one, this is from Gokeys' 1976 Fall Sportsman Catalog.

Women's Hiking Slacks and Shorts

For the Lady hiker, camper or vacationer in a choice of 2 fabrics: 50% Polyester–50% Cotton Twill or 100% Cotton Pin Wale Corduroy. Machine washable. Specially cut and tailored to give a trim fit. Four front pockets give all the room you need for carrying necessities—no back pockets. Slacks come in ample inseam length so that you may set them to any desired length. Shorts have 4-½" inseams and are hemmed and cuffed. Twill colors: Light Blue or Beige. Corduroy color: Slacks, Beige only. Sizes 8 to 18. Give fabric, color and size when ordering.[2]

Facts such as those presented in these two Gokeys' ads provide credibility. Remember, too, in most cases you are appealing to both emotion and intellect—heart and brain. The heart may want something—like sheepskin boot socks—but the brain may overrule the desire unless it gets sufficient factual evidence. Notice, for example, how the ads for Mercedes-Benz automobiles emphasize the engineering marvels of the car. Truthfully, the people who can afford $20,000 for a car are more likely to be seeking status—a desire of the heart. But the brain needs to be told that the engineering features are worth the extra money, that the car has a high resale value, and so forth. We all rationalize our desires, and supporting facts make it easier for us to do so.

What kinds of facts can be used in persuasion? As we have already seen, physical description and functional characteristics are appropriate. You can mention the reputation of your company or product. You can point to long years of experience. You can offer test and performance data. You can give testimonials from satisfied customers. You can show the product or service in action. The famous Charles Atlas ads used action. For years they showed skinny weaklings how to build their bodies. The ads always

[2]Reprinted by permission.

ended by showing the skinny weakling, now grown into a man rippling with muscle, knocking down the bully who had picked on him at the beginning of the ad—the service in action.

A more subtle use of the same in-action principle is at work in this coat ad from Norm Thompson Outfitters Fall and Winter Catalog:

> The Imperial possesses a unique elegance you'll wear with pride. It was designed primarily for town and travel, but it's so adaptable, you can team it up with casual and country clothes for a look that's bound to turn heads your way.

Before writing a sales message you should research your product or service as thoroughly as possible. Dig out as much information as you can. Then try to choose those facts that give you an edge over the competition. Just be sure your claims are credible and true—that what you are selling will live up to your description.

GETTING ACTION

If you want action from your reader, you must ask for it. In most sales letters it's desirable to ask your reader to do something: if not a major action, such as buying your product, at least an intermediate step, such as sending for a brochure or filling in a questionnaire. Make the action as easy to do as possible. Provide specific details on how to order, for example. Or provide specific information on how to reach your place of business, even using a map if necessary. Notice how even the small Gokeys' catalog ads call for action through statements like "Indicate shoe size when ordering." Sometimes the calls for action can be extensive. The end of a sales letter from *Writer's Digest* concludes with no less than five calls for action. Count them:

> Return the Half-Price Savings Certificate enclosed and try Writer's Digest *without risk*. If after sixty days you don't feel it can help you become a better writer, just let me know and I'll see you receive a *full refund* of your subscription payment.
>
> Rejoin us as a subscriber now and we'll send you the next year of Writer's Digest for *just half the regular subscription price*.
>
> You get the next twelve issues of Writer's Digest for only $6. And you have my personal guarantee of *satisfaction or your money back*. I challenge you to become a better writer this year. And through Writer's Digest, I can help you do it.
>
> So please check the "YES" box on the enclosed Savings Certificate and return it to me today. I've enclosed a postage-paid envelope for your convenience.
>
> I will look forward to your reply.

>   Sincerely,
>
>   John Brady
>   Editor

PS. I'd be very much interested to learn of your experiences as a writer and of your reactions to the changes we're making in Writer's Digest. So please take this opportunity to rejoin us at the special half price rate, and let me hear from you soon.

PPS. If, for some reason, you are no longer interested in writing, I'd like to know that too. If you aren't interested in seeing how the new Writer's Digest can help you, please check the "NO" box on your Savings Certificate and return it to me at my expense. Thanks.

PUTTING IT ALL TOGETHER

Figure 5-1 is a sales letter sent to its members by the National Geographic Society. Read it over before you read the discussion that follows.

In the National Geographic letter the attention step is the question printed in the box above the salutation. The use of an actual headline is a fairly common practice in sales letters. Of course, the same question would work well as the opening sentence after the salutation. The attention-getting approach in the letter is curiosity. Our immediate reward for reading on is to find out what a pack rat, a campfire, a hornet's nest, and dolphin trainer have in common.

Once into the letter, the reader is put into the picture with the phrase, "The 4-through-8-year-old children in your life." The audience is now selected, and it's a wide audience when you consider that parents, grand-parents, uncles and aunts, even older brothers and sisters could have 4-through-8-year-old children in their lives.

The writer immediately begins to give specific information to hold reader interest and to build desire for the adventure books.

Reading the letter, you learn about the books' contents and that the books were pretested on children. You learn that the print is big. You find out the size of the books, the number of pages in each, and the cost of the set. You learn that in only four years nearly five million of these sets have been purchased—a striking testimonial to their worth.

The letter closes with a request for action: "Simply complete the enclosed postage-free form and drop it in the mail." Note how easy it is for the reader to act. No money needs to be sent. The Society will bill later.

The letter is simply written, but it does not talk down to the reader. The average sentence length is just short of 15 words. Frequent ellipsis points (. . .) make the longer sentences seem even shorter. Paragraphs run three or four lines long. The longest is only six lines. Indented material is used, both to emphasize certain facts and to break up the page. The shorter paragraphs and the indentations make the page inviting to the eye.

With few exceptions simple subject-verb, active-voice sentences are used (See Writer's Guide, pages 284–286). The language is mature without being jargony or overly difficult.

NATIONAL GEOGRAPHIC SOCIETY
17th and M Streets, N.W. Washington, D.C., U.S.A. 20036

Office of The Secretary

What do a desert pack rat -- a

campfire ... a hornet's nest ... and

a dolphin trainer have in common?

Dear Member,

The answer is — they're all featured in National Geographic's new Books for Young Explorers. Those wonderful, color-splashed books that we publish especially for the 4-through-8-year-old children in your life.

The titles of this year's four-volume Set V are WONDERS OF THE DESERT WORLD ... CAMPING ADVENTURE ... ANIMALS THAT BUILD THEIR HOMES ... and THE PLAYFUL DOLPHINS. These books are sure to become your children's favorite reading fun. And here's why....

The books' subjects were actually chosen by children in a special survey of preschool and elementary students. So they are books that children really want to read.

The text is fresh and friendly. It is printed in big, easy-to-read type. And it is written in the vocabulary and at the comprehension level of beginning readers. Yet -- unlike many books written for the younger reader -- these talk to your children, and never "down to" them.

The big, bright photographs that illustrate the text make these books a learning adventure -- even for the little folks who haven't yet begun to read.

Best of all, Books for Young Explorers Set V has the answers to the kinds of questions that kids ask -- the "gee whiz" facts that kids love to learn....

A dolphin can find things underwater -- even if it's

blindfolded! A badger can dig faster than a man

with a shovel! Cactuses as tall as trees live in

the desert! There are tiny plants (without leaves)

that grow on rocks!

Each book has 32 pages brimming with this kind of wonder. And -- each has

Figure 5-1 Advertising letter. (Courtesy Marian Reeser, National Geographic Society; reprinted by permission of the Society)

heavy, child-tested paper ... durable, hardbound covers ... easy-to-handle 8 3/4"-by-11 1/4" size ... and full color on every page.

And there's an additional bonus: Each four-volume set of Books for Young Explorers comes with a fascinating booklet for adults entitled More About....

This 24-page illustrated guide contains additional information about each book's subject ... more colorful photographs ... a look at how the books were created ... and a suggested reading list. A useful supplement that encourages discussion and further study.

And all this - four wonderful books plus More About... - is only $6.95! A National Geographic book bargain that we are very proud to be able to offer our members.

One of the reasons we can bring you this value is that Books for Young Explorers are sold only by direct order from your Society. Another is the enormous volume of sales these books generate. Since 1972, when the first set was published, nearly 5 million copies have been purchased! This kind of success allows us to offer them to you at a much lower price than books of similar quality available in bookstores.

And just wait until you and your children get a look at this year's Books for Young Explorers Set V. It's a winning combination of fun, learning ... and value.

The enclosed brochure will give you a small sample of the color, excitement, and child appeal in these books. Look it over ...

... then think of your children (nieces, nephews, grandchildren, neighbors) ... the occasions (Christmas, birthday, rainy days) ... and order the number of sets you'd like to give your young friends.

Simply complete the enclosed postage-paid order form and drop it in the mail. Send no money now. We will bill you for your order when it is delivered in October.

We know you'll be delighted with Books for Young Explorers Set V. And what's even better -- we know your children will love them ... and learn from them. And that's the best gift of all!

Sincerely,

Owen R. Anderson

Secretary

ORA/ab

P.S. For those of you who missed it, we are also making available the current Set IV of Books for Young Explorers. See the enclosed folder for details -- and, if you choose, check the Set IV box on your order form.

Figure 5-1 Advertising letter *(continued).*

All in all, it's a well-done letter—persuasive, yet done with the taste and dignity that befits the National Geographic Society.

Not all persuasive letters are selling a product or even a service. Sometimes they are directly trying to persuade the reader to an action of some sort. Read the letter in Figure 5-2. This letter attempts to persuade a member of a society to take over a hard task—to help run a national convention. While not as obvious as a sales letter, the letter in Figure 5-2 follows the AIDA format.

Attention is gained by the thought that even while an upcoming convention is being planned, planning for a convention still two years away has begun. Certain attractive things about the 1978 convention are pointed out, and the people already involved are named.

The responsibilities of the job are outlined. The point is made that the job may not be as difficult as it might seem if good panel moderators are chosen. Benefits to the reader and to the Society and the profession are pointed out.

An intermediate action is suggested: "If you have any questions, please call. . . ." It is made clear that the receiver will have to take the action of saying yes or no within a few days. The yes answer is suggested.

Notice again that sentences and paragraphs are short. Sentence structures and vocabulary remain mature but simple.

You will have many occasions in your life to write persuasive letters, sales or otherwise. When you do, remember AIDA—*attention, interest, desire, action*. Most persuasion is built around this basic pattern.

SUGGESTIONS FOR APPLYING YOUR KNOWLEDGE

Real examples of the material discussed in this chapter are all around us in newspapers and magazines and probably in our mailboxes. Ads and sales letters provide a rich field for short assignments. Here are some things you might try, both in class and out:

1. Write a sales letter for some product or service you are connected with in an off-campus job.
2. Analyze a sales message you have recently received. Pay attention to its vocabulary and sentence and paragraph structures. See how closely it follows AIDA.
3. Write a sales letter for some campus activity such as the cafeteria, student center, library, or audio-visual center. Remember, you must research an activity and its potential users before you can sell it successfully.
4. Analyze the distinctions between ads that appear in technical and professional journals and those found in popular magazines. Be particularly alert for differences in emotional and factual content. Which appeal mostly to the head, which to the heart?
5. Elsewhere in this book (pages 115–146) we discuss process and mechanism descriptions. Analyze a sales message that contains such description. See where it follows the techniques we have described and where it does not.
6. Write a letter persuading someone to take on a tough job or to make a contribution. Use AIDA.
7. Think of some of the many situations in which persuasive techniques are needed. Can AIDA help you in any of them?

Sundstrand Corporation

CORPORATE OFFICES • 4751 HARRISON AVENUE, ROCKFORD, ILLINOIS 61101 • PHONE (815) 226-6000 • TWX 910-631-4255

September 14, 1976

Dorothy Saxner
American Hospital Association
840 North Lake Shore Drive
Chicago, IL 60611

Dear Dorothy,

As the 24th ITCC planning continues at a fast pace, a few persons are beginning
to plan the 25th ITCC in Dallas -- and I am one of them.

The 25th ITCC will be quite a festive conference, I think. We are planning an
"in retrospect" theme. We have some ideas we want to try, but we need another
person to help make this ITCC a noteworthy event for STC. We think that person
is you.

Here's the program cast at present: Dr. Thomas E. Pearsall, professor at the
University of Minnesota, is program chairman; I am deputy program chairman;
Dr. Robert Weaver, professor at the Air Force Institute of Technology, is chairman of the writing and editing stem; and we are awaiting word on a graphics stem
chairman.

What we would have you do is to be the management stem chairman. Your tasks
would be to coordinate and plan your stem based upon the conference theme;
evaluate abstracts of papers submitted for presentation; select panel moderators;
and, in general, see that your stem is planned, organized, and is complete. You
will have to do a moderate amount of telephoning and you would have to attend
the Dallas ITCC, so you would need some support from your employer. If you
have selected "good" panel moderators, most of your work will be done by them.

I think the experiences you will gain will be similar in philosophy to your
other activities with STC: you will benefit professionally, STC will benefit,
and the field of technical communication will benefit. Please consider, and
if you have any questions, please call me at 815/226-7365.

After a few days, I will call you for your decision. I hope you say yes!

Sincerely,

-Dick

Richard E. Wiegand   cc: Dr. Thomas E. Pearsall
Supervisor
Communication Design

REW:dje

Figure 5-2 Persuasive letter (courtesy Dorothy Saxner and Richard E. Wiegand)

UNIT TWO
Reports

CHAPTER 6
Basic Principles of Reports

Successful business and industrial organizations get their jobs done. To do them, they gather information and move it to those who need it or to those whom they want to have it—employees, suppliers, customers. They transfer all kinds of information in all forms of letters and reports. Unsuccessful organizations don't keep records or transfer information efficiently. Productivity stops. Ignorance and guesswork replace knowledge and information. The idea is simple. The effectiveness of an organization is tied to its reporting.

Because good reporting is so important to an organization's functioning, all organizations are in the business of communication. No matter whether your job is in accounting, engineering, production, sales, or service, as an employee you can expect report writing to be an important part of your work. You won't work in a vacuum: you'll work with and through other people, and you'll have to communicate with them. Without the ability to inform, you will not be successful.

The major types of correspondence that you might be expected to write have been covered in Unit I. What we'll cover in this unit are the important types of reports.

But before we take up individual types of reports, we want to present helpful ways for you to look at specific types of reports and at your obligation to make reports as easy to understand as possible.

TYPES OF REPORTS

Reports carry information to those who want it or need it. The information is usually expected or requested by those receiving the report.

When you prepare a report—regardless of its length, content, and form, whether it's written or oral—you'll be presenting specific information to a specific audience for a specific purpose. What information you include and what relationship you establish with your audience will depend largely upon what purpose you have in reporting. Exactly what information does your audience need or expect? Of what use will the information be? The answers to these questions will give you a good idea of what your purpose should be.

Most reports either inform or inform and analyze. The informational report informs your audience what you have found out, and it includes little or no commentary and interpretation. The analytical report presents the facts together with an analysis of the facts. Learn to think in terms of the purpose or function the information in your report serves, and you'll know what to put in your report. You'll be able to decide better what information to include, what information to emphasize, and how to organize your report.

In Unit I we gave you a formula approach to important types of correspondence. In this unit we'll discuss the more complex task of reporting and show you the different choices you have to make while planning and preparing reports.

CONSIDERING YOUR AUDIENCE

How beneficial your report is to your audience depends on how well you meet their interests and needs and estimate their ability to understand what you're trying to tell them. So get to know your audience and their needs and keep them in mind while you're planning and preparing your report. If you really know your audience, you've got a leg up on the job. If you don't, there's no way you're going to prepare a good report—no matter how much you hack away at it.

Two important things to remember when considering your audience are that they are real persons like yourself, and that probably they'll be eager to gain the information you have for them.

But don't assume that just because your audience may be eagerly waiting for your report that they are captive. Don't let your knowledge of the subject and your convenience totally govern how you prepare the report. Prepare a "user-oriented" report, much as the engineer-designer gives prime consideration to the users of a highway or an electric drill.

Show Courtesy to Your Audience

In the heat of on-the-job reporting don't overlook the courtesy that you naturally owe your audience. You must get your report to them in plenty of time—when they need it or want it. By all means, if you have doubts about any aspect of the report, ask your audience if they have any special requests concerning the report. They may give you information that will help you cut down on their reading or listening time and increase their comprehension. There may be times when they make the conditions for the report and establish specific requirements concerning the content, organization, format, and publication procedure or delivery.

In such situations your anticipation of your audience's desires is relatively easy. You've got their point of view from the start. Sometimes, though, in the case of written reports, your readers may not be available for reference. In the absence of such clear identification of your readers' needs, there still exist a number of techniques you can use to achieve a good level of legibility and readability.

Make Your Report Legible

Legibility relates to how easy or difficult your report is to read once it's on the printed page. Keep these points in mind:

- Use good quality paper heavy enough to make the typing stand out. Type your report on white bond paper, 20-lb. weight, 8½ by 11 inches.
- If copies are required, make them by the best reproduction process you have available. Carbon copies are generally undesirable.
- Maintain one-inch margins all around.
- If you're going to put your report in a binder, leave two inches of margin on the left-hand side.
- If typed single space, allow a double space between paragraphs, above and below headings, lists, long quotations, and graphics.
- If typed double space, allow no extra space between paragraphs, but allow a triple space above headings and above and below lists, long quotations, and graphics.
- Use legible, nondistracting type. Avoid script and types with fancy lines and flourishes.
- Use typographical elements to make words, phrases, and sentences stand out. Catch your readers' attention by using italics (underlining), all-capital letters, and different colors. But don't overdo such devices.
- Enclose graphics in boxes.
- If the sequence of a list is random (as this list is) or arbitrary, use bullets (•) or dashes(—). If the order is important, use arabic numerals (1, 2, 3 . . .).
- Keep paragraphs fairly short (under 100 words) to break the page vertically.

Don't let your report fail because of physical obstacles.

Make Your Report Readable

Making reports readable is a subject that strikes a responsive chord in persons who have to read and write reports as part of their work. To judge from the responses received by Prof. Richard M. Davis of the Air Force Institute of Technology in a recent study[1] students in technical writing courses should learn to write readable reports. Below are five typical answers from business people to Davis's question, "What should be the main emphasis in a course in technical writing—the most important things that a student should learn or be able to do as a result of taking it?"

[Learn] the ability to present concise writing . . . using technical verbiage or terms only where necessary to communicate the content to the reader in the most expeditious manner.

> Roy L. Aach, President
> Roy L. Aach & Associates
> Clayton, Missouri

Learn to write in understandable terms for upper management consumption. Write from the user's viewpoint and be brief and specific.

> Guy J. Bacci, II, Manager
> Corporate Industrial Engineering
> International Harvester Company
> Hinsdale, Illinois

Prepare written material in a clear, concise, and well-organized manner—not wordy but in sufficient detail to ensure that subject is adequately presented.

> G. L. Hancock, Jr.,
> Production Advisor
> Gulf Oil Company—U.S.
> Houston, Texas

[Learn] to communicate technical work in a simple language which will allow a nontechnical manager to be able to understand and act on the information.

> James E. Mahoney, Director
> Office of Management Planning
> Office of the Secretary
> Department of Health, Education and Welfare
> Washington, D.C.

Learn to write clearly and briefly, and to include essential support for opinions.

> John E. Slater
> Executive Vice President (Ret.)
> American Export Lines
> Essex Falls, N.J.

Clarity. Conciseness. Content. Organization. These appear to be the major ways to make your reports more readable. We'll talk about content and organization for specific reports as we come to them. Here we want to talk about clarity and conciseness.

[1]Richard M. Davis. *Technical Writing: Its Importance in the Engineering Profession and Its Place in Engineering Curricula—A Survey of the Experience and Opinions of Prominent Engineers.* Wright-Patterson AFB, OH: Air Force Institute of Technology, September 1975.

Readability relates to how easy or difficult, how pleasurable and interesting or unpleasant and dull, your report is to read. It all boils down to how long it takes your readers to read your report and how much they retain after reading it. As one 19th-century writer put it:

> The writer does the most who gives his reader the most knowledge and takes from him the least time.

Much research has been done in the past fifty years to find out what makes writing more readable. A lot of the research has been concerned with the number of syllables per word, the number of words per sentence, the number of sentences per paragraph, and how personal and direct the writing is. Conclusions from this research boil down to two simple principles: Don't reach for long words, and keep an eye on general sentence length.

The first five principles behind Robert Gunning's Fog Index[2] are worth noting because as long as you follow them you'll be on safe ground. They apply in most cases to speaking as well as writing.

- Keep Sentences Short
- Prefer the Simple to the Complex
- Prefer the Familiar Word
- Avoid Unnecessary Words
- Put Action in Your Verbs

Keep sentences short   Everybody knows the difference between a short sentence and a long one. Right? A sentence of 11 words is a short sentence. A sentence of 35 words is a long sentence. Right? Not necessarily. Let's look at an 11-word sentence.

> There is a direct line connecting us with the Seattle office.

If we count only the number of words in the sentence, we might call this a "short" sentence. But if we count the number of words needed to make up the thought, we would have to call this a "long" sentence. Why? Because the 11 words communicate a nine-word thought.

> A direct line connects us with the Seattle office.

Compare the following two sentences. Both contain 10 words.

> The high quality type soldering job was done by Carter.

> Because Carter did good soldering, he was promoted to supervisor.

The first sentence is too long. It uses 10 words to communicate a six-word thought: *Carter did the high-quality soldering.* Maybe even a three-word idea: *Carter soldered well.* The last two versions would not always be the

---

[2]Robert Gunning, *The Technique of Clear Writing* (New York: McGraw-Hill, 1952).

best possible sentences for the situation, but they are certainly better than the original 10-word sentence. The second sentence is short. It contains 10 words, too, but it says twice as much in the same number of words.

So what's a "short" sentence? What's a "long" sentence? A short sentence contains just the number of words necessary to communicate the idea. A long sentence contains more words than necessary. Do you begin to see what is meant by a short sentence?

Lots of bad habits make sentences long. Gunning's principles help keep sentences short. So pay attention to what they are and to what we say about using them.

Prefer the simple to the complex   Perhaps the original sin of unreadable writing is the writer's pride in his "special" knowledge. We once lived in a town where the weather reporter (who had no formal training in meteorology—or communication, it seems) for a local television station used to bamboozle viewers with complicated analyses of global movements of weather masses, technical terminology, and weather maps that looked like tangled spaghetti—all this to an audience that wanted to know whether or not to take an umbrella to work the next morning. Nobody was ever sure what the forecast was.

The former weather reporter's "reporting" is just one example of an unfortunate truth: Occupational writing is often more complex than it need be. The reason is often that many writers are insecure in their knowledge. The worst kind of gobbledygook comes from people trying to cover their ignorance. When secure in their knowledge, most writers improve at once. Learn to write simple, easy-to-understand language. Your readers will appreciate it.

Prefer the familiar word   Occasionally you might have to use words unfamiliar to your readers. Every trade and interest group has its own accepted and necessary technical language. Our quarrel is not with the words themselves, but with people who use those words without defining them in communicating with readers who don't understand them. Even worse are those who use pseudotechnical language to replace ordinary words that are just as good. Pseudotechnical vocabulary is language passed off as "necessary." But why would anyone need to call a garden "a personalized recreational eco-unit"?

A common source of pseudotechnical vocabulary is the substitution of long, heavy, formal words for everyday words. Sheer length is not what we're objecting to. It's addiction to long words that we are trying to break. Make it a practice to use the words in the right column instead of their more unfamiliar synonym in the left column.

Long, heavy, formal words	Everyday words
abate, abatement	drop, decrease, cut down
behest	request

cognizant	aware
delineate	draw, describe
facilitate	ease, help
germane	relevant
hiatus	gap, interval
impair	weaken, damage, hurt
lethal	deadly, fatal
multitudinous	many
nadir	low point
obviate	prevent, do away with
palpable	obvious, visible, clear
remuneration	pay
salient	important
terminate	end
utilize	use
vicissitude	change
wherewithal	means

The list can be extended, but you get the idea. As you can recognize, not all the words in the left column are long or unfamiliar. Some readers will even know all the words. But even when they understand the big words, they may regard those who use them as word snobs or show-offs.

A second common source of unfamiliar words is the unnecessary use of foreign phrases when English equivalents exist.

Don't use	**Use**
bona fide	genuine
chef d'oeuvre	masterpiece
in toto	altogether
ipso facto	by the very nature of the case
milieu	surroundings, environment
modus operandi	method
per annum	a year, each year
per diem	a day, each day
per se	as such
raison d'être	The primary reason for, the justification for
sine qua non	essential

You may occasionally have the urge to use a foreign phrase. Just remember that most readers will regard the phrase and you as pretentious and irritating.

Users of big words and unfamiliar words seldom stop at single words. Combinations of words to make meaningless phrases seem to have a special place in their hearts. But the impression made by such language is like that of pseudotechnical vocabulary—it's so much static. In fact, that's what is wrong with it. It's all noise and no meaning. Such phrase building is demonstrated ironically by Gerald Cohen's humorous Dial-A-Buzzword, a pseudotechnical vocabulary wheel that makes it easy to string words together until they register on the Richter Earthquake Scale.

The three dials rotate independently. From Figure 6-1 you might select combinations like "functional input compatibility," "operational systems environment," or "sequential output approach." A turn of the dials might result in the alignment shown in Figure 6-2 from which you could choose "overall communications implementation," "integrated performance analysis," or "conceptual interactive criteria." Joining the selected phrases produces jaw-breakers that say nothing.

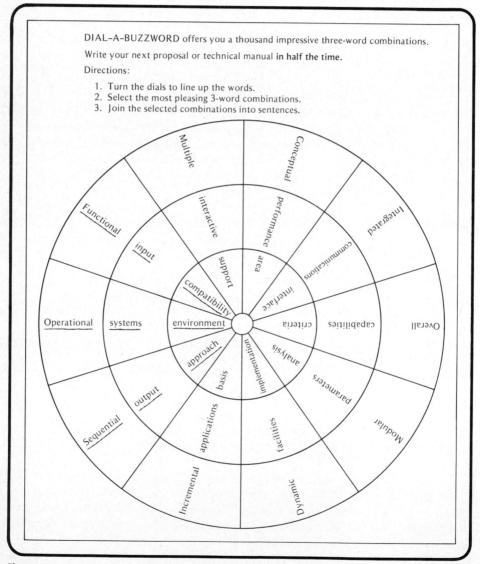

DIAL–A–BUZZWORD offers you a thousand impressive three-word combinations.

Write your next proposal or technical manual **in half the time.**

Directions:

1. Turn the dials to line up the words.
2. Select the most pleasing 3-word combinations.
3. Join the selected combinations into sentences.

Figure 6-1 Cohen's Dial-A-Buzzword. (Courtesy Gerald Cohen)

When unfamiliar language crowds out more familiar language, writing becomes especially difficult to read. The solution to such writing is to avoid technical vocabulary (unless you define it) when your readers don't understand it and to avoid pseudotechnical vocabulary all the time. Simply learn to live without it. You'll avoid a lot of foolishness.

The paradox of technical language is that while it provides an economical way to convey specialized information to those who understand the language, at the same time it blocks information to those who don't understand it. If a technical term is necessary and there's any doubt that your

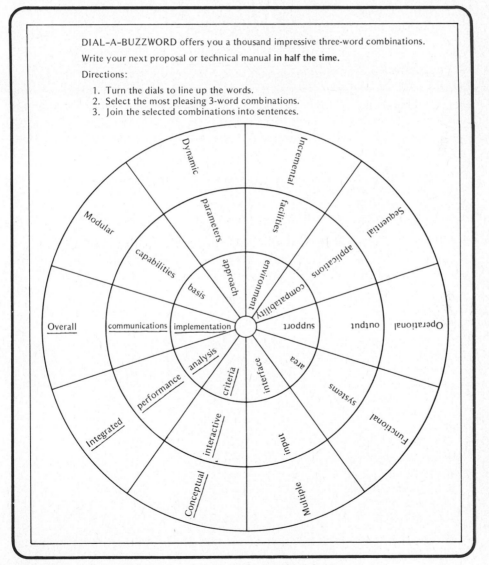

Figure 6-2 Cohen's Dial-A-Buzzword. (Courtesy Gerald Cohen)

readers might not understand it, make its meaning clear the first time you use it by providing a definition.

Avoid unnecessary words You've just seen how unfamiliar words create static. You'll now see how unnecessary words are like so much fat. To limit your writing to necessary words, you have to think thin.

Here are three tips for word dieting:

1. reduce fat verbal and prepositional phrases and conjunctions,
2. remove fillers,
3. cut out unnecessarily repetitious words.

Reduce fat verbal and prepositional phrases Certain verbal phrases produce globs of fat in your writing. Verbs like *have, give, take, be, do, get,* and *make* are innocent enough by themselves, but when connected with nouns ending in *-ance, -ence, -ion, -ity,* and *-ment,* they are loaded with calories. Dozens of them exist. Here are five that can be streamlined by single words:

to be in agreement with	agree
to give assistance to	assist, help, aid
to have a preference for	prefer
to be desirous of	desire, want

Likewise, fat prepositional phrases and conjunctions also bog down sentences like water-filled balloons. The following are typical heavy phrases that should be replaced by lighter ones:

in accordance with	with
in the event of	if
due to the fact that	due to, because
for the purpose of training	for training, to train
pursuant to	under
prior to	before
subsequent to	after
with regard to, in regard to	on, about
in order to	to
in view of the fact that	since, because
with reference to	about
at the present time	now
at this point in time	now
at that point in time	then
by means of	by
during the time that	that, while

The basic principle is to avoid verbs, prepositions, and conjunctions that consist of more than one word.

Remove fillers   *It* and *there* are often used as fillers, words that fill out a statement. When a filler is the subject of a sentence, it is followed by a linking verb and a word that is the logical subject of the sentence.

There are three trusses the beam rests on.
There is a suitable airplane available at Hopkinsville.
There were six workers absent from the night shift.
It is our plan to be in Chicago next Friday.
It is obvious *that* we must meet the deadline.

Such constructions as *there are, there is, there were, it is,* and *it is . . . that* anticipate the logical subject and verb and distract from the natural emphasis they should have. Since fillers take up space and delay the logical subject and verb, removing them replaces emphasis on the logical subject and verb and shortens the sentence.

The *beam rests* on three trusses.
A suitable *airplane is* available at Hopkinsville
Six *workers were* absent from the night shift.
We plan to be in Chicago next Friday.
Obviously, *we must meet* the deadline.

Cut out unnecessarily repetitious words   A word or phrase that repeats itself or says the same thing twice is a redundancy. A redundant system in engineering is a back-up system that provides alternative action if the primary system should fail. Redundant systems in space vehicles are desirable. Certain redundancies in writing are useful, too:

- An overview statement that gives the reader a good mental picture of the content and arrangement of a report.
- A heading system that identifies key topics that are restated and developed in detail in the report text.
- A graphic that repeats what is described in words, or vice versa.

But many expressions are so unnecessarily redundant as to be pointless. Examples are *red in color, rectangular in shape, large in size, return back, combine together,* and *25 in number.* Only the first word in each case should be kept. Other redundancies come early in phrases: *the month of July, the city of Elmwood, the field of biology,* and *a total of 30.* Only the last word should be kept.

  Another source of unnecessarily repetitious words is doublets: *any and all, each and every, revered and respected, unless and until, if and when, cease and desist,* and *give and convey.* These are perhaps the redundancies hardest to give up because we find ready-made phrases so easy to use; they flow so readily from the pen. However, they must be given up. If you write a sentence like "Each and every one of our employees and workers is ready and willing to work and toil long and hard," you should be eager to cut out one of each of the doublets. Such slices will result in a 50 percent weight loss.

Put action in your verbs The following pairs of sentences show how fat, sluggish verbs, general verbs, and passive voice verbs create unnecessary sentence length and sluggishness. Notice how the streamlined, specific, and active verbs bring the second sentence in each pair to life.

It is our intention to get the proposal *in* by the deadline.
We intend to submit the proposal by the deadline.

I won't be able to make the Denver meeting.
I can't attend the Denver meeting.

The demonstration *was seen by us.*
We saw the demonstration.

Earlier you saw how to get rid of sluggish verb phrases by replacing them with streamlined verbs. Simply reduce "It is our intention . . ." to "We intend . . ."

Verbs like *to get* and *to make* may not seem objectionable at first, and often they are the appropriate verbs to use. But the results are often poor when they are used extensively in the place of more specific verbs. A widely used desk dictionary lists 94 meanings for *get*. While *get* is often acceptable, especially in conversation, you should choose verbs more carefully in writing. Make the verb more important in the sentence.

General verb We hope *to get* a few more shipments this week.
Specific verb We hope *to receive* a few more shipments this week.
General verb We are certain that we *will get through* this job Friday.
Specific verb We are certain that we *will finish* this job Friday.
General verb We *will get a look at* the new antitank gun during the visit.
Specific verb We *will inspect* the new antitank gun during the visit.

A third way to put action in your verbs is to use the active voice. You frequently have a choice of making a particular noun either the subject or object in a sentence, with a resulting difference in verb form.

Active verb The company *gave* each employee a bonus.
Passive verb Each employee *was given* a bonus by the company.

In the active voice the subject acts. In the passive voice the subject is acted upon. The passive consists of some form of *be* plus the past participle (*is given, will be given, has been given*). Verb tense has nothing to do with whether the verb is active or passive.

In the active voice the actor is always identified because it's the subject:

The *company* gave . . .

In the passive voice the actor may or may not be identified:

Each employee was given a bonus *by the company*.
Each employee was given a bonus.

Most sentences use active verbs for a good reason: the logic of the active voice sentence matches the grammar of the sentence. Whoever or whatever controls the action is the subject of the sentence; whoever or whatever receives the action is the object.

There are times when the passive voice is effective:

1. When the actor is obvious or unknown:

The work will be completed in three months.
The office was robbed at 3 A.M.

2. When the receiver of the action is more important than the doer:

The bricks were then moved to the cooling chamber.
Sulphuric acid was poured into the container.
The letter has been filed.

There's really no surefire rule to follow about using the active voice. Try to put what you want emphasized in the subject slot. If the passive buries your main idea the way sluggish and general verbs do, use the active.

You should be able to extract enormous mileage from the few minutes it has taken you to view the first five principles behind Gunning's Fog Index. We believe that the biggest obstacle in the way of readable writing is the misplaced zeal to appear well-educated that makes persons feel uncomfortable making clear, direct statements that are easy to understand. Just remember—there are readers out there on the other end of the line. If you want to impress them, do so by making your writing readable.

To end this section on expression, we thought you might enjoy this brief article that appeared a few years ago in the St. Louis *Globe-Democrat* and other newspapers. We offer it without comment.

Ghost Editor Trims Memo on HEW Message Brevity
EVE EDSTROM

WASHINGTON—There's a person at the Department of Health, Education and Welfare who should be writing all government memos. He or she just polished the newest "HEW gem"—a memorandum attempting to say that HEW Secretary Robert H. Finch wants his top staff to send him shorter briefing memoranda.

Finch's executive assistant, L. Patrick Gray III, who has a considerable Pentagon background, tried to get the message across in a memorandum that was officially circulated. An unknown recipient translated Gray's memo for personal distribution, and showed that the word count could have been reduced by about two-thirds.

For example, Gray's opener was: "As a general rule, and certainly not applicable in all situations, the briefing memoranda forwarded to the secretary have been loaded with an excessive amount of verbiage."

The translation read: "Most of the briefing memoranda forwarded to the secretary have been too wordy."

Gray's memorandum continued: "In the future, the briefing memoranda should highlight the issue, set forth alternative courses of action or approaches to resolve the issue, and finally, a recommendation regarding the action to be taken by the secretary should be made with reasons therefor."

Translation: "Briefing memoranda should highlight the issue, state alternatives to resolve the issue, and the action to be taken by the secretary."

Gray said: "It is envisioned that this sort of writing will not require more than a page and a half to two pages at the most."

Translation: "No more than two pages should be required."

An equally terse translation—"Supporting data may be appended"—was offered for Gray's statement that "Additional supporting data, information, comments, and supporting documentation may be included beneath the writing referred to above, as deemed necessary."

Gray concluded with: "The secretary does not, in any way, intend that the free flow of information to him be restricted or limited; however, he does desire that the central issue be highlighted and acted upon in the manner set forth in this memorandum."

Translation: "The secretary does not want the flow of information to him restricted. He does insist that the central issue be highlighted and presented as described above."[3]

SUGGESTIONS FOR APPLYING YOUR KNOWLEDGE

1. At the end of the introductory chapter, we suggested that you start gathering examples of occupational writing. Examine one of the examples you have collected and write a report for your teacher and classmates that explains

   - what type of report it is
   - who its intended audience is
   - what features aid or hinder legibility
   - what features aid or hinder readability.

2. For each of the following words and phrases substitute a more familiar word or phrase that means the same thing.

assuage	inchoate
delectable	nadir
demeanor	neophyte
domicile	palpable
eschew	promulgate
geotome	remuneration
germane	substantiate
impecunious	vitiate

a natural geologic protuberance
a geriatose female of the Homo Sapiens species
totipalmated feet
observed in a state of rapid locomotion

[3]Reprinted by permission; © The Washington Post.

a sampling of fluid hydride of oxygen
a member of the team precipitantly descended

3. Verbs should be muscle words. Remove the fat from the following sentences by substituting a one-word verb for the verb phrase. Be sure to keep the same verb tense.

 1. We are in agreement that new circuit breakers should be installed.
 2. These payments are in excess of those specified by the contract.
 3. Mr. Donleavy was supervisor of the parts department when we conducted an inventory of unassembled equipment.
 4. Our staff has done a survey of health needs of the five surrounding counties.
 5. The night clerk is supposed to make a record of the daily activities.
 6. The committee will give consideration to alternatives.
 7. Figure 3 is a list of the centrifugal pump replacement parts.

4. Fillers weaken verb power and distract from the logical subjects of the following sentences. Strengthen these sentences by removing the fillers *it* and *there,* rewriting to emphasize the logical subjects and verbs.

 1. There are many mechanics who own their own tools.
 2. It was noticed by the pilot that the ground speed indicator was malfunctioning.
 3. There are two screws that fasten the cover to the wall box.
 4. There is a house at 212 Normal Avenue that is being converted into a day-care center.
 5. It is evident that the time needed to repair the hoses is still too long.
 6. There are two grooves that run the length of the handle.
 7. There are several different types of needles that can be used.

5. Eliminate the unnecessary words in these sentences.

 1. This morning at 8 A.M. the prisoners were transferred away to the prison facility by means of a bus.
 2. In view of the fact that the two companies are not in agreement with each other about the important essentials, it is the consensus of opinion of the board that advance planning is of great importance.
 3. It is absolutely essential that the scalpels be sharp-edged in order to bisect the specimens in two.
 4. Prior to the conductance of these tests, we made a decision to make use of disposable culture plates in lieu of glass ones due to the cost factor involved.
 5. I am of the opinion that the city and county agencies are at this point in time cooperating together.
 6. A total of ten (10) registered nurses will be needed to staff the proposed new intensive-care unit.
 7. The locking device that has suffered breakage is triangular in shape and red in color.
 8. Remove any and all foreign objects from the sensor mechanism.
 9. Either one or the other of the timetables is totally acceptable.
 10. The received message is decoded into two separate and distinct signals for correct and positive identification purposes.

6. Rewrite verbs in these sentences to make them active voice. Be sure to keep the same verb tense.

1. A review of the case by the appeals board was requested by the representative.
2. For the final test five dyes were used.
3. At our Newark plant semiconductors are manufactured.
4. The causes of wood warping are discussed in Part 4.
5. A 1 percent earnings tax is imposed by the new ordinance.
6. They are in the section in which the metal disks are housed.
7. The necessary equipment for constructing a battery eliminator is listed in Part 1 of this manual.

CHAPTER 7

Bibliographies and Literature Reviews

The day when you could carry all the information you needed under your hat is gone. There's no way you and your coworkers can know all the information you'll need to face the situations you come up against. Even your entire organization cannot hold all the information you need. Fortunately, though, it's not what you know that's important so much as knowing how to find out. You know whatever you can look up, for the chances are good that the information you'll need is in some published work.

To illustrate the value of knowing how to find published information, consider the case of an enterprising retailer trying to decide whether or not to give premiums with her merchandise to attract more customers. She needs information to make the decision. What's the cost of giving premiums? What percentage of retailers using premiums increased their volume of business with premiums? How much added volume is needed to meet the cost of giving premiums? Is it best to use nationally distributed premiums? Which premiums—nylons, cases of soft drinks, dishes, beach balls, other items that can be handled with small profit—increase business most? Are certain premiums more appropriate for certain products? Are there local, state, and federal laws that control or restrict the use of premiums?

The sources for answers to these questions are many. The retailer could, of course, rely solely on information from firms proposing to supply premiums to her. But the danger of depending only on the seller is obvious. The retailer could ask her business colleagues about their experience with premiums. She could hire—for a fee—a consultant. But she also could spend a little time in a library checking to see what information has been published on the use of premiums to improve business. If she spends 20 minutes looking *in the right places,* she'll find that dozens of articles have been published on the subject in a five-year period.

Under the subject headings of *Coupons, Premiums, Trading Stamps,* and other related words in the 1970–1975 volumes of *The Reader's Guide to Periodical Literature* and *Business Periodicals Index,* she'll find articles with titles like these:

- "Do Premiums Pay? How? Where? A New Look at the Pros and Cons"
- "Sales Incentive—Fastest Growing Use of Premiums"
- "How to Set Premium Plan Objectives"
- "Inflation Hikes Premium Appeal, But Boosts Costs"
- "Giving It Away—Profitably"
- "Premium Offers Boosted Shell Gas Sales Over 10%"
- "Arco Likes Glasses, But Isn't Afraid of New Premium Ideas"
- "Promotional Variety Aplenty is Displayed at NY Premium Show"

If the retailer looks under the same subjects in the library card catalog, she might find entries on books. And in very little time our retailer will be on the way to published material that will help her decide what kinds of bait to dangle before customers.

For a more detailed account of specific procedures for conducting library research, see Annex C, Library Research. Here, in the following pages, we will concentrate on the techniques of compiling various types of bibliographic reports.

If the information you gather is for yourself, the end product might be an information storage and retrieval system designed for your own needs. Such a system would be kept up to date to keep you informed about current information on particular subjects. The system can be as elaborate as you want to make it, but a relatively simple and efficient one might consist of two separate files of 3-by-5 note cards. One file would include annotated bibliography cards—one for each item to be entered into the system—and key-word cards.

Each annotated card (see Figure 7-1) would contain bibliographical information and a summary of the book, article, or report. It would be filed alphabetically by the author's name.

Each key-word card (see Figure 7-2), arranged alphabetically, would consist of a key word or words and a list of the authors whose publications deal with the subject of the key word. To find the information you're seeking, you'd consult the key-word file to identify the authors who have written on the subject, find the annotated bibliography card that contains the information, and pull it.

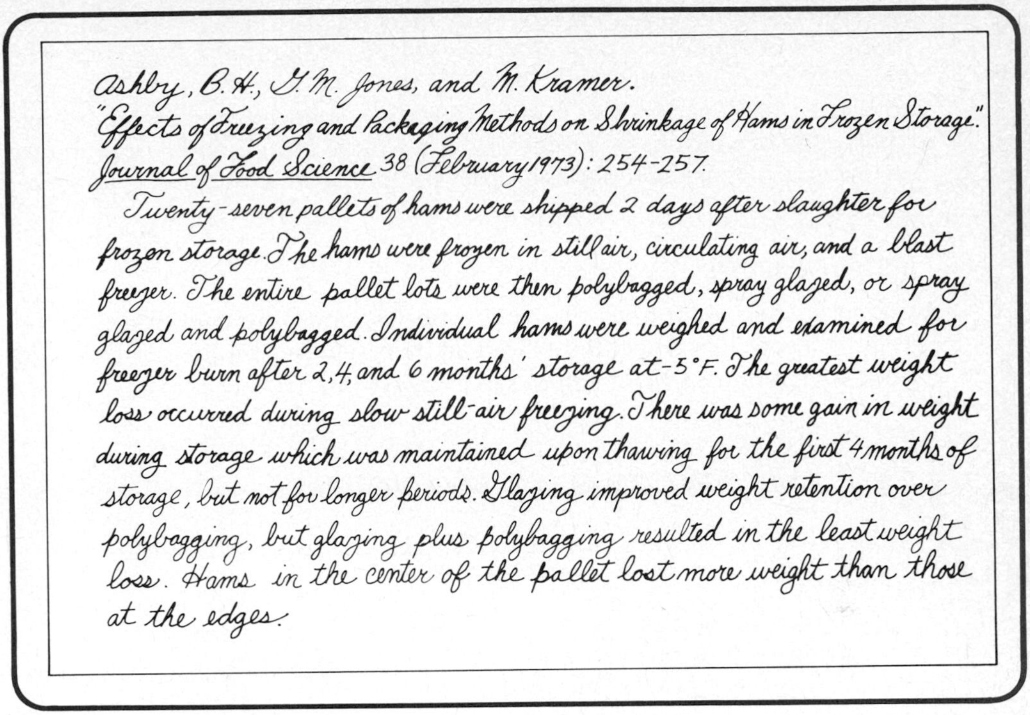

Ashby, B. H., G. M. Jones, and M. Kramer.
"Effects of Freezing and Packaging Methods on Shrinkage of Hams in Frozen Storage."
Journal of Food Science 38 (February 1973): 254-257.

  Twenty-seven pallets of hams were shipped 2 days after slaughter for frozen storage. The hams were frozen in still air, circulating air, and a blast freezer. The entire pallet lots were then polybagged, spray glazed, or spray glazed and polybagged. Individual hams were weighed and examined for freezer burn after 2, 4, and 6 months' storage at -5°F. The greatest weight loss occurred during slow still-air freezing. There was some gain in weight during storage which was maintained upon thawing for the first 4 months of storage, but not for longer periods. Glazing improved weight retention over polybagging, but glazing plus polybagging resulted in the least weight loss. Hams in the center of the pallet lost more weight than those at the edges.

Figure 7-1 Annotated bibliography card.

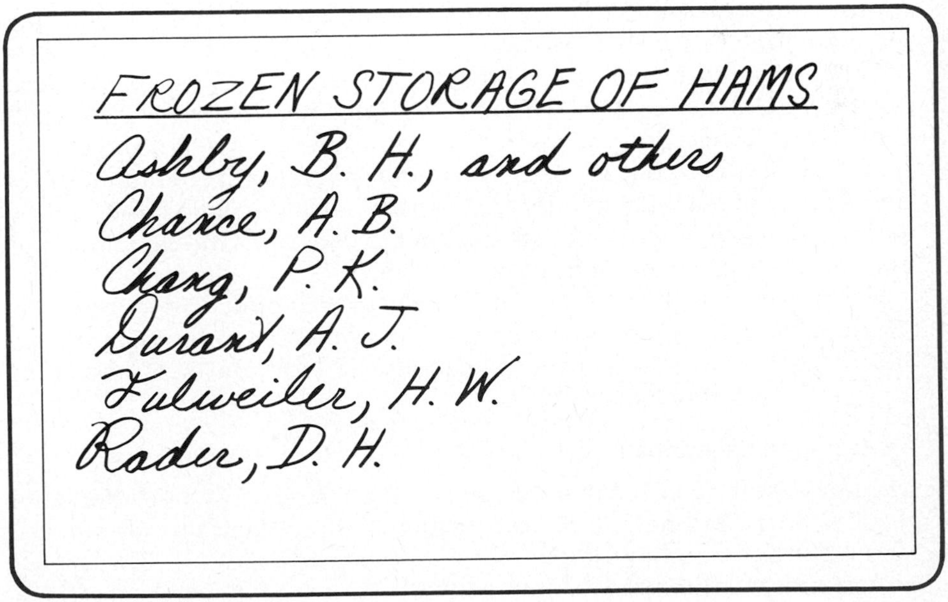

FROZEN STORAGE OF HAMS
Ashby, B. H., and others
Chance, A. B.
Chang, P. K.
Durant, A. J.
Fulweiler, H. W.
Rader, D. H.

Figure 7-2 Key word card.

If the information is for others, you'll have to prepare a bibliography, an annotated bibliography, or a literature review. The potential value of bibliographies and literature reviews is not to be underestimated. Their purpose is to give readers the information they need to increase their own knowledge of a particular subject. Which type of bibliography or literature review you prepare will depend upon the purpose the report is to serve.

BIBLIOGRAPHIES

If your readers want a list of articles, books, and other publications concerning a specific subject they can read themselves, a bibliography will do. Here's what entries from a bibliography look like:

```
Goodman, E. "New Personal Care Items Bowing at Premiums
     Show." Merchandising Week 102 (May 4, 1970): 1+.

Meredith, G. Effective Merchandising with Premiums.
     New York: McGraw-Hill, 1962.

"Shell Canada Begins Medallion Giveaway; Other
     Refiners Split on Promotion Views." Advertising
     Age 41 (March 16, 1970): 43.
```

The publishing information in the entry assists your readers in identifying and locating material. Many suggested forms for bibliography entries exist, and most provide the same information, but in slightly different form. The existence of these different forms shouldn't bother you. Just learn the form you're expected to use and stay consistent.

The form used above is based on the standardized and widely used form of *A Manual of Style*, 12th edition (Chicago: The University of Chicago Press, 1969). Unless you're required to use another form, learn and use this one. Format (the layout of the information on the page) should make the entries easy to read. Double- or triple-space between bibliography entries and use hanging indentation—that is, begin lines after the first line of an entry five spaces to the right of the first line.

We think it's easier for you to observe the uses of punctuation, underlining, and format in the following examples and imitate them than it is for you to learn from theoretical explanations. So look, observe, and learn. (See also pages 106–108, 113, 327.)

Arranging Bibliographies

Like any report, your bibliography must be arranged in some order easily recognized by and helpful to your readers—chronologically; by subject; alphabetically by author's last name; or by type of publication. The last two arrangements are the most common.

Alphabetical   As shown in Figure 7-3, a bibliography may be arranged alphabetically by author, surname first. If the work has no author given, the title of the work is used. If there's more than one work by the same author, they are arranged alphabetically by title, under the author's name. For the second and subsequent entries by the same author, an underline of seven spaces replaces the author's name.

Type of publication   As shown in Figure 7-4, a bibliography also may be arranged by type of publication (book, periodical, report, etc.). Each categorized list is placed under a separate heading. The entries under each heading may be arranged alphabetically by author (as in Figure 7-4), chronologically, or by publisher (for books) or title of periodical.

ANNOTATED BIBLIOGRAPHIES

If your readers want to know more specifically what the contents of the bibliography items are, or which items are more relevant to their needs, or what the differences are between one entry and another, an annotated bibliography will be particularly desirable. An annotated bibliography contains a description or summary of each item in the list.

A descriptive annotation looks like this:

```
"Shell Canada Begins Medallion Giveaway; Other
      Refiners Split on Promotion Views." Advertising
      Age 41 (March 16, 1970): 43.

      Explains Shell Oil of Canada's plan to give
commemorative medallions bearing portraits of Canada's
prime ministers and describes the policies of other
Canadian oil companies.
```

A summary annotation looks like this:

```
"Shell Canada Begins Medallion Giveaway; Other Refiners
      Split on Promotion Views." Advertising Age 41
      (March 16, 1970): 43.

      Shell Oil of Canada plans to give commemorative
medallions that bear portraits of Canada's prime
ministers during a 16-week campaign. One medallion will
be given free with a purchase of $3 or more of gasoline.
Customers will have no choice of medallion portraits,
but plans are being made to set up exchange centers for
customers who want to swap portraits to complete their
set. There will be no Shell identification on the
medallions. A. G. Gunther, Shell's coordinator of
```

Bibliography
on
The Use of Premiums to Stimulate Retail Sales

Compiled by

Mary K. Richards

"Be Sure Premium Program Is Above Reproach: Warren to PAAA." <u>Advertising</u>
    <u>Age</u> 41 (April 6, 1970): 4.

Churchill, G. A., and others. "Trading Stamp—Price Relationship." <u>Journal</u>
    <u>of</u> <u>Marketing</u> <u>Research</u> 8 (February 1971): 103—106.

Fulop, C. <u>The</u> <u>Role</u> <u>of</u> <u>Trading</u> <u>Stamps</u> <u>in</u> <u>Retail</u> <u>Competition</u>. London:
    Institute of Economic Affairs, 1954.

Geitner, A. J. "How to Set Premium Plan Objectives." <u>Advertising</u> <u>Age</u> 45
    (October 14, 1975): 57+.

Giges, N. "Promotional Variety Aplenty Is Displayed at New York Premium
    Show." <u>Advertising</u> <u>Age</u> 41 (May 11, 1970): 26.

————. "Return to Stamps Seen as Promotional Area Shows Growth."
    <u>Advertising</u> <u>Age</u> 45 (February 11, 1974): 2+.

"Giving It Away—Profitably." <u>Modern</u> <u>Packaging</u> 46 (January 1973): 34—36.

Goodman, E. "New Personal Care Items Bowing at Premium Show." <u>Merchandising</u>
    <u>Week</u> 102 (July 8, 1974): 1+.

Haugh, L. J. "Nostalgia Still in Vogue Among Premium Users." <u>Advertising</u>
    <u>Age</u> 45 (June 16, 1975): 65.

————. "T—Shirts Turn Fashionable and Advertisers Cash In."
    <u>Advertising</u> <u>Age</u> 46 (June 16, 1975): 60—61.

McConnell, R. M. M. "Do Premiums Pay? How? Where? A New Look at the Pros and
    Cons." <u>Banking</u> 66 (September 1973): 74+.

Mahaney, E. "Inflation Hikes Premium Appeal, But Boosts Costs." <u>Advertising</u>
    <u>Age</u> 45 (October 14, 1974): 44+.

Meredith, G. <u>Effective</u> <u>Merchandising</u> <u>with</u> <u>Premiums</u>. New York: McGraw—Hill,
    1962.

"Premium Offers Boosted Shell Gas Sales Over 10%." <u>Advertising</u> <u>Age</u> 43
    (February 4, 1972): 12.

"Shell Canada Begins Medallion Giveaway: Other Refiners Split on Promotion
    Views." <u>Advertising</u> <u>Age</u> 41 (March 16, 1970): 43.

"Trading Stamps: Most People Like Them." <u>Financial</u> <u>World</u> 138 (July 5,
    1972): 9+.

Figure 7-3 Example of bibliography report.

```
                              Bibliography
                                   on
                 The Use of Premiums to Stimulate Retail Sales

                                   by

                             Mary K. Richards

      Books

      Fulop, The Role of Trading Stamps in Retail Competition. London: Institute
          of Economic Affairs, 1964.

      Meredith, G. Effective Merchandising with Premiums. New York: McGraw-Hill,
          1962.

      Articles

      "Be Sure Premium Program Is Above Reproach: Warren to PAAA." Advertising
          Age 41 (April 6, 1970): 4.

      Churchill, G. A., and others. "Trading Stamp-Price Relationship." Journal
          of Marketing Research 8 (February 1971): 103-106.

      Geitner, A. J. "How to Set Premium Plan Objectives." Advertising Age 45
          (October 14, 1974): 57+.

      Giges, N. "Promotional Variety Aplenty Is Displayed at New York Premium
          Show." Advertising Age 41 (May 11, 1970): 26.
```

Figure 7-4 Bibliography arranged by type of publication.

advertising, states "We call it third-generation
promotion; we have progressed beyond tumblers and
games." Imperial Oil Ltd. reaffirms its policy not to
have giveaways. Gulf Oil of Canada continues to offer
bargain-priced products (steak knives, thermos cups,
etc.) to its customers. Texaco Canada continues to give
china sets and stemware to customers.

As you can see, the descriptive annotation describes the general coverage of the published item. The summary annotation is a brief summary of
the important ideas of the published item.

Annotated bibliographies are set up the same ways as bibliographies—
usually either alphabetically or by type of publication. The annotation is in
paragraph form (usually ranging from one or two sentences to ten
sentences), with the first line indented five spaces, the second and subsequent lines beginning on the normal left margin. The annotation is separated from the bibliography entry by a double space. An annotated bibliography is shown in Figure 7-5.

Annotated Bibliography
on
The Use of Premiums to Stimulate Retail Sales

by

Mary K. Richards

Geitner, A. J. "How to Set Premium Plan Objectives." _Advertising Age_ 45 (October 14, 1974): 57, 60, 62.

   According to Geitner, Director of Sales Promotion, Thomas J. Lipton, Inc., "inflation brings out the shopper in all of us. Premiums, offered in conjunction with another product, represent better value for the money." So premiums are a natural for times of inflation. Before starting a premium plan, a thorough review should be made of overall marketing objectives, of the competitive climate, of customer profiles, of product usage patterns, and financial resources the brand has to draw on. Premiums can be used to reach new users, hold current users, load current users, and trade up (get users to buy larger sizes).

Giges, N. "Promotional Variety Aplenty Is Displayed at New York Premium Show." _Advertising Age_ 41 (May 11, 1970): 26.

   The annual New York show has 1,000 exhibitors showing premiums in the forms of books, records, housewares, appliances, towels, linens, key chains, lamps, electronic air purifiers, audio and optical equipment, antiquing kits, vibrating cushions, and dry lubricators for zippers, keys, etc.

Mahany, E. "Inflation Hikes Premium Appeal, But Boosts Costs." _Advertising Age_ 45 (October 14, 1974): 44, 46, 48.

   There's good news and bad news in using premiums. The good news is that today's cash-short customer is eager to accept "legitimate money-saving premium offers." The bad news is that with inflation it is "difficult to 'lock in' on firm costs to put a program together." A good premium stimulates consumers, retail trade, and sales force. Trends are toward better quality, more expensive premiums, more multiple-choice premium assortments, multiple proof-of-purchase requirements (especially for "free" write-in premiums), credit card option as payment more often, more premiums related to product with which they're offered, and more "custom" premiums.

"Premium Offers Boosted Shell Gas Sales Over 10%." _Advertising Age_ 43 (February 7, 1972): 12.

   Shell Oil's gasoline sales increased from 10 percent to 25 percent with the aid of premium offers of glassware, coffee mugs, and steak knives. According to Michael Turner, Sr., Vice-President of the Houston office of Ogilvy & Mather (Shell's agency), five guidelines should be used in selecting a premium: (1) continuity—the premium should be part of a collection that encourages the customer to complete; (2) value—the premium must look like it's worth something; (3) dealer acceptance; (4) price—the premium costing over ten cents is risky; (5) research—the premium should be tested for durability, usefulness, etc.

Figure 7-5 Example of annotated bibliography.

LITERATURE REVIEWS

Unlike the annotated bibliography, the literature review takes the form of an essay. It is usually arranged by topical sections, which may be further divided by subtopics or chronology. Arranged this way, the literature review is perhaps the most helpful kind of bibliographical report because it describes the context of the work reported on. But it also requires you to take on the greater responsibility of organizing and perhaps even analyzing the results of your literature search.

Following is an excerpt from a review or survey of recent literature on technical writing. Such a review may appear in almost any form depending on the purpose, occasion, and audience. This one is in article form and reviews the literature on technical writing that appeared from 1965 to 1973. It consists of six sections: an introduction; four sections devoted to the topics of readability, profiles of professional technical writers, information transfer, and miscellaneous; and the list of references cited. Included in this excerpt are the introduction, the section on readability, and that part of the references section related to readability.

A Survey of Scholarly Works in Technical Writing

JAY J. GOLDBERG

Commentary

This article reviews scholarly literature, as opposed to professional readings, in the field of technical writing during the past nine years. Included in the review are articles describing experimental and humanistic research of the subject.

This excellent introduction starts by explaining the purpose, subject, and scope of the literature review.

It would seem, considering all of the areas of possible research, that relatively little has been done. I would suggest, though I have no study to back this up, that the reason for the plethora of professional articles and dearth of scholarly works is a result of the ratio of practitioners to scholars. That is, most technical writing activities are in industry; very few schools are involved in that field.[1]

Paragraph 2 speculates on why so few "scholarly works" on technical writing have appeared in the past nine years.

My review is for the period from 1965 to 1973. This time frame was selected because the years 1950 through 1965 are covered in *An Annotated Bibiliography on Technical Writing, Editing, Graphics, and Publishing: 1950–1965,* edited by Theresa A. Philler, Ruth K. Hersch, and Helen V. Carlson.[2] Although not exhaustive, the bibliography does contain 2000 entries (1500 articles and 500 books), and is therefore a useful point of reference.

Paragraphs 3 and 4 justify the scope of the literature search and cite the need for the survey.

A need for an updated bibliography does exist; one

Reprinted by permission from *Technical Communication* 22 (First Quarter 1975): 5–8, published by the Society for Technical Communication, 1010 Vermont Avenue, N.W., Washington, D.C. 20005.

has been called for by Donald H. Cunningham, associate professor of English, Morehead (Kentucky) State University, in his recent article in the *Journal of Technical Writing and Communication.*[3] My survey does not fulfill his request, though it may help. That project is presently being undertaken by the Society for Technical Communication, which is planning to update the bibliography cited in reference 2.

Sources for research included A. J. Walford's *Guide to Reference Material,* Theodore Besterman's *World Bibliography of Bibliographies, Bibliographic Index, Applied Science and Technology Index,* and the *National Union Catalog.* I was able to uncover only one research document and two theses printed in book form. Most research is reported in periodicals such as *Technical Communication* (formerly *Technical Communications* and *STWP Review*), journal of the Society for Technical Communication (STC), which was formerly the Society of Technical Writers and Publishers (STWP); *IEEE Transactions on Professional Communication* (formerly *IEEE Transactions on Engineering Writing and Speech*), publication of the Institute of Electrical and Electronics Engineers (IEEE) Professional Communication Group (formerly IEEE Engineering Writing and Speech Group); *Journal of Technical Writing and Communication; Proceedings of the Institute of Technical and Industrial Communications;* and *Proceedings of the STC International Technical Communications Conference* (ITCC).

Research falls into three general areas: readability, including studies in comprehension from poor text, typography, and layout; profiles, including education, job area, salary, and experience; and information transfer, including user's selection of technical materials, indexing, and retrieval of technical data. These three subjects, plus a few miscellaneous professionally oriented studies of work habits, comprise the four sections of this article.

Readability. Experimentation in this broad area seems to be dominated by Dr. Richard M. Davis of the Air Force Institute of Technology, Wright-Patterson Air Force Base, Ohio. In a series of experiments he has varied different discrete components in technical writing and has measured the results of comprehension and reading speed. His first set of three experiments was begun before the reporting period of this article; however, the reports of those experiments have been printed in several articles that appeared later.

Effective Technical Communications, Mechanical Description, Experiment II is the earliest article of *this* re-

Paragraph 5 lists the titles of the sources used in the literature search.

Paragraph 6 ends the introduction by identifying the areas of research to be included in the review—readability, profiles, information transfer, and "miscellaneous professionally oriented studies" —thus providing an overview of the four sections of the article. The reader now knows what the major topics are and in what order they will be discussed.

As you go through this section on readability, note how transitions are used to pull together the discussion and to keep the reader posted on the progress of the discussion.

The section summarizes the research of Richard

porting period.[4] In the experiment, Davis used several different descriptions of a simple teaching machine written by the same author. The descriptions contained the following variables: presentation of physical description of the machine verbally versus illustrations, presence or absence of introduction material, and presence or absence of headings. Effectiveness was measured by comprehension, reading time, and reader's impression of author's knowledge of subject and competence as a writer. The experiment indicates that introductions, headings, and other publication aids contributed little to the effectiveness of the publication.

In the third experiment of this study, reported in *Effective Technical Communications, Mechanical Description, Experiment III*, Davis extracted, from the same data base, the reader's impression of the author's knowledge of the subject and his competence as a writer.[5, 6] The two audiences tested consisted of men who had been instructed in technical writing, and men who had not been so instructed. The results of the experiment suggest that deviation from a standard format lowers the reader's impression of the author's knowledge of the subject. This suggestion was pursued by Davis in further experiments.

The three experiments are summarized in "Experimental Research in the Effectiveness of Technical Writing" in the *IEEE Transactions on Engineering Writing and Speech.*[7]

Follow-on experiments relating to credibility in regard to standard presentation were the subject of a paper presented by Davis at the 15th ITCC in 1968. However, as the experiment was still in progress at the deadline for printing the *Proceedings*, only a summary of the work appears in that volume. The paper, "The Effect of Departures from Standard Upon the Effectiveness of a Written Technical Message," discusses that part of the experiment that was completed prior to the deadline. In the experiment, he varied sentence length (19.6 words per sentence versus 36 words per sentence), agreement in number between subject and verb (20 errors in agreement in half the passages), and shifts in point of view (44 shifts in person, tense, and mood placed in half the passages). The results were inconclusive; no difference in readability was observed. However, Davis felt this might have been due to the pressure under which the tests were taken, and indicated further testing with that in mind. The results of this experiment are reported in *Effective Technical Communications Expression: Experiment 1, Final Report.*[8]

M. Davis, Hans Alenius, and James Allen Carte. Paragraphs 1–6 report the work of Dr. Davis. Paragraph 1 is an overview of his research. The next five paragraphs summarize this research in the order of its publication.

A more recent experiment of Davis is reported in "Sloppy Typing and Reproduction in a Written Technical Message—An Experiment" in the *Journal of Technical Writing and Communication*.[9] In this experiment, Davis altered the test document with sloppy typing and reproduction. In each case studied, he found the unaltered (good typing and reproduction) form to be more effective.

At the 15th ITCC in 1968, Hans Alenius, (Swedish) Royal Army Materiel Administration, reported on two experiments performed by the Swedish army in comprehension of instructions.[10] In the first experiment, "The Effect of Different Designs of a Small Manual," army personnel were given three presentations of illustrative material. In conventional manuals, when a figure accompanies text and contains items that must be called out (items that are mentioned in the text), the items are either numbered, with a listing below relating the numbers to nomenclature, or the nomenclature is presented right on the figure. In this experiment, those two methods were tested against a third (experimental) method, in which a line was drawn directly from the figure item to its reference in text. This, of course, required shifting words to make room for the leader lines. However, the experiment indicated that the extra effort was worthwhile. Tests showed that, although technically advanced persons did equally well with all three methods, persons not so accustomed to technical presentations did significantly better with the new method.

This and the next paragraph review the research of Hans Alenius.

In his second reported experiment, "Are Coloured Illustrations Superior to Black-and-White for Rapid Identification of Technical Objects?" Alenius indicated that experiments showed no difference in the audience's ability to identify an object in a black-and-white, natural color, or three-color print. In fact, the three-color print seemed to be worse than the black-and-white illustration.

"Filtering Typographic Noise from Technical Literature" (*Technical Communication*[11]) by James Allen Carte is a presentation based on material he studied for his master's thesis. In this article he discussed significance of type size, line width and spacing, font, line justification, hyphenated words, and type/paper color combinations as distractions to the reader. This article is not an experiment report, but rather a study based on his research of literature. However, the article does indicate that his thesis is on the same subject. Those interested might wish to pursue this thesis (from West Virginia University) when it is published.

The final paragraph of this section summarizes the work of James Allen Carte.

References

1. Thomas E. Pearsall, editor, "University Programs in Technical Communication," *Technical Communication*, 20(1): 2 (1973).
2. Theresa A. Philler, Ruth K. Hersch, and Helen V. Carlson, editors, *An Annotated Bibliography on Technical Writing, Editing, Graphics, and Publishing: 1950–1965*, Society of Technical Writers and Publishers, Washington, and the Carnegie Library of Pittsburgh, 1966.
3. Donald H. Cunningham, "Toward a Comprehensive Bibliography of Technical Writing," *Journal of Technical Writing and Communication*, 3(1): 39 (1973).
4. Richard M. Davis, *Effective Technical Communications, Mechanical Description, Experiment II*, NASA Report N66-28314, Air Force Institute of Technology, Wright-Patterson Air Force Base, Ohio, 1966.
5. Richard M. Davis, *Effective Technical Communications, Mechanical Description, Experiment III*, NASA Report N67-16342, Air Force Institute of Technology, Wright-Patterson Air Force Base, Ohio, 1967.
6. Richard M. Davis, "Effective Mechanical Description: Experiment 3," *Technical Communications*, 14(3): 28 (1967).
7. Richard M. Davis, "Experimental Research in the Effectiveness of Technical Writing," *IEEE Transactions on Engineering Writing and Speech*, EWS-10 (2): 33 (1967).
8. Richard M. Davis, *Effective Technical Communications Experiment: Experiment 1, Final Report*, NASA Report N69-39900, Air Force Institute of Technology, Wright-Patterson Air Force Base, Ohio, 1969.
9. Richard M. Davis, "Sloppy Typing and Reproduction in a Written Technical Message—An Experiment," *Journal of Technical Writing and Communication*, 2(1): 43 (1972).
10. Hans Alenius, "Two Experiments," Paper I-12, *Proceedings of the 15th International Technical Communications Conference*, Society for Technical Communication, Washington, 1968.
11. James Allen Carte, "Filtering Typographic Noise from Technical Literature," *Technical Communication*, 20(3): 12 (1973).

At the end of the article is this list of the publications in the order they were referred to or discussed. Complete bibliographical information is provided in this easy-to-use form should the reader like to locate the references.

SUGGESTIONS FOR APPLYING YOUR KNOWLEDGE

1. Arrange the following information as if it were a bibliography.

   —"Smart Traffic Lights Prevent Errors" in the July 5, 1973, issue of <u>Electronics</u>, vol. 46, pp. 68–69, written by G. Sideris.

   —"Development of Boston's Computerized Traffic Control System" by G. W. Casper and several other persons, in <u>Traffic</u> <u>Engineering</u>, the April 1975 issue, vol. 45, 22–24+.

--<u>The</u> <u>Computer</u> <u>Impact</u>, edited by Irene Taviss, and published in 1970 by Prentice-Hall, Inc., of Englewood Cliffs, New Jersey.

--"Automated Traffic Control Software; How Much Does It Cost?" by E. J. Kligman, in <u>Traffic</u> <u>Engineering</u>, the October 1973 issue, vol. 44, pp. 49-53.

--The Computer Revolution, written by Edmund C. Berkeley, and published by Doubleday of Garden City, New York, in 1962.

--"Basic Considerations for Selecting a Computer System for Traffic" by B. L. Kellett, the February 1974 issue of <u>Traffic</u> <u>Engineering</u>, vol. 33, pp. 20-23.

--"Midwest City to Install Computerized Traffic-Control System" in <u>Machine</u> <u>Design</u>, the November 14, 1974 issue, page 10, vol. 46.

--"Environment-Proof Microcomputer Enhances Traffic Control" in vol. 14, p. 90, the August 1975 issue of <u>Computer</u> <u>Design</u>.

2. You may have to do library research in conjunction with a report for your occupational writing course or some other course. Prepare a bibliography of published material that relates to the subject of the report.
3. As part of a progress report on a library research project, write an annotated bibliography on published material that relates to the project. Or in a periodical index locate five articles on a topic that interests you, look up the articles, read them, and write an annotated bibliography on them.

CHAPTER 8

Mechanism Description

Mechanism description explains the purpose, appearance, physical structure, and sometimes the operation or behavior of a mechanism. The word *mechanism,* as used here, applies to anything that takes up space and behaves in a predictable manner or performs work. In this sense a driver's license is as much a mechanism as is a clutch or an automobile. A mechanism can be small or large, simple or complex, man-made or natural. Handtools (scissors, pen, nail punch), devices (oil pump, telephone, bicycle, CB radio), and natural objects (egg, knee joint, flower, kidney, volcano) represent the wide range of mechanisms. In addition, layouts of plants, buildings, or rooms might also be regarded as mechanisms.

Regardless of the mechanism to be described, the main problems confronting you when you describe it are (1) how much information to include; (2) how best to create a picture of the mechanism in your readers' minds; and (3) how to arrange the details of the description.

DECIDING HOW MUCH INFORMATION TO INCLUDE

Two familiar considerations face you right away when you prepare to describe a mechanism: What is the purpose of your description? Who is your audience? Mechanism description is always selective. You would never describe a mechanism just to be describing it. What information you include about the mechanism depends upon whether you're describing it to readers who will make it, or buy it, or ship it, or operate it, or repair it.

Describing a Familiar Mechanism

If your purpose is to remind readers of the major features and parts of a mechanism with which they are somewhat familiar, you can rely on graphics to describe its appearance and on a few words to describe materials, connections, and functions. Figure 8-1 is a description of a device provided by the manufacturer to acquaint customers with their purchase.

   The description, appearing at the front of the customer's manual for the blender, is brief, yet sufficient for its purpose, and well organized. The mechanism is described in terms of its major parts and their functions. The two-column format, placing an exploded view of the blender to the right of the written description, enables readers to move back and forth from the writing to the pictures with ease. Notice also how helpful the headings and numbered parts are in helping readers identify parts.

Describing an Unfamiliar Mechanism

Often your purpose will be to acquaint readers with mechanisms they are unfamiliar with. In such cases you'll need to explain more thoroughly the purpose, physical structure, and use or operation of the mechanism. Let's assume, for instance, you're introducing a group of beginning drafting students to an instrument they'll have to know backwards and forwards— the hinged ruling pen. You'll need to blend as much functional description with visual description as you think necessary to acquaint them with the mechanism.

```
                   HINGED RULING PEN


        The hinged ruling pen is a precise drawing
   instrument used by the draftsman for the purpose of
   inking architectural and engineering drawings. It is
   designed for drawing ruled lines and not intended for
   free handwork. The hinged ruling pen is 4½ inches long
   and resembles a surgical knife. The pen consists of
   three main parts: the handle, two blades, and the
   graduated screw adjustment as shown in the drawing
   below.
```

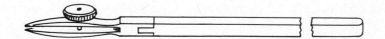

Know Your
Osterizer
LIQUEFIER-BLENDER ®

This Osterizer blender is designed for household use only.

1
2
3

cover

The cover for your Osterizer blender consists of two parts, the plastic feeder cap (1) and the vinyl cover (2). The cover is self-sealing and is made of vinyl and resistant to absorption of odors and stains. The feeder cap is removable for use as a measuring cap and provides an opening for the addition of other ingredients.

container

The 5-cup container (3) for the Osterizer blender is graduated for easy measurement and is molded of heat and cold resistant material. The convenient handle and pouring lip permit easy removal of liquid mixtures, while thicker mixtures are more easily removed through the bottom opening.

agitator or processing assembly

4
5
6
7

Consists of three parts: (4) a sealing ring of neoprene used as a cushion between the container and the agitator; (5) agitator of high-grade stainless steel; (6) a threaded container bottom.

motor and motor base

The powerful multi-speed motor is the heart of the appliance and designed just for this unit. It is completely enclosed within the housing (7).

The Osterizer blender motor uses a "free-floating" feature to reduce noise and wear. This feature allows the square post which protrudes from the motor base to move slightly from side to side.

Your Osterizer blender contains a powerful food processing motor, but it can be overloaded. To avoid this possibility, closely follow the instructions and the quantities specified in the recipes in this book.

The illustration and photography of Osterizer blenders found in this book do not necessarily depict the particular model Osterizer blender that you have purchased. These photographs are merely a guide to illustrate the versatility of your Osterizer blender.

care and cleaning of your Osterizer blender

Never store foods in your Osterizer blender container. Always remove the agitator assembly and wash and dry container and agitator assembly thoroughly after you have finished blending. Re-assemble container after cleaning so it will be ready for future use. Never place processing assembly on motor base without the container. See page 2 for proper assembly and tightening instructions.

Osterizer blender parts are corrosion resistant, sanitary, and easily cleaned. Wash in warm, soapy water and dry thoroughly. DO NOT WASH ANY PARTS IN AN AUTOMATIC DISHWASHER.

NEVER IMMERSE THE MOTOR BASE IN WATER. It does not require oiling. Its outside can be cleaned with a damp cloth (unplug cordset first).

©Oster Corporation. 1975. Milwaukee. Wisconsin 53217   *Oster. Osterizer. Pulse-Matic. T.M. Mini-Blend. Cyclomatic. Spin Cookery

203287-Rev.-N   [1]

Figure 8-1 The first page of manufacturer's booklet describing a product. (Courtesy Oster Corporation)

The <u>Handle</u>

The handle consists of a polished aluminum shaft, threaded for attachment to the blades. The handle is cylindrical, having a diameter of 3/8 inch and a length of $2\frac{1}{2}$ inches. At the point where the handle is attached to the blades, grooves $\frac{1}{2}$ inch long are placed around the handle. This grooving provides a textured surface to hold the pen firmly between the fingers.

The <u>Blades</u>

The blades, made of carefully tempered steel, are coated with nickel. The width of the blades is 1/4 inch at the handle, tapering to a semi—elliptical point 1/32 of an inch wide. The overall length of the blades is $2\frac{1}{2}$ inches. Both blades must be the same length in order to hold and deliver the ink properly. The upper blade is actuated by a spring similar to that of a pocket knife. The spring permits the upper blade to be held open at right angles to the fixed blade for cleaning purposes, or holds it firmly against the other blade.

The <u>Graduated</u> <u>Screw</u> <u>Adjustment</u>

The graduated adjusting screw is steel with a diameter of 1/16 inch. The adjusting screw is 5/16 inch long and threaded so that it screws into the upper blade. Attached to one end of the screw is a cylindrical head made of steel and nickel plated. The head is 9/32 inch in diameter and 3/32 inch high. The head has vertical grooves around the outside so that it can be turned with the fingers to adjust the distance between the blades and thus regulate the line width.

The description of the hinged ruling pen provides more detail than does the description of the Oster liquifier-blender. The extent to which a mechanism should be described (and, consequently, the length of the mechanism description) depends on what readers need to know about the mechanism. If your purpose were to provide specifications so that someone could make the mechanism, you would need to include detailed information that would provide a pattern to be copied. Not even the most minor dimensions or features could be omitted. So it's important to establish in your mind the purpose of your description and what your readers need to know of the mechanism. Otherwise you won't know what to include in your description, sometimes putting in too much information, sometimes not enough.

HELPING READERS VISUALIZE THE MECHANISM

It's natural for you to want to show readers what a mechanism looks like. The three common methods of doing this are to use pictorials, analogies, and geometric shapes.

Pictorials

When visual understanding is involved, pictorials (photographs and drawings) are the most exact method of communication. Verbal language—written or spoken—simply doesn't measure up to visual language in showing physical appearance and spatial relationship.

The old saying that "one picture is worth a thousand words" is true only if the picture is a good one and if it communicates better than words. Unless you're skilled in photography and drawing, you'll need to get help in making pictorials. If you work for an organization that has a presentations department that will do your pictorial work for you—count your blessings. If you don't, you'll have to hire someone to do them. However, even when others prepare pictorials for you, you should know what makes a good pictorial. You may be required to supply preliminary sketches that are to be made into finished pictorials.

Choice, execution, and placement of pictorials should *not* take a back seat when you plan your description. Determine what aspects of the object you want to convey, so that you can decide which type of pictorial best illustrates what you want to show. The following information on photographs and drawings should help you make such choices.

Photographs Photographs present the exact appearance of actual objects. Realism is their greatest asset. They are often essential in showing the appearance of newly created objects, objects readers have never seen before, objects at the end of a particular stage of development, and worn or damaged objects. They are also useful in comparing sizes of objects by scaling them against more familiar objects, such as a hand or coin, or an actual scale like a ruler.

Photographs are indispensable for showing the exact appearance to validate the condition of an object. Figure 8-2 shows how photographs are used to show pest damage to apples. Figure 8-3 illustrates how photographs contrast the appearances of strong, vigorous tobacco plants and damaged tobacco plants. Drawings would not be suitable in these instances, because they would not provide realistic appearances and would be time-consuming to prepare.

Take care in preparing a photograph for a report. It should be no larger than the other sheets of your report. Use rubber cement to attach the

Figure 8-2 Pest damage to apples. *Above:* Inside the fruit, maggot trails are brownish lines which meander through the flesh. *Below:* External signs are depressed "sting" marks and sunken, discolored areas over the maggot trails under the skin. (Agricultural Extension Service, University of Minnesota, St. Paul)

photograph to your paper. Don't use staples or paper clips. If you make notations on the back of a photograph, mark lightly or the marks might show through.

Figure 8-3   Tobacco plants. *Above:* Strong vigorous plants. *Below:* Cutworm injury in plant beds. (Cooperative Extension Service, University of Kentucky College of Agriculture, Lexington)

Drawings   Like photographs, drawings show what objects look like. Unlike photographs, they can be made to show different aspects of an object. The four most commonly used views are external, cutaway, sectional, and exploded. They may be freehand or ruled, drawn to scale or not.

An external view, like a photograph, shows the outside of an object to give readers an idea of its appearance. The outline is a special kind of external view that shows, as the name suggests, an object in outline form. The clear appearance of outline drawings avoids the realistic clutter of photographs and makes them useful for emphasizing significant features and for showing shapes and dimensions. Figure 8-4 is an outline drawing showing the shape, dimensions, and parts of a garden trowel.

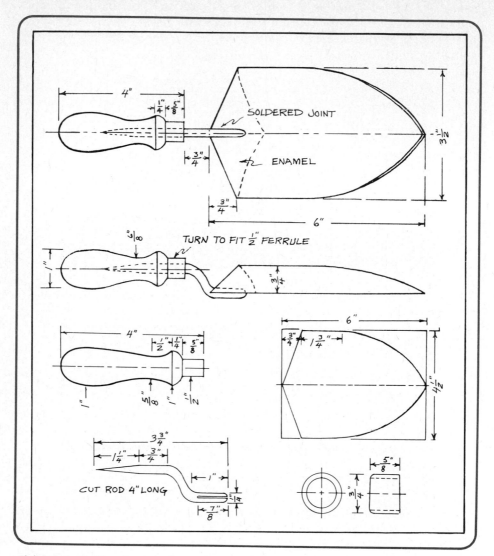

Figure 8-4 Outline drawing of a garden trowel. (Courtesy Norman Roberts)

Photographs and external views do not show the inside parts of objects, how parts fit together, or the transportation of material through a machine. Hidden lines, which may be used with any kind of view, help show features that can't be seen. The unseen features are represented by short dashes. Hidden lines are used in Figures 8-4, 8-6, and 8-7.

When interior parts cannot be shown well by hidden lines, cutaway and sectional views are used. They are very useful when objects contain so much housing that all readers see is the outside covering.

A cutaway view, as the name implies, shows an object as if some part of its exterior nearest the viewer had been cut away. It's used to show both internal and external construction in the same drawing. In Figure 8-5 the door and the covering for the wave guide channel of a microwave oven

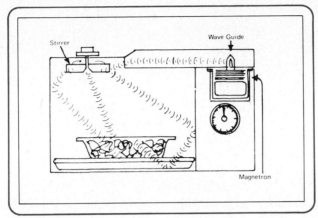

Figure 8-5   Microwave oven. (Agricultural Extension Service, University of Minnesota, St. Paul)

have been removed. Figure 8-6 illustrates the use of hidden lines and a cutaway view to show unseen rear parts and interior parts of an ammunition magazine of an M-14, A-1 military rifle that would not be visible in an external view. Notice also the exploded view to show the bottom plate.

A sectional view, as the name indicates, shows an object as if some section of the object nearest the viewer had been removed. The sectional view may be partial or full; that is, the sectional cut may be through just a portion of the object or may run completely through it. A cross-sectional view, which runs completely through the object, shows an object as if it had been split down the middle and the half nearest the viewer removed.

A phantom view suggests the way the object may look in an alternative position. Figure 8-7, a drawing of an adjustable beam compass, illustrates many of the drawing techniques we've been discussing. Hidden lines indicate the existence of the beam inside the center pin and writing head. Break lines cut the beam in two to shorten the view. A partial sectional view shows the inside of the coupling device, indicating that the base beam and the extension beam are separated by a partition. (Notice that the portion of an object cut through in a sectional drawing is represented by diagonal lines.) A phantom view indicates where the writing head would be on the extension beam.

Analogies

Suppose we want to describe something we've seen for the first time or that our readers have never seen. How do we describe the unknown? Usually the best way is by comparing it to the known.

Can you remember the tremendous feeling of excitement when you first

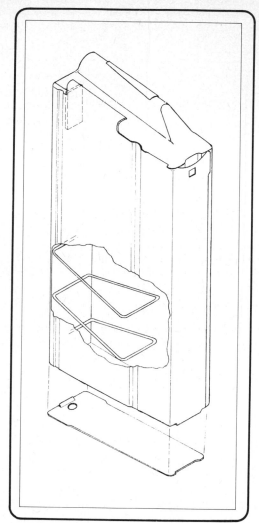

Figure 8-6 View of ammunition magazine M-14, A-1 military rifle. (Courtesy Betty L. Bradford, Drafting Instructor, Rowan County Vocational School, Morehead, Kentucky)

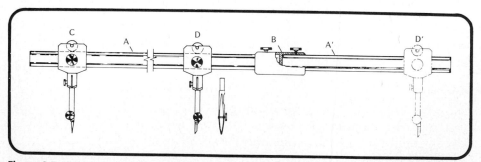

Figure 8-7 View of adjustable beam compass. (Courtesy Betty L. Bradford, Drafting Instructor, Rowan County Vocational School, Morehead, Kentucky)

looked at things under a microscope? Those magnified images revealed a world that had been hidden from you before. In 1665 Robert Hooke, a seventeenth-century English scientist, constructed a microscope that allowed him to examine many things that had never before been seen by the human eye. One of the things he looked at was a piece of outer bark of the cork oak. Part of his description of what he saw with his microscope is shown here as he recorded it in *Micrographia* (1665). The type looks quaint to us, but once you notice that some of the s's look like f's, you fhould have little trouble reading it.

Obferv. X V I I I. *Of the* Schematifme *or* Texture *of* Cork, *and of the* Cells *and* Pores *of fome other fuch frothy Bodies.*

I Took a good clear piece of Cork, and with a Pen-knife fharpen'd as keen as a Razor, I cut a piece of it off, and thereby left the furface of it exceeding fmooth, then examining it very diligently with a *Micro-fcope*, me thought I could perceive it to appear a little porous; but I could not fo plainly diftinguifh them, as to be fure that they were pores, much lefs what Figure they were of: But judging from the lightnefs and yielding quality of the Cork, that certainly the texture could not be fo curious, but that poffibly, if I could ufe fome further diligence, I might find it to be difcernable with a *Microfcope*, I with the fame fharp Pen-knife, cut off from the former fmooth furface an exceeding thin piece of it, and placing it on a black objeft Plate, becaufe it was it felf a white body, and cafting the light on it with a deep *plano-convex Glafs*, I could exceeding plainly perceive it to be all perforated and porous, much like a Honey-comb, but that the pores of it were not regular; yet it was not unlike a Honey-comb in thefe particulars.

First, in that it had a very little folid fubftance, in comparifon of the empty cavity that was contain'd between, as does more manifeftly appear by the Figure A and B of the X I. *fcheme*, for the *Interftitia*, or walls (as I may fo call them) or partitions of thofe pores were neer as thin in proportion to their pores, as thofe thin films of Wax in a Honey-comb (which enclofe and conftitute the *fexangular cells*) are to theirs.

Next, in that thefe pores, or cells, were not very deep, but confifted of a great many little Boxes, feparated out of one continued long pore; by certain *Diaphragms*, as is vifible by the Figure B, which reprefents a fight of thofe pores fplit the long-ways.

Hooke used two conventional methods to convey impressions of what he saw. As his references to "Figure A and B" indicate, he used drawings. His comparison of the cells to "Honey-comb" and "little boxes" shows that he relied on analogies to describe what the cells looked like.

Take a lesson from Hooke. When an object resembles something else your readers are more familiar with, analogies can be helpful in explaining its shape, size, and structure. A common way to do this is to use metaphors of shape based on the letters of the alphabet: A-frame, C-clamp, I-beam, O-ring, S-hook, T-square, U-bolt, Y-joint, and so on. Another way is to name parts of objects after parts of anatomy: head, eyes, ears, mouth, teeth, lip, throat, tongue, neck, shoulder, elbow, arm, leg, foot, heel. Gears and saws have teeth; pliers and vises have jaws; needles have eyes. A third way is to use resemblances to other well-known objects: a mushroom-shaped anchor, a barrel-shaped container, a canister the size of a tube of lipstick.

Analogies also can be used to suggest structure and size.

- Each stair tread on an escalator is like a small four-wheel truck.
- Some bearing sleeves are porous and under a microscope look like very fine sponges, but are rigid.
- The simplest portable hair dryer looks a little like an oversized handgun in which a small fan blows hot air out of a screened nozzle.
- The tape-recording head is a small C-shaped electromagnet the size of a dime.
- The barometer case looks like a small metal shoe box with a glass lid.
- The islands hang like a loose necklace from the entrance of the bay.
- The combustion chamber is shaped like a fat figure eight.

If you can't make the comparison by using a well-known and easily visualized analogy, you can often compare a new mechanism with an older one or a more complex one with a simpler one.

- Disposable syringes are just like rubber ones except they are made of plastic and can be discarded after use.
- An automobile battery is a much larger and chemically different version of the battery that powers a flashlight.

How good an analogy is depends on how well the comparison clarifies the object being described. It wouldn't do to describe something as looking like a pair of dividers or a lemur unless your readers could be expected to know what a pair of dividers or a lemur looks like. You'd be describing the unknown by the still more unknown. Furthermore, an analogy can mislead rather than clarify if it doesn't suggest the right features. For instance, comparing an object to a circle is ineffective if the object looks more like a wheel or a donut. Likewise, comparing an object to a funnel is misleading if it is only cone-shaped. So be sure your analogy is familiar, appropriate, and reveals as many characteristics as possible.

Geometric Shapes

When an object has an easily identifiable geometric shape, you can refer to that shape—assuming that you and your readers know geometrical terminology. However, if your readers can't be expected to know what a rhombus or a parallelepiped is, don't refer to them. And if the object you're describing is three-dimensional, don't refer to a two-dimensional shape. For instance, if your readers look at a two-dimensional drawing of a three-dimensional object, they might mistake a cone for a triangle. You must either provide a three-dimensional view or explain that the object is conical.

Let's review some of those terms from your geometry class that you've put away because you thought you weren't ever going to use them. They are very useful terms in mechanism description.

Two-dimensional shapes Two-dimensional shapes include angles, polygons, and circles.

Angles: Angles are shapes formed by two straight lines that meet. When two straight lines meet at a 90° angle, the angle is said to be a right angle. Angles less than a right angle are called acute angles. Angles greater than a right angle are called obtuse angles (see the figures).

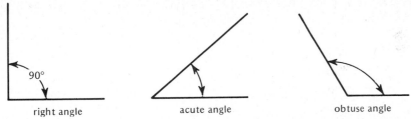

| right angle | acute angle | obtuse angle |

Polygons: Polygons are two-dimensional shapes bounded by straight sides. The most usual kinds of polygons are illustrated below:

Number of sides	Name of shape	Shapes		
3	triangle	△ equilateral	△ isosceles	◁ right
4	quadrilateral	□ square		▭ rectangle
		▱ parallelogram		◇ rhombus
5	pentagon	⬠		
6	hexagon	⬡		

Most of these shapes exist around us. The face of an Egyptian pyramid is a triangle. A musical percussion instrument, the triangle, is an example of an equilateral triangle. If you fold a square sheet of paper diagonally so that two of its opposite corners meet, you've made a right triangle. The courthouse square in county seats is laid out on a square parcel of land. The face of a length of board is a rectangle if the length exceeds the width. Home plate on a baseball diamond and the five-sided building in Arlington, Virginia, that is the headquarters for the U.S. armed forces are pentagons. The cells in a honeycomb are hexagons.

Circles: A circle is a shape bounded by a curved line that is at all points at an equal distance from its center. A hula hoop, the face of a coin, and wedding rings are circular shaped.

A half-circle, or semicircle, is half a circle with a diameter line connecting the end points. Half a circle without a diameter line is a type of arc.

An oval is a shape that looks like a stretched-out circle. The orbit of a satellite and the layout of a race track are examples of ovals.

Three-dimensional shapes   Technically speaking, a three-dimensional object is a solid object. For our purposes in mechanism description, however, the object doesn't have to be solid—it's the shape that we're concerned with. For example, a container or housing for a piece of machinery may be referred to as cubical or cylindrical even though the object is not solid. The most common three-dimensional shapes are polyhedrons, cylinders, cones, spheres, and ellipsoids.

Polyhedrons: Polyhedrons are "solid" objects bounded by plane surfaces. The most familiar type of polyhedron is the cube. Children's blocks, dice, and even some kinds of ice "cubes" are cubes.

Cones: Cones are shapes that look like tepees. The upper part of a funnel, the nose "cone" of a space capsule, cinder-coned volcanoes, and even some kinds of ice cream "cones" are examples of cones.

Cylinders: Cylinders are shapes that look like jars, glasses, cans, and tubes.

Spheres: Spheres are "solid" objects bounded by a surface that is at all points the same distance from its center. Tennis balls, globes, and marbles are examples of spheres. A hemisphere is half a sphere.

Ellipsoids: Ellipsoids are egg-shaped objects. An egg, a football, and various seeds and pills are examples of ellipsoids.

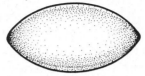

ARRANGING THE DETAILS OF THE DESCRIPTION

Because you have more than one thing to tell readers about a mechanism, and because a mechanism has more than one part, it is impossible to describe it all at once. Thus, you'll have to lead readers through a particular order of presentation. The following three-part arrangement will usually be satisfactory:

1. An introductory overall description of the function and appearance of the entire mechanism.
2. A description of the function and appearance of each major part of the mechanism.
3. An explanation of how the mechanism operates or is used.

What you're doing, in effect, is explaining what the mechanism does and looks like, what each part does and looks like, and how the mechanism as a whole works. Proportion of the description usually works out this way: For a mechanism composed of five major parts, the presentation will have seven main sections—an introduction, five sections describing the five functional parts, and a concluding section describing the operation of the mechanism. Figure 8-8 shows the basic organizational pattern.

The title is usually no more than the name of the mechanism being described: *Multipurpose Police Vehicle, Field-Effect Transistor, Underground Gasoline Storage Tanks,* and so on.

The Introduction

The introduction provides a frame of reference and overview for the entire mechanism. It names the mechanism again, explains its function or behavior, describes its overall appearance, and lists its individual parts. Let's examine an introduction that does these things.

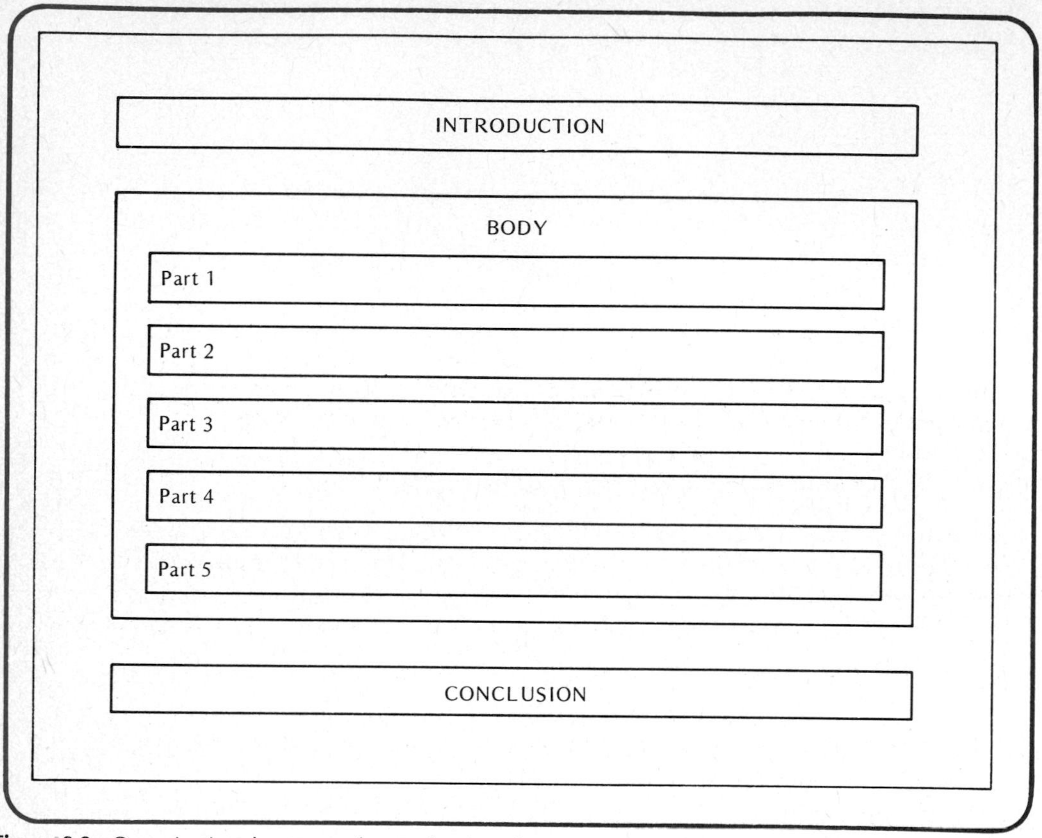

Figure 8-8   Organizational pattern of a mechanism description.

A volcano is a cone-shaped mountain with a crater in the top that from time to time erupts, spewing gases, rock, ash, and molten lava. The main features of the volcano are its crater (the opening in the earth's surface), and the conduit connecting the opening to the interior of the earth which contains magma (hot, molten lava). The largest active volcano in the world is Mauna Loa in the Hawaiian Islands, which towers more than 13,500 feet above the island floor.

The most important statements you make about a mechanism early in your description relate to its function, parts, and appearance. Since you'll be familiar with the mechanism, you'll likely take it for granted that your readers share your knowledge. But you'll have to remind yourself that most readers will need information about what the mechanism does, what it looks like, and what its major parts are. Let's look at a few more explanations of the function and listings of the parts of mechanisms:

A hand hacksaw is a metal-cutting saw of three parts: a handle, a C-shaped frame, and a thin, narrow blade fastened to the open side of the frame.

An amoeba, a one-celled animal found in fresh water, consists of a nucleus, the surrounding protoplasm, and an enclosing outer membrane.

A cantaloupe is a small melon having a ribbed, netted rind, yellow, delicately flavored flesh, and seeds.

A microwave oven consists of a housing, power unit, magnetron, wave guide, and oven cavity.

The steering system of a sailboat consists of the rudder, the rudder post, and the tiller.

Venetian blinds, which are horizontal slatted window shades that can be adjusted to control the amount of sunlight that enters a room, from unimpeded sunlight to nearly complete darkness, may be divided into the following parts:
1. control cords to lift and lower the blinds.
2. control cords to control the tilt of the blinds.
3. slats resting on crosspieces between pairs of tapes.

A rifle cartridge consists of a bullet, a case, powder, and primer.

A miter box is a device used to guide a saw in cutting stock to form angle joints. The simplest form consists of a wooden trough having saw cuts through the sides usually at angles of 45 degrees and 90 degrees.

The heart consists of four chambers (two atria for receiving blood and two ventricles for pumping blood), valves to prevent a back flow of blood, and numerous vessels that help this part of the circulatory system to work.

Every mechanism is designed or has the form to fulfill a particular function. Sometimes you can explain that function in the first sentence of the introduction, as in the example of the hand hacksaw, venetian blinds, miter box, and the heart. At other times you'll have to devote a sentence or more to explain the function:

A draftsman's compass is designed for drawing circles, arcs, and ellipses.

A torque wrench is used to tighten bolts to a specified degree of tightness.

In explaining the function, be sure to describe all of the important functions the mechanism is designed to perform. For instance, the function of an air conditioner is to do more than cool a space. Most air conditioners also circulate the air, remove moisture from the air, and filter the air. An explanation of the function of an air conditioner should fully reveal the kinds of "conditioning" the air conditioner is designed to do.

When the object you're describing is part of a larger mechanism—say, an ammunition clip or magazine of a rifle, the points in a distributor (or the distributor itself), or the speaker system of a stereo—you should explain how the mechanism relates to the larger whole. For example, readers unfamiliar with the distributor on an automobile would benefit from knowing that it, along with the battery, spark-plug wires, and spark plugs, is part of the ignition system of the engine.

Your reader always needs to have a notion of the size, shape, and general appearance of the mechanism. Size can be explained by giving dimensions (the metal plate is 2″ × 3″ × ¼″) or comparisons (the film canister is about the size of a tube of lipstick). Shape can be expressed by geometric shapes (the book end is shaped like an equilateral triangle) or comparison to shapes of letters of the alphabet and numbers. A drawing that shows the entire mechanism is often placed in the introduction to give readers some idea of the general appearance of the mechanism as a whole and to orient them to the physical viewpoint from which they are viewing the mechanism.

Partitioning the mechanism into its major functional parts usually doesn't present any problems, unless the mechanism is extremely simple or complicated. In either instance you'll have to make some arbitrary decisions. Try to come up with not less than two parts and not more than five or six.

Every mechanism has at least two parts. Something as simple as a piece of chalk, when thought of as a mechanism, has two ends for marking on a chalkboard and a cylindrical body used for a handle (unless some kind of handle is provided). Just because the mechanism is in one piece is no sign that you should not look for at least two functional parts. Do not confuse a physical piece with a functional part. Similarly, if a mechanism has lots of parts, you should group several of them under one larger part. For example, an adjustable beam compass can be separated into as many as 30 pieces, but it can be regarded as having only three major functional parts: the writing head, the center pin, and the beam. The thirty separable pieces are grouped as subparts of these major functional parts.

The list of parts will indicate the order in which the parts will be discussed. the order may be one of three sequences:

1. *Function:* the parts are described in the order of their activity—Part A moves Part B, which moves Part C, etc.
2. *Space:* the parts are described from left to right, top to bottom, outside to inside, front to back, etc.
3. *Importance:* the parts are described from the most significant to the least significant.

Random order of parts is seldom satisfactory.

The Body

The body of mechanism description explains each major part in the order indicated by the list of major functional parts in the introduction. The parts description provides much the same information for each part that the introduction did for the mechanism as a whole. Simply think of the part as a miniature mechanism. Give at least one section of details for each major part. Use the first few sentences to describe the part's function, appearance, and, if necessary, to list its subparts. In the rest of the section give whatever details of material, finishes, weight, and connections are needed to give readers a visual and functional understanding of the part.

The Conclusion

The conclusion explains how the mechanism works or is used. Here you divide its function or behavior into meaningful stages and explain what happens in each. If you have included this information in the introduction, you need not write a separate conclusion. To explain how the mechanism works or is used, you explain the principles involved in its action and how the major parts work together. For instance, an air conditioner cools a space by removing heat from it. (The next chapter discusses process description, of which mechanical processes are a major type [pages 139–140].)

To draw together the principles presented in this section, we include another example of mechanism description. As you read it, identify the purpose, situation, and audience it is designed for, and note the strategies that help the reader understand its function, appearance, parts, and operation.

The Adjustable Beam Compass

The adjustable beam compass is a drawing instrument used by draftsmen and technical illustrators to draw large arcs and circles that cannot be obtained with a regular bow compass. Depending on the number and length of beams, it can draw circles up to five feet or more in diameter. In spite of the variety of beams, the adjustable beam compass consists essentially of four major parts: (1) the beam, (2) the coupling attachment, (3) the center pin, and (4) the writing head. [See our Figure 8-7, page 124.]

The Beam. The beam (A) makes up the main body of the compass and forms the channel for the center pin (C) and writing head (D), which can be adjusted to obtain the desired diameter. Made of various types of metal or wood, the beam comes in several lengths—ranging from 6″ to 36″—which are graduated in inches to 1/32″. Metal beams look like miniature I-beams, approximately 5/16″ thick. Wood beams look like flat rulers, approximately 7/32″ thick. The potential radius of the beam compass can be extended by connecting "extension" beams (A') to the base beam with coupling attachments.

Coupling Attachment. The coupling attachment (B) is a double-locking device that rigidly connects beams for desired diameter lengths. A rectangular opening, slightly larger than the beams, is cut into the ends of the coupling attachment so that the beams fit inside. Two knurled tension screws serve to hold the beams rigidly.

The Center Pin. The center pin (C), consisting of an interchangeable leg assembly and a divider point, serves as a pivot for drawing arcs and circles. The interchangeable leg assembly (so-called because it is identical to the one used to hold the drawing point) mounts on the beam by the beam passing directly through its rectangular center. The knurled thumb roller, which is like a geared wheel riding against the beam top, allows the leg to be minutely adjusted. The locking screws maintain the exact setting of the leg on the beam and hold the center pin in place. The center pin (like the writing head) extends only one inch below the beam.

The Writing Head.   The writing head (D), as its name suggests, is the part of the compass that marks the desired curve. It consists of an interchangeable leg assembly (identical to the one on the center pin) that holds either a pen, lead, or scriber.

Adjustable Beam Compass in Use.   The number of beams necessary to obtain the diameter are connected, the center pin and writing head are adjusted and locked into position, and the proper marking point is put in the writing head. The center pin is then set at the center of the arc or circle to be drawn. The remainder of the beam compass is rotated to draw the desired curve.

SUGGESTIONS FOR APPLYING YOUR KNOWLEDGE

1. Explain the analogy behind the name of each of the following:

alluvial fan	hammerhead shark
bandsaw	hip roof
claw hammer	kangaroo rat
caterpiller gate	kettledrum
deadman	kidney bean
death's head moth	leaf spring
dining ell	monkey wrench
disk brake	needle-nose pliers
dovetail joint	organ pipe cactus
fiddlehead fern	pineapple
fiddler crab	rocker arm
forklift	sea cucumber
foxhole	T-hinge
gateleg table	U-bolt
hair spring	wing nut

2. Explain the analogy behind the names of five items from your field of study.
3. Choose some mechanism you are familiar with, partition it into not less than two and not more than six major parts, and explain what order of parts you would use to arrange your description.
4. Write a description of some mechanism you are familiar with, and be prepared to explain to other students in the class the intended audience, the purpose and the arrangement of the description, and the methods to help readers visualize the object and its parts.
5. Form a panel with two others in your class to give an oral description of a mechanism all three of you are familiar with. Arrange to have a drawing or drawings of the mechanism

itself in class. Decide who will make the initial introduction of the mechanism, who will describe its major functional parts, and who will describe the way it operates. Time: 10-15 minutes.

6. Write and illustrate a description of a mechanism you are familiar with for readers who need or want to know its function, its parts, and its operation or use.

Suggested topics:

automobile jack	nail punch
balance	odometer
ball peen hammer	paring knife
bookend	pipe wrench
bowsaw	plumb bob
caster	propeller
chisel	pump
coffee mill	resistor
crescent wrench	rubber stamp
earring	safety razor
felt-tip pen	screwdriver
file	shock absorber
fishing float	spring clothes pin
flashlight	student I.D. card
foot ruler	tinsnips
fuse	toggle bolt
hair brush	trowel
human organ	T-square
hypodermic needle and syringe	vise
keyhole saw	volcano
magnet	

CHAPTER 9

Process Description

A process is a specific series of actions that brings about a specific result. Process is essentially chronological, sequential—this happens, then this, then that. Because business and industry are concerned with processes, much of the writing and speaking you may do will be explaining processes. You may need to explain to a coworker, a supervisor, or a customer the way something happened, the merits of a particular process, or the way a mechanism works.

Obviously, such explanations are useful only if they're clear. Thus, you'll have to plan your explanation carefully.

PURPOSE OF THE DESCRIPTION

You'll have to decide first on the purpose of your explanation. You must distinguish between explaining a process and giving instructions for performing it. If you expect your readers to perform the process, you should write a set of instructions. We will take up writing instructions in the next chapter. If you don't expect your readers to perform the process but only to understand it, you should write an explanation of it. After reading your explanation, your readers should know the process well enough to understand what happened during a chain of events, to evaluate the reliability or efficiency of a process, or to understand the operational sequence of a mechanism.

Explaining How Something Is Done or Made

Much process description tells how something is done or made: how ships are mothballed, how coal is mined, how money is coined or printed, and how riots are controlled. Organizations use process description to tell the story of their product. For example, see the following excerpt from a pamphlet titled *All About Tuna,* published by the Tuna Research Foundation.

Apart from the fishing, a can of tuna also represents an exciting story of science and modern production which make possible a year-round supply of economical tuna for all Americans, regardless of how far inland they live.

A fishing vessel returning from a fishing trip heads straight for the docks behind the canneries for unloading. The unloading operation begins immediately and is accomplished by means of huge buckets which are lowered by derricks into the holds of the vessels, are filled with tuna, and unloaded on conveyor belts which carry the fish to the cannery.

The fish, after thawing and cleaning, are pre-cooked in steam ovens at a temperature of 218°F. for three to six hours, depending on the size.

Once cooked, the fish are cooled for ten to twelve hours, and then moved to the cleaning tables where the bones, skin and dark meat are removed. Only the tender flavorful loins, or lateral muscles, of the tuna are used in the canned tuna we buy. The rest provides nutritious pet food. Between 2.2 and 2.3 pounds of raw fish make one pound of canned tuna.

A special machine shapes the loins into cylinders and cuts them to size for the solid pack. Chunk-style tuna is cut into bite-size pieces before canning. The grated and flake packs are composed of small or irregular pieces of tuna, but meet the same standards of flavor and color as the other pack styles.

In the final steps, salt and vegetable oil, high in polyunsaturates, are added to the cans after the tuna has been packed. Then the cans are sealed and processed in huge pressure cookers at 240°F. or 250°F. for about 40 minutes to almost 4 hours, depending on the can size.

Processing is done by licensed operators under rigid standards. Equipment and processing operations are double checked by both the retort operators and automatic continuous checking devices not only to assure adequate sterilization of the food but also to provide an extra margin of safety. State inspectors are on hand at all times to check the processing operation, sample the batch and approve each lot. The canner's own quality control department also checks sample cans from each batch.[1]

The first paragraph, which serves as the introduction to the explanation of how tuna is canned, accomplishes three things. First, it serves as a transition to move the reader from an explanation of how fishing fleets fish for tuna to an explanation of how tuna is canned. Second, it tells the reader that the process is based upon the latest in canning technology. Third, it explains the importance of the process—it makes available year round and everywhere a supply of canned tuna.

[1]Reprinted by permission from *All About Tuna,* Tuna Research Foundation, 1972, pp. 8–9.

The next five paragraphs, which constitute the body of the process description, explain what happens in each major step of the process. The arrangement is chronological—that is, according to the occurrence of action in time. Notice how paragraphing marks off the separate steps.

The last paragraph concludes the explanation by pointing out the care taken during the process.

Process description also explains how research or tests were conducted. Research reports often contain a section describing the work done so that readers can evaluate, even reproduce, the methods. Thus, the explanation should be complete and clear enough that readers could use it as a guide to repeat the original investigation or experiment. Such a section is shown in the following excerpt from an article that describes the results of an experimental process to improve the baking characteristics of frozen par-fried French fries.

Preparing the Product. To evaluate the baking characteristics of the surface-treated fries, the product was prepared as follows:

• **Preparation.** Russet Burbank potatoes (commercial processing quality, specific gravity 1.086–1.096) held at 45°F were cut into ⅜-in.-square and ¼-in.-square × 3½- to 4-in.-long strips with a hand-operated French fry cutter. Shorter strips ⅜-in.-square × 1½- to 2-in.-long were also cut for use in precooked frozen dinners. The cut strips were washed and held briefly in tap water until used.

• **Surface Freezing.** The potato strips were placed on a dripping rack and then immersed and agitated in R-12 held in a Dewar flask (Nonaka et al., 1972). The immersion time in R-12 (−21.6°F) was standardized at 7 sec.

• **Leaching.** The ⅜-in.-square surface-frozen strips were leached in 125°F water for 15 min. and the ¼-in.-square strips for 10 min. The strips were immersed in heated water contained in a steam-jacketed kettle and agitated with a rotating propeller-type stirrer. The strips were not rotated.

• **Par-frying.** A Wells fryer using 5 qts. vegetable oil heated at 365°F was used for par-frying. The duration of par-frying was varied depending upon whether the French fries were to be baked on a cookie sheet or in a frozen dinner such as a TV dinner. Duration was also varied to change the degree of final crispness.

For the product to be baked alone, a par-fry time of 1 min. at 365°F was used to more or less duplicate the conventional practice of the industry. However, durations of 1 to 2½ min. will increase the crispness of a ⅜-in.-square fry. For a ¼-in.-square fry, a most desirable product was obtained with a 1 min. 15 sec. par-fry.

For the product to be baked with a precooked frozen dinner, the par-frying time was lengthened to 2, 3, and 4 min. to produce varying degrees of crispness. Frozen dinners are cooked for a specified length of time under conditions of steam heating, and the French fry must withstand this environment and still maintain the quality of a desirable fry.

• **Final Freezing.** The par-fried French fry was frozen in a tunnel blast freezer for 15 min. at −34°F and held at −10°F until used.

• **Baking.** The surface-treated fries were baked in the usual manner—placing the fries in a single layer on a cookie sheet and baking them in an oven. The ⅜-in.-square par-fries were baked 7 min. at 450°F, then turned and baked an additional 8 min. The ¼-in.-square par-fries were baked 4½ min. at 450°F, then turned and baked an additional 4½ min.[2]

Each of the six steps in preparing the potatoes for evaluation is set off by a heading. The writers discuss the materials, equipment, and methods in enough detail so readers know exactly what was done. Notice the writers' use of passive verbs:

"Russet Burbank potatoes . . . were cut . . ."

"The cut strips were washed and held briefly . . ."

"The potato strips were placed . . ."

Passive voice is used often in research reports to focus attention on the action, not the researcher. Readers assume that the researcher performed the action.

Explaining How Something Works

Process description also explains how mechanisms work: how a laser measures inaccessible, and sometimes invisible, points; how an image is telecast; how a CB radio communicates; how an inclinometer works. When you explain mechanical processes, you emphasize the interaction of parts and the underlying principles of those interactions that take place during a cycle of the mechanism's operation. Figure 9-1 is the description of how the parts of a tire pressure gauge work together. Notice how the explanation concentrates on the operation, not on the physical hardware. Pictorials, not words, carry visual features.

The description of how the tire pressure gauge works consists of an introductory paragraph and three paragraphs of descriptive details. The introduction explains the importance of the pressure gauge, its appearance, and its overall operation. Each of the other paragraphs explains the movement of the gauge's parts as it operates.

The large cutaway drawing, placed diagonally across the illustration, helps familiarize readers with both the external and internal features of the gauge. The drawing of the person using the gauge is an effective use of "window dressing" to attract readers' attention. The cross-sectional drawings, showing what happens in each step of the gauge's operation, illustrate the changing positions of the expanding chamber of air, the plunger, spring, and bar indicator.

ARRANGING THE DETAILS OF THE DESCRIPTION

As you have seen, process description is the method of the storyteller. You have to do more than merely explain a process. In fact, one of the biggest

---

[2]Reprinted by permission from M. Nonaka and M. L. Weaver, "Texturizing Process Improves Quality of Baked French Fried Potatoes." *Food Technology* 27 (March 1973): 50.

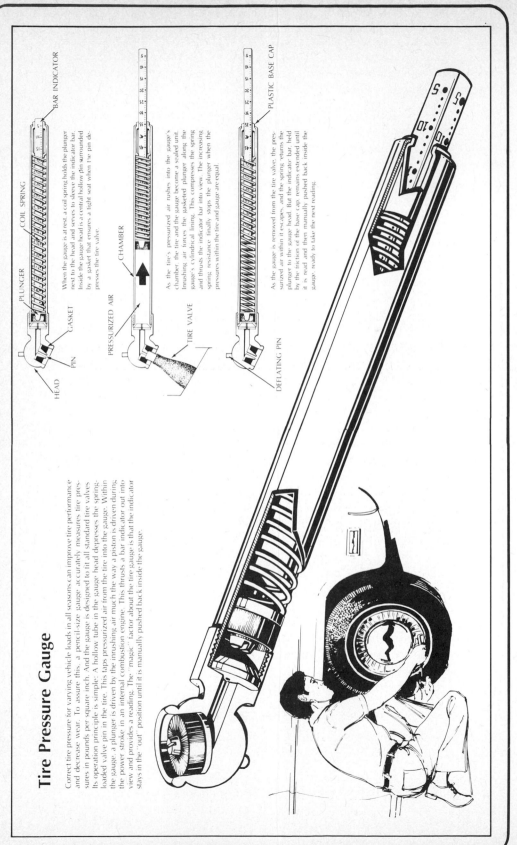

Figure 9-1 Description of how a mechanism works. (Reprinted from *How It Works Illustrated: Everyday Devices and Mechanisms* by Rudolph Graf and George J. Whalen; published by Popular Science Books)

problems readers have in following the explanation of a complex process is being thrust into the first step of the process without orientation. So it is not always best to explain the initial step without first giving readers some information to help them get their bearings. If you move too quickly, you're likely to lose readers.

To help you describe complex processes that require more than just a "then-this-happens" story, let's study the arrangement and the kinds of information that will aid readers in following your explanation.

The following three-part arrangement (Figure 9-2), very similar to the one used in mechanism description (see page 130), will usually be satisfactory for describing a process.

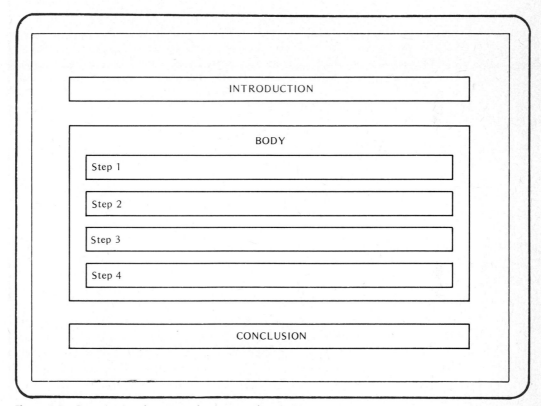

INTRODUCTION

BODY

Step 1

Step 2

Step 3

Step 4

CONCLUSION

Figure 9-2 Organizational pattern of a process description.

The Title

Your title doesn't have to be terribly snappy, but it should be specific enough to identify the process. If submerged welding techniques is the subject of your explanation, include those words in the title.

The Introduction

The introduction, which may run one paragraph or several, prepares readers for the details of the process. It identifies the process, states its purpose and significance, and traces briefly the main course of the process by naming its major steps. A well-written introduction may be the key to your readers' understanding of the process, so spend some time working on it.

Identifying the process   Often just naming the process is adequate (taping an ankle, how sediments build up on the ocean floor, recruiting personnel). Sometimes, though, you'll have to spend a sentence or more explaining the nature of the process:

> Like a refrigerator, an air conditioner cools a space by removing heat from the air and pumping it elsewhere.

> Electrons are so light and small that they can stop and reverse direction in no time. It is sometimes convenient to generate electricity (that is, supply pressure to push electrons out of your wall plug) if it is made alternately to push and to pull the electrons through the wire. For 1/120 of a second the electricity goes one way around the circuit, for the next 1/120 of a second it reverses and goes the other way. A full cycle is repeated 60 times each second, and so it is called a 60-cycle alternating (ac) current to differentiate it from the unidirectional, direct (dc) current.[3]

Remember to remind or inform your readers of the general principle behind what's familiar to you but little understood by them.

Going through the main steps   Readers will always find it easier to follow the explanation of a process when they have been given an overview of the process first. The process is divided into its major steps, which are listed in the order they occur. The process may involve many separate actions, so to keep your readers from getting lost in the forest of little steps and to protect them against a monotonous "and-then" sequence, group closely related steps as a single main step. For instance, preparing burley tobacco for market involves dozens of activities, but the major steps of the process are five: (1) removing the tobacco from the barn; (2) stripping and sorting the leaves; (3) pressing and bulking the stripped leaves; (4) loading the stripped leaves; and (5) unloading the stripped leaves at the warehouse. Each major step consists of several substeps. The second step—stripping and sorting the leaves—consists of sorting the plants, grouping the leaves, and tying the leaves into "hands."

You may present the overview two ways—by list or flow chart.

Let's first look at a few examples of sentences that list the major steps of a process:

> Executive recruitment consists of six steps: (1) making the position opening known to potential applicants, (2) screening the applicants, (3) interviewing qual-

---

[3]Richard M. Koff, *How Does It Work?* (New York: Doubleday & Company, Inc., 1961), pp. 73–74. Copyright © 1961 by Richard M. Koff. Reprinted by permission of Doubleday & Company, Inc.

ified applicants, (4) selecting the best qualified applicant, (5) offering employment, and (6) responding to the candidate's decision.

A fuse "blows" when the electrical current through the fuse becomes too great, creating heat that melts away the narrow center strip of the fuse, thereby interrupting the operation of the electrical circuit.

Making paper consists of four major stages:
1. preparing the pulp;
2. removing impurities from the pulp;
3. turning the pulp into paper strips;
4. wrapping the paper around a roller or cutting the paper into separate sheets.

Making a jigsaw puzzle consists of three main steps—mounting the picture on a sturdy material, cutting or sawing the mounted picture, and finishing the pieces.

Barbecuing chicken consists of four steps: preparing the fire, preparing the chicken, preparing the sauce, and broiling the chicken.

The shield budding method of grafting involves five steps:
1. A bud is cut from a twig.
2. A T-shaped cut is made in the bark of the stock.
3. The bark is raised to admit the bud.
4. The bud is placed in the cut.
5. The stock and bud are wrapped.

As you can easily see from some of the above examples, listing the major steps in a column makes them easier to see, to remember, to refer to—primarily because of the attention drawn to them by the surrounding white space.

To make a list:

Make the items in the list grammatically parallel; that is, use words or groups of words of the same grammatical type. (See also Parellelism, pages 275–276.) Here's an ungrammatical list of the steps in forming wood laminated bowls and plates:

1. making a plastic form
2. the veneering is then cut to fit the form
3. build up the laminations
4. to cure the laminations
5. finishing the laminations

A grammatically parallel list would read like this:

1. making a plastic form
2. cutting the veneer to fit the form
3. building up the laminations
4. curing the laminations
5. finishing the laminations

Single-space each item in the list. If any item is more than a line long, double-space between each item in the list.

Quite often a flow chart or other graphic gives an overview of the general activity of the process. The block diagram, the simplest form of flow chart, shows the steps of a process by means of labeled blocks connected by arrows. The arrows indicate the direction of the activity flow.

Most flow charts are designed to be read from left to right, and if more space is needed, from first row to second row to third. If you were to describe the process of changing a tire, your flow chart might look like this:

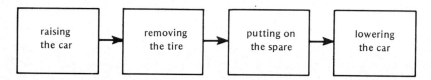

If the flow chart illustrates a cyclical process, it is very often a circle, designed to be read clockwise. If you were to explain the operation of a four-stroke gasoline engine, your flow chart might look like this:

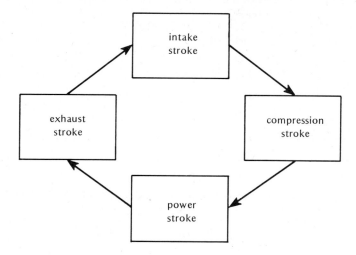

Flow charts used in computer programing almost always go from top to bottom.

Some flow charts use pictorials or schematic symbols to indicate activity at specific points in the process. A pictorial flow chart (Figure 9-3) is an interesting way to provide a broad overview of a process. But flow charts consisting of schematic symbols and formulas should be used only if your readers can understand them. For example, $2H_2 + O_2 \rightarrow 2H_2O$ may be an efficient way of summarizing a chemical process. But if your readers can't read the formula, you'll have to use language that they understand, such as, "When two molecules of hydro-

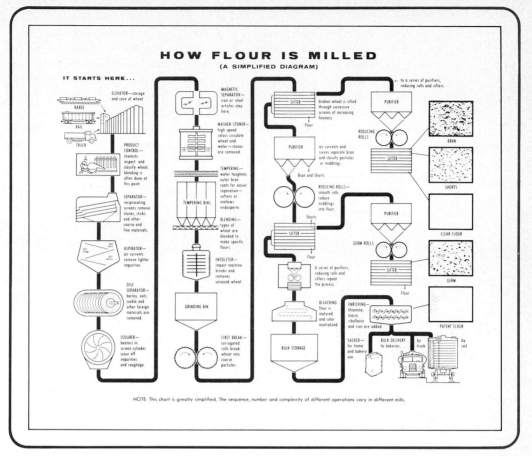

Figure 9-3   Pictorial flow chart. (Copyright 1976, Wheat Flour Institute)

gen are reacted with one molecule of oxygen, two molecules of water are formed.''

You should know how to make a block diagram—the simplest kind of flow chart—because it is relatively easy to make and to read. Here's the way to make it:

1. Draw geometric figures to represent steps in the process. Make each one large enough to hold the name of the step it represents.
2. Label each geometric figure with the name of the step it represents.
3. Connect the geometric figures using straight lines with arrows that show the direction of activity flow.
4. If desired, rule a boundary around the flow chart.

The Body

The body of the process description describes each step in the order given by the list of steps or the flow chart in the introduction. The step-by-step description provides much the same information for each step that the introduction did for the process as a whole. Again, as we suggested when we discussed mechanism description, simply think of a single step of the process as a miniature process.

If the steps are complex or lengthy, introduce them with headings. Give each step proper emphasis by devoting at least a paragraph or section to it. Early in each paragraph or section explain what the step is and what happens. If the step is complex and the detail is necessary, provide an overview of its substeps just as you did for the process as a whole. Topic sentences should explain what the result of each step is or what takes place in the step. The topic sentences of a series of paragraphs describing the preparation of text for letterpress printing might read like this:

> First, the manuscript goes to the Linotype operator, who types the text into individual, justified lines. . . .
>
> Second, each assembled, justified line goes to the casting section of the Linotype machine, where it is cast into metal as a single unit. . . .
>
> Third, the lines so cast are stacked and then "locked up" in a metal frame called a *chase* on a *stone*, a flat granite or steel table, by the compositor. . . .
>
> Fourth, the pressman mounts the chase on the bed of the press, where inked rubber rollers run over the raised type and leave a coat of wet ink wherever the type stands high. . . .

And so on to the end of the process. Each of the above sentences starts a paragraph that may be expanded to the length and degree of detail the writer feels the reader should have.

The Conclusion

The end of the process description may simply be an explanation of the last step, a summary of the steps (if the process is complex and difficult to follow), or additional comments on the process as a whole (if you feel the need to find some way to end the description gracefully).

SUGGESTIONS FOR APPLYING YOUR KNOWLEDGE

1. Choose a process you are familiar with, partition it into its major steps and the major steps into substeps. Submit for your instructor's evaluation: (1) a sentence listing the major steps; (2) sentences listing the substeps for each major step; (3) a flow chart depicting the major steps.

2. Team up with a classmate to give an oral explanation of a process both of you are familiar with. Prepare the necessary graphic aids large enough to be seen by the rest of the class. One of you make the initial introduction of the process; the other describe the steps in the process.
   Time: 10 minutes.
3. Write an explanation of a process you are familiar with:
   A. Explain how something is made:

beer	nylon
bricks	paint
butter	paper
clay flower pots	pencils
coins	printed circuits
glass	shingles
honey	soap
nails	wire

   B. Explain how something is done:

   an auction is conducted
   a beginning driver is taught to drive a vehicle
   a credit rating is checked
   a letter goes through the mail
   an organization hires an employee
   a student registers for courses at your school

   C. Explain how something works:

chain saw	pump
circuit breaker	remote controller
drill	rotary engine
EKG machine	sewage-treatment plant
fireplace	solar heating system
gall bladder	speedometer
heart	telephone-answering machine
light bulb	toaster
odometer	vise grips
pancreas	

   D. Explain how some natural process occurs:

digestion of proteins	lightning
earthquake	pollination
fog	sound
growth of a particular plant	volcano
growth of a particular animal	yawning
hail	

CHAPTER 10
Instructions

Learning how to do something new can be either enjoyable or frustrating. The key is how clear and complete the instructions are. Some instructions, written by persons who do not know how to do the job themselves, are full of misinformation. Other instructions, written by persons who know very well how to do the job and assume that everybody else does too, contain general directions that are hazy to readers. Good instructions are written by persons who know the job inside out and who know how much detailed instruction their readers need.

When you become good at giving instructions, you also become one of your organization's most valuable people. For good instructions can aid your organization two ways: they can be an effective customer-relations tool, helping customers use the goods they purchase; they can also be useful in helping employees learn to do many jobs. Instructions can be oral or written, but they should be put in writing when a mistake in a procedure is likely to be serious or when it is inconvenient or impossible to communicate orally with your audience.

Written instructions come in all sizes. They range from terse directions on bottle caps and the sides of packages to longer forms like manuals and books. It's impossible, of course, to cover every conceivable means of written instructions. Nevertheless, in this chapter we'll discuss the more frequently used written instructions—instructional panels on packages, instructional sheets and leaflets, and instructional booklets and manuals.

INSTRUCTIONAL PANELS ON PACKAGES

Instructions frequently appear on the side of containers, as illustrated by these brief directions for putting a mantle on a kerosene lamp.

Directions

+ Without touching fabric, remove mantle from box by wire frame and handle by ears. NEVER TOUCH FABRIC.

+ Fit mantle to burner gallery and lock by turning clockwise.

+ Taking care that match does not touch mantle, apply light to base of mantle to burn off protective coating. TAKE CARE THAT MATCH DOES NOT TOUCH MANTLE.

+ Lock chimney in burner gallery by turning clockwise. DO NOT FORCE.

The instructions for installing a mantle on a kerosene lamp are written in the imperative voice. That is, the reader is ordered to perform some action as in "Remove mantle from box" and "Fit mantle to burner gallery." Notice that the imperative is simply the "You" sentence form—"*You* remove mantle from box"—with the "you" missing. Imperative sentences sound a bit brusque when taken out of context as we have done here, but they don't really trouble anyone. You've read imperative-voice sentences many times in instructions, we suspect, and we're sure you've never been disturbed by them. Remember that instructions tell how to do something. Your readers rely on you to tell them what they're expected to do and how to do it.

Notice, also, that the sentences are short and to the point. They run from a low of three words to a high of 19. They average about 10 words each. From 9 to 14 is probably about the average you want in instructions.

Each step is emphasized by its being separated from the others by paragraphing, plenty of white space, and the little plus marks. Capital letters are used to warn or caution the reader about potentially troublesome or dangerous phases of the procedure.

INSTRUCTIONAL SHEETS AND LEAFLETS

Instructions also appear on sheets or leaflets enclosed with goods, as shown by the material in Figure 10-1 that tells how to mount decorative ceiling hooks for hanging flower pots, chimes, or chains for swag lamps.

Usually the first thing readers see when they look at an instruction sheet is the title. (In fact, that's usually what they're looking for.) The title should be specific enough to assure readers that they have the right information for the right job. Words like *directions, instructions, procedures, how to . . . ,* signal the type of document it is. Also, it helps to name the procedure in the title, as "How to Install Ceiling Hooks." Warnings and cautions should be placed where they cannot be overlooked easily.

HOW TO INSTALL CEILING HOOKS

CAUTION: Do not use hooks on radiant-heating ceiling. Do not drape electrical wire on the hook. Slide the chain link only over the hook. Weight of object should not exceed 15 pounds.

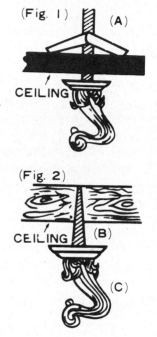

FOR PLASTER OR PLASTER BOARD CEILINGS (Fig. 1)

1. Drill hole in the ceiling to the same diameter as the closed flaps of the enclosed toggle bolt assembly (A).
2. Insert flaps and bolt into the ceiling with the toggle bolt protruding through the ceiling.
3. Lock the assembly by screwing on the hook as shown.

FOR WOOD OR ACOUSTICAL TILE CEILINGS (Fig. 2)

1. Screw steel screw (B) into hook (C).
2. Screw the assembly into the wood.

Figure 10-1 Sample of instructional sheet.

If there are several steps or series of steps, a numbering system can replace bullets(●), dashes(—), or other marks. As readers look over the instructions, they should see down the left margin each instruction beginning with an arabic numeral and period (or some other mark).

Graphics that help readers understand and follow a direction should be placed as close as possible to the direction. Call-outs (references to graphics) and captions should be included to identify graphics and relate them to the text. Otherwise, readers may not refer to them at all.

Another type of instructional sheet is instructions designed as a checklist for readers in their performance of routine daily tasks (see Figure 10-2).

Following is such a checklist used by employees of a service station. Notice how the vertical list functions as a checklist. Lined spaces to the left of the direction replace the numbering or designation system. When readers complete the step, they check it off.

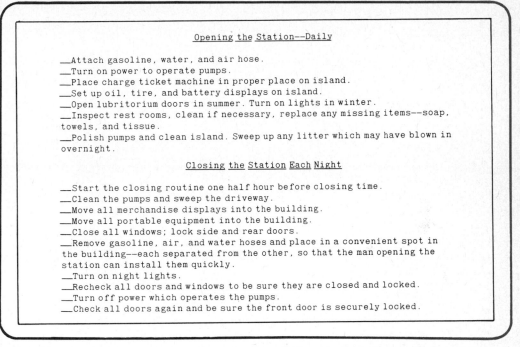

<u>Opening the Station--Daily</u>

__Attach gasoline, water, and air hose.
__Turn on power to operate pumps.
__Place charge ticket machine in proper place on island.
__Set up oil, tire, and battery displays on island.
__Open lubritorium doors in summer. Turn on lights in winter.
__Inspect rest rooms, clean if necessary, replace any missing items--soap, towels, and tissue.
__Polish pumps and clean island. Sweep up any litter which may have blown in overnight.

<u>Closing</u> the <u>Station</u> <u>Each</u> <u>Night</u>

__Start the closing routine one half hour before closing time.
__Clean the pumps and sweep the driveway.
__Move all merchandise displays into the building.
__Move all portable equipment into the building.
__Close all windows; lock side and rear doors.
__Remove gasoline, air, and water hoses and place in a convenient spot in the building--each separated from the other, so that the man opening the station can install them quickly.
__Turn on night lights.
__Recheck all doors and windows to be sure they are closed and locked.
__Turn off power which operates the pumps.
__Check all doors again and be sure the front door is securely locked.

Figure 10-2 Sample of checklist worksheet. (J. C. Chatfield and I. A. Mathias, *Profitable Oil Jobbing.* Scarsdale, N.Y.: 1966, p. 88)

INSTRUCTIONAL BOOKLETS AND MANUALS

As you can see by reviewing the samples in this chapter, the layout and design of instructions are important. You must think carefully about the amount of space they will occupy. Sometimes instructions have to be squeezed into small panels on the side of a box. Sometimes they fill a manual. Instruction manuals share many characteristics with briefer forms of instructions: directions are given in short imperative sentences, are separately paragraphed, are emphasized by surrounding white space, numbering, and different typeface, and are supported by graphics.

Figure 10-3 shows the first seven pages of a typical instruction manual, *Singer Instructions: Scholastic Zig-Zag & Stretch, Sewing Machine/Model 717 (Form 21717 [Rev. 575], 1973)*. Notice that the title is specific about the manual's contents: a specific manufacturer, type of machine, and model number. Readers thus know exactly what machine the manual describes.

As the Singer instructions illustrate, the most notable additional features

CONTENTS

Figure 10-3 Instructional manual. (Copyright © 1973 The Singer Company; all rights reserved; reproduced by permission)

1. GETTING TO KNOW YOUR MACHINE

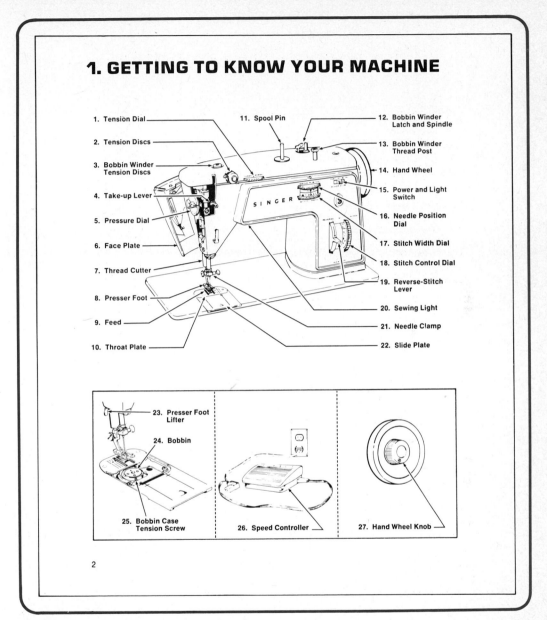

1. Tension Dial
2. Tension Discs
3. Bobbin Winder Tension Discs
4. Take-up Lever
5. Pressure Dial
6. Face Plate
7. Thread Cutter
8. Presser Foot
9. Feed
10. Throat Plate
11. Spool Pin
12. Bobbin Winder Latch and Spindle
13. Bobbin Winder Thread Post
14. Hand Wheel
15. Power and Light Switch
16. Needle Position Dial
17. Stitch Width Dial
18. Stitch Control Dial
19. Reverse-Stitch Lever
20. Sewing Light
21. Needle Clamp
22. Slide Plate

SINGER

23. Presser Foot Lifter
24. Bobbin
25. Bobbin Case Tension Screw
26. Speed Controller
27. Hand Wheel Knob

2

Figure 10-3 Instructional manual *(continued).*

principal parts and what they do

1. **Tension Dial** lets you select just the right tension for your stitch, thread, and fabric. The numbers eliminate guesswork in duplicating settings.

2. **Tension Discs,** controlled by the tension dial, regulate the amount of tension on your needle thread.

3. **Bobbin Winder Tension Discs** regulate thread tension for bobbin winding.

4. **Take-up Lever** controls flow of needle thread.

5. **Pressure Dial** regulates presser-foot pressure on fabric. It has an all-purpose sewing setting plus settings for extra-light and extra-heavy pressure and for darning.

6. **Face Plate** swings open for access to threading chart and pressure dial.

7. **Thread Cutter** is built into presser bar for safety and convenience.

8. **Presser Foot** holds fabric against feed.

9. **Feed** moves fabric under the presser foot.

10. **Throat Plate,** secured by magnets, lifts out for removal. Guidelines on right and left sides of plate help you keep seams straight.

11. **Spool Pin** holds spools of various sizes.

12. **Bobbin Winder Latch and Spindle** let you fill bobbin quickly and easily. Latch disengages when bobbin is full.

13. **Bobbin Winder Thread Post** guides the thread when winding the bobbin.

14. **Hand Wheel** controls movement of take-up lever and needle. *Always turn it toward you.*

15. **Power and Light Switch** turns on machine and sewing light simultaneously. **FAST** and **SLOW** speed range settings let you choose the best sewing speed for your work.

16. **Needle Position Dial** places needle in either **L** (left), **▲** (center) or **R** (right) stitching position.

17. **Stitch Width Dial** controls the width of zig-zag stitching and positions the needle for straight stitching.

18. **Stitch Control Dial** allows for a variety of stitch lengths; also has a special **STRETCH** setting for straight or zig-zag stretch stitching.

19. **Reverse-Stitch Lever** instantly reverses stitching direction at the touch of your finger.

20. **Built-in Sewing Light** illuminates sewing area. Pull-down bracket makes it easy to replace bulb.

21. **Needle Clamp** is designed to make needles self-setting and eliminate the possibility of inserting needle backwards.

22. **Slide Plate,** opens easily, lets you see bobbin. Seam guidelines (extended from throat plate) have cross lines to help you turn square corners.

23. **Presser Foot Lifter,** at back of machine, allows you to raise and lower presser foot. Extra-high lift position permits easy placement of bulky fabrics.

24. **Bobbin** shows thread supply, is easily removed for winding.

25. **Bobbin Case Tension Screw** regulates bobbin-thread tension. Seldom needs adjustment.

26. **Electrical Connections and Speed Controller** are designed for your convenience and safety.

27. **Hand Wheel Knob** engages hand wheel to sewing mechanism. Loosen knob for bobbin winding.

3

Figure 10-3 Instructional manual *(continued).*

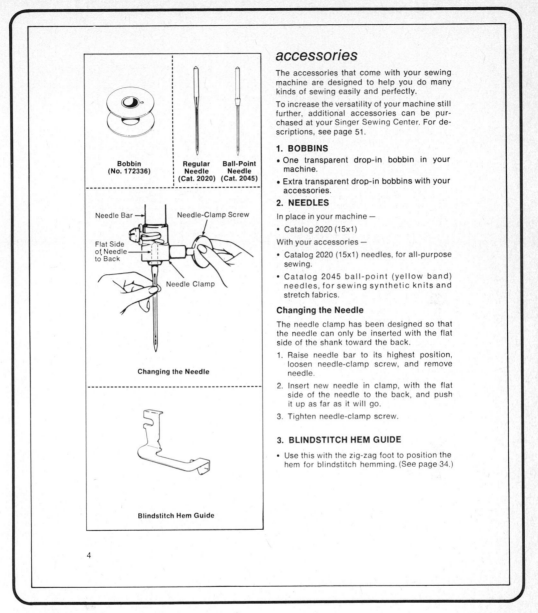

accessories

The accessories that come with your sewing machine are designed to help you do many kinds of sewing easily and perfectly.

To increase the versatility of your machine still further, additional accessories can be purchased at your Singer Sewing Center. For descriptions, see page 51.

1. BOBBINS

- One transparent drop-in bobbin in your machine.
- Extra transparent drop-in bobbins with your accessories.

2. NEEDLES

In place in your machine —

- Catalog 2020 (15x1)

With your accessories —

- Catalog 2020 (15x1) needles, for all-purpose sewing.
- Catalog 2045 ball-point (yellow band) needles, for sewing synthetic knits and stretch fabrics.

Changing the Needle

The needle clamp has been designed so that the needle can only be inserted with the flat side of the shank toward the back.

1. Raise needle bar to its highest position, loosen needle-clamp screw, and remove needle.
2. Insert new needle in clamp, with the flat side of the needle to the back, and push it up as far as it will go.
3. Tighten needle-clamp screw.

3. BLINDSTITCH HEM GUIDE

- Use this with the zig-zag foot to position the hem for blindstitch hemming. (See page 34.)

Image labels:
Bobbin (No. 172336) — Regular Needle (Cat. 2020) — Ball-Point Needle (Cat. 2045)

Needle Bar — Needle-Clamp Screw — Flat Side of Needle to Back — Needle Clamp — Changing the Needle

Blindstitch Hem Guide

4

Figure 10-3 Instructional manual *(continued)*.

5. GENERAL PURPOSE FOOT AND THROAT PLATE

The general purpose foot and the general purpose throat plate are in place on your machine. Ideal for all utility sewing, these fittings can be used for either straight or zig-zag stitching. *Always use them together* when alternating between straight and zig-zag stitching.

6. STRAIGHT STITCH FOOT AND THROAT PLATE

The straight stitch foot and the straight stitch throat plate are used when your fabric or sewing procedure requires close control. Especially useful for:

- Precision stitching of curved and scalloped edges, top stitching, edge stitching, etc.
- Stitching on delicate or spongy fabrics, synthetics, and knits.

7. ZIPPER FOOT

The zipper foot is used to place stitching close to a raised edge. Thus, it is as useful for corded seams and tubular cording as it is for zipper insertion (page 32). It can be adjusted to either the right or left side of the needle and may be used with the straight stitch or general purpose throat plate.

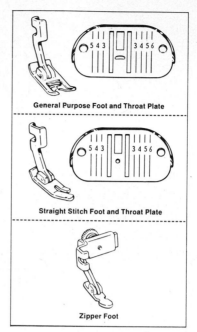

General Purpose Foot and Throat Plate

Straight Stitch Foot and Throat Plate

Zipper Foot

Changing Presser Foot

1. Raise needle to its highest position and raise the presser foot.
2. Loosen presser foot screw and remove the foot.
3. Hook new foot around the presser bar and tighten presser foot screw.

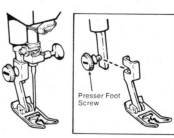

Presser Foot Screw

Changing Presser Foot

5

Figure 10-3 Instructional manual *continued).*

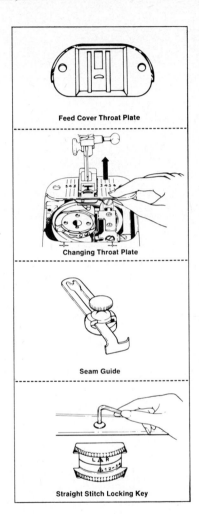

Feed Cover Throat Plate

Changing Throat Plate

Seam Guide

Straight Stitch Locking Key

8. FEED COVER THROAT PLATE

The feed cover throat plate replaces the throat plate when fabric feeding is not desired. Use it for button sewing (page 24) and free-motion darning (page 37).

Changing Throat Plate

(NOTE: Remove bobbin if it contains thread in order to prevent thread being caught when throat plate is replaced.)

1. Raise needle to its highest position and raise presser foot.
2. Open slide plate. Remove throat plate by placing thumb under plate and lifting it up and out.
3. Position new plate over the two pins and release. (Throat plate is drawn into position by magnets.)
4. Close slide plate.

9. SEAM GUIDE

The seam guide will help you to stitch seams of perfectly uniform width. It is especially useful for curved seams or top stitching, when absolute accuracy is required. Also, because it allows you to guide stitches at any distance between ⅛ inch and 1¼ inches from fabric edge, it is useful for very narrow or unusually wide seams.

Attaching the Seam Guide

Place screw in hole to the right of the slide plate; line up straight edge of guide with the throat plate guideline for desired seam width, and tighten screw.

10. STRAIGHT STITCH LOCKING KEY

The locking key furnished with your accessories is used to remove the pin that locks the dial controls for straight stitching in center needle position. Insert key into locking pin and turn key counter-clockwise to remove pin. To "lock" the machine in straight stitch position, set dials at ▲ and ▲ , insert pin from top through both dials and turn key clockwise.

6

Figure 10-3   Instructional manual *(continued).*

2. GETTING READY TO SEW

preliminary steps

1. CONNECTING MACHINE

Before plugging in your machine, be sure that the voltage and number of cycles indicated on top surface of face plate conform to your electrical power supply.

To connect a classroom machine, insert the power-line plug into your electrical outlet.

To connect a conventional household machine, push the machine plug into the plug receptacle. Then insert the power-line plug into your electrical outlet.

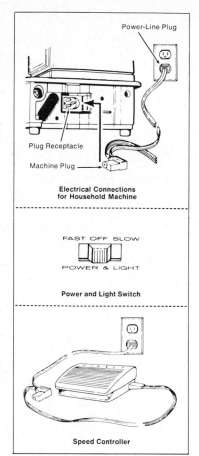

Power-Line Plug

Plug Receptacle

Machine Plug

Electrical Connections for Household Machine

FAST OFF SLOW

POWER & LIGHT

Power and Light Switch

Speed Controller

2. OPERATING MACHINE AND CONTROLLER

To turn on both the machine and sewing light and set speed range, slide the power and light switch to the selected range.

- The **FAST** setting allows for full speed capacity of the machine. It is best for long, straight seams, easy-to-handle fabrics, and general sewing where a variety of speeds is needed.

- The **SLOW** setting allows for maximum control at lower sewing speeds. Use this setting for special jobs such as button sewing, buttonhole making, and where construction details require close control.

CAUTION: We recommend that you turn off the power and light switch before changing needles, presser feet or throat plates and when leaving the machine unattended. This eliminates the possibility of starting the machine by accidentally pressing the speed controller.

To run the machine, press the speed controller (or knee lever). The harder you press, the faster the machine will sew within the selected speed range.

7

Figure 10-3 Instructional manual *(continued).*

of manuals are prefatory and introductory sections and the extensive use of graphics, bold type, and a heading system. Annex B, Formal Elements of Reports, will tell you how to use these in your writing.

The length of the introductory section depends upon the information your readers need before they can perform the action. At the front of the Singer manual are a table of contents that gives an overview of the information contained in the manual and a section that introduces the machine and accessories. If you write a manual consisting of several major sections and having more than a half-dozen or so pages, you should include a table of contents.

The introduction in instructional manuals also normally lists tools and equipment needed to perform the procedure. When the instructions explain how to operate a machine, the introductory section also includes descriptive information about the machine. The first section of the Singer manual describes the appearance and explains the function of the parts and accessories of the sewing machine.

Notice also the heavy reliance on graphics, bold type, and the heading system throughout the pages. The double-column format allows graphics to be placed next to the written instructions they illustrate. Earlier we discussed redundancies as contributors to wordiness. But here we see how graphics are valuable redundancies that clarify instructions. So take a clue from the Singer manual—use lots of graphics. And use lots of heads and subheads. They are extremely important in helping readers keep their place as they look back and forth between their work and the instructions.

The preceding examples are "on-the-job references"—sets of instructions to be followed by readers actually performing a process. There are also general how-to-do-it references that teach new techniques and skills to readers in the calm of their offices or homes. About the only differences between these two types are the more leisurely pace and longer introductory section of the latter. Such a pace and introduction often appear in informational pamphlets, such as the passage on pages 160–161 from a United States Coast Guard publication, *(Almost) Everything You Ever Wanted to Know About Boating—But Were Ashamed to Ask*. (Washington, D.C.: U.S. Coast Guard, February, 1972).

The first five paragraphs of this passage make up the introductory section of this particular set of instructions. The writer works primarily on motivating readers to follow these directions by describing common mistakes and dangers. If you think that your readers need to understand why they are to do something in a certain way, explain why. But keep the instruction and the explanation distinct. It's particularly important when giving instructions that you analyze the job from the point of view of readers unfamiliar with—perhaps even totally ignorant of—the job. This advice also applies when you give a specific command. Ask yourself whether a general command such as "Remove the oil filter" is clear enough, or whether the action of removing the oil filter will have to be broken down into a subroutine—into the smallest possible steps. Re-

Over half of the boats that got into an accident did so by smashing into another boat or some immovable object. If you think that's bad news — then how about the fact that most of these accidents happened because the operator of the boat *wasn't even looking ahead!* It would seem that these people, from the time they stepped into their boats were no better than an accident going somewhere to happen. In other cases the operator was looking ahead but he *didn't know what to do!*

It can be truly said that there are old boatmen.....and there are bold boatmen.....but there ain't no old, bold, boatmen. Not for long anyway.

To keep from running into things with your boat you must learn and use the "Rules of the Water Roads". In this little program we can only give you the smallest amount of all those things you need to know about the rules. For the rest, take an advanced boating course from the Coast Guard Auxiliary. OK, here we go.....

There are many different sets of rules of the road. Which set *you* use depends on *where* you are going to use your boat. You must understand that conditions are often very different on various water areas. The Coast Guard Auxiliary course, and other advanced courses will give you the straight scoop and we can promise you it *all* makes good horsesense.

There are three *general* situations where you will be meeting, crossing, or overtaking another boat. By learning these rules the rest should be easy. OK then, case number one....

1. Meeting head-on

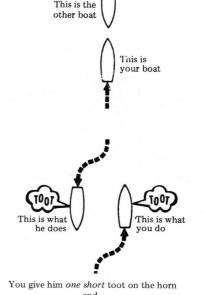

This is the other boat

This is your boat

This is what he does

This is what you do

You give him *one short* toot on the horn
and
He gives you *one short* toot back

member, just as some people who have boats don't know anything about maneuvering them, some people who have cars don't know how to remove an oil filter. Spell things out; don't be afraid of being too simple.

The writer of the Coast Guard manual ends the introduction by providing an overview of the series of directions to come, by mentioning the conditions or circumstances in which certain procedures are to be followed, and by leading into the first circumstance. The remainder of the passage is divided into the three series of commands to perform the maneuvers.

And now a final word.

Regardless of their size or shape, sets of instructions and directions must

OR, as in this case....

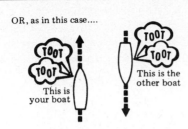

This is your boat

TOOT
TOOT

This is the other boat

TOOT
TOOT

You steer straight ahead.....so does he,
and

You give him *two short* toots on the horn
and

so does he.

How about that?

2. Crossing

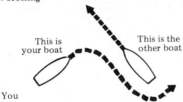

This is your boat

This is the other boat

You

1. Slow down
2. Turn right
3. Pass well behind the back of the other boat.

This means that you are *BURDENED* with the responsibility of slowing down, steering to the right, and passing to the rear of the other boat. The other boat is *PRIVILEGED* and *must* hold the same direction and speed.

3. Overtaking and passing.

OK, here's the situation

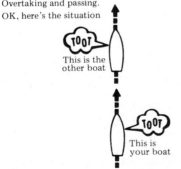

This is the other boat

TOOT

This is your boat

TOOT

If you want to pass *you* are called the overtaking boat and you are *BURDENED* with the responsibility of making the signals, making the steering changes, and passing the other boat. You can pass him on either side.

The best side is the safe side. Suppose that his right side is best....

You
give one short toot on the horn

This
tells him you want to pass on his right side....

He
looks ahead for you and if clear and safe he gives you one short toot on the horn..

This
means the way ahead is clear and he will hold his course and speed....

You
turn to the right, increase speed, cross his wake *carefully*, and pass on his right side like this....

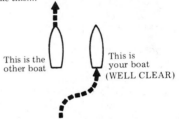

This is the other boat

This is your boat (WELL CLEAR)

To pass on the left side you give *two* toots on the horn.....he gives two toots back. You increase speed, turn out to the left, cross his wake carefully and pass well clear on his left side.

Finally, always stay well clear of sailboats. In almost every case they have the right of way.

do their job well or trouble will result. So try out your instructions after you've written them. Quality control is as important in the writing of instructions as in the production of material. Your instructions must be failure proof. Remember that your writing will be your readers' instructor.

They will read it for one reason—to learn how to do something. Don't let them go away confused or dissatisfied.

To illustrate once again the elements of effective instructional writing, here are two sets of instructions. The first is a very terse set of directions printed on the envelope a decal came in. The second, on preparing blood smears, is much like the material in instructional booklets and manuals.

APPLICATION INSTRUCTIONS

NOTE: Do not moisten sticker.

1. Thoroughly clean number plate.
2. Remove protective paper by bending decal over index finger paper side up and peeling at scoreline.
3. Place sticker in lower-<u>right</u>-hand corner of plate.
4. Firmly rub sticker and edges down with thumb.

Procedure: Preparing Blood Smears

General Comments

Correct preparation of blood smears is a fundamental technique in hematology. The information gathered from the examination of the blood smear is extremely important. It helps to furnish the diagnosis of blood diseases such as leukemias and anemias. It may serve as a guide to the physician in his prescribed therapy for the patient, and as an indicator of harmful effects of chemotherapy and radiotherapy.

One of the main uses of the blood smear is the differential cell count. In this test, the different kinds of white blood cells are counted and the appearance (morphology) of the red and white blood cells is reported. The reliability of the information obtained depends to a considerable extent on the quality of the smears. Properly prepared blood smears are essential to accurate work.

The method of preparing a blood smear is to place a small drop of blood near one end of a clean glass slide. Using a second slide as a spreader, the blood is streaked into a thin or a thick smear and allowed to dry. It is then stained with dye.

There are certain requisites for preparing good blood smears. The slides must be perfectly clean and free of grease. Precleaned slides of good quality are preferred. Additional cleaning is unnecessary if one is careful to touch only the *edges* of the slide.

The drop of blood that is placed on the slide should be no larger than 1/8 to 3/16 inch in diameter (about twice the size of a pinhead).

The task of spreading the drop of blood into a film must be done quickly before coagulation begins.

Materials and Equipment
Fresh sample of blood
Two glass slides, 3 inches by 1 inch, clean and dry
Ten milliliter (ml) syringe
One No. 21 or No. 22 needle

Preparation of a Thin Blood Smear

1. Using a 10 ml. syringe with needle attached, draw about 3 ml. of blood from a tube of oxalated (nonclotted) blood.

2. Add one small drop of whole blood from the syringe to the center of one end of a clean or new glass slide. Proceed *immediately* to the next step because in actual practice the blood will not contain an anticoagulant and will therefore clot rapidly.

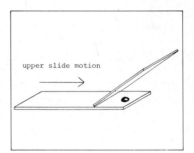

3. Hold a second clean slide above the first slide at a 30° to 40° angle and a few millimeters in front of the drop of blood. Move the upper slide back toward the drop of blood until the end of the upper slide touches the drop and the blood spreads by capillarity along the edge of the slide in contact with the blood. Just *before* the blood spreads along the entire edge of the upper slide, proceed to step 4.

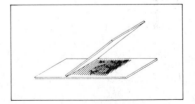

upper slide motion

4. Keeping the entire edge of the moving slide in contact with the stationary slide, move the upper slide rapidly in the opposite direction. In this way the blood spreads over the slide in a thin film. The blood is *drawn,* not pushed, across the slide. When the end of the blood film is reached, lift the upper slide away from the lower edge.

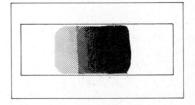

5. Wave the slide in the air rapidly to dry. The thin blood film should look as it does in the illustration at the right. The slide is now ready to be stained and examined.

Preparation of a Thick Blood Smear

1. Repeat steps 1 through 4 of Preparation of a Thin Blood Smear, but use a larger angle (65° to 80°) between the two slides. The greater the angle between the slides, the thicker the blood film will be. Conversely, the smaller the angle, the thinner the film. A thin film is desirable for the examination of red blood cells, while a thicker film is often preferred for differential white blood cell counts. A thick film is used when a slide for malarial parasites is requested.

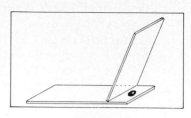

2. Wave the slide in the air rapidly to dry, or allow it to dry in a slide holder, using a small fan if one is available.

3. The slide is now ready to be stained and examined.

SUGGESTIONS FOR APPLYING YOUR KNOWLEDGE

1. Your career course textbooks probably contain many examples of instructions. Bring one example to class to examine in the light of the information in this chapter.
2. Discuss a hobby procedure that you recently learned. Who instructed you? Were the instructions oral or written? Did you have any initial problems following the instructions?
3. Write a set of instructions for one of the following procedures:

   change a tire
   rotate tires
   antique a piece of furniture
   construct a gravel walk
   winterize a swimming pool
   set up a roadblock
   handcuff a prisoner
   fix a leaky faucet
   insulate the attic
   set up and remove a Christmas tree
   prune roses
   build a bird feeder
   start a compost pit
   plant new roses
   repair a garden hose
   remove oil stains from concrete driveway
   restore old paint brushes
   collect blood sample (venipuncture or capillary puncture)

replace an appliance plug
prepare a clinical specimen for a test
make a solder connection on a printed circuit
cut out a garment for sewing
change oil and oil filter in an automobile
replace a screen in a door or window

CHAPTER 11

Periodic Reports, Accident Reports, Trip Reports, and Minutes

Somebody once joked that Charles Lindbergh's nonstop solo flight across the Atlantic was relatively easy. A more difficult task, according to the joke, would have been to have five persons aboard, with each one partly responsible for flying the airplane.

Perhaps there is no other feature in which individual work and organizational work differ more than in the need to coordinate the activities of several individuals and to keep everybody informed of what's happening. When Charles Kettering, the American inventor and automotive manufacturer, worked in his backyard developing an electrical starter for his automobile, he kept no records of materials, labor, or progress. He simply worked until he achieved what he set out to do. He knew exactly what his objective was, he didn't have to coordinate the work of others, he built what he needed, and he didn't have to tell somebody else what his costs were or how he was spending his time.

But the work of an organization is different. Its activity, like Lindbergh's and Kettering's, is directed toward achievement of objectives. However, its objectives are achieved through the coordinated efforts of several individuals. As we mentioned at the beginning of Chapter 6, Basic Principles of Reports, successful organizations achieve their goals by getting information to those who need it. A knowledge of the types of reports discussed in this chapter—periodic reports, accident reports, trip reports, and min-utes—will help you write the effective reports your organization needs to achieve coordination.

PERIODIC REPORTS

Periodic reports are records of work over a specific period of time—a day, a week, a month, etc. Their intervals are determined by management needs or customer requirements. They frequently build up from workers' daily logs or job reports to supervisors' weekly, monthly, or quarterly reports. Higher-level periodic reports pull together these other reports to present information to organizational officers or customers.

These reports are vital documents that give an organization the neces-sary information upon which to base decisions. If they are not used or are not well written, organizations can have many problems. Persons respon-sible for the work, but perhaps removed from the actual work, can find it difficult to keep abreast of expenditures of time, money, and materials, and to evaluate work. Persons responsible for long-range planning can be deprived of valuable records of their organization's capabilities and per-formances.

Because periodic reports are often preliminary to other reports and are important as references, they should be designed so readers can retrieve information from them easily. And while no set format exists for periodic reports—they may be transmitted as memos, letters, informal, or formal reports—they are often so routine that their arrangement can be regu-larized into printed forms.

Printed Periodic Report Forms

Printed periodic report forms are useful because the type of information to be included in them seldom varies. New data is simply put in the existing categories. For instance, monthly periodic reports on the activities of a government agency contained the following categories: (1) Liaison with Department of Transportation, (2) Assistance to County Planning Commis-sions, (3) Assistance to Bureau of Recreation, and (4) Supervision of Youth Conservation Corps Programs. Since the work of the agency was restricted to these four categories, a printed form was a great convenience in making monthly periodic reports. Any time the activities of an organization change significantly, the printed periodic report form can be changed accordingly.

Figures 11-1, 11-2, and 11-3 show the use of printed forms to report routine information periodically. As you can see, the information filled in consists mostly of numbers and phrases. Sometimes, as in the "Remarks" space of Figure 11-1, the information is presented in phrases, sentences, or paragraphs. All printed periodic report forms have two advantages: the organization of a particular report is always the same and the spaces en-courage complete reporting of essential data.

WILLIAMS-NICKELL TRANSPORT CO., INC.

MOREHEAD, KY. 40351

Driver	Date
Arthur Baldridge	*February 22, 1977*

Out	In	Delay
12:50 pm	*7:45 pm*	

		Gasoline	✓	Straight Load	✓
Louisville	✓	Oil		Split Load	
		Fuel Oil		Straight Load	
Ashland		Oil		Split Load	
Route		West Liberty		Town	
#5 Fuel		Destination	*Morehead*		

Truck Number	Fuel Used	
# 4	Number of Gallons	*60 gal.*

Beginning Mileage	*204,697*	Ending Mileage	*204,987*

Remarks *I-64*

1650 gal. Super Regular
2500 gal. Super Shell
Morehead Car Wash 2500 gal. Shell Regular
Plant 1650 gal. Super Shell

Figure 11-1 Printed form to be filled in by truck drivers after each trip. (Courtesy Agnes Williams)

ATTENDANCE RECORD

Floor: **3A** Month: **February**
Librarian: **Wiggs** Total: **4855**

Date Time

	8	9	10	11	12	1	2	3	4	5	6	7	8	9	Total
1	7	19	31	26	23	28	19	20	9	11	5	8	14	6	226
2	11	17	25	25	19	23	20	24	10	10	6	3	8	4	205
3	9	15	27	24	20	26	23	20	14	12	10	13	18	11	242
4	6	13	19	20	23	20	16	11	5	5	4	3	4	2	151
5	3	9	16	11	8	7	5	9	4	4	—	—	—	—	76
6	—	—	—	—	—	—	9	8	10	7	11	8	10	5	68
7	9	20	28	27	29	25	17	22	11	12	7	6	10	8	231
8	15	20	29	27	25	28	17	21	10	14	8	3	13	10	240
9	10	16	27	33	28	25	19	26	20	10	4	5	15	10	248
10	11	18	34	31	26	17	20	20	19	10	14	15	22	16	273
11	8	12	17	21	20	23	19	15	8	4	4	6	3	5	165
12	1	4	12	10	9	11	8	5	3	3	—	—	—	—	66
13	—	—	—	—	—	14	10	6	8	6	10	15	11		80
14	10	26	35	30	31	25	20	26	12	8	10	5	17	13	268
15	8	24	28	23	29	21	23	16	12	11	5	3	10	4	217
16	14	17	20	21	20	18	14	20	18	17	9	2	6	6	202
17	15	29	39	33	36	23	26	25	18	14	8	10	16	11	303
18	8	17	17	28	27	19	15	11	10	3	7	3	5	4	174
19	2	5	11	12	8	10	17	15	9	3	—	—	—	—	92
20	—	—	—	—	—	—	—	—	—	—	—	—	—	—	
21	—	—	—	—	—	—	—	—	—	—	—	—	—	—	
22	15	18	23	24	20	17	16	28	12	11	14	9	6	5	218
23	14	21	28	33	29	20	16	23	11	8	9	14	11	9	246
24	9	13	16	21	20	32	31	23	18	14	9	18	18	14	256
25	6	12	19	23	24	18	18	11	15	8	5	3	3	2	167
26	5	13	12	14	13	11	8	5	5	5	—	—	—	—	91
27	—	—	—	—	—	20	16	9	5	7	13	10	7		87
28	12	19	19	30	27	31	39	26	19	11	8	10	6	6	263
29															
30															
31															
Total	208	377	532	547	514	478	469	456	297	228	170	170	240	169	4855

Figure 11-2 Sample report to be filled in hourly and submitted monthly.

72A089
5-72

Commonwealth of Kentucky
DEPARTMENT OF REVENUE
Frankfort
40601

LICENSED GASOLINE DEALER'S MONTHLY REPORT

Name and Address of Dealer

Report for month of _____ , 19 ___

License No. _____

Schedule A - Report of Gasoline Received	Detail Gallons	Total Gallons
1. Gasoline purchased in Kentucky (tax paid by consignee) (Form 72A080)		
2. Gasoline imported into Kentucky (Form 72A081)		
3. Taxable gallons from terminal storage report (Form 72A090 Line 20)		
4. All other receipts (attach statement of explanation)		
5. TOTAL GASOLINE TO ACCOUNT FOR (Lines 1 through 4)	xxxxxxx	
Deductions		
6. Gasoline exported from the state (Form 72A084 in duplicate)		
7. Gasoline sold to Kentucky licensed dealers (tax paid by consignee) (Form 72A085 in duplicate)		
8. Sold to U. S. Government (Form 72A077).		
9. Lost through accountable losses (Form 72A078)		
10. TOTAL AUTHORIZED DEDUCTIONS (Lines 6 through 9)	xxxxxxx	
11. Total gasoline taxable (Line 5 less Line 10)		
12. Less: Allowance for evaporation and loss (2¼% of Line 11)		

Schedule B - Computation of Tax		
13. GASOLINE SUBJECT TO TAX (Line 11 less Line 12)		
14. TAX DUE (Line 13 times 9¢ per gallon)		$
15 Credits for previous payments (attach copy of authorization)		
16. NET AMOUNT DUE or (overpayments)		$

AFFIDAVIT

The affiant, a principal officer of the above-named dealer, swears that this report (including any other information submitted during the month), is to the best of his knowledge and belief a true, correct and complete report made in good faith.

Subscribed and sworn to before me this _____ day of

_____ , 19 _____

_____
Signature of Affiant

_____
Notary Public

My commission expires _____

_____
Title of Affiant

This report must be filed on or before the twenty-fifth day of the month following the month
for which the report is prepared unless Form 72A103 is filed.

Figure 11-3 Sample report to be filled in monthly.

Progress Reports

If you've ever had something repaired or built, you've experienced a keen interest in keeping posted on how the work was going. And probably as long as you didn't make too big a pest of yourself, the contractor very cordially kept you up to date. That same desire to know accompanies practically every endeavor, large or small: knowing what's happening on a project that's underway, but not yet completed, is essential.

The pressing need to know is satisfied by a special kind of periodic report—the progress report. The obvious purpose of progress reports is to record work completed and to outline work planned so everybody who needs to know (managers, customers, coworkers) will know just what the situation is at the time of the report. Thus, a lot of important persons need to have progress reports available.

There are three ways of timing progress reports. First, like periodic reports, they may be submitted at specified time intervals—weekly, monthly, quarterly, or whatever regular interval has been decided upon—until the project is completed. Second, they may be submitted when major stages of work have been completed rather than at definite time intervals. Third, they may be submitted in response to requests by persons who want to know what progress is being made on a project.

Like other periodic reports, progress reports have no set format and are usually multilevel. That is, in projects of long duration there may be different formats for different levels of progress reports. A work log may be submitted each day; a letter or memo or informal report may be submitted each quarter or semiannually. Such a report schedule accumulates information at different times and uses different formats for different audiences.

Organizing and developing progress reports   Regardless of the submission schedule or format, progress reports tell how a project is going, how much has been completed, and how much remains to be done. To report these three things, the following arrangement is quite suitable:

- An introduction explains the period of work covered by the report, the work that had been planned, and, if appropriate, the authority to do the work. If expected by readers, the introduction may also assess the progress to date.
- A discussion section (body) provides a detailed account of what has been accomplished, and, if appropriate, how.
- A conclusion explains what work is planned for the future and gives an overall appraisal of the progress to date.

This three-part arrangement may suggest the actual headings in some progress reports: Introduction, Discussion, Conclusions. Of course, what arrangement and headings are used will depend upon two important factors: the practices of the organization, and the data-submission plan that may be part of the contract with a customer or sponsoring agency. To appreciate how varied headings may be, consider the following headings gathered from just four progress reports:

Statement of Problem	Introduction
Current Progress	Job Description
Future Work	Work Completed
Assessment of Progress	Work Remaining
	Overall Appraisal

Period of Report	Introduction
Discussion of Work Completed	Project Progress
Roster of Personnel	Project Problems
Expenses Incurred	Logistics
Work for the Next Period	
Conclusions and Recommendations	

In these four report outlines you can readily see that time is the major arrangement. The sample progress report in Figure 11-4 uses time as the major organizing principle. The report, written by the person in charge of a large commercial poultry farm, is an example of a simple, straightforward progress report that evaluates the progress, covers each task in the detail necessary, and then looks ahead and tells what the plans are for the future.

Although the progress report on the poultry plant expansion is arranged chronologically (work completed, work unfinished) with subsections on specific tasks (laying house, brooder house, processing room, drying yard), progress reports are sometimes arranged according to specific tasks, with subsections arranged chronologically. Organized by tasks, the report outline looks like this:

I. Laying House
  A. Work Completed
  B. Work Unfinished
II. Brooder House
  A. Work Completed
  B. Work Unfinished
III. Processing Room
  A. Work Completed
  B. Work Unfinished
IV. Drying Yard
  A. Work Completed
  B. Work Unfinished
Conclusions

Most of the progress reports you'll write will use a straight time arrangement, but if the tasks you're reporting on are large enough to be regarded as mini-projects in themselves, you might consider arranging your report by tasks.

PROGRESS REPORT
EXPANSION OF THE MEDINA POULTRY PLANT
MARCH 1–MARCH 31, 1977

During March we made good progress toward completing the expansion of the poultry plant. The addition to the processing room has been completed. We should complete the entire expansion project by May 15, nearly two weeks ahead of schedule, which will give us additional time to review our late summer and fall production schedules, and will allow us to conduct a tour of the plant for the Farm Advisory Committee at its annual meeting.

Work Completed

Laying House
1. The new 150' X 34' laying house has been completed.
2. 4500 hens (2500 Leghorns and 2000 New Hampshires) were added to the laying flock and were housed in the new laying house. Pockman cages (12" X 16") were installed to hold two hens each. The New Hampshires were housed at the front of the building because they are less easily frightened than the Leghorns.

Brooder House
1. The new 150' X 40' brooder house has been completed, except for installing the automatic feeding and watering system.
2. A portable sprayer has been ordered.

Processing Room
1. The 25' X 40' addition to the processing room has been completed.
2. A new Eggomatic sorting machine has been installed to handle the anticipated increase in egg production.

Drying Yard
1. The drying yard has been doubled in size.
2. The yard has been regraded so that no liquid runoff goes onto adjoining property or into underground water.

Work Unfinished

Laying House
1. During the first week of April, we will cull the nonlayers from the new hens. We anticipate approximately 300 to be culled and marketed.
2. Experiments will be conducted to determine the best lighting.

Brooding House
The automatic feeding and watering system should arrive about the middle of April, and it will take about three days to install.

Processing Room
The processing room is complete.

Drying Yard
1. Marion Harris, Assistant Poultry Plant Supervisor, will visit the Poultry Experimental Stations at State University and Western University, April 14 and 15, to study the work at these stations in controlling flies and maggots in large manure drying yards. He will make recommendations on further environmental control of our drying yard. Until then, we will continue spraying every two weeks.
2. Invitations for bids to remove manure on a monthly basis will be announced April 27, 28, and 29. Bids will be opened at 2 p.m., May 10, in the poultry office.

Figure 11-4 Sample progress report.

The degree of detail included in progress reports will depend on your readers' needs. For most simple projects brief statements like those in the progress report on the expansion of the Medina poultry plant sufficiently inform readers of what's been done and what will be done. In more complex projects it may be necessary to use tables and charts to report a mass of data, especially numbers. But don't interrupt your discussion with too many charts and tables. Place them in an annex at the end of your progress report, commenting on them and referring to them in your discussion.

ACCIDENT REPORTS

Unlike periodic reports, the remaining three reports discussed in this chapter are written when special situations require them.

Accident reports are written when failures, breakdowns, accidents, or anything that interferes with normal work occurs. Such reports are important for two reasons. First, they are indispensable for persons responsible for the performance and operation of personnel and machinery. Second, they are often required as legal documents for reporting injuries, deaths, and damage. Various state and federal agencies' regulations and state and federal law (workman's compensation law, for example) provide reporting guidelines that explain what accidents should be reported to what authorities, who is required to report, what reports are required, and the penalties for failure to report.

Regardless of what kind of accident is being reported, certain information must be reported objectively and specifically:

- What the accident is
- When and where the accident occurred
- Who was involved
- If there was injury, what was done to provide medical treatment, where and by whom
- Who reported the accident, and when
- What caused the accident
- What has been done to correct the trouble
- What recommendation or suggestions are given to prevent recurrence of accident

In fact, information required for accident reports has become so standardized that an accident report form can be designed to handle most routine situations. Figures 11-5 and 11-6 show two such forms. Figure 11-5 is to be filled out by hospital employees who are injured, so that the proper insurance claims can be filed on their behalf. Figure 11-6 is to be filled out by a physician or nurse when an accident to a patient happens in a hospital or nursing home.

If accident report forms are not available for you to use or if the situation requires you to write the accident report from scratch, the following outline will be a suitable pattern to follow:

ST. AGNES MEDICAL CENTER
Stillman, Kentucky

EMPLOYEE'S FIRST REPORT OF INJURY

Hospital personnel who are injured while working must complete this form and turn it in to the Personnel Office. This form is for the protection of the employee, that he or she may report an injury and the proper insurance claims can be filed for the employee's benefit.

Name of injured employee _____

Home address _____

Home phone number _____

Date of injury _____ Time of injury_____a.m. or_____p.m.

Where were you when injured? _____

_____

Describe what you were doing when injured _____

_____

_____

What caused the injury? _____

_____

Describe your injury (e.g., cut on rt. index finger, etc.) _____

_____

Did you receive medical treatment? If so, where and by whom? _____

_____

Were X-rays taken or lab work done? _____

Were you paid in full for the day of injury? _____

Did you report this injury to your supervisor?_____E.R. nurse?_____

Date of report_____ Signed _____
                                              Employee
NOTICE: If you are unable to work because of the injury on any day after the
         day of injury, you must contact the Personnel Director.

Figure 11-5 Injury report form.

ST. AGNES MEDICAL CENTER

ACCIDENT OR INCIDENT REPORT

Name:last   first   middle   Age   Sex   Room No.   Adm. No.

                                                                              a.m.
Date of accident or incident_____19_____ Time _____p.m.

Diagnosis_____

Name of attending physician_____Name of nurse in charge_____

Was physician notified?_____Time of notification_____Notified by_____

Describe accident or incident _____

_____

_____

_____

_____

_____

Was there apparent injury?_____Was treatment rendered?_____

If yes, describe _____

_____

_____

Answer the following with "Yes," "No," or "N/A" (not applicable):
  BEFORE THE ACCIDENT:
Was patient in bed?_____ Was patient in chair?_____ Was floor
dry?_____ Was patient restrained?_____ Was call light on?_____
Were side rails up?_____ Was patient on sedatives?_____ Was patient
confused by nature of illness or condition?_____ Was patient post–op
under 24 hours?_____ Record any factors pertinent to cause or
environment of incident_____

_____

_____

Were corrective measures taken to prevent a further accident or incident of
this nature? _____

Describe _____

_____

Date report written_____19_____ Signed _____
                                                   Physician or Nurse

Figure 11-6   Accident report form.

- Description of the accident. Get right to the point: explain what happened, to whom, when, and where. Explain how you learned of the accident.
- Explanation of what was done to correct situation. Explain how the injured were treated or cared for, how the damage was repaired, how the troublesome situation was corrected.
- Discussion of situation. Analyze what happened, trying to explain reasons for the accident.
- Recommendations. If called for, explain what corrective measures should be taken to prevent recurrence of this particular accident.

TRIP REPORTS

Trip reports, often called travel reports, are records of business or worl trips. They are primarily used to keep supervisors, managers, directors, and sometimes customers informed on the progress of projects, work done, or meetings attended out of town. Trip reports also share information with fellow workers on a project. This is especially helpful if the project is later transferred to another person or group.

Trip reports are written all the time, and the circumstances that call for them are endless. A large company with several branches or offices frequently sends employees from the home office to other branches to exchange information about projects with their counterparts. A company may send a technician to train customer personnel to operate a system sold to them. Or an employer may send an employee to a two-week school or to a convention.

The observations you make, the information you gather, and the work you do during a trip do not always fall into clear categories or are not always relevant to the purpose of the trip. Your job is to select only that information relevant to the trip and to organize it in some helpful way for the reader.

Trip reports don't usually follow any predesigned format. They may be in the form of a memo, a letter, or a formal report. However, there are certain features that you should keep in mind when you write trip reports:

- Use headings to show your organization.
- Record accurately dates, times, places, and the names and titles of people you met.
- Emphasize what was covered during the trip that was relevant to its purpose.
- Include conclusions, recommendations, and evaluations, if appropriate.

As you'll see in the trip reports in Figures 11-7 and 11-8, these features are arranged much in the order listed.

March 21, 1977
To: Professor Lewis Phillips
     Department of Corrections and Social Work

Reed Grant

From: Reed Grant
       Corrections Major—Senior

Subject: Visit to Bryson City Training Center, March 17, 1977

Purpose

    As a member of the SW 429 class, I visited the Bryson City Training
Center (BCTC) to learn how a typical juvenile correctional facility
operates. BCTC is one of six such facilities under the jurisdiction of the
State Division of Human Resources.

    The visit consisted of a briefing by Dr. James Mitchell,
Superintendent of BCTC; a tour of the inmate dormitories; lunch with staff
and inmates; and a tour of classrooms and workshops.

Agenda

    9 a.m. to 10:30 a.m.: Dr. Mitchell gave us a brief history of the
establishment of juvenile correctional facilities in the state and the
history of BCTC. He described the progress of a typical inmate's stay at BCTC.

    10:30 a.m. to noon: Mr. Stan Fralex, a resident counselor at BCTC, gave
us a thorough tour of the dormitory area.

    Noon to 1:00 p.m.: Lunch in mess hall with staff and inmates.

    1:00 p.m. to 1:30 p.m.: Mr. Tom Weaver, BCTC Coordinator of Education
and Training, briefed us on BCTC's educational and training programs, which
consist of classes in English, arithmetic, mechanical drawing, automotive
maintenance, and woodworking. All inmates take English and arithmetic and
one of the vocational classes every day. A new water pumping station and
sewage disposal plant are planned for the facility, and a course in water
resources technology is to be added to the curriculum.

    1:30 p.m. to 2:30 p.m.: Mr. Weaver led us on a tour of the educational
and training area. We visited classes in session.

    2:30 p.m. to 3:30 p.m.: Mr. Raymond Bissell, a BCTC counselor,
explained how Positive Peer Culture was used as part of the rehabilitation
process at BCTC. All inmates are assigned to a group that meets daily to work
on the personal problems and conflicts of the members of the group.

Evaluation of Trip

    I learned a lot from the visit. The BCTC staff was very courteous and
helpful in explaining the way the facility operates. However, I would
recommend that two additional items be added to the agenda of future trips:

    1. An opportunity to visit privately with some of the inmates. The
subject of inadequate recreation and sports programming came up during
lunch, but most of the inmates were reluctant to say much about it since the
staff members were present.

    2. An opportunity to discuss more thoroughly the responsibilities of
resident counselors at BCTC. Since I am considering serving my practicum at
one of the juvenile correctional facilities, I believe such a discussion
would help prepare me better for such service.

Figure 11-7 Sample trip report 1.

June 13, 1977
To: Ron Pelfrey

Alex

From: Alex Williams

Subject: Quarterly Inspection of Martinsburg Bulk Plant,
          June 11, 1977

<u>Results</u>

1. The perimeter area is in good shape. The fence and spur track are well maintained. The grass was cut and trash containers are being used. No spills or leaks were evident.

2. The tank battery is working well. All valves and meters and pumps are working. <u>The</u> <u>ladder</u> <u>on</u> <u>Tank</u> <u>#3</u> <u>needs</u> <u>new</u> <u>skid-proof</u> <u>surfacing</u>.

3. The tank car loading dock is in good shape. All grounding and bonding cables are in good shape. However, <u>the</u> <u>lubricating</u> <u>schedule</u> <u>for</u> <u>the</u> <u>rotary</u> <u>pump</u> <u>on</u> <u>the</u> <u>truck</u> <u>loader</u> <u>was</u> <u>missing</u>.

4. Fire-fighting equipment is in working order. The equipment and the bulk plant were inspected last week and approved by the state fire marshal.

5. The warehouse and offices are well arranged and clean.

6. The three tank trucks and the pickup truck are in good running order. <u>The</u> <u>accident</u> <u>report</u> <u>kit</u> <u>and</u> <u>supply</u> <u>of</u> <u>flares</u> <u>are</u> <u>missing</u> <u>from</u> <u>the</u> <u>pickup</u>.

7. I met with John Waltz and the employees (except for Chris Rodman, who was not at work due to an illness in his family). I told them that I was pleased with the condition of the plant. We discussed hiring somebody for the summer to help with mowing, washing the trucks, and other general duties while people were away on vacation. I told John he could hire somebody to work four hours each morning, five days each week, at $2 an hour.

<u>Action</u>

1. Replace skid-proof surfacing on ladder to Tank #3.

2. Post new lubricating schedule for the rotary pump on the truck loader.

3. Replace accident report kit and supply of flares for the pickup.

4. Find out from John who was hired for the summer.

cc: John Waltz

Figure 11-8   Sample trip report 2.

Our first example trip report (Figure 11-7) is a fairly common report required by instructors to get feedback about class trips. The information in the report is arranged under three headings: *Purpose, Agenda,* and *Evaluation of Trip.* The first section identifies the site of the visit, the purpose of the trip, and a brief summary of the visit (which even in this brief memo provides a handy overview of the visit). Notice how the subheads and paragraphing guide the reader through the report. The third section, which briefly evaluates the trip, transmits two recommendations made by the writer as a result of the trip.

Our second example trip report (Figure 11-8) is a memo detailing a periodic inspection trip to a branch plant. Since the occasion of the report is obvious, there's no introductory material or background information other than that given in the memo heading. The information is arranged under two headings: *Results* and *Action.* The first section provides an area-by-area account of the inspection and describes the conditions the writer found. Notice the underlining to emphasize conditions needing attention. The second section gathers in a convenient list the action the reader needs to attend to.

MINUTES

Often you will take part in many types of meetings. Occasionally you may be called upon to serve as secretary to take the minutes of the meeting—the official record of action taken by the group. While groups may set up their own rules for conducting meetings and recording their actions, most groups follow the suggestions in *Robert's Rules of Order.*

When you serve as secretary, you should sit near the chairperson. Most of the discussion and all official motions will be aimed toward the chair, making it easier for you to hear what you need to record. Record the meeting as well as you can. When the meeting is over, write out the minutes fully from your notes (conferring with the chairperson if you're not sure of a particular item of information), and give the minutes to the chairperson for distribution.

A fairly well-established format for minutes has developed, so your biggest concern will not be how to organize or lay out the minutes. What may prove bothersome, though, is determining the degree of detail required to make the minutes complete. But even here the solution is fairly simple. Remember that minutes are *the official record of action taken by the group during its meetings.* It is mainly a record of what was done, not what was said by the members. Sometimes, however, especially in the case of reports by group members or of debates on an important issue, you may be required to summarize what was said. What you record should be written down objectively and factually, without your opinions being reflected.

The minutes of a meeting should contain the following information, in the following order:

1. Name of the group holding the meeting.
2. Kind of meeting (regular, special, etc.).
3. Date (and place, if not always the same) of the meeting.
4. Subject of the meeting.
5. Names of persons attending, including the fact that the regular chairperson and secretary were present, or in their absence, the names of those persons who substituted for them.
6. Time the meeting was opened.
7. Whether the minutes of the previous meeting were read and approved (as read, or as corrected).
8. Reports of members of the group.
9. Action of the group, with special attention to stating exactly what motions were made and their disposition (carried, defeated, tabled, etc.). It is conventional to include the names of persons making motions, seconding motions, or making amendments to motions. It is also conventional to explain the voting on a motion—how the vote was conducted and so on. If a roll call vote is conducted, the minutes should include a roster of members and how each voted. Going beyond this information may be recording too much. However, the group should decide how much detail the minutes should include.
10. The time of adjournment and the time and place of the next scheduled meeting.
11. The signature of the secretary (as well as the chairperson, if so desired).

Minutes of a meeting are shown in Figure 11-9.

SUGGESTIONS FOR APPLYING YOUR KNOWLEDGE

1. Collect samples of different types of periodic reports and study the format and types of information that have been categorized by headings. Design a periodic report form that would be suitable for reporting recurring kinds of information.
2. Write a progress report to your advisor showing your progress toward completing a degree or receiving a certificate or license.
3. If you are working on a project in a course, write a progress report to your team leader or instructor showing your progress.
4. Collect samples of different types of accident reports and study the format and types of information that have been categorized by headings. Design an all-purpose accident report form that would be suitable for reporting almost any kind of routine trouble an organization might experience.
5. If you take a field trip in a course, write a trip report addressed to the teacher of the course.
6. Take complete notes on a class meeting and write a report explaining what was done during the class period.
7. If you belong to an organization that holds regular formal meetings, attend a meeting, take notes of the business conducted, and write a set of minutes. If you don't belong to such an organization, attend a meeting of an organization that holds such meetings, take notes of the business conducted, and write a set of minutes.

G. G. WARREN AND ASSOCIATES—HOTELIERS

Minutes of Regular Meeting of the Committee on New Construction

May 19, 1977

SUBJECT: Review of Items of Work on The Flowers House,
Houston, Texas

ATTENDEES: Howard Dickinson, Chairman   Don Jones
William Drummond,   Charles Meiners
Willoughby Fulweiler   Wanda Smith
Richard Hudson, Secretary

AGENDA:

1. The meeting was opened by the chairman at 1:15 p.m.

2. The minutes of the previous meeting were accepted as read.

3. Charles Meiners briefly summarized the status of work on The
Flowers House project. The basic situation is as follows:
A. The project is ahead of schedule.
B. Cooperation has been excellent between the general contractor,
his superintendent, and the major subcontractors.
C. An adequate work force has been maintained. No appreciable
delays or work stoppages have occurred.
D. All items have been delivered on schedule. There are no
anticipated delays. Some difficulty was encountered in obtaining shop
drawings on the marble and granite facing material for the exterior of the
building. But that problem has been resolved and the first phase of the
material has been released for shipment.

4. Don Jones stated that he now believes the wood veneer to be applied
to the drywall panels in the dining room is too thin. He said that the
subcontractor told him that the specified wood veneer might buckle, because
he had seen it happen before on other jobs. After some discussion, it was
moved by Wanda Smith and seconded by William Drummond that Charles Meiners
check with the subcontractor on changing the work order to include a heavier
wood veneer if the cost were not more than $3 per panel. Motion carried.

5. Willoughby Fulweiler reported that an incandescent downlight over
the head table area in the banquet room has been incorrectly connected to
the circuit supplying the fluorescent lights in the area. He said that the
problem was not observed until this week, and therefore has not appeared on
any previous work-change order. It was moved by Willoughby Fulweiler and
seconded by Don Jones that Charles Meiners check with the electrical
subcontractor to have the light corrected. Motion carried.

6. The chairman reported that all the documents needed to close the
contract on The Flowers House, with the exception of the general
contractor's statement concerning the full payment of accounts, are in the
hands of the architect. After some discussion, it was moved by Wanda Smith
and seconded by Richard Hudson that the chairman request the architect to
attend the next meeting of the group to discuss the procedure for closing
the contract. Motion carried. The chairman said he would notify the
architect by telephone.

7. There being no other business, the chairman closed the meeting at
3:00. The next regular meeting is scheduled for May 26 at 1:15.

Richard Hudson

Richard Hudson, Secretary

Figure 11-9 Minutes of meeting.

CHAPTER 12

Analytical Reports

You have been analyzing facts and coming to decisions since you were a child. When you stood before a candy showcase weighing the merits of buying four licorice sticks at ten cents against buying five jawbreakers also at ten cents, you were analyzing. You were comparing and contrasting alternatives. You were doing a cost analysis—four for ten cents versus five for ten cents. You remembered the flavor of the two candies and realized that the licorice in your estimation was superior. You weighed quantity versus quality. You reached a series of conclusions:

The jawbreakers were cheaper.
Each piece of candy lasted ten minutes.
The jawbreakers would give you fifty minutes of pleasure.
The licorice would give you forty minutes of pleasure.
However, the flavor of the licorice was superior.
For you, forty minutes of superior pleasure were better than fifty minutes of inferior pleasure.
Therefore, for you, the licorice sticks were a better buy.

If you then proceeded to plunk down your dime for the licorice, you were backing your conclusions with a decision.

As you grew older, your analyses became bigger and more complicated. Perhaps, you had to choose between two bicycles. You considered cost, naturally. You also considered the comparative weights of the bicycles. You compared ten-speed bikes against three-speed bikes. You made these comparisons not merely in an abstract way but by considering them against your own needs. For a serious biker who planned long trips through hilly country, the lighter, more expensive ten-speed might be the answer. On the other hand, an occasional bike rider who simply wanted to combine some exercise with transportation around the flat streets of town would probably choose the heavier, less expensive, three-speed bike.

So it goes. Analysis is how we move from the facts of a situation to the conclusions that can be drawn from those facts. During analysis, we seek out the relationships among our facts. The human mind can move with such lightning speed that often we are not always precisely sure how we have reached a conclusion. If your thought processes are good, this may do you no particular harm. But in the world of work, unlike the world of candy or bike buying, you often have to justify your conclusions and your decisions. Often you have to persuade someone to accept them. When such occasions arise, you need the analytical report—a rational way of showing your facts and how you sifted through them in reaching your conclusions and decisions. As soon as we have made a few more generalizations about analytical reports, we'll show you, through examples and explanation, how analytical reports are put together.

INFORMATION SOURCES

Where does the information for analytical reports come from? Three major sources stand out: personal and professional experience, library research, and original research.

As we live and experience and practice a vocation, we fill our minds with facts. A young man who becomes a mechanic learns his vocation in various ways. He may attend a school for mechanics. Following school, he may work side-by-side with an older, more experienced mechanic. Through the trial and error of doing various repair jobs, he learns which methods work the best. By the time he is thirty years old, he would be hard pressed to tell someone where, precisely, any specific piece of knowledge he possessed came from. But he would know what he knows and be able to put his knowledge to work. For example, if he devises a superior new procedure, he should be able to tell someone why his procedure is the best. He could probably do so without drawing on any knowledge but that of his own experience.

No matter how extensive our living and working experience, however, more knowledge exists than any of us can ever hope to store in our minds. When we need such knowledge, the library is our best source. For example, suppose you were thinking of making jam. You perhaps have some friends who make their own jam, and they seem to enjoy the hobby. Their jam tastes good to you. You wonder exactly what is involved in terms of cost, time, equipment, storage space, and so forth. Your friends and the people who sell jam-making equipment can help some. But they naturally will be somewhat biased in favor of jam making. A trip to the library will get you information to analyze the situation more accurately. You can weigh the facts of jam making against your own interests and capabilities and decide if home jam making is for you.

Chapter 7, Bibliographies and Literature Reviews, and Annex C, Library Research, will tell you how to conduct your library search.

Often original research is the only answer. Suppose you were a highway technician who needed to know accurately and precisely the noise levels in a certain tunnel. Personal experience would not give you the information with precision. Neither would any book. You would have to set up test equipment at various points in the tunnel to measure the noise levels. Likewise, agronomists interested in the effects of a new fertilizer must set up experimental plots where they can measure its effects under controlled conditions. Political analysts measure the attitudes of citizens toward issues and people by various polling and question techniques. At both simple and complicated levels much of our knowledge comes from experimentation. Often, of course, all three sources of information—personal, library, and experimental—are combined in one analysis.

FORMATS

No one format exists for analytical reports. They may be transmitted as memos, letters, formal reports, informal reports, printed brochures, and even oral reports. The more formal reports require apparatus such as title pages, abstracts, tables of contents, references, and so forth. For help with such things see Annex B, Formal Elements of Reports.

As is usually the case, your audience, purpose, and message will probably be your best guide to proper format. For example, take the matter of whether to state conclusions first or last. An audience of busy executives would likely prefer the conclusions stated first. Therefore, in this case, audience decides the issue. If you had an audience of customers outside a company, message and purpose might decide the issue. Your purpose might be to persuade your customers to accept a change in company policy. If the change would be seen as good news—say, interest rates on loans are being lowered—state the pleasing conclusions first and then give the supporting details. If, as may be more likely, you are announcing bad news—perhaps a price hike—give the analysis first, followed by your conclusions. In other words, follow the good news—bad news strategy described in Chapter 1, Basic Principles of Correspondence.

Analytical reports are perhaps the most difficult and most interesting that you have to do. They call upon all your skills of fact-finding and organizing. Through examples, we'll show you how some people go about this important task. In a practical way we'll demonstrate some organizational patterns such as comparison and contrast, cause to effect, argumentation, general to particular, and particular to general. Don't be put off by our rhetorical terminology. As you see the patterns, you will recognize that you have used every one of them in everyday situations.

SAMPLE REPORT 1

Our first sample analytical report is a fairly straightforward comparison. It's an article from *Consumer Reports*[1] that compares the merits of some electric drills. The information in the report is based primarily on original research supplemented by professional knowledge. The purpose of the report is to provide consumers with enough information to make a wise choice of an electric drill suitable for their uses. The audience is considered intelligent but not particularly informed about test equipment or even electric drills. All of these factors influence the way the report is organized and written.

In comparing things to each other, you need a set of standards—a way of measuring how one thing stacks up against another. The success or failure of your comparison will depend on how well you choose these standards and on how well you define them. Once the standards are chosen and well defined, you know what you are looking for in your comparison. And, of course, when it comes time to report your comparison, you must explain your standards carefully to your audience. In fact, explaining the standards, in some cases, could be the major part of the report. Once that is done, the actual results can often be presented very simply, perhaps in a summary table. A table has the advantage of cutting down the wordage needed and of making the comparison easy to follow. Often, however, you will accompany the table with a prose explanation—perhaps explaining the table and pointing out the significance of some of its facts. Let's see how the report on drills illustrates these points.

### Electric Drills	*Commentary*
A good electric drill is virtually indispensable for any kind of do-it-yourself work. Its basic job, of course, is to drill holes. However, with the right accessories, a drill can also let you sand, grind, and polish. Considering the versatility it offers, a good electric drill is probably the first power tool anyone should buy.	The introduction to this report comes immediately to the point. It tells you why electric drills are important and what types of drills were tested. It also
For this report we tested drills with a ⅜-inch chuck	distinguishes between

[1]*Consumer Reports* is a publication of Consumers Union, an organization whose purposes are "to provide consumers with information and counsel on consumer goods and services, to give information on all matters relating to the expenditure of family income, and to initiate and to cooperate with individual and group efforts seeking to create and maintain decent living standards."

capacity—that means they can take drill bits with shanks up to ⅜ths of an inch in diameter. Each drill has a pistol grip and an on-off trigger switch that can be automatically locked in the "on" position for continuous work. Most units are double-insulated—made with two levels of protection between you and the electrical circuits. Seven models were purchased in Canada; four of those were twins of U.S. models (all are listed in the Ratings).

Of the 31 drills CU tested, 13 are single-speed models, 17 are variable-speed units, and one—the *Black & Decker 7109*—offers two speeds. In theory, optimal drilling speed depends on the material being worked, the bit material, bit size, and other factors. But in practice, single-speed drills are perfectly adequate for most ordinary jobs. For one thing, you don't really have to drill at optimal speed to get most jobs done. For another, a single-speed drill generally tends—as it should—to run faster with small bits and slower with large bits. (Friction is lower when you drill with a small bit.) The single-speed drills ranged in price from about $12 to $45.

The variable-speed models run from near zero revolutions per minute (rpm) to their maximum speed. Typically, you adjust the speed by varying your squeeze on the trigger, which doubles as a speed control. Very slow speeds are a boon when you want very precise control of the drill, when you use a screwdriver bit, or when you start a hole in masonry, metal, or hard-surfaced ceramic materials without first punching a starting place. Most of the variable-speed units are reversible, which is especially handy in certain circumstances—when you're removing screws in quantity, for example. Understandably, you generally pay more for the versatility of multi-speed, reversible models; ours ranged in price from $29 plus shipping to $57.

THE THREE IMPORTANT QUALITIES

Nearly any drill will do the easy jobs. What you need for the more difficult ones is plenty of raw power, the ability to resist stalling, and little tendency to overheat. To test for these qualities, we used a dynamometer, a device that put each drill under load while it measured the drill speed in rpm. Our Ratings were based primarily on the results we found in these three tests:

Maximum power output. This is the measure of how much power—torque (twisting strength) multiplied by rpm—a tool can deliver. For hard jobs, such as drilling tough wood with an outsize bit or sanding with a disk-sanding attachment, you should have a drill judged as

single-speed and variable-speed drills and states some of the advantages of each. Notice also the definition of the term "double-insulated."

As is often the case, some standards take priority over others. In this case, three standards are labeled the important ones. Each is carefully explained and, when necessary, technical terms such as "dynamometer" are defined.

medium or better (see Ratings). The tougher the jobs you plan, the higher power rating you should reach for in one of these drills.

Stalled torque. Increasing the load on a drill slows down its speed. Stalled torque is the measure of the twisting effort a drill exerts when loaded to a point where the chuck quits turning. That's important in such jobs as drilling sheet metal, since the bit may stick and stall if it takes too big a bite just before breaking through. With very high torque at low rpm a drill can usually meet a short, severe ordeal and follow through without stalling. Models noted as having very high stalled torque (see Ratings) should be able to continue drilling under those circumstances.

Notice the use of two levels of headings to guide the reader through the report.

Overheating. We put each drill under a load that slowed its rpm by 25 percent, then measured its temperature. The top-rated *Black & Decker 7154* showed very little tendency to overheat. That, in combination with its high maximum power output, would let you run it steadily at peak power with little risk of overheating. When a drill overheats, its motor can burn out or be damaged. Drills with plastic housings are particularly susceptible to damage since their relatively cool handles mask the overheating of the motor.

OTHER OPERATING FACTORS

We tested for several other important aspects of performance (see Rating for results):

Operating factors of lesser importance are simply labeled "other." Again, terms that may be unfamiliar to the reader, such as "no-load speed," are defined. Some results of the testing are given.

Maximum no-load speed. When you run a drill's motor without actually drilling, the shaft can reach the top rpm that motor and gears allow because the chuck is free to turn—the shaft doesn't have a load to fight. The drills we tested (including the variable-speed models set at their speediest) ran at maximum no-load speeds ranging from about 740 to 1290 rpm, about average for drills of this chuck capacity. Those that ran at relatively high speeds would do somewhat better with very small bits.

Speed under load. As a drill is put under load, the drop-off in speed will be steeper with some than with others. Under what we calculated as a typical load, maximum speeds ran from about 560 to 940 rpm—a range that should ensure satisfactory performance. However, drills that run fast can be hard to control, and vibration with large bits can result in off-center, ragged, or oversize holes and possible damage to the bit from overheating.

The rationale for some of the testing is given.

The user can, to some extent, control a drill's speed under load by varying the pressure he or she applies to the drill (feed pressure). But too much feed pressure means increased fatigue for the operator, off-round holes in sheet metal, or possible breakage of bits. On balance, CU believes drills that are geared to run slow to achieve a high stalled torque are better for all-round use. And, in fact, the gearing in most of these tools seems designed to hold down operating speed.

Noise. Running these tools produces plenty of noise. We measured the decibel (dBA) level of each drill at its noisiest and got readings that ran from a noisy 92 dBA to a howling 104 dBA. We'd recommend you get hearing protectors (see our report on page 618) to wear when using one of these electric drills for any extended period.

The terms "92 dBA" and "104dBA" would not be meaningful to many in the audience, so the helpful adjectives "noisy" and "howling" are added.

ELECTRICAL SAFETY

Power tools are inherently dangerous, but shock hazard is an additional threat to users of portable power tools. You grip a drill tightly, sometimes with both hands moist from perspiration. You may be working outside or in a basement or garage, where a damp floor sometimes acts as an electrical ground. A short circuit in a drill, under those circumstances, could be lethal.

The *Wizard 2H5208,* the *Stanley 91048,* and the *Stanley 91041* have metal cases and handles, which could be dangerous, but are made with three-prong grounding plugs to protect against electrical shock. However, those plugs protect you only if the third (ground) wire is properly grounded. If the electrical outlets in your home won't take a three-prong plug, you'll need an adapter, which must itself be grounded correctly. (See page 91 of the 1975 Buying Guide Issue.) Any extension cord used with these drills must also be the three-wire grounding type.

Double insulation gives much better protection against shock. It ensures that no exposed part will be electrically live if the internal insulation fails, and it eliminates the need to ground a power tool. All of the double-insulated models have plastic handles, and most of them have a full plastic housing as well. We prefer them over those that have some metal in the housing, in the remote possibility that you may drill into live-wire cable in a wall.

"Electrical safety," a key standard, is given a section by itself. Certain hazards are explained and ways to guard against them given. Good communicators educate their audiences whenever necessary, as this report well illustrates.

CONVENIENCE IN USE

A variety of features add to the ease of use of the drills. The more important ones are:

Lock buttons. To lock the on-off switch in the "on" position you squeeze the trigger fully on and press a button on the left side of the handle with your thumb. If a drill gets caught in the work or somehow "gets away" from a user, pulling the trigger a second time releases the lock. All the drills have such lock buttons—the minor variants are noted in the Ratings. The variable-speed drills lock "on" at their top speed, and almost all have a trigger lock for an intermediate speed (see Ratings for exceptions).

Trigger pinch. If space between the trigger and the housing is minimal, there should be little chance of pinched fingers. Flanged or contoured triggers (and handles) also help keep fingers clear of the pinch area. The Ratings note whether or not the trigger was judged to be the nonpinching type.

Handles. A drill's handle should be long enough and full enough to be gripped firmly, without crowding your fingers against each other. The handle's contour should fit a clenched hand naturally and easily. Handle surfaces should have no sharp ridges or edges. Plastic handles are preferable to metal ones—they insulate better from both hot and cold.

The handle's location also affects the ease with which you can use a drill. Handles mounted just under or a bit forward of the motor housing—rather than behind the housing—provide better balance and reduce fatigue in prolonged drilling. Most models have a rear-mounted handle; that makes them somewhat nose-heavy when held horizontally. The Ratings give our judgment of each unit's handle comfort, based on such details. But comfort is a very personal matter—we recommend that you grip a drill before buying it to see how comfortable it feels to you.

Matters open for interpretation or shortcomings in the testing should be explained to the reader as they are here.

Auxiliary handle. A second handle gives you a firmer, more comfortable grip; you use your free hand to steady a drill's housing. Some models came with an auxiliary handle; it's available in a kit that's an option with the two *Rockwell* units and by itself as an option with the *Mastercraft 54-2843*. A few drills have screw-in sockets for this handle on both sides of the housing. Six models (see Ratings) have only a left-side socket, useful mainly to right-handers.

Cord length. Most drills come with a line cord at least five feet long. If you need an extension, get the length the manufacturer may recommend. Lacking a recommendation, consider the following: For cord lengths up to 50 feet, drills with a 2- to 3-amp rating take 18-gauge cord; those rated at 3 to 6 amps, 16 gauge. And any extension cord should be the heavy-duty variety, not ordinary lamp cord. Four drills (noted in the Ratings) come with short, stubby cords and must be used with extension cords.

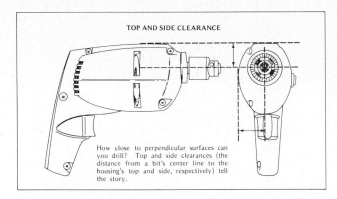

TOP AND SIDE CLEARANCE

How close to perpendicular surfaces can you drill? Top and side clearances (the distance from a bit's center line to the housing's top and side, respectively) tell the story.

The concept of "dimension," difficult to explain in prose, is easily explained in an illustration. Many concepts are better explained in some combination of words and graphics than in words alone.

Dimensions. The overall length and height of a drill are not so crucial. However, the ability to work in cramped quarters may depend on a drill's *clearance.* Top clearance (the distance between the bit's center line and the top of the housing) is the most important clearance dimension; it determines how closely you can drill to a perpendicular surface, as when boring holes in the floor next to a wall. Side clearance can be important for comparable reasons (see diagrams, opposite). Ratings give top and side clearances.

Chuck key. Every drill has a geared-key (Jacobs-type) chuck and comes with a key for tightening the chuck around the drill bit. It was sometimes difficult to get a good grip on the keys, especially those with an L-shaped handle. If you have similar problems, we'd suggest buying a high-quality T-shaped key. Some drills came with a strap for fastening the key to the line cord. If your drill doesn't, improvise something out of tape or cord.

Brushes. The brushes, which deliver electrical power to a drill's rotating armature, eventually wear out. If worn-out brushes let other internal components touch the armature, heavy sparking and possibly damage to the drill will result. No such mishap is possible with the *Black & Decker* units and the *Stanley 91041* thanks to "self-limiting" brushes, a useful design. The Ratings also note six units that have visible brushes; you can inspect for wear without having to dismantle the drill.

MAINTENANCE AND GUARANTEES

Proper maintenance and timely repair can prolong any tool's useful life. Some drills come with detailed instructions for periodic lubrication; dedicated do-it-

ELECTRIC DRILLS

Listed in order of estimated overall quality, based primarily on power output, stalled torque, and tendency to overheat. All have a pistol grip, a trigger switch that can be locked at maximum speed, and a ⅜-in. Jacobs-type chuck, and come with chuck key. Except as noted, all have power cord at least 5-ft. long, are double insulated, variable-speed models

KEY: E, Excellent; VG, Very Good; G, Good; F, Fair; P, Poor.

	Maximum power output	Stalled torque	Tendency to overheat	Maximum no-load speed	Speed under typical load	Decibels of noise
BLACK & DECKER 7154 (Black & Decker Mfg. Co., Towson, Md.) $40. 3 lb. 8 oz.	High	Very high	Low	1130 rpm	730 rpm	100 dBA
SKIL 917C (Skil Canada, Ltd., Toronto) $57. 3 lb. 11 oz.	High	Very high	Medium	740	620	99
SHOPMATE 2151 (McGraw-Edison Portable Electrical Tool Div., Geneva, Ill.) $45. 3 lb. 4 oz.	High	Very high	Medium	890	710	97
SHOPMATE 2151 (McGraw-Edison of Canada, Ltd., Toronto) $47. Identical to U.S. Shopmate 2151, preceding.	High	Very high	Medium	890	710	97
WIZARD 2H5208 (Western Auto) $45. 4 lb. 5 oz.	High	Very high	Medium	970	730	102
WARDS Cat. No. 9215 (Montgomery Ward) $32 plus shipping. 3 lb. 2 oz.	High	Very high	Very high	1190	900	96
MILLERS FALLS SP3139 (Millers Falls Co., Greenfield, Mass.) $41. 2 lb. 15 oz.	High	Medium	Medium	1260	940	95
STANLEY 91048 (Stanley Power Tools, New Bern, N.C.) $45. 3 lb. 12 oz.	Fairly high	Very high	Medium	1100	770	94

Figure 12-1   Part of the table used with the *Consumer Reports* article "Electric Drills." Once the rating standards have been explained, little needs to be done except to show the comparative results in some easy-to-follow way. Here, as is often the case, a table is used—both for ease of comparison and for cutting down on the wordage. Notice that information needed to read the table is given. Notice also that each of the rating items used in the article is given a vertical column and each drill a horizontal one. Additional comments that don't fit into any of the rating categories are simply handled in an extra column labeled "Comments." Given the explanations of the rating categories that make up the main body of the report and this table, most readers should be able to make a wise choice.

yourselfers and owners of expensive drills will doubtless follow those instructions. There's no need for that with some units that appear to have "lifetime" lubrication. And, for safety's sake, manufacturers of double-insulated drills recommend that all maintenance be done by a service shop.

Some units come with a one-year guarantee covering parts and labor: In some instances the guarantee provides for over-the-counter replacement by a dealer; others provide repair or replacement at the dealer's option. Other models offer coverage for an "unlimited time" exclusive of normal wear and abnormal use. That's really no guarantee at all.

RECOMMENDATIONS

Drills are often sold at discount—and most of the high-rated models would be good values if available at

In this report recommendations are limited to pointing out which drill is the best buy, depending

with a reverse feature, and can be adjusted to lock at any intermediate speed. Prices are list, rounded to the nearest dollar; discounts are generally available. A maple leaf desig-

nates Canadian models; their prices are in Canadian dollars. All were judged Acceptable.

Non-pinching trigger	Handle position	Handle comfort	Auxiliary handle position	Clearance		Comments
				Top	Side	
No	Rear	F to G	None	1 in.	1¼ in.	Exposed metal on housing. Roller bearings on chuck shaft, an advantage. Locking button under trigger judged slightly inconvenient. Line cord can be unplugged when storing drill. Self-limiting brushes (see story).
Yes	Rear	P to F	Left	1	1¼	Exposed metal on housing. Ball bearing at rear of motor shaft and roller bearing on chuck shaft, advantages. Very heavy-duty chuck. Visible brushes (see story).
No	Middle	F	Either side	1⅛	1⅜	No comfortable resting place for thumb; thumb hits either reverse lever or locking button.
No	Middle	F	Either side	1⅛	1⅜	No comfortable resting place for thumb; thumb hits either reverse lever or locking button.
Yes	Rear	G	Left	1¼	1½	Not double-insulated. Judged rather unbalanced. Visible brushes (see story).
No	Middle	G	Either side	1	1¼	
No	Rear	F to G	None	1	1¼	
Yes	Rear	F to G	None	⅞	1¼	Not double-insulated. 1 speed. Nonreversible. Visible brushes (see story).

Ratings continued ▶

prices lower than list. If you have plenty of uses for an electric drill and take your do-it-yourself jobs seriously, the high-powered, variable-speed reversible models are certainly your best bet. At $40, the top-rated *Black & Decker 7154* is hard to beat. If you can't find that model (or want to spend less), consider the *Wards 9215;* it lists at $32 plus shipping. A good choice for Canadians would be the *Skil 917C,* at $57.

People who want this size drill mainly for small jobs around the house should probably buy a single-speed model with double insulation. The *Rockwell 4100* is certainly the first choice in that category: Low price—just $13—in tandem with good quality made it a Best Buy.

on how serious a "do-it-yourselfer" the reader is. The complete results are printed in an easy-to-read table that we have partially reproduced in Figure 12-1.

In the electric drill article most of the information comes from original research supplemented by professional knowledge. However, comparisons can also be based on library research. No matter what the source of the information, the key to writing a good comparison report is to bring together the items compared with the standards. After the introduction to the electric drill article, the standards are explained and the comparative results are presented in a simple table. In more complicated reports that require more written explanation, organizational plans might look like one of the following:

Plan Based on Standards
  I. Introduction
  II. Explanation and description of things to be compared
  III. Comparison by standards
    A. Standard A
      1. Item 1   Standard A is explained
      2. Item 2   and then applied to the
      3. Item 3   items compared.
    B. Standard B
      1. Item 1   Standard B is explained
      2. Item 2   and then applied to the
      3. Item 3   items compared.
    C, D, E, etc. As many repetitions of A and B as needed.
  IV. Conclusions
  V. Recommendations

Plan Based on Items Compared
  I. Introduction
  II. Explanation of standards
  III. Comparison by items compared
    A. Item A
      1. Standard 1   Item A is described and
      2. Standard 2   each standard is applied
      3. Standard 3   to it.
    B. Item B
      1. Standard 1   Item B is described and
      2. Standard 2   each standard is applied
      3. Standard 3   to it.
    C, D, E, etc. As many repetitions of A and B as needed.

In a plan prepared for busy executives who might be more interested in conclusions and recommendations than in a recital of all the facts, either of the plans might be presented this way:

Introduction
Summary of Data   In smaller reports, these
Conclusions   sections might be combined into a single section.
Recommendations   bined into a single section.
           ANNEXES   tion.
  I. Explanation of Items to be compared
  II. Comparison by Standard A
    A. Explanation of Standard A
    B. Application of Standard A to items compared
  III. Comparison by Standard B
    A. Explanation of Standard B
    B. Application of Standard B to items compared
  IV, V, VI, etc. As many repetitions of I and II as needed.

Any organizational plan may be formalized by the addition of a title page, table of contents, and so forth. See our Annex B, Formal Elements of Reports, for guidance in such manners.

SAMPLE REPORT 2

Our second sample is a portion of the 1975 Annual Report to the policyholders of the United Services Automobile Association (USAA). As we analyze the techniques being used, notice that in this more complex report no one simple, all-purpose technique is used. Rather, it uses a coordinated combination of many techniques.

Commentary

Last year, I reported to you that 1974 was the worst year in the property and casualty insurance industry since 1932. Most executives in the industry felt that 1975 would also be poor, but few correctly forecast it would be so bad that 1974 would almost look good by comparison. To illustrate this fact, in 1974 the industry's total loss amounted to $2.7 billion. In 1975, it escalated to $4.5 billion.

In the face of this tide of adversity, *USAA returned $33 million to its members in dividends during 1975, and still managed to post a slight net gain, and an $8 million increase in surplus.* Most other property and casualty companies experienced significant losses from their operations.

Several important developments flowed from this deterioration of financial results.

- No fewer than 30 companies became insolvent. While none of these was a "major" company, some were large enough to cause significant shock waves within the industry.
- Many companies, seeing their underwriting losses soar and their reserves dissolve, sharply curtailed their writing of new policyholders—even those persons once considered reasonably good risks.
- A large number of companies—some bearing prestigious names—had their coveted A+ top financial rating lowered by A. M. Best & Company. *I am pleased to report that USAA was not among them.*

Why was 1975 such a disastrous year for our business? There are no simple answers, but the major problem was inflation. Very frankly, premiums charged for most types of insurance have lagged far behind the increases in the cost of goods and services paid for by insurance dollars. This has been especially true in the case of automobile insurance.

The report begins with a general statement about the adverse position the property and casualty industry finds itself in. The statement is immediately particularized by the contrast of 1975's losses with 1974's. Moreover, most of the report will enlarge upon the problems in the industry and their significance to policyholders. The "I" of the report is Robert F. McDermott, President of USAA.

Through contrast to other companies, USAA's stronger position is pointed out. Good management is implied.

The report uses cause-to-effect here. The cause is the "deterioration of financial results." Each of the effects is spotlighted by being indented and given a bullet.

At this point the strategy reverses, and now effect-to-cause is used. The effect is stated as a rhetorical question: "Why was 1975 such a disastrous year for our business?" The causes are given as follows:

Reprinted by permission of the United Services Automobile Association.

In the past two years, the Consumer Price Index has increased 19%. Automobile repair costs (parts and labor) have gone up 24%, and medical and hospital costs 25%. During that same period, automobile insurance rates have increased only 9%, with most of this coming in 1975.

It requires no special acumen to forecast the results of this massive wrongway cash flow. Insurers already beset with poor management, or with a weak reserve or surplus structure, were most vulnerable to failure. Others, with better management or a stronger financial position, could at least anchor themselves against the ebb.

The vast majority of companies survived, but, as I have mentioned, some were forced into insolvency. The result of such insolvencies was that "Guaranty Funds" in existence in most States were called upon to pay claims owed by the defunct insurers. The money for these payments is derived from assessments against still-solvent insurers, such as USAA. In normal times, these assessments are nominal. For example, from 1969 through 1974 USAA was assessed a total of only $413,000, and most of that in 1974. However, in 1975, USAA's insolvency fund assessments totaled $1,061,000, an amount more than double that of the past five years combined.

A more common consequence of widespread financial losses within the industry has been a tightening of insurance markets. More simply stated, some companies have become much more selective in whom they will insure and, consequently, have significantly curtailed their acceptance of new policyholders. The natural result has been a substantial increase in the number of people who must look to State-established "Assigned Risk" plans for insurance. Under these plans, all insurers are required to provide insurance to their proportionate share of persons otherwise unable to obtain auto insurance. USAA at year-end insured approximately 45,800 assigned risks, and experienced an estimated loss of $11,082,000 on all nonvoluntary business in 1975.

This combination of increased insolvency fund assessments and enlargement of the assigned risk populations has served to further aggravate the already difficult financial circumstances of many companies. It could, in fact, be responsible for forcing additional marginal companies into insolvency. Such insolvencies would mean more assessments and assignments for the rest of the industry, and the awesome cycle would continue.

How can this all happen? Why can't the insurance industry do something to level itself out? There are several factors contributing to the complexity of this problem.

Inflation. Notice here, too, the general-to-particular development frequently used so well in this report. The general statement about inflation is immediately followed by particular facts about the rising Consumer Price Index and rising repair and medical costs.

Increased guaranty fund assessments—which are, in turn, the result of companies forced into insolvency.

Enlargement of "assigned risk populations," both an effect of poor financial times and a cause of further financial problems, illustrating the snowballing nature of the problem.

In analysis, you attempt to anticipate your audience's questions and

One is the very fact that insurance companies have, in general, been relegated a "black hat" status by some so-called consumer advocates, and by many politicians. Every try at levelling out automatically is fraught with public suspicion.

This climate helps to explain some of the difficulty insurers have had in adequately pricing their products. Insurance companies have a unique pricing problem, in that the cost of services to be rendered (claims) is unknown at the time the price is set. In an inflationary environment, insurance rates always lag behind increases in the price of products and services the insurance dollar buys (crash parts, hospital bills, etc.). This problem is compounded by the fact that it often takes considerable amounts of time to secure regulatory approval of needed rate increases. Even after approval is received, it takes up to 12 months to reflect increases in renewal policies. By then, of course, inflation has long since passed where it was when the rate increase was originally requested.

Coupled with the problem created by rapid inflation, there has been a significant rise in the number of auto accidents (up 6% from 1974), thefts and fires. The accidents, regrettably, have been made worse by virtue of the fact that more small cars carrying more passengers have been involved than was true in the past. So we find we are paying substantially more claims and that each of them is costing much more money.

There was a thin silver lining for the industry in 1975. The securities market turned upward, and most insurers were able to realize increased gain on their investment portfolios. Had this not occurred, had the market continued its dismal 1974 performance, a far greater number of property and casualty insurers would have found themselves in desperate financial condition.

The life insurance industry, while not affected nearly as severely by 1975's economic environment as property and casualty insurers, was nevertheless not completely immune.

Historically, life insurance sales have increased at an annual rate of about 6%. So consistent has this been that many companies have counted on 6% when budgeting their ensuing years. In 1975, the sales increase rate dropped to 2%—a 4% "gap" which, in a multi-billion-dollar industry, is serious. Several companies lost the A. M. Best & Company top ratings, but so far as we know, none failed. I will elaborate later, but should mention now USAA LIFECO garnered top ratings in every category, and enjoyed a 6.7% sales increase.

You may wonder why I have belabored you with a long

reactions. This section does precisely that. It begins with the questions, "How can all this happen? Why can't the insurance industry do something to level itself out?" The problem is presented not as insoluble but as one of "complexity."

One cause of the complexity is the suspicion under which insurance companies operate. This, in turn, has an effect that further complicates the issue—it slows the possibility of swiftly adjusting for inflationary change.

The final cause given is the "significant rise in the number of auto accidents." Essentially, what you have from the question, "How can all this happen?" to this point is an application of the argumentation mode. The mode consists of a major statement supported by a series of minor statements that are usually themselves supported by evidence. Something like this:

Major: The problem is complex.

Minor: A unique pricing problem exists.

—support—

Minor: The accident rate is rising.

—support—

President McDermott at this point gives one of his

recitation of the troubles experienced by the industry during 1975. I have done so for a very fundamental, and partially self-serving, reason. I think it's important for USAA members to understand the very difficult environment in which the Association had to operate during 1975. It is only against this backdrop that our accomplishments during 1975 can be properly evaluated. In summary:

- As I have indicated, the USAA Property and Casualty Group ended the year with a slight net gain, even after dividends. This, in and of itself, was a major accomplishment in light of the experience of most other companies.

- Our financial condition continued to be one of the strongest in the industry.

- In contrast to some insurers, we did not close the door to new policyholders. We closed the year insuring approximately 88% of the total active duty officer corps—a record accomplishment that attests to member satisfaction with our prompt and fair claims service and relatively low net cost.

There are certain facts which we must recognize as inescapable lessons of 1975. We would be doing our members a disservice if we did not recognize those facts.

First of all, there is no way in which we can avoid seeking needed rate increases in 1976. The dilemma created for insurers by rapid inflation makes such action inevitable. While we like to think of ourselves as "special," we cannot escape the economic forces which impact all other companies in the industry.

Secondly, we are going to have to reevaluate some of our underwriting practices. USAA has long had a reputation for insuring virtually everyone who is eligible for membership. Once attaining membership, extraordinarily few members have had policies canceled or nonrenewed. We have to recognize, however, that no matter how desirable the majority of our members may be as insurance risks, there are some who do not live up to such expectations. Consequently, we have begun a very careful process of evaluating applicants and existing policyholders who have poor driving records. The objective of this effort will be to protect the vast majority of our members from having to subsidize poor drivers.

An even more extensive change in attitude is required in the case of ex-dependents of USAA members. As you know, USAA-CIC began insuring these young people in 1973 after receiving many requests from parents to take such action. It was our hope that driving records of ex-dependents would reflect their parents' records. Unfortunately, this proved to be an overly optimistic expec-

purposes for the "long recitation of the troubles"—to serve as a backdrop for USAA's accomplishments. Why did he wait so long to state his purpose? Audience analysis provides the answer. In persuasion, it is often self-defeating to begin by telling your audience that you intend to convince them of something. You often stiffen their resistance by doing so. Rather you let the weight of your argument convince them first.

The positive accomplishments are stated and made to stand out by indentation and bullets.

At this point another purpose for the catalog of troubles emerges. A series of troubling decisions are to be announced:

- rate increases
- reevaluation of coverage
- extensive tightening in insuring ex-dependents of members

These decisions are the necessary results of the "inescapable lessons of 1975." Following the bad-news organizational plan, the decisions come near the end of the report.

Here again you see how audience and purpose affect organization. If this were a formal report to President McDermott's fellow executives, the organization would likely be reversed. That is, the de-

tation. While many of our CIC insureds have shown themselves to be good drivers, others have not. In order to continue to provide insurance to ex-dependents at low cost, we had to start tightening our standards for accepting new insureds and continuing the present ones.

I know our decisions in this area will be difficult for some parents to accept. I hope it will be understood, however, that we are taking this action with the best interests of USAA and CIC in mind.

cisions might have been announced first, followed by the justification for them, perhaps, in this fashion:
Introduction
Summary
Conclusions
Recommendations/
Decisions
———
Annexes containing supporting information

The last part of the USAA report, which we have not reproduced here, presents further evidence of good management and tells of plans for holding down costs as much as possible. The placing of such information after the announcement of the unpleasant decisions is again part of the bad-news organization. You try to reserve some good news to announce at the very end to soften the blow a little.

The information in the USAA report came primarily from company records and from published reports about the condition of other companies. Mixed in as well was the knowledge that comes from professional experience.

The analytic techniques used were primarily cause-to-effect, effect-to-cause, and argumentation. The purposes of the report were twofold:

- To establish that under trying circumstances USAA was managing better than most other companies.
- To persuade policyholders that costly changes were necessary.

Neither the electric drill article nor the USAA report was presented here as a rigid, inflexible way of handling analytical reports. The reverse is true. We have presented these quite different reports to indicate the flexibility you have. Remember that your best guides to good organization are always material, purpose, and audience.

GRAPHICS

Tables and graphs frequently play an important role in analytical reports. Figure 12-2 illustrates the use of line graphs in a report on economic effects. Notice that the graphs are introduced and their significance pointed out. You cannot assume that your readers will pay attention to a figure unless you draw attention to it. Nor can you assume that they will see its significance before you make it clear.

Another useful graph in analytical reports, particularly for showing percentages, is the pie graph. Figure 12-3 shows how a pie graph is used to illustrate the breakdown of heat losses from a house. Notice that the per-

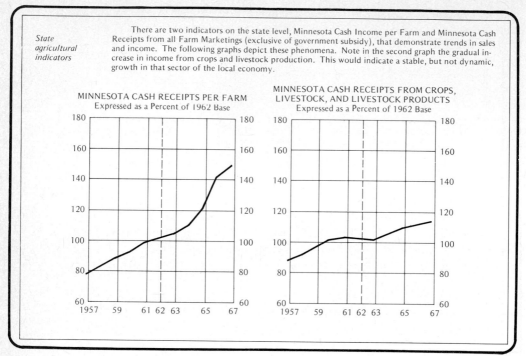

State
agricultural
indicators

There are two indicators on the state level, Minnesota Cash Income per Farm and Minnesota Cash Receipts from all Farm Marketings (exclusive of government subsidy), that demonstrate trends in sales and income. The following graphs depict these phenomena. Note in the second graph the gradual increase in income from crops and livestock production. This would indicate a stable, but not dynamic, growth in that sector of the local economy.

Figure 12-2 Line graphs. (*Minnesota Agricultural Statistics,* Minnesota State Department of Agriculture)

centages and explanations are placed inside the pie when there is room. When room is lacking, as in the 10 percent loss, the information is placed adjacent to the slice.

Small graphs are frequently integrated right into the prose rather than being set aside in separate figures. Figure 12-4 illustrates such integration. In it, notice also that the percentages are labeled directly on the graph. Such labeling is a good idea, particularly for nonexpert audiences. It assures that the reader will see the information correctly.

Tables of all sorts play an important role in analytical reports. Sometimes the tables are really rather informal listings incorporated into the text, as in Figure 12-5.

More complicated tables are often set apart from the text, either through the use of double lines or by being placed on a separate page. When separated, tables are usually given titles. If more than three or four tables are used in a report, they are probably also given numbers. Figure 12-6 illustrates a separate table. Notice how the footnotes and sources are handled within the table itself.

Keep graphs and tables basic and simple. Don't overload them with information. When a graph or table gets overly complex, find a way to divide the information among several graphs or tables rather than putting it all into one. (For additional information on tables and graphics see pages 4–6, 119–124, 144–145, 237–245, 308–318.)

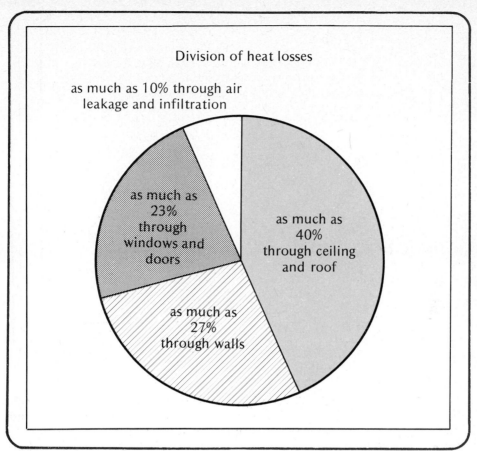

Division of heat losses

as much as 10% through air
leakage and infiltration

as much as
23%
through
windows and
doors

as much as
40%
through ceiling
and roof

as much as
27%
through walls

Figure 12-3 Pie graph.

A WORD OF CAUTION

Some pitfalls in the use of logic lie in wait for the writer of analytical reports. Probably the most common and perhaps the most dangerous is to generalize from insufficient information. We are all guilty of this mistake from time to time. Perhaps we read in the newspapers about the scandalous conduct of a few United States congressmen. We shake our heads and imagine Washington, D.C., as a hotbed of skulduggery. This would be generalizing from insufficient evidence. As Aristotle long ago pointed out, one swallow does not make a summer. Neither do several scandalous congressmen indicate that all our representatives behave badly. Walk carefully when you make conclusions, and make only those conclusions justified by your evidence.

Be careful not to argue in a circle. A politician who says, "You can trust me, because I'm trustworthy" is arguing in a circle. What is needed is evidence of that trustworthiness. And don't attempt to fool others (or

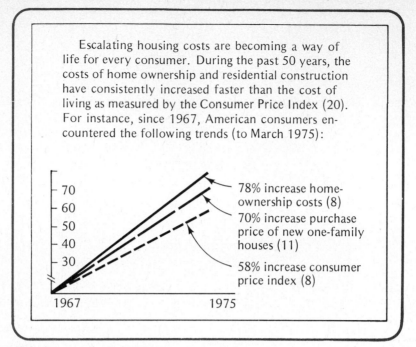

Escalating housing costs are becoming a way of life for every consumer. During the past 50 years, the costs of home ownership and residential construction have consistently increased faster than the cost of living as measured by the Consumer Price Index (20). For instance, since 1967, American consumers encountered the following trends (to March 1975):

78% increase home-ownership costs (8)

70% increase purchase price of new one-family houses (11)

58% increase consumer price index (8)

Figure 12-4   Integrated graph. (*Housing Costs in the Mid-Seventies,* Agricultural Extension Service, University of Minnesota, 1975)

yourself) by building assumptions into the questions you ask about your material. Everyone is familiar with the old joke in the question, "When did you stop beating your wife?" which illustrates this pitfall well. The question, "Why do men make better business executives than women?" assumes a proposition that might call down considerable disagreement.

Finally, be careful of the error that logicians call *post hoc ergo propter hoc.* In this error you make the faulty assumption that because *x* follows *y,* *x* must have been caused by *y.* Other associations besides sequence have to apply. For example, if a man fell sick after eating his wife's potato salad, that would not prove that the salad caused his sickness. There would have to be other evidence, such as other members of the family also falling sick after eating the salad, or a chemical analysis that showed the salad to be contaminated.

CONCLUSION

We have not attempted in this chapter to tell you that analysis and writing analytical reports are easy. They most certainly are not. They are difficult and challenging and require great care and effort. But by starting with the

INITIAL OCCUPANCY COSTS

Whether a family rents or buys a home frequently depends upon the individual's ability to accumulate adequate financial resources to pay initial occupancy costs. Whereas initial requirements for rent are modest and may include simply the advancement of a month's rent and posting a security or damage deposit, the costs of buying a house may be quite staggering. According to a 1971 study conducted by the Department of Housing and Urban Development, the national average cost of buying an $18,000 house financed with an FHA or VA mortgage included the following costs (13):

— Title examination	$116
— Title Insurance	129
— Attorney's fee	102
— Preparation of documents	28
— Survey	42
— Closing fee	47
— Miscellaneous fees and inspection	225
— Transfer tax	70
Total	$759

These expenses, which must be paid by the average buyer at the closing, amounted to 3.8 percent of the purchase price.

Figure 12-5 Informal table. (*Housing Costs in the Mid-Seventies,* Agricultural Extension Service, University of Minnesota, 1975)

candy example and by pointing out to you that you frequently engage in analytical thinking, we have attempted to put the process into perspective. The rhetorical techniques used in analytical reports—comparison, cause to effect, particular to general—are techniques you do use day to day. Therefore, they should not be mysterious or foreign to you. In analytical reports we should use these techniques more carefully than we normally do. We attempt to avoid the sloppy thinking all of us sometimes engage in. We check and double-check to be sure the associations we think we see really do exist. We take care not to fall into some of the more common pitfalls of logical thinking. Given these precautions, good analytical reports should be within the reach of most people.

TABLE II

Percentage Distribution of Residence Type by College

College	Live with parents/ relatives (Avg: 27%)	Apartment/ off-campus housing* (Avg: 57%)	University residence hall (Avg: 11%)
Agriculture	15	72	13
Biological Sciences	33	53	14
Business Administration	34	57	9
Dental Hygiene	23	58	19
Dentistry	6	82	12
Education	26	68	6
Forestry	30	61	9
General College	38	53	9
Graduate School	6	86	8
Home Economics	30	58	12
Institute of Technology	35	49	16
Law	12	81	7
Liberal Arts	37	50	13
Medical Technology	18	64	18
Mortuary Science	17	83	—
Nursing	11	86	3
Occupational Therapy	—	100	—
Pharmacy	30	59	11
Physical Therapy	20	60	20
Public Health	11	78	11
University College	28	72	—
Veterinary Medicine	2	96	2

*Includes categories of rent apartment, own or rent house, rent room, work for rent, married student cooperative, and private commune or coop.

Source: *Housing the University Student, 1973–1974,* published by University of Minnesota Housing Office.

Figure 12-6 Formal table.

SUGGESTIONS FOR APPLYING YOUR KNOWLEDGE

Analytical reports present the opportunities for a wide range of reports from one- or two-page letters to major term reports. As usual, message, audience, and purpose will govern how extensive your treatment is. If you decide to give some subject a formal report treatment, be sure to consult Annex B, Formal Elements of Reports.

One useful assignment is to take a piece of analytical writing and make an analysis of it as we have done on pages 186–193 and 195–199. These analyses can be done orally or in writing. *Consumer Reports, Popular Science, Popular Mechanics, Scientific American,* and *Business Week* are all good sources of analytical reports. Well-done, rational advertisements of the type found in trade and professional journals are also good examples. Look for the organizational patterns used, such as comparison and contrast, cause to effect, argumentation, general to particular, and particular to general.

See if you can spot any errors of logic such as generalizing from insufficient evidence, circular argument, and *post hoc ergo propter hoc.*

Examine the graphics and tables used. Are they well integrated into the analysis? Are they identified and referred to? How well do they support the analysis? Will the intended audience understand them?

You can do analytical reports of your own. Comparison and contrast papers in which you analyze two or more tools, procedures, careers, schools, politicians, and so on are good possibilities.

You could write a sales letter in which through analysis you develop the good points of a product and compare it favorably to the competition.

Is someone concerned about your progress in school? Write a progress report (see pages 171–174) for that person. Compare and contrast your present level of effort and success with that of previous years.

Causality papers provide a good opportunity for library research, particularly in almanacs and yearbooks (see pages 331–333). You could browse through *The Statistical Abstract of the United States* looking for significant trends that interest you. For example, what is happening to the American family farm? Are farms growing in size? Does this growth correlate with a drop in farm workers and a rise in crop yields? Do these last two trends correlate in some way with an increase in the use of machinery on the farm with a consequent rise in energy consumption? Could there be some causal relationship among all these trends?

Are the number of women in the work force increasing? Are more women seeking higher education? Are women marrying later in life? Is the birth rate dropping? Is there a correlation among all these trends? Is there evidence of causality? Enormously interesting, fact-filled papers can be done on such subjects. They can also be used for class discussion. Be careful in writing causality papers not to press the causality beyond the supporting evidence. Be temperate in your judgments.

For any analytical paper be sure you have a purpose and audience for your message.

CHAPTER 13

Proposals

One excellent essay on the proposal defines it this way:

> In the conversation of the sexes a proposal is considerably different from a proposition. In the conversation of business, however, a proposal is simply a formalized proposition. Written out in rather elaborate detail, the proposal merely says, in effect, "Here's what we will do for you at this time for this price." In this sense it is no different from the proposition of the horse trader who says, "I'll tell you what I'll do: I'll throw in the saddle and the bridle with the horse, just to make a deal today."[1]

Proposals are made for many purposes and come in many sizes and formats. An insulation contractor, for example, called in to examine an old house may make a proposal to the house's owner. He may outline the quantity and type of insulation needed and describe how the job will be done. He'll estimate how soon the job can be done and set a price for it. If he's a good salesman, he may give the names and phone numbers of satisfied customers. He may give an incentive for quick action: "For the rest of August, we can give you our summer discount of 10 percent. In September our prices go back up." The whole proposal or bid, as it may be

---

[1]Frank R. Smith, "Engineering Proposals," in *Handbook of Technical Writing Practices*, Vol. 1, eds., Stello Jordon, Joseph M. Kleinman, and H. Lee Shimberg (New York: Wiley-Interscience, 1971): 494.

called in this instance, may be contained on one page. At the other end of the scale, an aircraft manufacturer proposing to build a new fighter airplane for the U.S. Air Force may submit a proposal that fills several large books. The aircraft proposal will contain information on plans, facilities, schedules, costs, key engineering and management personnel, and much more.

Proposals fall into two general categories—solicited and unsolicited. A solicited proposal is in answer to a request for a proposal. An unsolicited proposal is made on the initiative of the proposer. We'll look at solicited proposals first.

SOLICITED PROPOSALS

A request for a solicited proposal, will state rather carefully what goods or services are wanted. It will specify how the proposal should be organized. You can learn a good deal about how to organize and write proposals by looking at such requests. A 1975 National Science Foundation (NSF) solicitation requested proposals for student-originated studies. The solicitation began by laying down rather careful guidelines as to what NSF wanted. We reproduce these instructions in part here.

Student-Originated Studies
GUIDE FOR PREPARATION OF PROPOSALS

I. Introduction. In conducting a competitive program for the support of student-originated studies, the National Science Foundation is pursuing three closely related goals:

(1) to provide talented students with science learning opportunities above and beyond those normally available in most formal science education programs in the Nation's universities and colleges,

(2) to increase the variety of instructional modes and of institutional patterns of instruction by demonstrating to both students and faculties the capacity of students to be motivated by independence and thus to accept greater responsibility for planning and carrying out their own learning activities, and

(3) to encourage college students to express in productive ways their concern for the well-being of our Nation by applying their scientific and technological expertise to the study of significant societal problems.

To request Foundation support through Student-Originated Studies, student groups will submit proposals that describe the scientific or technological studies they wish to carry out and that give details as to the funds required for that purpose. In almost every academic institution there are faculty members who are familiar with this "proposal process" who can provide information to interested students. There are also officials in the institution's business office who are experienced in estimating the cost of projects. Although the competition requires that proposals be developed by students, the Foundation recognizes their

Office of Experimental Projects and Programs, *Student-Originated Studies* (Washington, D.C.: National Science Foundation, 1975): 1–2.

need for faculty and business office advice, and has no objection to applicants' obtaining this sort of assistance.

Guidelines for the Student-Originated Studies Program are being kept as brief and straightforward as possible to encourage diversity and flexibility in the supported projects—within the general framework outlined below:

- Each project proposed is to be problem-oriented—to deal with a local problem (or set of associated problems) that has immediate relevance to society, and that poses yet-unanswered questions of a scientific or technological nature on which the student group can collect meaningful data. Ideally, a prospective user of the project's results is identified in advance, so that this user's needs become a relevant consideration in the design and conduct of the project.

- The approach to understanding the problem(s) and the search for solution are to be *interdisciplinary* or *multidisciplinary* in nature, hence,

- Each proposed study or set of studies is to be conducted by a *group* of students (a minimum of 5 students, but usually not more than 12)—primarily made up of undergraduates, although some graduate students may be included within each group.

- Projects proposed are to be *student*-originated, *student*-planned, and *student*-directed, and are to be carried out under the leadership of one of the students in the group (hereinafter referred to as the *Student Project Director*). In discharging his duties, the Student Project Director may be assisted by a Steering Committee chosen from and by the group of participants. The extent to which each group seeks consultation with one or more college faculty members or members of the community at large is a matter for decision by the students, but it is required that there be associated with each grant a specifically-named *Project Advisor* who is a member of the science faculty of the host institution.

- Projects are to be planned to occupy fully the time of the student investigators (predominantly undergraduates) for an uninterrupted period of 10–12 weeks. This means that most projects will be conducted during the summer, although projects may be conducted at other times in institutions with schedules that provide 10 to 12 uninterrupted weeks for individual work or independent study during the academic year.

- Proposals for the SOS competition must be received *at* the Foundation on or before November 10, 1975. Awards resulting from this competition will be announced early in March 1976. Therefore, projects may be scheduled to operate during any 10–12 week period available to the students for full-time participation between April 15, 1976, and May 31, 1977.

- Each project will be required to file a final report of its activities and accomplishments, and to be represented at an SOS Symposium in Washington, D.C. during the post-Christmas week of 1976. For projects completed by October 1, 1976, final reports will be due on or before December 31, 1976.

When you answer a solicited proposal, pay careful attention to the guidelines. For instance, in this case there would be no use in your submitting a proposal for a study by a single student. The request specifies a group of from five to about twelve. Nor would you want to ignore the advice that the project is to last "for an uninterrupted period of 10–12 weeks."

The NSF solicitation also lays out with care the content of the proposal and how it should be organized:

Commentary

CONTENT OF PROPOSAL

A proposal consists of the following items arranged in the order given: (A) Cover Sheet, (B) Summary Budget Page, (C) Budget Explanations, (D) Abstract, (E) Narrative, (F) Appendices.

The NSF guidelines for content and organization are fairly standard. They request the information needed in most proposals.

(A) Summary Cover Sheet—prepared in strict accordance with the sample on page 15.

See Figure 13-1.

(B) Summary Budget Page—see format, page 16.

(C) Budget Explanations—This section must provide a brief but convincing justification for all direct costs listed on the Budget Summary Page (except participant stipends). Items should appear in the same order as entries in the Budget Summary, with corresponding numbering. In drawing up the budget, only essential costs should be included.

See Figure 13-2. Budget information is high in importance. What will the proposal cost, and what will the money be spent for?

(D) Abstract—a not more than one-page summary of the problem(s) to be investigated and the proposed experimental approach(es) or study plan(s).

(E) Narrative—the following points should be addressed in the order indicated: (Although there is no limit on number of pages, proposers should remember that a concisely written document will present a stronger case for support than one distinguished primarily by its wordiness.)

Abstracts are needed in all but the shortest proposals. Proposals are often read by busy executives who want to get the big picture early.

In describing the work to be done the proposal writer has to strike a nice balance that provides enough detail without being wordy.

(1) A one-paragraph description of the host institution and its science program, including local experience in project-type studies, if any.

(2) A brief description of the institution's surroundings (natural and social), if these are relevant to the proposed problem(s).

(3) A description of the problem or group of problems, and of the methodologies to be employed in the study. The several coordinated disciplinary approaches that are to be applied must be outlined in all proposals. Provide any maps or other aids needed by reviewers seeking to understand the project plan. This analysis of the problem and the detailed discussion of the students' plan for attacking it form the core of the proposal. It is here that a merely "good idea" is fleshed out into a competent strategy. *Sufficient detail must be provided* to enable reviewers to reach an affirmative finding as

Notice the call for any graphics that may be needed.

The salesmanship required in writing good proposals is pointed up

to the adequacy and scientific merit of the proposed study.

(4) Evidence that the project's findings hold promise for utilization by civic, governmental or industrial entities responsible for planning and/or decision-making in matters related to the project. This evidence should be as specific as possible, naming persons and organizations contacted, quoting or attaching to the Appendix (see F below) their expressions of interest and the like.

(5) A description of the student group who organized the group submitting the proposal and how this was accomplished. (Was it, for example, a science club, an individual, an informal group of concerned students, or who?); how the topic or topics were selected:

—the number of participants for whom support is being requested (with any special justification required);

—who has already been selected to participate in the project (a brief curriculum vitae for each principal participant should be included in the Appendix, emphasizing any previous experience in research or project-oriented studies);

—the disciplinary distribution and balancing of skills to be sought in filling remaining vacancies on the SOS team, by what criteria the remaining participants will be chosen, methods for recruiting participants from other institutions if this is to be done (or if not, the factors that decided the group against it); the function of the Student Steering Committee or reason for not having such a committee;

—any other details that will assist reviewers to understand the personnel aspects of the project. (Curricula vitae should appear in the Appendix.)

(6) Pre-summer preparation of individuals and coordination of their efforts prior to formal initiation of the study.

(7) A time schedule for the project in outline form, sufficient to convince reviewers that realistic consideration has been given to the amount of work contemplated relative to available time and manpower.

(8) The Project Advisor—name; description of the process by which he was nominated by the students; statement of institution's confirmation of the nomination; curriculum vitae showing highlights of his academic training, scholarly prod-

by NSF's call for "Evidence that the project's findings hold promise for utilization by civic, governmental or industrial entities responsible for planning and/or decision-making in matters related to the project." In writing a proposal, keep your eye on what your work will do for the people paying the bills. Try to find and show something unique about the goals or service you can provide—something that your competition can't duplicate.

In many proposals you are really selling the services of people. Therefore, it's important to provide details about previous education and relevant experience. (The term *curriculum vitae* used here refers to such significant biographical data.) Buyers of services are often willing to pay more for people they feel sure they can trust to do a job properly and on time. Here again strive for uniqueness.

Time and work schedules are important. They show that you know where you're going and how you intend to get there.

More personnel information.

uctivity and other qualifications for advising the group.

(9) A description of the institutional facilities (including library) and equipment, specifically identifying what is to be available for use in the SOS project, and its adequacy for the project's needs.

(F) Appendix—

(1) Curricula vitae of Student Project Director and other principal participants already selected, following the format set forth on page 17.

(2) Supportive statements or materials that bear on the expected quality of the proposed project. This evidence should be as specific as possible. Testimonials are useful only if written by local authorities who possess detailed factual information concerning the problem and current efforts to deal with it. Broad, general statements of support from officials remote from the problem or policy issue under investigation are of little value. For any statement to affect the evaluation of the proposal, it must be received before the review panels convene on December 11, 1975. Later submissions cannot be considered.

(3) Bibliography of sources consulted in background research during preparation of the proposal. The inclusion of key references here will assure reviewers as to the thoroughness of the group's preliminary study.

Facilities are important. If you can't prove that you have the facilities and equipment to do the project, you are not likely to get your proposal accepted.

See Figure 13-3.

Detailed information about personnel, facilities, and other aspects of the proposal is often presented in an appendix. Note, too, the possibility of including testimonials, again a good selling technique.

In many instances a bibliography can be a good way of showing that you have done your homework.

Most of the information found in proposals of any size at all is requested in this NSF solicitation. NSF requests information on cost, people, facilities, and schedule. It wants to know precisely what will be done and why. NSF is particularly interested in the significance and value of what is to be done. (As is so often the case, the answers to the journalist's questions of *who, what, when, where, why,* and *how* will provide much of the information required.)

Remember that the proposal is a sales document. Emphasize the value and quality of your own products and services. Point out the unique advantages offered by the experience and education of your people. If possible, provide testimonials covering your previous work.

While the proposal is a sales document, it is also a rational analysis. Therefore, don't shout too loudly in the manner of a huckster selling cheap souvenirs. Let your facts speak for themselves, but present them in a thorough and attractive manner.

When preparing a solicited proposal, take care to follow the suggested organization precisely—even if you don't like it. The requesters will be looking for information in the places where they have specified they want

COVER SHEET

1. Program: STUDENT-ORIGINATED STUDIES

2. Descriptive Title of Study: _____
   (Maximum: 12 words)

   _____

3. Host Institution: _____

   Address: City _____ State _____ Zip Code _____

   Grant to: _____
              (Full official name of institution to which grant should be made)

4. A. _____ _____ _____
      Student Project Director's name   Social Security No.   Department

   Telephone: _____   _____
                 Summer Office Number   Number where you may be reached during current academic year

   B. _____ _____ _____
      Faculty Advisor's Name   Social Security Number   Department

   Telephone: _____ _____ _____ _____
               Area Code   Office Number   Department Number   Home Number

5. A. Major Disciplinary Code: IN

   B. Field of Science and Engineering: 9900000, OTHER NEC

   C. Field(s) of Interest and Application*: _____

   D. Type of Project: NEW

6. Period of Full-time Participation: _____197____ to _____197____
                                          Starting Date   Ending Date

7. Does the host institution intend to grant academic credit in appropriate amounts and levels for work
   on this project?
                   (   ) Yes   (   ) No

8. Participants and Cost of Proposed Project:

                    FULL TIME

   No. of Weeks   No. of Participants   Amt. Requested

   _____   _____ $ _____
                                   (Budget Item 32)

9. Signatures:

   _____   _____
   Signature of proposed Student Project Director   Signature of authorizing official

   _____   _____
   Signature of proposed Project Advisor   Typed name and title of official authorized to sign
                                                                  for institution

10. Date of Submission: _____

*List 1 to 3 codes with their abbreviations, in descending order of importance. See pages 13, 14.

15

Figure 13-1 Summary cover sheet.

SUMMARY BUDGET PAGE

Institution: _____

_____

Project Director: _____

_____

NUMBER OF PARTICIPANTS		
Full Time		Acad. Year
19___		
19___		
19___		

A.   PARTICIPANT SUPPORT

_____ Participants for_____ weeks @ $_____ /wk.
(Minimum 10 weeks; Maximum 12 weeks); (Maximum $90/wk.)

10.   Total Participant Support . . . .

B.   OPERATING COST
Salaries and Wages
12.   Staff* *(Faculty Advice)* . . . .
13.   Assistants and Technical Personnel* (No._____) . . . .
15.   Secretarial and Clerical* . . . .
16.   TOTAL SALARIES AND WAGES (12, 13 & 15) . . . . . .
17.   Staff Benefits *(When charged as direct costs)* . . . .
18.   TOTAL SALARIES, WAGES AND STAFF
               BENEFITS (16 & 17) . . . .
20.   Staff *(Faculty Advisor's)* Travel* . . . .
21.   Field Expenses* . . . .
22.   Laboratory and Field Materials* *(Consumables)* . . . .
23.   Office Supplies, Communications, Publicity* . . . .
24.   Fees† . . . .
25.   Insurance, Health Services & Activities Fees* . . . .
26.   Permanent Equipment* *(Note Restrictions)* . . . .
27.   Publication Costs and/or Miscellaneous Expenses* . . . .
28.   TOTAL DIRECT OPERATING COSTS
               (18 thru 27) . . . .
29.   INDIRECT COSTS_____ % . . . .

30.   TOTAL OPERATING COSTS (28 & 29) . . . .

C.   TOTALS
31.   Total Budget *(Participant Support (10) + Total Operating
         Costs (30))* . . . .
32.   TOTAL REQUESTED FROM NSF
               (Round to nearest $50) . . . .

_____

* *Itemize in "Budget Explanations", with adequate justifications.*
† *Justify in "Budget Explanations". Other operating costs (lines 12–29) must be reduced to fully offset this item.*

Figure 13-2   Summary budget page.

CURRICULUM VITAE FORMAT FOR
STUDENT PROJECT DIRECTORS AND PARTICIPANTS

Name: _____ Age: _____
　　　　　　(Last)　　　　　(First)　　　(Middle)　　　　　　(As of May 1, 1976)

Present Institution: _____ Sex:　Female _____ Male _____

Other Institutions Attended: _____

　　　　　　　　　　　　　　　　　　　　　　　　Marital Status:
Major Field(s): _____ Minor(s): _____ Single _____ Married _____

Class (as of May 1, 1976): _____

Courses already completed which are relevant to proposed project (Faculty advisor will please submit in confidence grades for students in those institutions where policy prohibits their being shown to students.):

Course Title	Grade	Course Title	Grade

Additional relevant courses to be completed before summer of 1976:

Previous experience in research or project-oriented studies:

Skills, hobbies, interests pertinent to the proposed study:

Please note briefly why you wish to participate in the projected studies:

Figure 13-3 Curriculum vitae format.

it. When preparing an unsolicited proposal, you can devise your own organization.

UNSOLICITED PROPOSALS

Unsolicited proposals are very much like solicited ones. Essentially the same information is required with one major difference. In a solicited proposal the solicitors recognize a need. Therefore, you don't have to sell them on the need, only on your ability to understand and interpret the need and to meet it. In an unsolicited proposal you must first convince the audience the need exists. If you can't, they will have no particular interest in your goods or services.

For example, a roofing contractor called in by a homeowner to bid on reshingling a roof does not need to establish the need for the job. But an enterprising contractor who sees a roof in need of repair may have to convince the owner that reshingling is really necessary. Often establishing need calls for a problem-solution organization. The problem establishes the need. Your goods or services supply the solution.

A small, simple unsolicited proposal might fall into five parts:

1. Introduction, which establishes need.
2. Overview section, which defines the process to be followed or describes the goods to be furnished, or both.
3. Work and management plan, which outlines the tasks to be done and schedules their accomplishment.
4. Detailed budget, which gives precise information on costs.
5. Personnel section, which briefly gives the relevant qualifications of the people involved.

Very often, short proposals are drafted in the form of a letter or memorandum. Even so, captions and applicable graphics should be used—particularly easy-to-read informal lists and tables.

The proposal in Figure 13-4, modeled after an actual successful proposal, follows the five steps outlined above. Take the time to read it now. The bracketed letters in the model proposal refer to the comments below.

A. The proposal is set up in a letter format frequently used for short proposals. Executives like to have a concise statement of a proposal before they study it in detail. You will impress them favorably if you compress the major points of your proposal into a short abstract.

B. The beginning of the introduction defines the subject, peer advising, and points out its successful use elsewhere.

C. The survey shows that early and careful planning has taken place. The results of the survey do not show that an outright problem of student dissatisfaction exists. But they do show that students might feel more com-

BATTLE CREEK COMMUNITY COLLEGE

Kellogg, Michigan 48108

DEPARTMENT OF CRIMINAL JUSTICE STUDIES

10 December 1977

TO: Janice H. Grumbacher, Director
               Center for Educational Development
               317 Clark Library
               Battle Creek Community College
               Kellogg, MI 48108

FROM: Martin A. Doyle, Student, Criminal Justice Studies

SUBJECT: Request to Center for Educational Development for funding a Peer
               Advising Program for Criminal Justice Studies Students.

ABSTRACT: A survey shows that students and faculty in Criminal Justice
               Studies (CJS) favor the concept of peer advising. Peer advising
               is being successfully used in other colleges in the United
               States. This proposal requests $2114.00 to set up an operational
               experiment in peer advising in CJS. The experiment would run for
               13 months from May 1978 through May 1979. The experiment will be
               monitored by senior CJS faculty. Evaluative reports will be
               written and disseminated at the end of the experiment. **[A]**

INTRODUCTION

    A new development in many two- and four-year colleges is the
successful use of students for advising their fellow students regarding
course registration, program development, and job opportunities. Called
peer advising, this new development supplements but does not replace normal
faculty advising. **[B]**

    In the fall of this year, I surveyed the faculty and students of the
Department of Criminal Justice Studies (CJS) regarding their opinions about
peer advising. A complete copy of the survey results, "Response to Peer
Advising in the Department of Criminal Justice Studies," is available from
me upon request. But the results can be summarized briefly:

    —Rightly or wrongly, many students feel they are imposing upon their
     advisers' time by seeking assistance. Some students view their
     advisers as having more important matters to contend with.

    —Students feel that peer advisers will be better able to relate to the
     problems of their fellow students.

    —Students stated frequently that they would feel freer and more
     comfortable in bringing their problems to peer advisers.

    —Faculty acceptance of peer advising was high. Most felt it would be a
     welcome addition for both faculty and students.

Figure 13-4 Model proposal.

The study showed such strong support for peer advising among faculty and students that such a program seems to have a good potential for success. **[C]** In the remainder of this proposal, I'll present a methodology for establishing the program, a work and management plan, a detailed budget, and the qualifications of the key personnel involved.

METHODOLOGY **[D]**

If instituted, peer advising will be conducted for 13 months as an operational experiment. A peer advising unit of two students will be set up in the spring of 1978. Mr. William Morrell, Chief Adviser for CJS, has agreed to train the two peer advisers and to supervise the program through the year. Beginning in the fall of 1978, regular office hours will be maintained with one or both peer advisers present at all times.

The peer advising unit will deal with

- —registration and scheduling difficulties
- —guidance on classes and instructors
- —sequence of classes and prerequisites
- —recommended classes
- —questions on the CJS program
- —information for potential majors
- —information on jobs and placement
- —information on University services and agencies

The peer advising unit will work closely with:

- —current faculty advisers
- —the Head of CJS
- —Admissions and Records

The peer advising unit will collect statistics and information on

- —number of students helped
- —types of problems dealt with
- —where/who solved problems
- —feedback from CJS students and faculty

In the spring of 1979, the peer advisers will prepare a full evaluation consolidating all the data collected and presenting conclusions concerning the potential of peer advising in CJS. Mr. Morrell will prepare a separate evaluation of the program. Both evaluations will be submitted to Dr. Carlos Montoya, Head, CJS; Dr. Mary Baker, Dean of the College; and your office.

Dr. Montoya and Dean Baker will arrive at a decision concerning the continuance of peer advising in CJS. Dean Baker will also consider the possibility of peer advising in other departments of the college.

WORK AND MANAGEMENT PLAN

This section provides detailed treatment of facilities, the task breakdown, and management.

Figure 13-4 Model proposal *(continued)*.

<u>Facilities</u> [**E**]

Dr. Montoya has agreed to provide an office for the peer advising unit. The office will be located in an area easily accessible to CJS students. CJS will furnish the office with a desk, telephone, filing cabinet, bookshelves, a swivel desk chair, three straight chairs, a typewriter, and a typewriter table. The peer advisers will have the use of CJS office supplies including stamps and stationery. CJS secretaries will furnish clerical assistance not to exceed three hours a week.

<u>Task</u> <u>Breakdown</u> [**F**]

There will be three major tasks: training, maintaining office hours, and evaluating the program. The accompanying graph shows the task timetable.

<u>Training</u>. May, 1978. Mr. Morrell will give the two peer advisers 10 hours of training in advising procedures to include filling out registration forms and procedures for adding and dropping courses. He will provide information concerning other college programs, particularly those that provide aid in needed study skills such as note-taking, reading, listening, and library research. He will aid the peer advisers in learning the interpersonal communication skills needed for effective advising.

<u>Office</u> <u>hours</u>. 3 September 1978–28 May 1979. Office hours with at least one person present will be scheduled from 11 a.m. to 2 p.m., five days a week, holidays and school breaks excluded. During each of the heavy advising months of September and January, an additional 20 hours of advising time will be scheduled to allow two advisers to be present during peak hours.

<u>Evaluation</u>. 1–30 April 1979. During April 1979, the two peer advisers will consolidate the information they have gathered throughout the year and write their evaluation report. A total of 16 hours is scheduled for this task.

<u>Management</u> [**G**]

Mr. Morrell will supervise the entire peer advising experiment as part of his duties as Chief Adviser for the CJS program. He will be readily accessible to the peer advisers. He will monitor their procedures and provide advice and counsel when needed. Throughout the year he will provide informal reports to Dr. Montoya. At the end of the experiment he will provide an evaluation of the peer advising program.

Figure 13-4 Model proposal *(continued)*.

DETAILED BUDGET [H]

Because CJS is furnishing office space, office supplies, and clerical help, the entire budget needed is for salary for the two peer advisers. The normal student hourly wage of $3.50 per hour is requested. The budget breaks down in the following manner:

Training time:	Salary for 2 peer advisers, a total of 20 hours	70.00
Office hours:	Salary for 3 hours of peer advising a day for 176 days, a total of 528 hours	1848.00
	Salary for 40 additional advising hours in September and July	140.00
Evaluation time:	Salary for 16 hours	56.00
	TOTAL	$2114.00

The budgeted $2114.00 would be divided approximately equally between the two peer advisers. If this grant request is approved, your office is requested to transfer $70.00 to the CJS budget in April of 1978 and the remaining $2044.00 in September 1978. Normal college accounting procedures will be used by CJS to account for expenditures. [I]

PERSONNEL [J]

I request that I be one of the peer advisers. In March of 1978 the other peer adviser will be chosen from among applicants for the job by a secret ballot of the CJS students.

My qualifications are as follows. After graduation from high school in 1966, I served four years in the U.S. Air Force as an air policeman, leaving the service with the rank of sergeant. From November 1971 to the present I have been a sheriff's deputy in Bad Axe County. I am currently working half-time while I complete my CJS studies. I have a special interest in counseling. To develop myself in this area, I have taken Social Science 1104, Dynamics of Small Groups, and I am currently taking Social Science 2111, Interpersonal Communication. My current grade point average is 3.2.

Mr. William Morrell, who will supervise the experiment, is Chief Adviser for CJS. Before taking his degree in Criminal Justice Studies at the University of Washington, Mr. Morrell was a police officer with the Seattle, Washington, Police Department for eight years. He also has a Master's Degree in Educational Administration from the University of North Dakota. With CJS for the past six years, Mr. Morrell has been Chief Adviser since 1976.

CONCLUSION [K]

Evidence gathered at other schools indicates that peer advising is successful—a positive benefit to students, faculty, and the school. I have reports concerning established programs at two major universities that I will send to you at your request. Preliminary studies here indicate that both faculty and students favor peer advising in CJS.

If successful, peer advising will remove a significant burden from the CJS faculty, freeing them for additional time to pursue their teaching and professional development. The experiment may lead to similar innovative advising techniques in other departments of the college.

Figure 13-4 Model proposal *(continued)*.

I will be happy to discuss this proposal with you at your convenience.
And I will be open to any modifications in the plan you might suggest.

Sincerely,

Martin A. Doyle

Martin A. Doyle

cc: Mr. William Morrell
    Dr. Carlos Montoya
    Dean Mary Baker

Figure 13-4 Model proposal *(continued).*

fortable with another approach. The survey results also set to rest the thought that the faculty might object.

D. The methodology section outlines the strategy and some of the timing of the operational experiment. Again it shows that a good deal of thought has gone into the proposal. The final paragraph suggests the money spent for the proposal may result in a new and more desirable advising procedure than currently exists. Such a development is likely to please the Center for Educational Development, an organization charged with developing innovative methods to improve the college's educational process. As in all selling, you consider the self-interest of those you are selling to.

E. Facilities have to be explained somewhere. In a simple report like this one, the work and management plan is a good location. If facilities are extensive, they would, of course, rate a section of their own.

F. The tasks to be accomplished are presented in a chronological sequence. A simple graph shows the time relationship of the tasks.

G. Proper management is always a concern. People want to know the spending of their money will be overseen by experienced, responsible managers.

H. The budget is presented in a simple table form. Don't overlook any possible expenses. Figure 13-2 provides a good checklist.

I. If appropriate, specify the time and method of payment. Tell how the money will be accounted for.

J. In a simple proposal a short narrative biography that gives relevant education and experience is usually enough. But use your salesmanship here. The facts chosen for the student's biography emphasize his maturity and experience. The two courses listed establish an interest in counseling that is a real selling point for the project. The information on Mr. Morrell establishes his credibility as a supervisor and points out that the project will have high-level direction.

K. The conclusion resells the proposal. It emphasizes previous successes for peer advising and offers to provide evidence for this claim. Indicating flexibility and the willingness to negotiate is also important. Often proposals can't be carried out exactly as proposed.

Proposals are unique documents. They combine the skills needed for information giving, analysis, and persuasion. Remember, too, they are legal documents. Whatever you say you are going to do, you can be held legally accountable for doing. But the satisfaction of writing a successful proposal is considerable. When someone gives you money on the strength of a proposal you have written, you have direct evidence of your writing and persuasive skills.

SUGGESTIONS FOR APPLYING YOUR KNOWLEDGE

Proposals provide a rich field for both long and short writing assignments and for class discussion.

- Short proposals can be essentially bids. You can bid to furnish products or services in carpentry, plumbing, interior design, food service, health services, and so forth. You could bid to build a porch, install track lighting, furnish carpets or drapes, or cater a party. The possibilities are enormous. The proposals can come from school work or off-campus work or some combination of the two. Just include the information absolutely relevant to the bid, such as what is to be furnished, by whom, and at what cost. You might also include a few salesmanship touches like experience and testimonials.
- Long proposals could be a term project. Like short proposals, they could relate to major fields of study or to off-campus work. They could relate to community problems. They could involve extensive research in the area involved, perhaps even including surveys and interviews, as in our model proposal about peer advising. In long proposals you would get into more sections, such as facilities, equipment, schedules, and personnel. You would have to establish the need for the product or service offered. You would have to provide and analyze a large body of information. You would have to sell your ability to fulfill the terms of the proposal. You would have to devise an organization and a format that present your proposal in the best way possible.
- Long proposals can also be team or even class projects. There are certainly enough sections to go around. You could even try a proposal that is for real and not just an exercise. Most colleges have an office that deals in grants. You could go to the grants office in your college and see if they have any student-oriented requests. The NSF solicitation we use as an example in this chapter is just such a request. If you find such a solicitation, you might have a stimulating project for a group that could end in real accomplishment.
- Long proposals can often be combined with speeches. Proposals often have to be sold orally as well as in writing. They provide good applications of persuasive speaking skills.
- A good deal of material can be gathered for class discussion. Your grants office will likely have on hand out-of-date requests for proposals they would be happy to let you have.

These requests can furnish material for good class discussions as you analyze the types of information, organization, and format they call for. They provide fine examples of our constant theme: Occupational writing provides specific information for a specific audience for a specific purpose. Compare and contrast the organizational plans and formats called for. You can learn from all of them, but try to decide which ones are best, and why. You may also find it possible to obtain actual proposals submitted by various units of your college or by companies in your area. Discussion of how they were researched, organized, and written can be a great way to learn how to do your own proposals. The originator of the proposal might be willing to enter into the discussion.

CHAPTER 14
Oral Reports

Speaking at a convention, Robert T. Oliver of Pennsylvania State University said:

> Winston Churchill with a rifle in his hand, crouched behind an earthen rampart along the Dover coast, might have repelled two or three Nazi Invaders. But the same Winston Churchill, speaking with his matchless oratory, was able to marshal the global resources and inspire the will to victory that toppled Hitler's empire and preserved the democratic civilization of the Anglo-American world.[1]

Professor Oliver's point is important. Through communication you can enlarge your own resources many times over. You can teach others to know what you know and to do what you can do. You can persuade others to help you do what you do. You can seek understanding for your beliefs. The people we communicate with become extensions of ourselves. Because of its personal, live nature, spoken communication is something rather special. Even in an age of technology, speech making is still a highly effective way of communicating, necessary in almost every professional occupation. It's worth doing well.

Our purpose in this chapter is to guide you from the moment you know you have to give a speech to the moment you step from the rostrum after completing your successful speech. We talk about how to prepare a speech, how to integrate visuals into it, and how to deliver it.

[1]Annual Convention of Toastmasters International, New York, 1965.

223

"Great! But where does he stand on environmental protection?"

Drawing by Mulligan; © 1976 The New Yorker Magazine, Inc.

PREPARATION

Preparation is much more than gathering material for a speech and even more than organizing that material. Successful preparation involves, first, considering whom you're talking to and where. What is the occasion for your talk? After you know the audience and the occasion, you can consider your purpose in the speech. When you know audience, occasion, and purpose, then you can select the right material to satisfy all three and organize that material. It's these important matters that we discuss in this section.

Context

Conversations differ depending upon where you are, what you're doing, and whom you're with. A conversation between a man and a woman in a dimly lit restaurant differs from the conversation between two men at a football game. A conversation with a potential employer is not the same as a conversation with your girlfriend or boyfriend. You don't use the same tones or language at a noisy party as you do in church or in a library. As the context changes, so do the content of your conversation and the manner of its delivery.

So, too, do speeches differ with context. Specifically, we refer to occasion and audience.

Occasion   When you are invited to speak, find out as much about the occasion for your speech as you can. What is the purpose of the occasion? Is it social, business, some mix of the two? Are you the only speaker? If there is a program of speakers, where do you fit in? Why were you specifically invited to talk? What is expected from you? These are the questions you should try to get answers for. Without knowing the answers, you can be led into terrible traps. A speech entirely suitable for one occasion may be utterly unsuitable for another.

> **Case in point:** Teachers from colleges around the country are gathered at a major university for a three-day conference. The first meeting of the group occurs at an evening cocktail party and dinner. The group meets, drinks, and eats a heavy meal. A dean of the university is introduced to give the group a welcoming talk. He proceeds for forty minutes to deliver an excellent, informational talk about programs at the university, complete with statistics, success-failure ratios, and so on.
>
> How successful was the dean on this occasion? He was a complete flop. He was at a social occasion, but he treated it like a business meeting. He put half his audience to sleep and made the other half too annoyed to sleep. He delivered a speech that would have been successful and appropriate on another occasion—say, the annual report to the board of regents. What was called for at the dinner was a short, light talk of perhaps five to ten minutes' duration in which he welcomed the group and told a humorous anecdote or two.

It is also important to know the physical location of where you are going to talk. What size is the room? Does the room fit the number of people in the expected audience? It can be more depressing than you may think to talk to 40 people in a room meant to hold 200. Conversely, it's often exciting and successful to talk to an overflow crowd of 40 in a room meant for 30 people. What kind of equipment is available? Is there an overhead projector or a blackboard if you need it? Will you have a lectern and a light?

> **Case in point:** A prominent writer is invited to give an after-dinner speech to a group of writing teachers. It's expected that the talk will be fairly serious. The writer is respected and the teachers want her opinions about writing. The writer

comes with her speech written out. The banquet room is dimly lit. There is neither lectern nor light at the writer's place. While she gives her speech, she holds her manuscript about 10 inches from her face in order to see it. She gives up trying to read in the dim light and tries to give the speech extemporaneously. However, she has quotes she has to read, and when she tries to find them from the manuscript, she loses her place. Finally in frustration she sits down to light, polite applause.

What should have been an excellent talk was ruined by a lack of equipment. One of two preparatory actions would have prevented the disaster. The writer could have let the dinner's organizers know that she had to have a light and a lectern. If for reasons beyond control, light and lectern were not available, she should have been warned in ample time. She could then have prepared an extemporaneous speech. Speaking from a brief outline, as one does in extemporaneous speech, she could have survived in the dim light. Her quotes could have been typed in large type on separate, numbered cards and placed in the order she needed them.

The moral in the tales of the dean and the writer is clear. Know beforehand what you are getting into and plan accordingly. If you have any control over the situation, ask for needed changes: the right-sized room or the necessary equipment, for example. If you can't get the changes you want, at least you will be forewarned. You can probably make appropriate plans that will give the proper results.

The occasion also has much to do with the mode of speech you choose—impromptu, memorized, written, or extemporaneous.

- **Impromptu** As the name implies, impromptu speeches can't be prepared. Or rather, you can't plan the specific speech. Your preparation is knowledge of the subject matter. At a social occasion you may be asked to give a little impromptu speech to introduce yourself. Or at a business meeting you may be called upon to stand up and discuss an arrangement, a contract, or the operation of your shop. At a union meeting or a school board meeting you may stand up to protest or support an action. Some of the things we say about content and organization later will help some, but to deliver a good impromptu, you had better know your subject thoroughly.

- **Memorized** Memorized speeches have extremely limited uses. They probably serve the best when you have to repeat a speech many times. For instance, the guides at places like Disneyland memorize their patter: "Good afternoon, ladies and gentlemen, we're about to enter darkest jungleland. If you're fainthearted. . . ." Experienced lecturers, actors, and politicians go about the country giving the same speech over and over. In the late nineteenth century Dr. Russell Conwell earned over seven million dollars by giving a speech he called "Acres of Diamonds" more than 6,000 times. That was a speech worth memorizing. But for most of us it's not worth memorizing a speech. It's too much effort and can get us into trouble. When you learn something word for word and forget a word, the whole speech can depart from your mind—instant blank.

- **Written**   Written speeches are quite suitable for some occasions. People running for political office often write their speeches. Having the speech written prevents them from making misstatements of fact or overheated spur-of-the-moment statements that may plague them later. Businesspeople often write their speeches for the same reasons. But rarely should speeches for social occasions be written out. Usually, the desired light, adlib effect is destroyed by a written speech. And often, as in the case of our writer in the dimly lit room, conditions are not right for reading.
- **Extemporaneous**   The most suitable speech for the widest variety of occasions is the extemporaneous speech. This mode calls for a good deal of preparation. You organize, outline, and rehearse it, but you do not write it or memorize it. You know what ideas and facts you're going to work with and have them well in hand. But the actual wording of the speech is left for each delivery of it. It's a good speech mode— sound, safe, and flexible. It's the primary mode that we consider.

Audience

Find out as much about your audience beforehand as you can. First, how many people will there be? For twenty people you might plan an informal speech that is mainly discussion—a short talk followed by an extensive question-and-answer period. For a large group meeting in an auditorium discussion might be unwieldy, so you would plan for a longer well-organized speech. But most of your decisions based on audience, regardless of its size will be based on the social context and the audience's knowledge and expectations.

How closely do you relate to your audience?   For instance, is it composed mainly of friends and coworkers? Is it an audience with which you have many shared interests? Are you a student talking to students? A nurse to nurses? A policeman to policemen? If so, in some ways your job is easier. Your language can be a bit casual, your speech patterns relaxed. You can leave some things unsaid, because everybody knows them anyway. On the other hand, speaking to this group can be tough. They are likely to question your expertise. The old notion that prophets are not listened to in their own countries is often true. People know them too well to take them seriously. So you may need more evidence to prove your points with this audience than with another that doesn't know you as well.

Groups that don't share your experiences present different kinds of problems. They may expect less relaxed, more formal language from you. They may not take you seriously because you are too young or too old. When you move out of your normal social context, expect difficulties. Your speech will have to be well prepared to overcome them.

What does the audience know about your subject?   If they already know all the basics, you can start at a more advanced level. If not, you may have to give background information. We all learn a vocational vocabulary with the jobs we are trained to do. Sometimes we forget that others don't share that vocabulary. An engineer speaking about horizontal and vertical curves may forget that nonengineers would call the first simply *curves* and the second *hills*. When you can, use simple expressions for a nonexpert audience. If you can't, define the needed terms.

But judge your audience correctly. An audience that doesn't need background, simple language, or definitions will feel talked down to if you do supply them.

What does the audience expect of you?   In occupational situations most audiences can be classified as management, technical, or nontechnical. By *technical* we mean those people who work closely with whatever it is you're talking about.

Suppose you develop a new process in an auto shop for taking off old tires, putting new ones on, and balancing the wheels. If you were talking to management about this new process, they would expect cost data. Will this new process cost more or less than the old? Will it require fewer or more mechanics? Are there safety problems involved? The technicians would also want to know some of these same things. But they would also want more details about the process itself. How do you do it? What are the major steps in the process? Does it require new equipment? The nontechnicians primarily expect to be told how the process relates to them. In the case of new tire-changing techniques, the nontechnical customers of the garage would want to know two things: Will the new process be cheaper, and will it get cars in and out of the garage faster?

So it goes. You have to know your audience to do your best. For you can't get through to an audience unless it lets you get through. In that sense the audience is in control, not you. But don't despair if you can't always analyze an audience perfectly. Aristotle—the first person to write thoroughly and intelligently about speaking—said that credibility is inspired by a speaker having good sense, good moral character, and good will. With these three qualities you'll get along with most audiences. Without them all the analysis in the world probably won't do you much good.

Purpose and Content

Purpose and content are closely related, and of course both are closely related to occasion and audience. In broad terms you would normally wish to speak socially, to inform, or to persuade. Or you may have in mind some mixture of the three. For a specific speech to a specific audience you would narrow a broad purpose down to a specific one:

- I propose to welcome and amuse for a few minutes a group of 20 visiting salespeople.
- I propose to inform 20 visiting salespeople how the new billing system works.
- I propose to persuade 20 visiting salespeople that the new billing system is better than the old.
- I propose to inform 20 visiting salespeople about the new billing system and to persuade them that it is better than the old.

When you have your specific purpose clearly in mind, you have complete the criteria you need to choose your content. There are four questions you should ask about anything you intend to include in your speech:

- Will it meet the needs and expectations of my audience?
- Will it move my purpose forward?
- Does the occasion call for it?
- Does accurate presentation of the topic call for it?

Don't include any item that doesn't meet at least one of these criteria. Your best items will meet all four. The more criteria that each item meets, the more economical you will be of both your and the audience's time.

Time is always a problem. Accuracy may say to include an item. Time may say to leave it out. It's a conflict that goes on in all speaking and writing. Also, you must set priorities among your criteria because they will often be in conflict. For instance, an item that your audience really doesn't expect may be needed for accuracy. Which of these two criteria is your highest priority? In this instance you might be wise to remember Aristotle's comment about good moral character. Go for accuracy.

What sort of material makes up the content of speeches? Let's analyze a few excerpts from actual speeches to see.

Anyone engaged in publishing who thinks our English language is not changing is probably in the wrong business. English continues to change because it is a language used by living people, and living people are forever changing. Speech and writing are tools and reflect the lives of the people who use them. If you want an indication of the extent of the change, compare the novels and newspapers of the last century to their counterparts today. Style, vocabulary, structure—all of these have been affected by time. Even if your great-grandparents were born in America, you speak a different language than they did. Your great-grandparents would find today's newspapers extremely puzzling—we have a great number of words in the language that did

The speaker uses a general statement for an opening. He states an opinion.

With the "if" statement, the speaker begins a comparison that runs through the rest of the paragraph.

Opinion through here, but not controversial. Most people would readily accept this statement.

not exist more than a few years ago. Would great-grandpa understand stories dealing with dragsters, jets, extravehicular activity, lasers, or pushers? Could he identify a coffee break? Or understand this sentence: "The fuzz caught me with the grass and I got busted"?[2]

An accurate fact, although not statistically support-ed.

A series of short, factual examples drawn from modern language.

In this next example the speaker is talking about the danger of quacks in the teaching of technical writing. The speaker, Henrietta Tichy, herself a noted authority on technical writing, draws upon another authority for support.

The highly touted quacks who achieve such disastrous results are easy to recognize by their brazen advertising. The dangerous courses are also easy to recognize by their preposterous promises. Professor Siegfried Mandel warns,

The central statement of the paragraph leads up to the quote.

The quote is simply intro-duced.

In an attempt to crash through the barriers between themselves and good writing, many persons have fall-en into the attractive traps of the one-day circuses that come to town under the respectable label of "Insti-tute," or have pounced on the books that promise clear writing in a few easy lessons. Little except self-delusion can be gained by gunning one's intellectual apparatus and hoping to reach the top in a single spurt; the flesh may be willing, but the means are in-adequate.[3]

The quote is an appeal to authority.

Later in the same speech Professor Tichy uses an anecdote to illustrate a point:

However, even the most tenacious supervisors retire or change, and so do the writers of manuals. A few months ago a manager of that company asked me to write a new manual for the company.

"I didn't know whether you would talk to me," he said, "because when I once called to ask you to give a course based on our manual, you said that you would not prostitute yourself by using that book."

"I've forgotten those strong words," I told him, "but I'm sure that you are wise to plan a sounder book of instructions."

[2]James A. Woolf, "A Style Guide for the Future," *Proceedings 19th International Technical Communications Conference* (May 1972): 31. Reprinted by permission of the Society for Technical Communication, 1010 Vermont Avenue, N.W., Washington, D.C. 20005.

[3]Henrietta Tichy, "Teaching in Industry: The Consultant-Instructor Speaks," *Proceedings 19th International Technical Communications Conference* (May 1972): 66. Reprinted by per-mission of the Society for Technical Communication, 1010 Vermont Avenue, N.W., Washing-ton, D.C. 20005.

"Yes," he said, "but I should tell you that I was one of the writers of the old manual."[4]

An excerpt from another talk uses research data to support the opening general statement:

Someone once said, "It's not what you write that counts, but what you get others to read. Publicity sent does not equal publicity received."	General statement
A study conducted at the University of Wisconsin a while ago found that out of 300 releases received over a five-day period by a typical morning newspaper, 242 were rejected. The reasons given by the 61 editors polled were as follows:	Statistical data
• Limited local interest • No reader interest at all • Story poorly written • Disguised advertising • Apparent inaccuracy • Too thin[5]	Questionnaire results

The pattern is clear, we hope. General statements such as, "It's not what you write that counts, but what you get others to read," are made and then supported. The support can be almost anything and everything—facts, numbers and statistics, authoritative opinions, comparisons, examples, anecdotes, and so forth. All are suitable so long as they pass through the screen of your four criteria—audience, purpose, occasion, and accuracy.

Recognize that general statements need support unless (like Mom's apple pie) they're widely accepted. But there is a limit to the amount of support that you can supply or be reasonably expected to supply. When you reach the point where your material is adequate to satisfy a reasonable person, stop. We recognize, naturally, how subjective the word *reasonable* is, but speaking is a subjective business. Perhaps Mark Twain's story about his encounter with a fund raiser will help illustrate the meaning of *reasonable*. When the fund raiser had reached what Twain thought was a reasonable place to conclude, Twain was convinced he should give him ten, maybe even twenty dollars. Finally, though, when the man talked on for half an hour longer, Twain took fifty cents from the collection plate.

Organization

After you have considered context, purpose, and content, the next step is organization. In looking at the content of speeches, we saw that most moved back and forth between generalizations and support for the gener-

---

[4]Ibid., 67

[5]Arnold T. Koch, Jr., "Publicity for Better or Worse," *Proceedings 19th International Technical Communications Conference* (May 1972): 43, 44. Reprinted by permission of the Society for Technical Communication, 1010 Vermont Avenue, N.W., Washington, D.C. 20005.

alizations. Indeed, this general-to-particular or particular-to-general development is a good overall organizational plan, as you will see when we discuss argument. But most often a different organizational plan is laid over the internal general-to-particular movement. We have already discussed a great many organizational plans in this book. We've talked, for instance, about process and mechanism descriptions, good- and bad-news approaches, and analytical reports. Most of the organizational schemes good for writing are also good for speaking, so don't overlook any of them.

In this section we present briefly and schematically some organizational plans universally used in both speaking and writing. They may be used in isolation or combined with each other. When planning a talk, consider these plans as well as plans you already know. Choose the plan or combination of plans that best fits the same criteria we have discussed for content: audience, purpose, occasion, accuracy.

- **Chronological** The chronological or time approach is probably the oldest approach in existence. It's the storytelling approach—"Once upon a time, there was. . . ." You pick a point in history and move forward (or backward) from it. It's useful for giving the history of an action. It combines rather naturally with other plans such as cause and effect.

- **Cause and effect** In cause and effect your basic plan is that x has caused y. Naturally, discussions of causality lend themselves to a chronological approach. Variations exist for the basic plan, such as
  —If x continues, y will result.
  —y exists; its probable causes are u, w, x. . . .
  —In itself x is not undesirable, but its probable effect y will be.

- **Categorical** The categorical approach is often useful for handling large amounts of otherwise unmanageable material. For example, consider a group of 20 of your friends and acquaintances. You want to discuss them. Where do you begin? Well, categorizing may be a good start. The categories are infinite. You can categorize by sex, religion, age, income, grades, occupation, eye color, and on and on. In discussing a state's highways you might categorize by surface—gravel, asphalt, concrete. Or you might categorize by funding—city, county, state, federal.

  Choose whichever category or categories best help you work with your material. Be careful not to mix categories at the same level. The following categorization of highways is faulty:

concrete
asphalt
federal

The federal highways may be either concrete or asphalt. The following two-level combination is fine:

Federal
    concrete
    asphalt

State
    concrete
    asphalt

- **Problem-solution** Many talks are made about problems and how to solve them. The basic organization plan is quite simple. You present in turn

Problem
Solution
Effect of the solution

Defining the problem well is crucial. The traditional newspaper approach will help you cover most points. Looking at the problem, answer the questions who? what? when? where? why? and how? In stating your solution, the same questions are likely to apply. Who is involved in the solution? When and where will it occur? And so forth.

There are some variations to the basic plan. One, named for its developer, Professor Alan Monroe of Purdue University, is called the Monroe motivated sequence. It includes five steps:

—Draw attention to the problem
—Demonstrate need for solution
—Present a satisfactory solution
—Visualize the solution in action
—Call for action

Sometimes you have to choose among several solutions. Here the elimination plan is valuable:

—State problem
—State criteria to be applied to solutions
—State solution 1 and apply criteria
—State solution 2 and apply criteria
—Choose solution that best meets criteria

Be sure to apply all criteria evenhandedly to each solution. For instance, don't eliminate one solution because of a cost criterion and then fail to apply the cost criterion to the other solution.

- **Topical** Sometimes you simply want to inform people about a topic. You have no particular problems to solve or arguments to deliver. Here again the newspaper approach may prove useful. Suppose you wished to discuss 4-H clubs, for example. You might tell your audience the following:

—Who 4-H club members are
—What 4-H clubs do
—When the clubs meet
—Where they meet
—Why 4H exists—that is, its goals
—How 4H meets its goals

You could of course vary the order and eliminate steps not needed for your topic and purpose.

- **Advertising**   You can use the advertising organizational plan, AIDA, when you wish to persuade an audience to action—to buy, to vote, to attend a concert, whatever:

—Get **A**ttention
—Awaken **I**nterest
—Awaken **D**esire
—Call for **A**ction

- **Argument**   The form for argument is an elaboration of the general-to-particular plan. Begin with a major generalization, sometimes called the major thesis. Then support the major thesis with a series of minor theses—generally three, certainly no more than five. Each minor thesis is itself supported, usually by a combination of fact and authoritative opinion. An argument might look like this one:

Major Thesis: The 55mph speed limit should be maintained
   Minor thesis: It conserves energy
                  —support
   Minor thesis: It causes less damage to highway surfaces
                  —support
   Minor thesis: It is safer
                  —support

No argument is ultimately any better than the support you bring to your opinions. Two procedures are worth remembering: Put the strongest minor thesis at the end, the weakest in the middle. And if your opponents have a strong point, bring it up, discuss it, try to moderate it, soften it, or cast doubt upon it in some legitimate way.

The speaking outline   One of your organizational chores is to prepare your speaking manuscript or notes. If you were to write your speech, you would first outline it (see pages 272–274) and then write it, much as you would any other piece of writing. Knowing it was meant to be read aloud, you would be careful about a few things. You would take care to use shorter sentences than usual and try for a higher percentage of sentences that begin with the subject. You would avoid putting complicated phrases or clauses between subject and verb. You would use contractions except when you wanted emphasis.

If you are going to speak extemporaneously, stop at the outline stage. We recommend that two outlines be made, actually. The first one would look like the outline for written work, complete with subdivisions and sub-subdivisions. You'll need this complete outline to bring all your material into order. But such an outline is too complex to speak from. You'll depend on it too much and be forever peering at it and losing your place, thus throwing away the whole graceful effect of extemporaneous speech.

Cut the first outline down to fit onto several 4-by-6 cards. You don't need to go as far as did a history professor that one of us once had. One afternoon he lectured knowledgeably for two hours about the ancient Greeks. He had a small card before him that read, "Talk about the Greeks today."

No, you don't need to go that far. Make one card for each major division of your speech. Put just enough on each card to keep you on track, following the main points in the order you have planned. Print your outline in rather large letters (but not all capitals; they're hard to read) on the card. It might look like Figure 14-1.

With such simple notes, of course, you must rehearse your speech beforehand. But such notes enable you to see at a glance where you're going. Thus, most of the time you can keep your eyes where they belong—on your audience.

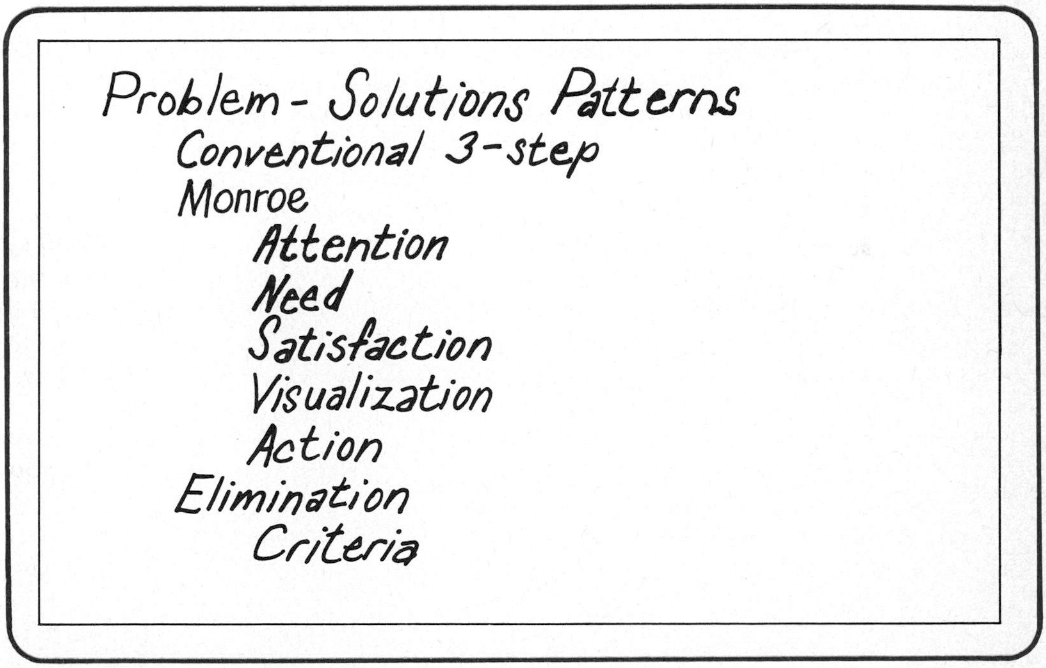

Figure 14-1 Speaking notecard.

Introduction and Conclusion

Both introduction and conclusion are very important to your speech; they should be well prepared.

Introduction Actually, most successful introductions come in two parts. The first part is often called the icebreaker. You want to slip gracefully from the introduction of you to the introduction to your speech. Various devices can be used. You can open with a quotation or an anecdote that illustrates your major point. The quotation about Winston Churchill that opens this chapter is an example of an icebreaker.

You can get audience participation in some manner. Ask for a show of hands: "How many people have had a hamburger in Larry's Diner in the last two weeks?" You can compliment the occasion or the audience. You have many options. We have only two warnings. Your quotations and stories should apply to your topic. Don't let them seem dragged in. Second, be careful of humor. If you can't handle it, don't touch it. And if the occasion for the speech is a serious one, humor would likely be seen as inappropriate.

After your icebreaker start, state your purpose and plan plainly and clearly:

> In the next twenty minutes, I'll explain to you why the national speed limit should be kept at 55 miles per hour. It saves gasoline, highway maintenance, and lives.

In this statement the audience is told the main purpose and the major subdivisions of the speech. All purpose statements, with one exception, should be this complete. The exception: If your purpose involves bad news, use the bad-news approach (see page 13). That is, build through a factual analysis to the bad news. Keep it out of the introduction.

Two other things can be done in an introduction. If your speech is going to include several key terms or theories not known to your audience, explain them at the beginning of your talk. Don't make people suffer from a lack of knowledge. And in a persuasive speech the introduction is often a good place to seek common ground with your audience:

> I'm sure we all agree on the need to conserve energy, money, and lives. Where we perhaps don't agree is on how to go about it. Let's consider . . . .

Conclusion Conclusions also come in two parts, sometimes three—all short. Once you move into a conclusion, move through it quickly. It should not take over a minute, even for a long speech.

Summarize your major points in a sentence or two:

> Driving at 55 miles per hour cuts gasoline use by 10 percent and cuts down highway maintenance bills by as much as 700 million dollars a year. Most important of all, it saves over ten thousand lives a year.

Note the repetition of the key points of the introduction, but with the addition of some important support data.

If your speech has been persuasive, you may wish to add a call to action to the summary:

> If I have persuaded you of the need for a 55-miles-per-hour speed limit, write your congressman today. You can be sure that the truck lobbies are bringing pressure to bear to raise the limit.

Sometimes you may also want to have something like the icebreaker—a memorable quotation or story—to close your speech. If you do use a story, keep it brief.

VISUALS

As in occupational writing, visuals are often indispensable in occupational speaking. Think of the words saved in describing how to tie a square knot by a simple illustration like the one here. Even when visual aids are not

absolutely necessary, they add variety and interest to your presentations. They support, clarify, and expand your points. They can snap a wandering audience to attention. They increase audience understanding and retention of your information.

What exactly is a visual? As in writing, it can be a graph, drawing, table, photograph, and so forth. But in speaking, the field broadens. Visuals can be models. Your pictures can be animated. And you can use objects—even people and animals. In this section we give some criteria for selecting effective visuals and a rundown on some of the most used visual tools.

Criteria

Good visuals enhance speeches, bad ones detract. In a valuable book, Professor James Connolly of the University of Minnesota has laid down some criteria for judging the worth of visuals—visibility, simplicity and clarity, and control.[5]

Visibility The notion of visibility in visuals seems obvious enough, but it is all too often overlooked. If your audience can't see your visual, it's worthless. A 9-by-12-inch photograph held in your hand and waved about does nothing for your audience. Because of the ease with which transparencies can now be made, speakers are tempted to reproduce printed

---

[5]*Effective Technical Presentations* (St. Paul, Minnesota: 3M Business Press, 1968), pp. 54–55.

pages and to show them on overhead projectors. Unfortunately, the print is usually so small that it's unreadable beyond the first few rows.

For printed material we can give you a simple rule. To be read, letters should be at least 1 inch high for each 25 feet between the visual and the audience. If you project a transparency on a screen, the letters on the screen should follow the same 1-inch/25-feet ratio. This means that you will have to prepare the originals for your transparencies using oversized type.

For other visuals, such as drawings, photos, graphs, and objects, the rules are not so easily laid down. You may have to experiment a bit. You should know beforehand how far the last row of your audience will be from your visuals. Stand that far yourself and see if you can understand the material presented. If you can't, it's too small. Don't use it. It is frustrating to an audience to have a speaker point knowingly to a visual that they can't see very well.

Clarity and simplicity   Visuals that are suitable in printed work may be too complicated for use in speaking. The reader, after all, can stop and study a visual. But in speeches the listener has only a limited time to take in the visual before the speaker sweeps it away and goes on to the next point. Therefore, the rule for speech visuals is to simplify and then to simplify again. Cut down to only absolutely vital information. The audience should be able to take in a visual's meaning at a glance. Use graphs to show the shapes of trends without worrying overmuch about the actual numbers. Break up tables and extract only needed information. Eliminate all unneeded features from maps. Use block diagrams rather than schematics.

The graph in Figure 14-2 is too complicated for use in a speech. Viewers must refer back and forth between the key and the surfaces to orient themselves. And surface graphs are difficult for many readers to interpret, let alone for a viewer who may only have a short glimpse of it. The graph in Figure 14-3 is more suitable. Here viewers can easily grasp the relationship between the two trends whether they absorb the dollar figures or not. Labeling the graph directly instead of using a key makes understanding the information even easier. And the speaker can easily draw attention to the dollar figures if they are important.

Figure 14-4 shows the layout of the interstate highway system in Minnesota. It would make a good transparency or poster. The lines are bold and the print large. The interstates, major cities, and state boundaries are clearly located. All other detail has been eliminated.

The top table in Figure 14-5 is far too complex to be of any use for a speech visual. The simplified, large-print bottom table would work well if made into a transparency.

What is obvious here is that few visuals found in books are satisfactory for use in speaking. So resist the temptation merely to reproduce them. You will usually have to redo them first. You will need to eliminate unneeded material and to provide bold lines and large lettering.

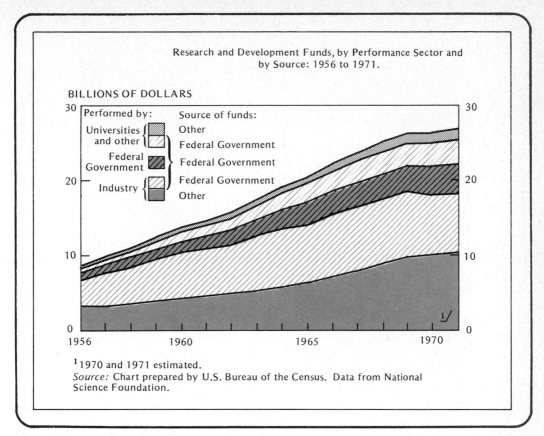

Figure 14-2 Complicated graph.

Control As a speaker, you should control your audience as much as you can. You don't want their minds wandering from you and your speech. Properly made and used visuals can increase audience concentration. They draw attention when you want them to and are invisible when you are through with them. Poorly made visuals distract an audience by drawing attention when you don't want them to.

For instance, large models or mockups of equipment are often excellent visuals. But they have the disadvantage of sitting there on the rostrum like a lump after you are done with them. The audience may stare at them, running over their operation, instead of attending to you. If possible, arrange to have them removed or at least covered when they are not in use.

Small exhibits passed through the audience are deadly for proper audience concentration. Members of the audience get involved in the mechanics of passing them about. They examine them when they receive them,

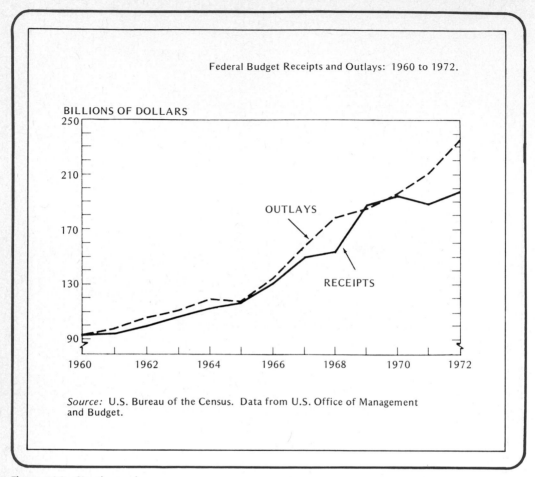

Federal Budget Receipts and Outlays: 1960 to 1972.

BILLIONS OF DOLLARS

OUTLAYS

RECEIPTS

Source: U.S. Bureau of the Census. Data from U.S. Office of Management and Budget.

Figure 14-3 Simple graph.

ignoring the speaker. Passed-around objects are perfect examples of visuals you can't control.

For proper control, then, you should be able to show or remove a visual at will. You'll be even farther ahead if you can easily change it by adding or deleting material.

Visual Tools

You have a wide range of visual tools to choose from—movies, 35mm slides, models, blackboards, flannelboards, and many others. We'll deal here with five such tools, all to be recommended for their effectiveness and ease of use: blackboards, posters, flipcharts, flannelboards, and overhead projectors.

Figure 14-4 Minnesota interstate system. (Minnesota Highway Department, St. Paul)

Blackboards Blackboards have the major advantage of being easy to use. They do not normally require extensive preparation beforehand. They also provide eye-appealing action as you move about, writing and drawing on them. Their major disadvantage is slowness. It takes time to produce your drawings, lists, or whatever on the board. You can, of course, put your visuals on the board *before* you talk. If you do, cover them until you use them and erase them as soon as you are done with them.

Write or print legibly and in large letters. Drawings can be crude but must be understandable. It takes experience to draw and talk at the same time. Do try not to talk to the board exclusively. Remember that you have an audience out there.

In an age of technology the old-fashioned blackboard's effectiveness is

DISTRICT LEVEL (REGIONAL) PROJECTIONS
of Population, Employment and Dwelling Units

Districts	LOCATION	1960			1970			1980			1990			2000		
		Population	Employment	Dwelling Units	Population	Employment	Dwelling Units	Population	Employment	Dwelling Units	Population	Employment	Dwelling Units	Population	Employment	Dwelling Units
52-69	Minneapolis	482,867	274,189	165,791	434,319	290,324	161,080	441,581	307,066	164,455	467,510	313,438	168,061	446,281	312,467	152,279
47	Richfield	42,523	5,554	10,893	47,228	10,328	14,797	44,960	11,547	15,203	38,736	12,525	15,103	45,554	16,027	17,761
48	Airport	898	7,460	150	624	14,888	105	838	22,265	106	884	12,351	106	939	15,554	106
49 & 50	Bloomington	50,498	7,978	12,035	81,961	33,955	21,816	93,555	46,209	28,548	118,424	53,165	37,679	131,655	60,951	45,773
19	Eagan	3,381	94	832	10,398	5,915	2,607	28,042	12,978	8,003	53,291	24,654	16,718	70,594	34,723	23,354
21	Burnsville	2,717	284	664	19,940	2,808	4,876	50,630	11,770	15,000	70,380	18,277	22,380	91,794	24,807	29,726
22	Apple Valley and Rosemount	2,596	1,295	634	12,536	2,834	3,056	19,802	5,563	5,197	34,393	13,246	10,612	52,518	22,225	17,082
24	Lakeville and Farmington	5,346	832	1,503	10,660	1,823	2,937	15,093	4,341	4,500	21,378	7,091	6,500	40,708	12,972	12,781
25	Empire Township	717	203	171	1,136	44	271	4,340	468	963	5,641	18,739	1,248	8,657	23,134	2,395
27	Eureka Township	2,924	4	708	3,453	84	865	6,082	300	1,588	10,464	600	2,882	16,735	1,956	4,815

POPULATION GROWTH

Community	1940	1950	1960	1970
Hennepin Co.	568,890	676,579	842,854	960,080
Dakota Co.	39,660	49,019	78,303	139,808
Apple Valley	—	—	5,143	8,502
Eagan	—	—	3,381	10,398
Burnsville	495	583	2,716	19,940
Bloomington	3,647	9,902	50,498	81,970

Figure 14-5   Two informational tables. (Minnesota Highway Department, St. Paul)

often underrated. It meets the important criterion of control excellently. You don't have to draw your visuals until the moment you need them, you have all eyes on you as you are drawing them, and you can erase them whenever you like.

Posters   Words, drawings, and graphics can be displayed on posters prepared ahead of time. Display the poster itself on an easel. Keep the poster a convenient size: 2 feet wide by 3 feet high is a common dimension. Be sure that all lettering is at least 1 inch high for every 25 feet from your audience. Do not use all capital letters. A normal mixture of capital and lower-case letters is easier to read. Check to be certain that all drawings and graphs are easily visible from the back row.

Posters are controllable and quite effective if you keep their contents visible and simple. Put them on the easel only when you need them. They require a good deal of advance preparation, but the wide range of brightly colored felt-tipped pens available today has speeded up the process considerably.

Flipcharts The flipchart in its simplest form is a large tablet (about 2 feet wide by 3 feet high) *securely* fastened to an easel. When you are through with one page, you flip the page over and reveal the next. When a blackboard is not available, the blank pages of a flipchart can be used instead. Or, if you want to prepare ahead, you can construct each page as you would a poster.

A combination of the two approaches is to draw your visuals lightly on the flipchart before your talk. (If you do it lightly enough, your audience won't see your sketches, but it won't particularly matter if they do.) Then, during your presentation you cover your light lines with bold strokes of a felt-tipped pen. This method effectively combines action with accuracy.

You have good control with a flipchart. Be sure to leave the top page blank, so that you can cover visuals when not using them.

Flannelboards A flannelboard is an inexpensive, effective, easy-to-make visual tool. You make it of fiberboard or light plywood. A good portable size is 3 by 4 feet. Cover the fiberboard or wood with flannel of an unobtrusive color such as light gray, green, or blue. To use it, place the flannelboard on an easel or hang it on a wall. Before your presentation prepare your visuals piece by piece. On pieces of poster cardboard print words or draw sections of a mechanism or whatever. Then back each piece with flannel or medium-grade sandpaper, which will stick to the flannelboard.

During your presentation you develop visuals by placing them piece by piece on the flannelboard. You have excellent control with a flannelboard. It's particularly effective for developing a time or organizational sequence. You place a step of the sequence on the board, discuss it, leave it in place, put up the next step, discuss it, and so forth. You might, for instance, build an entire sequence that ends up looking like Figure 14-6. Building the sequence piece by piece provides good action, draws attention to each new step, and yet allows the flow of the sequence to develop and be visible in its entirety when you are done.

Overhead projectors At the risk of sounding like salesmen for overhead projectors, we have to say that they are probably the most effective visual tool ever devised for speakers. This simple machine that allows you to project transparencies on a screen or wall has numerous advantages.

- *Ease of preparation.* Most of the photo reproduction machines readily found in offices and libraries make transparent copies as well as opaque ones. These transparencies are your visuals. It's so easy to reproduce almost anything for a transparency that you must guard against reproducing inappropriate material, such as pages of small print or complex graphs.

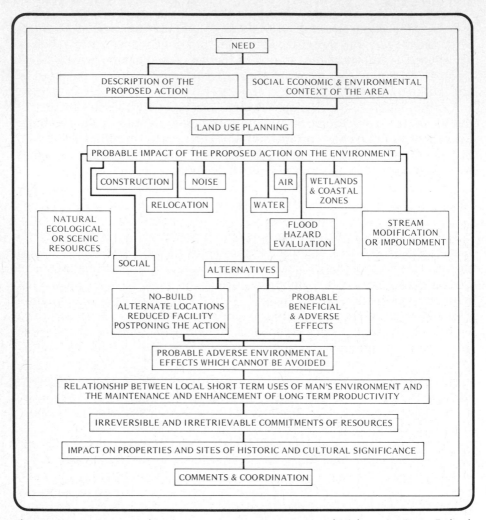

Figure 14-6 Environmental impact statement content. (National Highway Institute, Federal Highway Administration)

- *Ease of operation.* With your projector in the front of the room, you can remain in front of your audience and easily control your own visuals. You lay transparencies directly on the machine in a position that allows you to read them. Turn on the machine, focus the image, and you're in business. There are no trays of slides to jam. Room lights can remain on. You can project on either a light-colored wall or a screen. About the only thing that can go wrong with an overhead projector is a burnt-out light bulb. Keep a bulb handy and know how to change it, and you'll never lose more than a minute or two out of a presentation.

● *Ease of control.* Overhead projectors offer more control over your visuals than any other tool. You can prepare transparencies ahead of time. Or you can put a blank transparency on the projector and use it like a blackboard. You can prepare a transparency partly and finish it with a felt-tipped pen or a crayon while you talk. By sliding a piece of paper around on your transparency, you can reveal as much or as little of your visual as you like. You can prepare other transparencies to superimpose over a first transparency to add material as you go along. You can shut off the entire visual with a flip of a switch.

In preparing your transparencies, keep our criteria in mind. Keep your transparencies visible, simple, and clear. Your projected image must be of sufficient size to be seen in the back row. For printed material this generally means your letters have to be about twice the size of ordinary typewriter print. Many schools and offices now have oversized-print typewriters available. There is a way to use ordinary typewriter print. You can move the projector farther back from the screen or wall and thus enlarge the letters. But by so doing you may lose the option of changing and controlling your own visuals, one of the major advantages of the overhead projector.

A modern overhead projector is small enough that it will seldom block anyone's view. Place it in front of your audience and stand slightly to the side. Face your audience while you talk to them and work with your visuals. You may point to material on the transparency with a pencil. The pencil's shadow will point to the image on the wall. *Always* turn the projector off immediately when you are not using it.

Because of their effectiveness overhead projectors are in use in many schools and businesses. You almost certainly have the opportunity to see them in action. Observe carefully how they are used. Learn what to do from the people who use them well, and what not to do from those who use them poorly.

PERFORMANCE

Let's assume you have made all the preparations we have suggested. You've considered context, purpose, and content. You've organized your speech and either written it or made up a speaking outline for it. You've planned your visuals and integrated them into your speech. You now have only one task left—the performance of the speech itself. And make no mistake about it—standup speaking is a performance. Whether you choose a low-keyed conversational style or a more wide-open orator's style, you're giving a performance. In this section we talk about the preperformance period, the delivery of your speech, and the question-and-answer period that often follows a speech.

Preperformance Period

No matter whether you plan to give your speech from a manuscript or extemporaneously from cards, you must rehearse it. If you can find a sympathetic but critical audience of one or two persons, fine, but rehearse even if it's only in front of a mirror and, if possible, to a tape recorder. Play back the tape and listen critically to your pace and delivery. Listen for effective use of the techniques we'll discuss shortly under Delivery. Timing is critical. Tailor your speech to fit precisely into whatever time is allotted you. Running seriously under or over your allotted time can greatly inconvenience a good many people and gain you nothing but bad marks from your audience. Pay attention to the pronunciation of words. Rehearsal is the time to discover the words that you can't pronounce or that you feel shaky about. Look them up; practice them until you have mastered them. You will know your rehearsals are adequate when you can run through a speech comfortably—on time with no major hesitations and with all the words properly pronounced. You should feel comfortable in your movements and know how you're going to work with your visuals.

On the day of your speech pay some attention to your appearance. Dress for the occasion, whatever it is. Some occasions are shirt-sleeved affairs; others are more formal. But unless there are exceptional circumstances you should be neat and well groomed for your speech. The simple truth is that people feel better about themselves when they feel attractive, and proper dress enhances whatever nature gave us to work with.

Delivery

The moment arrives. You have done all you can to get ready. You are introduced, and it's time to make your way to the front of the audience. For many people this is an absolutely terrifying moment. For others it's a stimulating, enjoyable experience. In either case, however, the right delivery techniques will enable you to do a better job. Specifically, we tell you here about the beginning of a speech, some general techniques, and the ending.

The beginning Rule number one: don't hurry your beginning. Walk slowly to the lectern. Place your manuscript or notes in front of you and arrange them the way you want. Incidentally, don't try to hide the fact that you're speaking from notes or a manuscript. Use them openly. Pause, survey your audience pleasantly. If water is available, pour some and take a sip. All this business may take only twenty seconds, but if you're an inexperienced speaker, it may seem like an hour. This unhurried approach is essential. It gives you time to prepare yourself, and it relaxes your audience. It tells them they are about to listen to a calm, composed individual, and they will be happy for that.

Begin by greeting your audience in whatever manner is appropriate for the occasion. Perhaps a simple "Good evening, ladies and gentlemen" will do. On more formal occasions you may need to acknowledge the person who introduced you and greet important people in the room: "Thank you, Mrs. Robinson, for that kind introduction. President Weaver, Dean Goodding, faculty members, students. . . ."

Now begin firmly and authoritatively with your icebreaker. At this moment your adrenalin will be pouring into your bloodstream. You will be experiencing what physiologists call the fight-or-flight response. You can't fly, so let the response carry you not into fight but into vitality and enthusiasm.

At the beginning of a speech never apologize for conditions or set up a rationale for failure: "Despite having driven over a thousand miles in the pouring rain to be here with you today. . . ." No, have your icebreaker and the rest of your introduction well in hand and get on with your business.

Techniques

The expressions *good vibes* and *bad vibes* are familiar to most young people. When you have good vibes about someone, you feel comfortable and rate the person highly. With bad vibes the reverse is true. Researchers in communication are well aware of good and bad vibes. And they have found that they are produced by very subtle interactions between people. Body motions, or *body language,* and the way peoples' voices sound may be more important in producing good or bad vibes than what is actually being said. For instance, a man may be addressing you as a friend, but the whole tenseness of his body, the stiffness of his neck, may be shouting his hostility toward you. You will instinctively trust what his body says rather than believe his words. A great many politicians have ultimately failed over the years because, say what they would, they were never able to project sincerity through their bodies and voices. So proper body actions and voice sounds are important for success in speaking.

A stiff, motionless speaker comes across as a frightened speaker. Motion is important in convincing people—and even yourself, for that matter—that you are relaxed and assured. Use all the normal body motions while speaking. Shake your head yes and no. Indicate size with your hands and arms. Clench a fist for determination or righteous anger. Point for emphasis. Almost every gesture you would use in normal conversation, perhaps broadened a bit, is appropriate in speaking. Have a mobile face. Smile or frown as you feel like it. Move about the rostrum if you can. The use of visuals is important here; they encourage natural movement as you draw or write or move a poster or transparency.

Eye contact is an important part of body language for two reasons. First, people really don't feel that you're speaking to them unless they feel your eyes on them. They will feel you're insincere if you fail to meet their eyes. Second, if you are really looking at people, you can read *their* body language. You get feedback. People sitting alertly with faces pleasantly composed are giving you positive feedback. You can continue as you are. People slumping down, yawning, or looking away from you are giving you negative feedback. If that happens, don't panic, but recognize that something needs to be changed. The change might be a different speech rate, more motion, or more explanation. If it's a problem you can do something about immediately, do it. Perhaps curing the problem is beyond you for the moment. Then file it away as a lesson for next time. After the speech, analyze what you did wrong and try not to do it again.

The very sound of your voice carries part of your message. Obvious as it may seem, pay attention to whether or not you're being heard. Early in your speech look carefully at the back rows. If people there are frowning, stop and ask them if they can hear you. If not, crank up the volume. Besides volume, you can also control pitch and rate. High pitch and a high rate both suggest excitement and enthusiasm. But too high in either one suggests hysteria. Low pitch and rate suggest confidence and stability. Too low, however, and boredom sets in. Practice varying volume, pitch, and rate to get the effects you want.

Be careful to say your words clearly. A slovenly style of speech tells people you don't care; therefore, why should they care. Avoid what *New Yorker* writer John Davenport labeled "Slurvian." An example of Slurvian is the man who brings his "sweet as surp" wife "flars" for their anniversary. Or some human "beans" go to "Yerp" to visit "forn" countries.[6]

How can we sum all this up? Simply. Stand up straight, move freely, speak loudly and clearly, and look directly at the faces of the people in front of you. If you seem both vital and composed, people will take their cues from you and get good, not bad, vibes.

The ending   As we have said elsewhere, once you suggest you are going to end, end quickly. Have your final summary or quote or whatever firmly in mind or handy on a card so that you won't miss a beat when it's time to conclude. Close firmly, but don't hurry from the rostrum. As you did at the beginning, pause. Hold eye contact with your audience for five seconds. In certain situations applause can be expected and will come. Wait for it and take it standing on the rostrum, not back in your seat. In situations such as a classroom session or a company briefing applause is unlikely. But hold eye contact for five seconds anyway and then look away as you gather up your notes and move from the lectern.

Question-and-Answer Period

In many situations you will have a question-and-answer period following your prepared talk. In some business situations the entire talk, after a brief introduction, could be questions and answers. Sometimes a chairperson

[6]"Slurvian Self-Taught," *The New Yorker* (June 18, 1949): 24.

will take the questions; in other situations you will. In any case be sure everyone in the audience understands the question before you begin your answer. We can sum up what your behavior should be during the question-and-answer period with five C's. You should be courteous, correct, complete, concise, and careful.

Courteous   Give everyone in the audience a fair shake. Look around and answer questions from different parts of the room. Don't get zeroed in on one area or let one person monopolize you. Sometimes questions may indicate hostility to you or your ideas. Don't rise to the bait. Be polite and objective in your answer. But don't take abuse either. If someone is obviously more interested in harassment than information, say something like, "Under the present circumstances, I cannot answer that question objectively," and move on to the next question. Whatever you do, don't play for laughs at the expense of someone who may have innocently asked a foolish question. You embarrass the person needlessly, probably make a lifelong enemy, and lose the rest of the audience.

Correct   Be sure your answers are accurate. Quite frankly, in the excitement of playing expert speakers sometimes get carried away. They make up facts or give dubious answers rather than appear ignorant. Answer a question only if you can do so accurately. If you can't, don't be afraid of saying, "I don't know." Or get the questioner's name and address and promise to send the information. If you do, keep your promise.

Complete and concise   Complete and concise are obviously somewhat in opposition. Answer as fully as time allows and the question deserves. Questions often indicate that major points in your talk have not been understood or, worse, have been misunderstood. Elaborate as needed until you reach a correct understanding. In many situations you would be wise to bring additional material with you for the question-and-answer period—reports, tables, charts, and so forth. Take enough time if you have such material with you to look up the answers needed. Be complete, but keep your eye on the clock. Don't get carried away into a whole new talk. When you really have answered the question, stop.

Careful   Keep your head when answering questions. If you're not careful, you can get trapped into many unhappy situations. Be careful not to be angry or sarcastic. Be careful not to let playing expert lead you into inaccurate answers or into giving authoritative answers to questions outside your field. Be ready to say, "My opinion on that matter would be no better than anyone else's." Be careful not to make elaborate promises to people. In other words, be careful to be courteous, correct, complete, and concise.

SUGGESTIONS FOR APPLYING YOUR KNOWLEDGE

If there is time for it, speaking can be tied into many of the course writing assignments. A sales letter can easily be made into a persuasive talk. Descriptions of processes and mechanisms can be given orally as well as in writing. Proposals are often accompanied by briefings that cover the major points of the proposal. The possibilities are wide.

Often the major report of the term is given orally as well as in writing. Because the major term report is usually based on the information of a specific discipline, it furnishes a good opportunity for cooperation with other departments of your school. Teachers who are experts in the subject matter can be brought into the class to help evaluate the speech. Their presence in the classroom assures a combined audience of experts and nonexperts, a situation common in real life.

Try to go beyond the schoolroom situation of a student speaking to other students. Create a context for the talk, such as a sales meeting, a proposal briefing, a demonstration of a new process or mechanism to its users. Students can even role-play, becoming executives, technicians, members of community groups, and so forth.

Create a real-life situation in other ways. Have a lectern for the speaker. Put out a pitcher of water and some glasses. Invite guests. Schedule time for a question-and-answer period.

Speeches should not be considered complete without visuals. You can create transparencies if an overhead projector is available for their use. Flipcharts, posters, and flannelboards are all easily assembled. A blackboard is almost always available.

Annexes

ANNEX A
Writer's Guide

This annex is a handbook containing a series of little essays on various writing techniques, conventions, and problems. To see a complete list of what it contains, look at the back of the book. We have arranged the handbook alphabetically to make it easier for you to find your way around.

If you're in a writing class, your instructor may use the symbols in the back of the book in marking your papers. In this way your instructor will refer you to entries that should show you how to correct a problem in your paper.

But whether you are in class or not, you can use this handbook to help you with the revision of your writing. Revision is almost the last stage in the writing process. In the first stage you plan your paper and think about its purpose and content. Then you gather your information. With your information in mind you plan an organization for your paper—perhaps based on one of the many kinds of writing we describe in this book. Work in these early stages should be thorough.

In the stage just before revision you write your rough draft. Do the writing quickly. Don't delay to seek the right phrase or the correct spelling. Instead get your thoughts and facts on paper as fast as you can. It's this roughly written draft that you are going to revise. It is no less true for having been said many times: There is no good writing, only good rewriting.

First, check your paper for purpose. Is it clearly stated early in your paper, either explicitly or implicitly? If your paper requires a full-scale introduction, have you clearly defined and limited your subject? Perhaps you are answering a letter of complaint. Is your opening sufficiently friendly? Would it calm a tense situation or make bigger waves?

On into the body of your paper. Have you followed through on your purpose? Does everything in your paper speak to your purpose? Are there any gaps or digressions in your paper where you lose sight of your subject as you have defined and limited it? Are the purpose and subject of your paragraphs clear? Are you sure of all your facts? Are your sentences well structured? Is your diction appropriate to the occasion? For most occupational writing diction should be straightforward and unembellished—well mannered, neither heavy nor slangy. Good writing has a good sound to it. Read your work aloud. Does it sound right? Could you replace some of your writing with graphs or tables?

Be hard on yourself. Everything is for your reader's convenience, not yours. If your paper is faulty, cut it up. Literally, cut it up. Take a scissors to it and try to rearrange it for better organization. Insert better transitions or better-written sentences. For help with some of the decisions you have to make see the entries on Diction, Graphics, Paragraphs, and Sentences.

When you get the big things controlled to your satisfaction, look at some of the smaller things.

Get your dictionary off the shelf and check all those words you are doubtful about. If a word doesn't look right, check it out. If your paper is a typical piece of occupational writing, it probably contains numbers, abbreviations, and quotations. Have you handled them correctly and consistently? Do you have a consistent system for capitalization? Are there grammatical problems you know you have—faulty comma placement or dangling modifiers, for instance?

Now is the time to check anything that may be a fault in your paper. If you have checked the list of what is in this guide, you know we have entries to cover all these things and more. If this is a formal paper, you'll need to construct such things as title pages, tables of contents, and headings. See Annex B, Formal Elements of Reports, for explanations of these matters.

When you are fully satisfied, put your paper in whatever final form is required by the situation or your teacher. Before sending it on its way after it has been typed or whatever, look at it one more time. Proofread it for those little errors that may have slipped through despite all your care. Make whatever corrections are necessary. Then, and only then, send your paper on its way to its readers. And good luck.

ABBREVIATIONS

Abbreviations are much used in business and technical writing. However, they must be used with some care. Remember that abbreviations are primarily for the convenience of the writer. If they are likely to inconvenience the reader, they should not be used. Use without explanation only those abbreviations you are absolutely certain your reader will understand correctly. If you have any doubts at all, spell out the full expression the first time and follow it with the abbreviation in parentheses: *Trunk Highway (TH)*.

Any college-level dictionary will list the abbreviations you are likely to need. In most dictionaries the abbreviation will be listed twice—once as an abbreviation in normal alphabetical order, and once behind the word for which it is an abbreviation.

Guidelines concerning the acceptability of abbreviations vary from place to place, but the following rules are usable unless you have instructions to the contrary.

Accepted Abbreviations

Some abbreviations are generally known and accepted, even preferred, in all writing. The following is a representative list of such abbreviations.

Titles	Dr.		Mrs.
	Mr.		Ms.

(These abbreviated titles are used only before the name, as in *Dr. Smith*. By themselves, of course, titles are spelled out: The *doctor* drove a black car.)

Time	a.m.	B.C.	C.S.T.
	p.m.	A.D.	(Central Standard Time)

Academic degrees	A.A.	M.A.	M.B.A.
	B.A.	M.D.	Ph.D.

In most of your writing you may also abbreviate the names of organizations and countries when the names are long and unwieldy. Be careful to use a standard abbreviation and to spell it out the first time if it is unfamiliar to the reader.

CBS	Columbia Broadcasting System
FBI	Federal Bureau of Investigation
NASA	National Aeronautics and Space Administration
USAF	United States Air Force
U.S.A.	United States of America
U.S.S.R.	Union of Soviet Socialist Republics

Notice that the abbreviations of countries maintain the periods in the abbreviation. The abbreviations for organizations generally do not.

Some commonly known measurements expressed in two or more words are usually abbreviated without periods:

mpg
mph
rpm

Certain common Latin terms if used instead of their English equivalents are always abbreviated:

etc. (and so forth)
e.g. (for example)
i.e. (that is)

Abbreviations Accepted in Specialized Writing

Abbreviations are much more widely used in occupational writing, particularly scientific and technical writing, than in general writing. Measurement terms of two or more words such as *Brinell hardness unit* (Bhn), *British thermal unit* (Btu), and *cubic foot* or *feet* (cu ft) will be abbreviated both in lists and tables and in the textual prose. Business writers will use such abbreviations as *C.O.D.* (collect on delivery) and *F.O.B. (free on board,* meaning the receiver pays the transportation charges).

But even in technical writing some restraint is called for. A page that bristles with abbreviations intimidates the reader and slows understanding. Therefore, many technical writers do not abbreviate one-word measurements, such as *ounce* or *pound,* in their text. However, they may abbreviate them in lists and tables. (See Annex D, Metric Conversion Tables, which includes the abbreviations for many metric measurements.)

Internal consistency is important. Once you abbreviate a term, continue to do so throughout your text. A typical piece of engineering prose might look like this:

> The horizontal and vertical alignment of the highway is consistent with a freeway designed for 70 mph. The maximum mainline curve is 3°00′; steepest mainline gradient is 3%. Maximum speed on the frontage roads will be 30 mph and ramp termini will be designed for 10-second vehicles interval.

Abbreviations to Be Avoided

In any text, general or specialized, there are many abbreviations that you should avoid. We specify *text* because some of these abbreviations are suitable in lists, tables, illustrations, and addresses, where space may be limited.

In your text, you should spell out

Titles Colonel, not Col.
First names Charles, not Chas.
Geographical locations France, not Fr. New York, not N.Y. (Long names such as U.S.S.R. are an exception.)

Geographical terms street, not st.; road, not rd.; mountain, not mt.
Seasons, months, days winter, not wtr.; January, not Jan.; Monday, not Mon.
Common words government, not gov't; Protestant, not Prot.

APOSTROPHE

The apostrophe has three major uses: (1) to form the possessive case of nouns and indefinite pronouns; (2) to replace omitted letters and numerals; and (3) to form the plurals of numerals, letters, and symbols.

Forming the Possessive

To form the possessive of nouns and indefinite pronouns that do not already end in *s*, add an apostrophe and an *s*.

John's friend	anybody's guess
the umpire's call	another's child
the year's end	anyone's desire
my wife's traveling	neither's question

Pronouns other than the indefinite pronouns form the possessive without an apostrophe: *he-his, she-her-hers, it-its, you-your-yours, who-whose,* etc.

To form the possessive of words that already end in an *s*, add an apostrophe only.

The girls' hats were blue.
Jones' winning pleased everyone.
Moses' leadership was powerful.
The three countries' flags were raised.

Replacing Letters and Numerals

In contractions we omit letters, and in numerical expressions we sometimes omit numerals. In both these uses the apostrophe replaces the missing element.

He doesn't work here now.
It's Mary at the door.
He graduated in '72.

Forming Plurals

Use the apostrophe and an *s* to form the plural of letters, numerals, and symbols.

Omitted is spelled with one *m* and two *t*'s.
The 1930's were depression years.
There are four +'s in that equation.

This use of the apostrophe is for clarity—to prevent someone, for example, from confusing *a*'s with *as*.

BRACKETS

Brackets are limited to almost a single use—inserting material of your own into a quoted passage. Such insertion is sometimes necessary for various reasons: (1) to add a date or fact not obvious from the passage; (2) to indicate by the use of *sic* an error of fact or usage in the original and therefore not your error; or (3) to straighten out the syntax of a sentence you may have disturbed through the use of ellipsis (see entry on Ellipsis Points). Brackets are the accepted signal to the reader that the inserted material is not part of the original. Therefore, do not use parentheses for this purpose.

Most typewriters do not have a key for brackets, so you'll probably have to ink them in neatly. (Remember to leave space for them.) You can also make them by a combination of diagonals and underscoring.

> I was encouraged to engage in others [partnerships] . . . on the same terms with that in Carolina.
> He fell to erth [*sic*] from a plane.

CAPITALIZATION

Rules for capitalization vary from organization to organization, but the following general rules are fairly standard.

Proper Nouns

Capitalize proper nouns and the words that derive from them.

People   Charles Darwin, Darwinism
Geographic entities   England, English, Minnesota, Minnesotans, East 40th Street, the Ohio River, Mount Everest
Languages   French, Russian, Swahili
Religious terms   God (He), the Bible, the Old Testament, Protestant, Catholic, Judaism, Jews, Jewish, Muslim
Days of week   Monday, Tuesday
Months   January, February
Holidays   Easter, Independence Day
Specific buildings   Empire State Building
Organizations   United States Senate, United Nations, United States Air Force (USAF), American Legion
Certain historical terms   Magna Carta, Constitution, Revolutionary War, Renaissance
Brand names   Chevrolet, Polaroid, Ivory Snow, Xerox
Companies   International Business Machines (IBM)
Course titles   Scientific and Technical Writing
Ships   *U.S.S. San Pablo*

Titles of Books, Articles, Plays, Movies

Capitalize the first and last word of every title. Capitalize all other words *except* prepositions of fewer than five letters, articles, and conjunctions.

Maxims and Instructions from the Boiler Room
"Getting Inside Your Camera"
"What's a Camera For?"

Official Titles

Capitalize an official title when you place it before a person's name or use it to refer to a specific person.

Congresswoman Smith
Colonel Peter R. Moody
The President is in his office.

Do not capitalize a title used in a general way.

Most professors enjoy teaching.

See also entries for Colon and Quotation Marks.

COLON

The colon is a mark of introduction. You can use it to introduce quotations (particularly long inset quotations) and lists.

Quotations

The Environmental Impact Statement for I-35E clarifies the impact on wetlands as follows:

The most significant impact to water resources would be the direct displacement of wetlands. Of approximately 2,300 acres of wetlands in the study area, 28 acres would fall within the corridor of the proposed action and would be filled or altered.

Lists

There will be three final steps: a location-design hearing, a final EIS, and a Design Study Report.

The Metropolitan Council's long-range planning indicates that expansion of the urban service limit should involve the following areas:

—Existing urban service area
—Addition to the urban service area, 1975–80
—Freestanding growth centers

Do not place a colon between a verb or a preposition and the objects that follow. Both the colons in the following examples are INCORRECT and should be removed:

The three steps are: a location-design report, a final EIS, and a Design Study Report.
Public hearings have been scheduled for: Apple Valley, Eagan, and Mendota.

Place no punctuation at all after the verb or preposition:

Public hearings have been scheduled for Apple Valley, Eagan, and Mendota.

Following colons you may use a capital or a lower-case letter. Generally, a complete sentence would start with a capital, a subordinate clause or a phrase with a lower-case letter.

Conventional Uses of the Colon

Dear Mr. Rose:
6:22 p.m.
8:4:1 (expression of a proportion)

COMMA

Commas have so many uses that it's little wonder people despair of using them correctly. In this elementary guide we'll keep things as simple as we can and still cover the major rules.

Compound Sentences

When two independent clauses are joined by a coordinating conjunction (*and, but, for, nor, or,* and *yet*), use a comma before the conjunction:

Building the highway on the present alignment would have little impact on the north bluffs, but building it on the new alignment would create a severe impact.

See also the entries for Run-on Sentences and Semicolon.

Introductory Elements

We begin about 25 percent of our sentences with an introductory word, phrase, or subordinate clause. After such an introductory element, a comma is *never* wrong:

Unfortunately, the bridge will be seen as a man-made object.
Of the 36 Indian mounds, only 12 are well preserved.
As speed increases, foreground details fade rapidly.

Sometimes, when the introductory element is short, you would not be incorrect if you omitted this comma. Do so with care, however. Make sure you don't cause your reader to overread. Look at the following sentence:

Because foreground objects do not block viewing, bridge structures can provide an opportunity for outstanding vistas.

Remove the comma after *viewing* and readers will mistakenly read that the bridge structures are being viewed. When they realize their error, they have to back up and begin again.

Unless you're quite sure of what you're doing, you may want to use the comma always after introductory elements. Be careful, however, not to confuse a long, complete subject for an introductory element. This error could cause you to put a comma incorrectly between subject and verb. You would want no punctuation at all at the spot we have marked with brackets in the example:

Planned recreational development of the area[ ] includes a river valley trail system.

You may, of course, have a parenthetical element between the subject and the verb that would call for two commas, one on each side of the element:

This game refuge, as proposed, would cross the entire area.

Final Elements

Subordinate clauses or phrases that follow a main clause present more of a problem than do introductory elements. Generally, if they are not closely tied to the thought of the main clause, they are preceded by a comma. Definitely use a comma when the final element presents a turn of thought:

Railroads and highways have contributed to the area's urbanization, although much of the area is still undeveloped.

However, when the final element is closely tied into the preceding main clause, you are better off without a comma:

The highway will cross Indian mounds that have already been disturbed.

In this sentence the clause beginning with *that* is essential to the thought; therefore, a comma is not wanted. Reading aloud will usually help in this situation. If you pause before the final element while reading aloud, it's a good sign that a comma is needed.

Parenthetical and Interrupting Elements

When a word, phrase, or clause is parenthetical to the main thought of the sentence or interrupts the flow of the sentence, set commas around it:

The cultural features, mainly Indian mounds, are to the west of the highway.

The inserted phrase, *mainly Indian mounds,* adds information to the sentence, of course, but it's an aside. It interrupts the flow of the main clause. See also the entries for Dash and Parentheses.

The phrase *of course* is usually set off by commas. So are the conjunctuve adverbs such as *consequently, however, nevertheless, therefore,* etc.

The bridge is so high, of course, to allow river traffic to pass underneath.
However, the most expansive vistas are to the east.

Nonrestrictive Modifiers

Nonrestrictive modifiers are set apart from the rest of the sentence by commas. Restrictive modifiers are not. Sometimes, determining which is which is a puzzle.

A restrictive modifier is essential to the meaning of the sentence. For instance:

The design choices *for the Cedar Avenue Bridge* are all costly.

The italicized modifier defines and identifies which design choices, among all the possible design choices the writer could be talking about, are meant. The writer is not talking about the design choices for the Brooklyn Bridge or the Golden Gate Bridge. The writer is talking specifically and exclusively about the design choices for the Cedar Avenue Bridge. The modifier is therefore *restrictive*—it is essential to the meaning of the sentence. Look now at a nonrestrictive modifier:

> Old Shakopee Road, *which is a two-lane asphalt highway with narrow shoulders,* will be obsolete by 1986.

In this case the italicized modifier adds important and useful information, but it is not essential to the sentence. The road's name provides the limits or restrictions needed: It's not any road; it's the Old Shakopee Road. Therefore, the modifier is *nonrestrictive*.

If in doubt, try reading your sentence aloud. You will probably pause quite naturally at the breaks around nonrestrictive modifiers. These pauses are your clue to insert commas. See also the entries for Dash and Parentheses.

Series

Commas are the normal punctuation used when you are constructing a series:

> This seepage emerges as natural springs that feed *tributary streams, lakes, and marshes.*
>
> The components of the recreation system range from *mini-parks, neighborhood playgrounds, and community playfields* to *multipurpose parks, park reserves, and historic parks.*

For lists with internal punctuation see the entry for Semicolon.

Conventional Uses

The comma is the conventional mark of punctuation in several situations.

Informal salutation	Dear Dave,
Dates	November 13, 1959 is my . . . .
	(But *13 November 1959* and *November 1959* are both written without commas.)
Addresses	1269 River Valley Drive, Eagan, Indiana, is . . . .
Titles and degrees	Charles E. Norad, Department Head, is . . . .
	Charles E. Norad, M.D., is . . . .

DASH

The dash is essentially a mark of separation. On a typewriter a dash is made with two unspaced hyphens:

```
    For all three models--XL, XM, XN--you have your
choice of over forty lenses.
```

The dash is a rather peculiar but also rather useful mark of punctuation—so long as it is not overused. It is peculiar because it can be substituted for many other marks of punctuation, particularly the comma and parentheses. And, of course, it's this peculiarity that makes it useful.

When substituted for a comma, the dash indicates that the writer meant to be emphatic about the separation:

> The table lists the total acres of wetlands within the project—all of which would be eliminated.

Placing dashes around parenthetical material indicates a degree of formal separation greater than the comma would indicate and lower than parentheses:

> Several protective measures—wood fiber mats, mulches, and special seed mixtures—will prevent erosion.

You may also use the dash to emphasize items in a list or occasionally rather than a colon to introduce a list:

Several anti-erosion measures are available:
—wood fiber mats
—mulches
—special seed mixtures
—berms and dikes

> Several anti-erosion measures are available—wood fiber mats, mulches, special seed mixtures, and berms and dikes.

The dash's versatility may tempt you to overuse it. It would quickly lose its emphatic value if you substituted it too freely for other marks. Used discreetly it's a useful—even powerful—mark of punctuation.

DICTION

You have good diction when you choose words and expressions suitable to the occasion and express your thoughts as simply and clearly as possible.

Most people recognize that words suitable for some occasions are not suitable for others. The happy slang of locker rooms and poker games would be inappropriate in an annual business report. A paragraph from an annual report on student housing, for instance, reads this way:

> Dormitories were full and dorm waiting lists long as students began fall classes this year. More than 250 students were waiting to be assigned rooms. In some instances, students were temporarily housed in local hotels and motels.

The language is simple and serious and quite adequate to the occasion of the report. It's neither slangy nor heavy and pompous. Don't let the desire to be more formal lead you into windy pomposities like *viable interface* and *at this point in time* or tired clichés like *grim reality* or *Mother Nature*.

Your cleaned-up everyday language supported by whatever professional vocabulary both you and your readers need and understand will probably serve you well. You don't have to *ascertain reality* to write formally. *Finding out the facts* will serve just as well.

Your ear, as it is so often in writing, is a good guide. Read your work aloud. If it *sounds* foolish or pompous, it probably is. If you're sure you would not *say* something the way you have written it, don't write it that way either.

Faulty diction can also be caused by a lack of precision in choosing the words needed to express your thoughts. You may be *communicating* when *talking* is the more precise word. You may have confused *enormity* with *enormousness*. Perhaps you wrote the nonstandard *irregardless* for *regardless*. Perhaps you used *good* as in "Johnny played good" instead of "Johnny played well." You may have windily talked about *factors* when what is needed are some specific words to express what the factors really are.

You won't learn about good diction by reading about it. Rather you learn it by reading and listening to people who have it and by practicing what you have learned. And don't forget your dictionary—*diction* is its first name. (See also pages 88–97.)

ELLIPSIS POINTS

Ellipsis points consist of three or four spaced periods. They have several uses in occupational writing.

Use ellipsis points to indicate you have omitted something from a quoted passage. Use four periods rather than three when the omission comes at the end of the sentence, the fourth period being the period of the sentence. For example, the preceding sentence could be quoted as follows:

> Use four periods . . . when the omission comes at the end of the sentence. . . .

Notice we have removed supplemental material from the sentence but have been careful not to change its meaning.

On occasion you might use ellipsis points to substitute for *and so forth* or *etc.*:

> After the semicolon you often see one of the conjunctive adverbs: *consequently, however, therefore.* . . .

In a brochure or ad you might use ellipsis points as an emphatic mark of separation between statements:

> Be sure to get your copy. . . . ORDER NOW. . . . Mail the coupon below with your check or money order for the full amount.

EXCLAMATION POINT

The exclamation point is placed after a statement to emphasize the statement. Its presence indicates the information in the statement is particularly impressive, unusual, or emotional.

> The project engineer recommended the building site despite knowing it was unsafe!

If you don't have an exclamation point on your typewriter, make it with an apostrophe over a period.

The exclamation point has very limited use in occupational writing. Use it sparingly, and certainly never use more than one after a statement.

FRAGMENTARY SENTENCES

If you inadvertently punctuate a piece of a sentence as a complete sentence, you have written a fragmentary sentence. Fragmentary sentences most often lack a complete verb or are introduced by a relative pronoun or a subordinating conjunction.

Incomplete Verb

> The glaciers forming three striking and different natural features.

Correct this sentence by correcting the verb:

> The glaciers formed three striking and different natural features.

Relative Pronouns

The relative pronouns are *who, that, what, which, whoever, whatever,* and sometimes *as.* They signal that the clause they introduce needs to be connected to a complete sentence. When you make this connection, you have corrected the error.

> **Incorrect** The Minnesota River is an underfit river. That is too small for its valley.
>
> **Correct** The Minnesota River is an underfit river that is too small for its valley.

Subordinating Conjunctions

Subordinating conjunctions, as the name implies, connect a subordinate clause with a main clause. Therefore, their presence at the beginning of clauses marks the clauses as subordinate and unable to stand alone. Common subordinating conjunctions are *after, although, because, since, though, unless,* and *when.*

As with the relative clause, the answer here is to join the subordinate clause to the main clause.

Incorrect	Although the area is largely undeveloped. It does have some light industry.
Correct	Although the area is largely undeveloped, it does have some light industry.

Sometimes writers will deliberately write fragmentary sentences to gain some special effect. In the following example the writer attempts to catch the feeling of conversation:

Unbelievable? Not really. In *Highway to Life* you'll find out how modern, safe, multilane divided highways are reducing traffic fatalities by as much as 90 percent. For instance. . . .

The source of the example is an advertising letter where such use is appropriate. But use such devices with care, and be sure your deliberate use is so obvious it can't be mistaken for an error.

GRAPHICS

Graphs and tables play an important role in occupational writing. Whenever you have statistical data to present, consider presenting it graphically. Graphical presentation is particularly useful when you need to show comparisons and trends. We have integrated discussions of graphs and tables into our chapters in the places where we felt they would be the most useful to you. However, our major discussions of them are on pages 4–6, 119–124, 144–145, 199–201, 237–245, and 308–318.

HYPHEN

Hyphens are used in word division and in numbers. For these two uses see the entries for Word Division and Numbers.

In this entry we are concerned with the use of the hyphen to combine two or more words to make them function as one word. Some publisher's or newspaper style manuals devote dozens of pages to the use of the hyphen. We suspect that madness lies in that direction. We'll attempt to simplify matters by considering hyphens used in compound words and in compound modifiers.

Compound Words

In English we form many new words by compounding two existing words as in *wristband, wrist-drop,* and *wrist shot.* We experience no trouble in speaking such compounds, but we do have problems as soon as we attempt to write them. As our three examples rather maddeningly demonstrate, sometimes they're written as one word, sometimes hyphenated, sometimes as two words. There are no rules observed uniformly enough to be much help to us here. And most of us are not going to keep such fine distinctions in our heads.

What's the answer? When the piece of writing you are doing is important—perhaps a report or a letter of application—use your dictionary if you're not absolutely sure of the spelling. There is really no other way.

Compound Modifiers

Compound modifiers are obviously compound words also, but here our problems are eased some. Most compound modifiers, whether in the dictionary or of our own concocting, are hyphenated when used *before* the words they modify. Thus we'll see

> a coarse-grained texture
> a close-mouthed man
> a light-blue coat
> the ready-to-go-to-college woman

In informal writing we might see all of these examples and similar modifiers written without the hyphen. But in occupational writing it's a good idea to use the hyphen to avoid confusion. Take the example of *light-blue coat*. A *light-blue coat* is light in color. A *light, blue coat* is light in weight. If the hyphens were omitted, consider the possibilities for confusion in *new-house owner, used-car buyer,* and *pink-skinned pig.*

Note that we have specified that a compound modifier is hyphenated when it is placed *before* the word it modifies. In constructions where the modifier appears as a predicate adjective—that is, after a linking verb—it is usually not hyphenated:

> For the ready-to-go-to-college woman . . . .
> For the woman who is ready to go to college . . . .

If in doubt about the hyphenation of compound words, whether they are used as modifiers or not, consult your dictionary. If you don't find an entry for the compound, use your own good judgment and the principles we have given you here. Remember, your goal is to avoid confusing the reader.

ITALICS

In print, italics are a special typeface, like this: *Modern Photography.* When you type or write you italicize by underlining:

> Modern Photography

Italics (or underlining) have several conventional uses.

Emphasis

You can emphasize a word or several words by italicizing them:

> Do not place a colon between a verb or a preposition and the objects that follow.

Like all emphatic devices, italics quickly lose their value if you overuse them.

Foreign Words

We frequently incorporate foreign words into English. When they have been completely accepted—like "rendezvous," for instance—we do nothing to make them stand out. But if they are still considered exotic, we italicize them:

> The officer in charge of a firing squad has the unpleasant task of giving the *coup de grâce*.

If in doubt about how to handle a word, use your dictionary. Its entry for the word will indicate whether or not you should italicize it.

Italicize the scientific terms for things:

> American chars belong to the genus *Salvelinus*.

Words as Words

When you use words as words and letters as letters, italicize them to prevent reader misunderstanding. There are frequent examples of such uses in this book, for instance:

> *Omitted* is spelled with one *m* and two *t*'s.

Titles

Italicize the titles of books, journals, magazines, newspapers, films, and TV programs:

> *The Compact Edition of the Oxford English Dictionary*
> *Newsweek*
> *Wide World of Sports*

MISPLACED AND DANGLING MODIFIERS

Modifiers are words, phrases, or clauses that limit or restrict other words, phrases, or clauses. "Green" modifying "coat" limits the coat to that color. "The bridge that fell down" can't be a bridge that remained standing. "A boy moving downhill" can't at the same time also be a boy moving "uphill." For the most part we all use modifiers with little difficulty, seldom thinking about them. But if we become careless in their placement, we can create sentences that can be vague or misunderstood or, on occasion, accidentally funny.

Modifiers that are in the wrong position to modify the words the writer intended to modify are called *misplaced*. Modifiers that have nothing in the sentence to modify are called *dangling*.

Misplaced Modifiers

To correct a misplaced modifier, place it as close as possible to the words it modifies. Let's look at some examples:

The report about the resident students *of July 6, 1976,* reached me today.

Here the italicized modifier is located properly to modify "students" but incorrectly to modify "report." If "report" is to be modified, move the phrase:

The report of *July 6, 1976,* about the resident students reached me today.

Another example:

Many researchers are attempting to identify factors that contribute to student development *in residential college life.*

If we move the italicized modifier, we have quite a different statement:

Many researchers are attempting to identify factors *in residential college life* that contribute to student development.

Obviously, you the writer are in charge of the sentence. Get the modifier next to the words modified and say exactly what you mean.

Dangling Modifiers

Unlike misplaced modifiers, which modify the wrong word, dangling modifiers have nothing to modify:

Analyzing change during the first year of college, students who lived at home participated in fewer extracurricular activities.

At first impression this sentence leads us to believe that the students were analyzing change. But the sentence doesn't make sense that way. Looking at the sentence again, we realize that the word meant to be modified by the italicized modifier is not in the sentence. Let's say the missing word is "she." We can now correct the sentence:

Analyzing change during the first year of college, *she found* that students who lived at home participated in fewer extracurricular activities.

Any time you begin a sentence with a phrase of the type represented by "Analyzing change" or "To analyze change," be alert. Be sure you include the words you intend to modify.

NUMBERS

The point at issue in writing numbers is whether they are written as a figure (26) or a word (twenty-six). The rules we give you are generally, though not universally, accepted. Whether you use these rules or others, be consistent throughout any piece of work.

Figures

Most style and usage books call for a number to be written as a figure in the following instances.

Addresses   1262 Pater Road, Dayton, OH 45419
Dates   July 27, 1976 *or* 27 July 1976
Time (with a.m. or p.m.)   6:20 p.m.
Exact sums of money with $ or ¢ $106.52, 26¢
References to pages, figures, etc.   Page 6. See Figure 10.
Units of measurement   10 meters, 20 amperes, 42 feet, 9 tons
Identifying numbers   His telephone number is (212) 626-6934.
His social security number is 010-18-7806.
Decimals   6.42 kilometers, 3.5 liters
Percentages   61 percent, 61%
Fractions connected to whole numbers   42⅛, 6 5/6
Tables and illustrations   For reasons of space and clarity all numbers in tables and illustrations are normally written as figures:

Table 3. Historical Population Growth

Area	1870	1920	1950	1960	1970	1975
Apple Valley	216	361	377	5,143	8,502	15,315
Burnsville	361	419	583	2,716	19,940	31,274
Eagan	670	857	1,185	3,381	10,398	17,686
Mendota Heights	444	757	2,107	5,028	6,168	7,258
Study Area Totals	1,691	2,394	4,252	16,268	45,008	71,533
Metro Area Totals	109,340	759,518	1,185,694	1,523,956	1,874,380	2,031,000

Source: U.S. Bureau of Census

Words or Figures

The general trend in business and technical prose is to use figures more than words. However, there are still some instances where a word is preferred or an option.

Numbers over 10   In most business and technical prose all numbers under 10 are written as words, and numbers 10 and over are written as figures:

We have three choices in how to cross the valley.
Only 36 Indian mounds are well preserved.

Large numbers are written with commas every three numerals, counting from the right:

3,126,400,000

If numbers under and over 10 are linked together in a series, write them all as figures:

> Historical sites in the area include 36 Indian mounds, 2 Indian villages, and 3 pioneer cemeteries.

Numbers over 100   Contrary to the previous rule, some organizations and publications write textual numbers under 100 as words and over 100 as figures. Under this system, hyphenate the two-word numbers between twenty-one and ninety-nine. If numbers under and over 100 are linked in a series, all are written as figures.

> Only thirty-six Indian mounds are well preserved.
> In 129 historical sites, only 36 Indian mounds are well preserved.

Approximate numbers   Very often, numbers used in an approximate way are written as words, regardless of their size. The notion is that written as a figure the number might imply an exactness that is not meant:

> The bookstore sold over three thousand hand calculators during the fall term alone.

Numbers at beginnings of sentences   Do not write any number that begins a sentence as a figure. This is a sensible rule. In certain circumstances a hurried reader might connect the number to the period of the preceding sentence and so read the number as a decimal. If writing the number as a word will be cumbersome, rework the sentence:

> Five hundred and ten insurance policies were sold in September.
> In September, 510 insurance policies were sold.

Fractions   Fractions connected to whole numbers are always written as figures:

> 42⅛, 6 5/6

Small fractions are often written as words; if the fraction stands alone, write it as an unhyphenated compound:

> one fourth
> two thirds

Hyphenate a fraction written as an adjective:

> one-third speed

If the numerator or denominator of a fraction already is hyphenated, omit the hyphen between the parts:

> forty-two thousandths

This last circumstance will seldom occur because such large fractions are usually expressed as decimals.

Time (with o'clock)   We normally use the term *o'clock* only with the hour. And we generally write the hour as a word:

eleven o'clock

Compound-number adjectives   In occupational writing you frequently have two numbers functioning together as a compound adjective. When such is the case, to avoid confusion write one as a number, one as a word:

3 two-lane highways
two 12-foot driving lanes

Be very careful about hyphenating number adjectives. There's considerable difference between *100 gallon drums* and *100-gallon drums*. In fact, it would be far safer to write the first as *100 one-gallon drums*.

OUTLINES

Writers use many individual techniques to organize a paper, but almost all of them go through some sort of planning process. The intent of the process is to break down the main body of material into its major parts, and then the major parts into their subparts. (For a summary of often-used organizational patterns for both writing and speech, see pages 231–234.)

We can't honestly say that most writers end their organizing with a rigid formal outline. Most do not.* Many writers feel that rigidity and creativity do not go together. A writer's feelings in these matters are probably justified when no one else is to see the rough outline except the writer. But often a writer's plans have to be shared—with a coauthor, for example, or, if the writer is a student, with an instructor. In such instances a formal, easy-to-follow outline may be useful or even necessary.

To help you construct a formal outline, we present here an outline of a report you can see in final form in Figure 13-4, pages 216–220. To emphasize the rules of outlining, we have annotated the typewritten outline with notes in regular type and followed it with a few comments.

Sample Outline

Peer Advising Proposal   Title

The purpose of this report is to request funding
for a peer advising program to be established for
Criminal Justice Studies students. The report will be

---

*For a discussion of how professional technical writers go about organizing and outlining, see Blaine McKee's "Do Professional Writers Use an Outline When They Write?" *Technical Communication* (First Quarter 1972): 10–13.

sent to Janice H. Grumbacher, Director of The Center
for Educational Development. Purpose and audience
statement

I. Methodology 1st-level head, capital roman numerals
   A. Creation of peer advising unit 2nd-level head, capital letters

   B. Duties of unit No punctuation needed after any head

   C. Evaluation of unit

II. Work and management plan Capitalize only first letter of all heads and proper nouns

   A. Facilities
   B. Task breakdown
      1. Training 3rd-level heads, arabic numerals
      2. Office hours
      3. Evaluation
      4. Management
         a. Supervision 4th-level heads, lower-case letters
         b. Reporting

III. Detailed budget
   A. Training time
   B. Office hours
   C. Evaluation time

IV. Personnel
   A. Martin A. Doyle
   B. William Morrell

Comments

- Normally, you don't include heads in the outline for your introduction or conclusion. The organization of the body of your report is what concerns you. Some version of your purpose and audience statement is likely to end up in your introduction, however.
- Make your heads statements of substance. That is, use words that will give the reader of your outline a true idea of your material. Heads such as "Cause 1," "Cause 2" or "Example 1," "Example 2" are of little use.
- Put parallel heads into parallel grammatical form. (See also the entry for Parallelism.) All parallel heads must have the same phrase struc-

ture. They must all be noun phrases, for example, and not a mixture of noun phrases and infinitive phrases. Use whatever phrase structure best suits your needs, but stick to it. Our sample outline uses parallel structures. An example of IMPROPER form would be

A. Creation of unit
B. To accomplish duties of unit
C. How to evaluate the unit

- Logically, you can't divide anything without ending up with at least two pieces. This rule of logic holds true in outlining. Don't put just one subhead under any other head; you must have at least two. An outline entry like the following would be INCORRECT:

4. Management
   a. Supervision

If you have I, you must have II; if an A, you must have a B; and so forth.

PARAGRAPHS

A typical paragraph is a central statement followed by opinions and facts that relate to or support the central statement—as in this example:

Saint Anthony Falls, the only major cataract on the Mississippi and the original reason for the existence of Minneapolis, is the focal point of this historic district. Father Louis Hennepin, the first European to see the falls, viewed it and named it in 1680. In 1823, soldiers from the recently established Fort Snelling harnessed its power for grist and lumber mills. The first dam was built in 1847, the first big sawmill in 1848. Within another 10 years, four flour mills were in operation, and Minneapolis was on its way to national leadership in both lumber and flour milling.

Generally, the central statement comes first in the paragraph, as it does in this example. In this position it fulfills two jobs: It introduces the paragraph and provides necessary transition from the preceding paragraph.
Sometimes, however, the central statement may be placed last:

A check of auto-deer collisions recorded by the Department of Natural Resources within the Study Area showed 60 auto-killed deer in 1973 and 64 in 1974. Several locations had a high incidence of deer-auto collisions. These locations are within linear bands of vegetation extending from the river valley to various woodlots and agricultural fields within the Study Area. Deer follow these vegetational bands in their movements between the valley and the higher ground. The proposed highway bisects several of these bands. Therefore, it seems likely that auto-deer accidents will continue and perhaps increase.

Placing the central statement last is useful in persuasion. You allow the facts to convince the reader before you draw the conclusion. It's a device to be used sparingly, however. Used too often, it can leave readers wondering why they have to plow through so many facts without proper guidance.

Paragraphs come in many lengths. On occasion a paragraph may be used as a transition between longer units. Such a paragraph might be only a sentence or two long. On the other hand, a fully developed paragraph in a scholarly book might be 250 words long.

Paragraphs also vary in length depending upon where they are going to appear. Paragraphs in newspapers run about 50 words long, in magazines about 100 words. These lengths relate to the narrowness of the columns being used. Newspaper and magazine editors don't want long columns of print without a break. Therefore, they break the paragraphs at fairly slight shifts of thought. Nonfiction books of a general nature have paragraphs that run 100–150 words long. Probably for most occupational reports an average of about 100 words per paragraph would be appropriate. In typed work this would be about 2½ paragraphs to a page.

Paragraphs run shorter in letters and memos than in printed work. A one-page letter that was all one paragraph would look hard to read. Therefore, paragraphs in letters and memos may run only two or three sentences long—sometimes only one sentence.

Think of paragraphing as a way of guiding your reader through your material. Well-constructed paragraphs help the reader to spot your generalizations, usually the key to your organization. And, normally, your generalizations are your major statements—the ideas and opinions you want your reader to retain. And don't forget the visual impact of paragraphing. Large blocks of unbroken print may frighten off the reader. But too-short paragraphs may suggest a lack of organization. A middle road of paragraphs of varying lengths will probably present most material best.

PARALLELISM

When you start a series of sentence elements that serve the same function, put them into the same grammatical form. For instance, you will use many lists in occupational writing. Place all the elements of the list in the same form, as in this example:

Always consider the following factors in designing an exhibit:
—Distance of viewers from exhibit
—Average viewing time
—Material to be used
—Lighting conditions
—Visual acuity of viewers

In this example each item on the list is based upon a noun—*distance, time, material,* and so on. The writer would have had faulty parallelism if he had switched his grammatical forms, as in this faulty list:

—Distance of viewers from exhibit
—To consider viewing time
—What material should be used?

In this faulty list we go from a noun phrase to an infinitive phrase to a complete clause.

Use any grammatical form in your lists that is convenient for you. But stick to the same form throughout.

We have many paired constructions in English such as *both . . . and . . . ; either . . . or . . . ; neither . . . nor . . . ; not . . . but . . . ;* and *not only . . . but also . . .* that call for parallel forms after each part of the pair. Look at this example:

Design your exhibit *either for* a technically skilled audience *or for* the general public.

Both elements are based upon prepositional phrases and are correctly parallel. You would have faulty parallelism with this next structure:

Design your exhibit *either for* a technically skilled audience *or to please* the general public.

Here the parallelism breaks down with the introduction of the infinitive phrase *to please* in the second element.

In most compound sentences you'll be wise to keep both clauses in the same voice—active or passive (see the entry for Sentences). In this example both sides of the compound sentence are in active voice:

People want to excel, construct, and imitate; and they seek pleasure, recognition, friends, and security.

The reader would be disturbed if we switched to passive voice in the second clause:

People want to excel, construct, and imitate; and pleasure, recognition, friends, and security are sought by them.

The following pair of main clauses reads easily despite their length (thirty-six words) because all the elements in both clauses are carefully balanced:

Speeding drivers passing a billboard off the highway will be able to read nine words at most, but slow-moving students passing a sign in a cafeteria line will be able to read several hundred words.

Any time you have elements in any kind of series, take a hard look at them. Be sure you have them in parallel grammatical form.

PARENTHESES

Of the three marks of punctuation used to enclose parenthetical material (commas, dashes, and parentheses), parentheses are the heaviest. They separate the inserted material more definitely and can enclose longer elements—up to several sentences, if necessary—than the other marks. Look at several examples. Pay particular attention to the punctuation:

Norway spruce (*Picea abies*), a native of Europe, is similar to white spruce in most characteristics.

The model tree would have a straight central stem, normal taper (forming a cone the base of which is 70 to 80% of its height), and foliage that would be progressively less dense going from the bottom of the tree to the topmost whorl.

The primary purpose of shaping is to control height and width and to develop uniform taper. (Other purposes are to correct deformities, remove multiple leaders, and to prune lower branches to form a handle and a complete base whorl.) A variety of tools may be used in the shaping process.

Parentheses can be used to enclose any parenthetical material—scientific names, abbreviations, definitions, figure and page references, etc. The decision of what to enclose is really yours. Remember that there is a subjective limit, however. Too many parentheses, or too much material within parentheses, will distract the reader.

Notice how punctuation works with parentheses:

- Place no punctuation before the first parenthesis.
- Delay any punctuation needed after the last word before the first parenthesis until after the second parenthesis.
- Use any capitalization and punctuation required by the sentence structure inside the parentheses.
- Use no special punctuation around parentheses placed between sentences.

A special conventional use of parentheses is to enclose figures or letters used in lists:

The two main steps in shearing any species with a regular whorled branching habit are (1) regulation of the terminal whorl and (2) clipping or shearing of the side branches.

See also the entries for Comma, Brackets, and Dash.

PERIOD

Periods have several conventional uses illustrated below:

Abbreviations   Mr., etc., Jr.
Decimal point   .00236, $13.45
End stop   He bought the farm.
Initials   John H. Doyle
Leaders   A series of spaced periods to lead the eye are sometimes used in tables and tables of contents:

TABLE OF CONTENTS

See also the entry for Ellipsis Points.

PRONOUNS

Take care with pronouns in regard to agreement, reference, and case.

Agreement

Make a pronoun agree in number and gender with its antecedent—singular with singular, plural with plural, male with male, female with female, neuter with neuter:

John monopolized the meeting, but *he* . . . .
The *woman* walked through the lobby; then *she* . . . .
Set the *table* down and put the lamp on *it*.
The group *members*, when *they* meet . . . .

Traditionally, when we could be referring to either a man or a woman, we have used the male pronoun:

The *student* first gets a registration card; then *he* . . . .

The women's movement has made many people feel this construction is unfair or at least insensitive. One way around the problem is to use a plural construction when you can:

The *students* first get a registration card; then *they* . . . .

But English still lacks a neutral pronoun for such situations.

Be particularly careful with collective nouns (see the entry for Verb Agreement). They can be considered either singular or plural, depending on meaning. Make your pronoun agree with whatever number and verb you choose for the collective noun:

The committee *is* having *its* last meeting tonight.
The committee *are* arguing intensely among *themselves;* they . . . .*

Reference

Make sure your reader can tell without the slightest hesitation which word or word group your pronoun refers to. If you suspect any confusion, rewrite your sentence:

---

*See also the material on Collective Nouns, page 292.

The speaker should place the notes on the lectern provided. *He* should not wave *them* about.

> Despite the distance between the nouns and pronouns, the references are quite clear.

Both the group leader and the secretary are responsible for the proper recording of motions. *He* should keep an accurate record.

> This reference is unclear. It could go back to either *leader* or *secretary*. In cases like this repeat the needed noun: *The secretary* should keep an accurate record.

Group members should believe that all contributions are worth considering. *This* in itself will prevent many arguments and unhappy members.

> In this case *this* clearly refers to the broad concept of considering all contributions worthwhile.

A faulty fact can usually be identified when placed next to an accurate statement. But *this* may not occur.

> In this instance *this* is an unclear reference. We don't know what will not occur. We have three choices: (1) a faulty fact being identified; (2) a faulty fact being placed next to an accurate statement; (3) an accurate statement being made. A clear rewrite would be "But *this identification* may not occur."

As the last example demonstrates, you need to examine every reference for the possibility of misunderstanding. Remember that references clear to you may not be clear to your reader. Lean over backward to be clear. Be particularly careful whenever you are using *this, that, which,* or *it.*

Case

A brief lesson from the history of English is appropriate here. At one time in English—about 1,400 years ago—all nouns had case. A noun used as the subject of a sentence was in the nominative case, an indirect object in the dative case, and so forth. Thus a hound eating a bone was a *hund,* but a hound given a bone to eat was a *hunde.* Except for the possessive case—*a hound's bone*—these cases did not survive in nouns. Today word order and prepositions tell us whether a noun is subject (S), object (O), or indirect object (IO):

S   O   IO
John gave the bone to the hound.

But case did survive in pronouns. Correct case is seldom necessary for understanding. If someone incorrectly says, "John and me went fishing," we understand him as well as if he had correctly said, "John and I went fishing." If not necessary for understanding, case is still important. Quite frankly, status is involved. People who keep their pronouns sorted out correctly are considered by many other people to be more educated and cultured than those who do not.

A pronoun used as the subject of a sentence is in the nominative case—*I, he, she, we, they, who*. Pronouns used as objects of verbs and prepositions are in the objective case—*me, him, her, us, them, whom*. The pronouns *you* and *it* are the same in both cases.

Let's look at some examples:

> *He* hit *me*.
> *We* are going to *him* at once.
> *He* gave *her* the hat.
> *She* bought the car for *us* boys.
> *We* women want equality.
> *Who* is going to the fair?
> He gave the car to *whom?*

Many people have no trouble sorting out pronouns until they have to use a plural object. Then they go to pieces and use nominative case rather than objective, perhaps because it sounds more elegant to them. The following forms are CORRECT:

> He gave the book *to my brother and me.*
> It's a matter *between him and me.*
> She *sent them and us* an invitation.
> *Between you and me,* I think I understand it.

If in doubt about a double object, try it in the singular. Few people would say, "He gave the car to *I*." Therefore, "He gave the car to *my brother and I*" would be equally incorrect. "He gave the car to *my brother and me*" is correct.

There is only one tricky place in the whole sorting out of pronouns—the seldom-used predicate nominative. After any form of the verb *to be* (*is, are, was,* etc.), we use the nominative case rather than the objective:

> It is *she*.
> Is it *she?*

Despite this rule practically everyone says "It's me," not "It's I." As we say, this construction is little used, particularly in writing. And if you get it wrong, most people will not notice. But do pay attention to your other pronouns. They may be more important to you than you think.

QUESTION MARK

If you write a direct question, place a question mark at its end.

> How far must you drill to reach stable bedrock?

Polite requests may be punctuated with a question mark or a period.

> Will you please send me the noise analysis report before Tuesday? (*or* .)

Do not use a question mark after an indirect question.

The Sierra Club asked what the impact of the larger dam would be.

QUOTATION MARKS

Use quotation marks to set off quotations and certain titles. You may also use them to set off words used as words.

Quotations

Use quotation marks to enclose a passage repeated from an earlier statement, whether written or spoken. The quotation marks signal that you have reproduced the passage word for word:

Zoo director John Sikes wrote, "The Zoo Board believes that most of the traffic will originate from the metropolitan area and will use the major freeways to reach the Zoo."

You may make small, properly marked additions and omissions in quoted material, as explained in our entries for Brackets and Ellipsis Points.

If your quotation runs over three lines, don't put it inside quotation marks. Instead, indent it on the page in the following manner:

In a letter to the Highway Department, the Chairman of

the Rockport Environmental Council expressed the Council's

major concern concerning the new route:

The proposed route would cut a path across the marsh, destroying valuable habitat. Even though the new bridge would be supported by piers, the piers themselves and the associated construction activities would leave permanent scars and damaging effects to the landscape.

Note that in the example the quoted passage is not only idented but also single-spaced to contrast to the double-spacing of the text. Use a colon to introduce indented quotations.

Titles

Titles of works shorter than book length, such as magazine articles, short stories, and poems, are set inside quotation marks:

"Comparing Your Options in Home Insurance"
"An Episode of War"
"Frankie and Johnny"

Words as Words

Words used as words may be italicized (see the entry for Italics) or set inside quotation marks:

> What is meant by the term "shaping"?

Whichever method you choose, be consistent within a piece of work.

Quotation Marks with Other Marks of Punctuation

Fairly definite rules govern the use of other punctuation marks with quotation marks.

Introductory marks   Quotations that need an introduction are preceded by commas or, in more formal circumstances, by colons:

> The Rockport mayor said, "No major conflicts with plans for existing development are anticipated."

> The Rockport mayor supported alternative C with this statement: "All Rockport land use planning has anticipated the construction of alternative C. Therefore we strongly recommend this alternative."

See also the entry for Colon.

   When a quotation is closely integrated into a sentence, use no introductory mark of punctuation:

> The zoo director supports the building of the freeway because he feels "that most of the major traffic will originate from the metropolitan area. . . ."

The use of the lower-case letter at the beginning of the quote tells the reader that the preceding part of the sentence has been omitted. Therefore, no ellipsis is needed. However, an ellipsis is needed to signal the omission of material at the end of the sentence. See also the entry for Ellipsis Points.

Quotation marks within other quotation marks   When you use quotation marks within other quotation marks, use single quotes for the inside marks. When typing, use the apostrophe.

> In objection, the councilwoman said, "We question your use of the terms 'prudent and feasible' in this regard."

Commas and periods   A period or comma at the end of any words set inside quotation marks is *always* set inside the marks, even when logic indicates it should go outside:

> The councilwoman questioned our use of the terms "prudent and feasible."

Colons and semicolons   A colon or semicolon at the end of words inside quotation marks is *always* set outside the marks:

The councilwoman questioned our use of the terms "prudent and feasible"; we agree that the issue is open for interpretation.

Dashes, exclamation points, and question marks   Dashes, exclamation points, and question marks follow the logic of the sentence. When they belong to the quotation, they go inside the marks. When they belong to the sentence, they go outside:

Many new tree growers ask, "Why should trees be shaped?"
What is meant by the term "shaping"?

Note that in the first example the question mark also serves as end punctuation for the sentence.

RUN-ON SENTENCES

The rule for avoiding run-on sentences is simple enough: Don't join two independent clauses with only a comma or with no punctuation at all. Normal punctuation between two independent clauses is one of the following:

1. A period
2. A semicolon
3. A comma and a coordinating conjunction *(and, but, for, nor, or, yet)*

The trick is to recognize an independent clause when you see one. The following are all independent clauses. If you have difficulty with run-on sentences, commit these patterns to heart:

—Overhead projection is a dramatic method of presenting facts and ideas clearly, concisely, and effectively.
—The instructor controls the equipment with a switch at his fingertips.
—Put your overhead visuals on a transparent base.
—Most inks can be washed off easily.
—They are safe to use.

Placing a conjunctive adverb before an independent clause *does not* make it subordinate. Nor does the conjunctive adverb serve as a strong connective. Therefore, you must use normal punctuation as defined in this section before an independent clause beginning with a conjunctive adverb. The major conjunctive adverbs are *accordingly, also, anyhow, besides, consequently, furthermore, however, indeed, likewise, moreover, nevertheless, then, therefore.*
Observe carefully these examples of correct punctuation:

1. Most inks can be washed off easily. Therefore, they are safe to use.
2. Most inks can be washed off easily; therefore, they are safe to use.
3. Most inks can be washed off easily, and, therefore, they are safe to use.

See also the entries for Colon, Comma, Fragmentary Sentences, Period, and Semicolon.

SEMICOLON

The semicolon is used in certain situations between independent clauses and when internal commas make it necessary in a series. It really has quite limited uses. Don't confuse it with a colon. Don't use it to introduce lists or quotations, and don't use it after the salutation in a letter. See the entries for Colon and Run-on Sentences.

Independent Clauses

You can use the semicolon between two independent clauses at any time instead of the more normal period; however, the semicolon is most widely used when the link between the two clauses is one of the conjunctive adverbs: *consequently, however, nevertheless, therefore,* etc. In this situation the comma is not considered heavy enough punctuation, and the period perhaps too heavy:

> The outlet will be below water level; therefore, it will be entirely submerged and not visible from the bank.

Sometimes independent clauses between which you would use a comma and a coordinating conjunction already have heavy internal commas. In this case substitute a semicolon for the comma:

> The buildings, mainly flour and sawmills are gone; but foundations, penstocks, tailraces, and some machinery remain.

Series

When the elements of a series have internal commas, substitute a semicolon at the breaks where you would normally use commas:

> The schools examined were Normandale, a two-year public community college; Hamline, a four-year private school; and the University of Illinois, a four-year public school.

SENTENCES

Elsewhere in this Guide we tell you about various sentence faults (see the entries for Fragmentary Sentences, Misplaced and Dangling Modifiers, Run-on Sentences, Parallelism, and Verb Agreement). In this section we give you some positive advice about better sentences. Specifically, we're going to discuss choice of the proper voice, sentence length, sentence order, and directness.

Voice

English sentences come in two voices—active and passive:

Active The glaciers formed three striking and different natural features.
Passive Three striking and different natural features were formed by the glaciers.

In the active-voice sentence the subject acts; in the passive-voice sentence the subject is acted upon. Active-voice sentences use fewer words and state more directly what you have to say. With passive voice you run the risk of forgetting the final prepositional phrase—*by the glaciers*—and leaving the doer of the action unknown.

For simple instructions the imperative mood of the active voice is clearly superior to the passive. A passage in a safety brochure reads this way:

> Keep your distance. Never operate a crane beneath power lines without adequate clearance. Play it safe. Leave more than the minimum six feet required. Remember, too, a boom may rebound when a load is released.

The passage is crisp and direct and clearly says, "This means you!" Compare the active version to how it would be in passive:

> Distance should be kept. A crane should not be operated beneath power lines without adequate clearance. More than the minimum six feet should be allowed for safety reasons. It should be remembered that a boom may rebound when a load is released.

The second version is flabby, indefinite, and needlessly long.

A seemingly polite request expressed in the passive can sound rude compared to an active-voice request.

> **Compare**   It is requested that you send me a copy of your speech.
> **With**   I would appreciate a copy of your speech.

The second active-voice version is far closer to normal speech and far politer than the impersonal passive-voice version.

Passive voice has many uses. Use it when the person or thing acted upon is more important than the actor or when you wish to deemphasize the actor. But don't use passive voice by accident. Know it when you see it, and use it only when it is clearly better than the active-voice version of the same idea. (See also pages 96–97.)

Sentence Length

Professional writers average about twenty words a sentence whether they're writing for high school graduates or Ph.D's. For an audience with less than a high school education they might scale down to fourteen to eighteen words. You should take a lesson from the pros and work for similar averages. Remember that we're talking about averages. Don't cookie-cut a series of twenty-word sentences. Rather, let your sentences range over a spread of about ten to thirty words. Being conscious of your sentence length will prevent the two extremes of poor writing—too-short sentences and too-long.

Too-short results in disconnected, primer sentences:

> The glaciers formed the topography of the study area. They left an accumulation of glacial drift. This drift is from 100 to 500 feet thick. (25 words in 3 sentences)

Smoothly connecting the ideas, we get this result:

> The glaciers, leaving an accumulation of glacial drift from 100 to 500 feet thick, formed the topography of the area. (20 words in 1 sentence)

At the other extreme too-long sentences are too complex for the reader to follow. And sometimes, as in this example from a government document, the writer loses control over the material:

> As of the effective date of this memorandum, projects which have received design approval (as defined in PPM 90-1) may receive PS & E approval, if otherwise satisfactory, on the basis of past state highway submissions which identify and document the economic, social and environmental effects previously considered with respect to these advanced projects, together with a supplemental report, if necessary, covering the consideration and disposition of the items not previously covered and now listed herein in paragraph 4.b.

Seventy-eight words of gobbledygook!

Keeping track of your average sentence length is one of the easiest and most effective things you can do to improve your writing (see also pages 89–90).

Sentence Order

Normal English sentence order is subject first, verb second. Following the verb a wide range of objects, modifiers, subordinate clauses, and additional main clauses is possible:

S   V

Actual shearing techniques differ among growers.

S   V

Some prefer to begin trimming at the base of the tree and work upward to the terminal leader.

Research shows that professional writers begin about 75 percent of their sentences with the subject.[1] Another 23 percent of the time they begin the sentence with a simple adverbial opener, followed by the subject:

> *In the terminal whorl,* the grower will encounter some common situations that require corrective action.
> *However,* these are dangerous tools, and you should take extra precautions.

Less than 2 percent of the time professional writers begin with a subordinate clause or verbal phrase:

> *When the operation is repeated annually,* it has the effect of developing a shorter, well-shaped, and compact tree.
> *To use any herbicide safely,* follow the exact instructions on the label.

[1]Francis Christensen, "Notes Toward a New Rhetoric," *College English* (October 1963): 7–18.

Sentence openers before the subject usually serve as transitional devices, linking the sentence to a previous idea.

We appreciate professional writing because, being cast in normal sentence patterns, it puts no roadblocks between us and the thought. Follow the professional pattern and you'll put your main idea first most of the time. You'll avoid the difficulties of sentences like the following:

> If it appears logical to use the same shoulder width and surface type as that in place on adjacent projects, or if aspects of traffic growth or traffic assignment splits would justify a different selection, or if stage construction is a consideration, it may be desirable to deviate from standards.

This sentence, poor on several counts, puts its main idea—permissible deviation from standards—last. Readers wander through the conditions, wondering why they are reading them. Reverse the order and use a list and the result would be a far better statement:

> You may deviate from standards under these conditions:
> 1. If it appears logical to use the same width and surface type as that in place on adjacent projects.
> 2, 3. etc.

Directness

Write directly to your thought. Write to express ideas, not to line up words in a row. Don't follow old formulas that are word wasters. Don't *make application to,* simply *apply.* Don't *make contact with* people; instead, simply *see* them or *meet* them. Do you begin thank-you notes by saying, "I want to thank you for . . . ."? Why not simply say, "Thank you for . . . ."? It sounds faintly pompous to say or write *at this point in time* rather than *now.* If something happens *due to the fact that,* simply say *because.* If something is *in accordance with the regulation,* it is really only *under* or *by the regulation.* The list of such tired, indirect ways of saying things is unfortunately all too long. You'll avoid most of them if you *think* about what it is you want to say and say it in the most direct way you can.

We also waste a good many words by not recognizing the value of the verb in English.

Compare   What is the conclusion to be drawn from this research?
With   What can we conclude from this research?

The second sentence saves three words. How was this achieved? By taking the action idea in *conclusion* and putting it in the verb *conclude* where it belongs.

Besides using fewer words when you put your action into verbs, you'll make your writing more vivid. This first version of a sentence is pallid and indirect:

> A blockage of debris in the conduit could cause a flood in the upper pool.

By putting action into verbs, we have this far better sentence:

Debris blocking the conduit could flood the upper pool.

Look at the use of verbs and verb forms in the opening paragraph of an advertising letter (the italics are ours):

> *To help prevent* highway deaths, engineers *may* someday *control* traffic with computers. For long distances, the computer *may steer, accelerate,* and *brake* the car as *needed.* The driver can *lounge, read, play* cards, even *sleep* while *being whisked* safely down the highway.

The professional writer of this paragraph knew that verbs snap people to attention. He used verbs to express his ideas vividly and directly. He did not hide his ideas behind a smokescreen of needless words. (See also page 96.)

SPELLING

Spelling correctly is important. All too many people are quick to judge your competence and intelligence by how well you spell. A misspelled word or two in a letter of application may block you from a job as quickly as a lack of experience or education would. This may be unfortunate and even unwise, but it is one of the facts of life.

For many historical reasons, such as changes in pronunciation and the introduction of foreign words, English is a difficult language to spell. Nevertheless, there are certain rules to follow. Numerous books explain these rules. Look for them in your library—under either *spelling* or *orthography*—or in your bookstore. The rules really do help and are worth mastering.

If you have a dictionary handy, you probably spell the difficult words correctly. That is, you know you can't spell them, so you look them up. If you are like most people, it's the everyday words that you misspell the most. Most of us are reluctant to lift the heavy dictionary off the shelf when we need it only for the spelling of a common word. We'd rather take our chances. All too often our confidence is misplaced. May we suggest another approach. Most secretaries own small books, easily carried in a pocket, that list without definition twenty to thirty thousand of the most used words. These books also divide words into syllables, so they are useful for breaking a word at the end of a line. Any bookseller will be happy to find one for you. If you own one, you'll find it convenient to use, and you'll improve your spelling.

To give you some immediate help with these common words, we have provided a list of 544 words that college students frequently misspell. See also the entries for Abbreviations and Word Division.

List of Commonly Misspelled Words

absence	accommodate	accustomed	achievement
absorption	accompanied	ache	acquaint
accessible	accomplish	achieve	acquire

across
actual
actually
address
advice (*noun*)
advise(*verb*)
adviser
aerial
affect (*verb*)
against
aggravate
aisle (*of theater*)
alcohol
all ready
   (*all prepared*)
all right
almost
already (*so soon*)
although
altogether
always
amateur
among
amount
analysis
analyze
annual
anoint
answer
antiseptic
apparatus
apparent
appear
appearance
appetite
appropriate
arguing
argument
around
arouse
arrangement
article
ascend
assistant
athlete
athletic
author
auxiliary
awful
balance

basically
before
beginning
believe
benefit
benefited
breathe (*verb*)
brilliant
buried
business
busy
cafeteria
calculate
calculator
calendar
captain
carburetor
careful
carrying
category
ceiling
cemetery
certain
changeable
changing
characteristic
chief
choose
   (*present tense*)
chose
   (*past tense*)
climbed
clothes
collegiate
column
coming
commit
committed
committee
common
comparatively
competition
complement
   (*to complete*)
compliment
   (*to praise*)
conceive
conceivable
concentration
concern

conquer
conscience
conscientious
conscious
consider
consistent
continually
continuous
control
controlled
convenience
conversation
coolly
copies
corroborate
countries
course
courteous
criticism
criticize
crowd
crystal
curiosity
cylinder
dealt
decide
decision
definite
degree
dependent
describe
description
desirable
despair
desperate
destroy
determine
develop
development
device
didn't
diesel
dietitian
difference
different
dilemma
dining
disappear
disappoint
disapprove

disastrous
discipline
discoveries
discriminate
discussed
disease
dissatisfied
dissection
distinction
divide
divine
division
doesn't
dormitories
drunkenness
easily
ecstasy
effect
   (*usually a noun*)
efficiency
efficient
eighth
electricity
electronics
eligible
eliminate
embarrass
embarrassment
emphasize
enemy
engines
environment
equipped
equipment
especially
essential
etc.
exaggerate
exceed
excellent
except
exercise
exhausted
exhilaration
existence
expense
experience
experiment
explanation
extremely

familiar
fascinate
fascinating
February
finally
financial
flourish
forcibly
foreign
foresee
formally
　　(*in a formal way*)
formerly (*earlier*)
forth (*forward*)
forty
forward
fourth (*4th*)
friend
frightening
fundamental
further
gardener
gauge
generally
government
governor
grammar
grateful
grievous
guarantee
guard
guidance
hadn't
handle
hear (*sound*)
height
here (*place*)
heroes
heroine
holiday
hoping
humorous
hungry
hurriedly
hurrying
identify
imaginary
imagination
imitation

immediately
incidentally
increase
incredible
independence
independent
indispensable
inevitably
influential
initiate
inoculate
insistent
intellectual
intelligence
intelligent
interest
interfere
interpret
interrupt
invitation
irrelevant
irresistible
irritable
island
it's (*it is*)
its (*possessive*)
jealous
judgment
knew
knowledge
laboratory
laid
larynx
later
led
leisure
length
library
license
lightening
　　(*remove weight*)
lightning
　　(*and thunder*)
likable
likelihood
likely
literally
literature
loneliness

losing
loyalty
lying
machine
magazine
maintenance
manageable
management
maneuver
manual
many
marriage
married
mathematics
meant
mechanics
medicine
miniature
misdemeanor
merely
minutes
mischievous
misspelled
morale
mortgage
mournful
muscle
mysterious
naturally
necessarily
necessary
neighbor
neither
nickel
niece
ninety
ninth
noticeable
obstacle
o'clock
occasion
occasionally
occur
occurred
occurrence
official
omission
omit
omitted

operate
opinion
opportunity
optimism
optimist
optimistic
origin
original
oscillate
paid
panicky
parallel
particularly
partner
pastime
peaceable
peculiar
perceive
perform
perhaps
permanent
perseverance
persistent
personal
personally
perspiration
persuade
pertain
piece
plain
planned
planning
pleasant
poison
politician
possess
possesses
possession
possible
potato
potatoes
practical
practically
practicability
prairie
precede
preceding
predictable
prefer

preferable
preference
preferred
prejudice
preparation
prepare
presence
prevalent
primitive
principal (*main*)
principle (*a rule*)
privilege
probably
procedure
proceed
professional
professor
prominent
pronunciation
propeller
protein
prove
psychology
publicly
pursue
quantity
quarter
quiet
realize
really
receipt
receive
recognize
recommend
referred
relevant
relieve
religious
repetition

representative
resemblance
resistance
respectability
restaurant
rhythm
rhythmical
ridiculous
safety
salary
scarcely
scene
schedule
science
secretarial
secretary
seize
sense
separate
sergeant
several
severe
shepherd
shining
shoulder
sight (*seeing*)
signal
similar
simile
sincerely
site (*location*)
sophomore
speak
specimen
speech
statement
stationary
   (*not moving*)
stationery (*paper*)

stopped
straight
strategy
strength
strenuous
stretch
striking
studying
succeed
successful
suddenness
suppress
superintendent
surely
surprise
syllable
symmetrical
technician
technical
technique
temperament
temperature
tendency
than
   (*bigger than*)
their
   (*possessive*)
then
   (*at that time*)
there (*location*)
therefore
they're (*they are*)
thorough
thought
through
to (*toward*)
together
too (*also*)
toward

transferred
tries
truly
Tuesday
twelfth
two (2)
undoubtedly
university
unnecessary
until
unusual
using
usually
vacuum
vegetable
vengeance
vertical
villain
vitamin
weather
   (*climate*)
Wednesday
weird
where
whether
   (*which of two*)
wholly
who's (*who is*)
whose
   (*possessive*)
woman
women
won't
writing
written
you're (*you are*)
your
   (*possessive*)

UNDERLINING
See Italics.

VERB AGREEMENT
Make the verb agree with its subject. Normally, this won't be a problem for you, but some trouble spots do exist.

Intervening Prepositional Phrases

When a prepositional phrase with a plural object—*of the women*—comes between a singular noun or pronoun and its verb, writers often go astray and use a plural verb:

Incorrect The stack of letters are . . . .
Correct The stack of letters is . . . .

The pronouns most likely to cause difficulty in this construction are *each, everyone, everybody, either, neither, none, anybody,* and *somebody,* all of which take singular verbs. Grammar is often at war with meaning here, but grammar decides the verb:

Incorrect If *each* of the group members *have* . . . .
Correct If *each* of the group members *has* . . . .
Incorrect *Everyone* of the flowers *are* . . . .
Correct *Everyone* of the flowers *is* . . . .

Compound Subjects

Compound subjects connected by *and* take a plural verb:

Hydrogen and oxygen are . . . .

When you have a compound subject in an *either . . . or* construction, the noun closest to the verb decides the form of the verb. Note the reversal in the two examples:

Either the group members or the *leader is* . . . .
Either the leader or the group *members are* . . . .

Collective Nouns

We have a good many collective nouns in English, nouns like *audience, band, committee, group, company,* and *class.* Collective nouns can take either singular or plural verbs, depending on the meaning of the sentence:

The committee *is* having *its* last meeting tonight.
The committee *are* arguing intensely among *themselves.*

In truth, however, most Americans feel uncomfortable using a plural verb after a collective noun. (The British do it naturally.) We're more likely to say, "The committee *members* are arguing intensely among *themselves.*" See also the entry for Pronouns.

Plural-Sounding Nouns

Some nouns sound plural but are not—for instance, *electronics, economics, mathematics, physics,* and *measles.* Despite their sound such nouns take singular verbs:

Mathematics *is* necessary in . . . .

Nouns of Measurement, Time, and Money

Plural nouns expressing measurement, time, or money take singular verbs:

One hundred yards *is* the distance from goal line to goal line.
Ten years *was* the sentence.
Five thousand dollars *is* a lot of money.

WORD DIVISION

When you have to carry part of a word over to another line, break it between syllables and hyphenate it:

Even more important than the dormitory program is the . . . .

Your dictionary will show the syllable division of words:

croc · o · dile
gum · my
gra · cious

A few standard rules cover the proper way of dividing words:
—When a vowel ends a syllable or stands by itself, break after the vowel:

paro-chial
esti-mate (not est-imate)

—Break between double consonants, unless the double consonant appears in the root of the word:

occur-ring
bril-liant

but

spell-ing
toll-ing

—Don't carry over single letters or *ed* when the *e* is silent. For instance, you would not carry over the *y* of *brushy* or the *ed* of *bucked*. You could break *darted* before the *ed* because the *e* is pronounced. (However, usually it is better not to carry over only two letters. Leave them above or carry the whole word over.)

Formal Elements of Reports

Reports can be anything from four or five sentences scribbled on a notepad to a twenty-two-volume feasibility study on the development of a supersonic transport. No clear-cut distinction exists between informal and formal reports; simple problems and situations require only simple reports, perhaps resembling letters more than anything else. But, the more complex and lengthy the report, the further removed your audience is from the project you're reporting on, and the more valuable the report is as a long-term reference, the greater the need to formalize certain elements of the presentation to save readers time and effort and to prevent confusion. The formal elements help readers recognize the various units of a report, consequently speeding up the retrieval process by highlighting important information. In short, formalizing certain elements in a report fights against the loss of meaning, however slight, that inevitably takes place when a message is transmitted. But it would be an academic exercise of little importance to decide when a report was "formal" and when "informal."

Some companies and agencies use a rigid, standardized plan for long reports; others are more flexible. Our advice is that you learn whatever plan you are expected to follow. Our discussion of the formal elements of long reports is purposely general and flexible, so that you can design each report to fit its own subject matter, purpose, and audience.

The following list illustrates the commonly used formal elements of reports:

1. Prefatory Elements
   A. Title Page
   B. Letter of Transmittal or Preface
   C. Table of Contents
   D. List of Figures and Tables
   E. Abstract
2. Main Portions of Report
   A. Introduction
   B. Body
   C. Conclusion
3. Supplemental Elements
   A. List of References or Bibliography
   B. Appendixes

PREFATORY ELEMENTS

The prefatory elements initially present your report to readers before they come to the main portions of the report. Their function is to identify the report—its author, audience, date, subject, coverage, and organization. Prefatory pages are numbered in small roman numerals—iii, iv, v, etc.

Title Page

The title page gives identifying information about the report. It shows the title of the report, the name and position of the person or group for whom you prepared the report, your name and position, and the date you submitted the report. This information is important because it introduces the subject, identifies the primary audience and author, establishes the currency of information, helps in filing and retrieving the report, and makes it easy to refer to.

Here are suggestions on providing the necessary information for the title page:

1. *Title*—Think of your title as a one-phrase summary of your report. It should indicate the subject as briefly and specifically as possible. Make your title concise and emphatic: avoid unhelpful expressions like *A Report on* . . . , *A Study of* . . . , *An Investigation of* . . . . Four to eight words are usually enough. One or two words are often vague; more than ten work against easy comprehension. Here are some satisfactory titles that describe succinctly the purpose and subject of reports:

   Proposed Changes in Traffic Pattern in Lockwood Shopping Center

   Atomic Attack and the Nation's Water Supply

Comparative Merits of Copying Machines on the Market

Tooth Transplantation in Pediatric Dentistry

Battery Eliminators Save Money in the Shop

2. *Name and Position of Primary Reader*—Identify the audience of your report by name, position, and organization.
3. *Name and Position of Author*—Identify yourself by name, position, and organization.
4. *Date of Report*—Date your report according to when you submit it to your reader. Never abbreviate the date; give the month, day, and year:

November 16, 1978 or 16 November 1978.

Center each line on the title page. The vertical arrangement will depend on how much information you have to give in each part. Begin the title about one and a half inches from the top of the page. Divide the title into two lines if it looks too long for one line. The date line is about two inches from the page bottom.

The title page is understood to be page i of the prefatory elements, though it is not numbered.

The finished title page should look balanced, like Figure B-1, page 301.

Letter of Transmittal

The letter of transmittal officially transmits or presents the report to your readers. It may be in memorandum or letter form. Addressed to your readers, it provides sufficient background by:

- explaining the authorization or occasion for the report
- restating the title of the report (in case the letter is mailed separately from the report)
- explaining the features of the report that may be of special interest
- acknowledging special assistance in performing the study or preparing the report

Close the letter politely by stating your willingness to provide similar services in the future or to provide further information if the readers desire it, whichever seems appropriate.

If the letter is bound with the report, it is understood to be page ii of the prefatory elements, though it is not numbered.

The letter should look like Figure B-2, page 302.

Preface

The preface is almost identical to the letter of transmittal. It should contain statements about purpose, scope, and content of the report, and acknowledgment of assistance received. If you include a letter of transmittal, there's no point in including a preface, too.

Whether you use the letter of transmittal or the preface depends upon the audience of your report. Use the letter of transmittal when your audience is a single person or a well-defined group. Use the preface when your audience is more general and you don't know specifically who will be reading your report. The tone of the preface is often less personal than that of the letter of transmittal.

As the preface is relatively short, it should be centered on the page. Type the word *Preface* at the top of the page. When the preface takes the place of the letter of transmittal, number it as page ii of the prefatory elements. Center the number ii at the bottom of the page, ¾ inch up.

The preface should look like Figure B-3, page 303.

Table of Contents

The table of contents is a list of the headings and subheadings from the report. It provides a handy outline overview of the report that helps your readers locate any major section quickly.

Here are some suggestions for completing the table of contents:

- Place the words *Contents* or *Table of Contents* at the top of the page.
- Arrange information into three columns. The left column contains roman numerals as major division or section numbers. The center column contains the phrases that make up the headings or subheadings of the report. Wording, capitalization, and order should be exactly as in the report. Indent the side heading under each major heading. If there are paragraph headings, indent them under each side heading. The right column contains the page numbers on which the headings and subheadings appear. For numbers that have more than one digit, backspace so the numbers will be even on the right.
- Make headings and subheadings as informative as possible since they give your readers key-point identification at a glance.
- Use double-spaced dots, or leaders, to connect headings and subheadings with their respective page numbers.
- Double-space between entries and single-space any heading that is too long for one line.

Number the table of contents page as page iii of the prefatory elements. Center the number iii at the bottom of the page, ¾ inch up. From here on number all pages of the prefatory elements in sequence with little roman numerals.

A table of contents should look like Figure B-4, page 304.

List of Figures and Tables

The page that lists figures and tables shows your readers the location of graphics and tables. You should include it only if your report contains more than five figures or tables. If there are many figures and tables, you may group them into separate categories: "List of Figures," "List of Tables," and so on.

The list of figures and tables is set up just like the table of contents:

- Place the words *Figures and Tables* or *List of Figures and Tables*, or whatever is appropriate, at the top of the page.
- Arrange the information in three columns, similar to the table of contents: the left column contains the figure number or table number or letter; the center column contains the title of the graphic or table; the right column contains the number of the page it is on.
- Use double-spaced dots to connect titles of figures and tables with their respective page numbers.

The list of figures and tables should look like Figure B-5, page 305.

Abstract

The abstract is a brief, condensed statement of the most important ideas of your report. It provides your readers with a compressed overview of the report by mirroring both the content and organization of the report. It must be informative; that is, it should not simply describe the coverage of the report, but actually present what's in the report.

Its length depends on the length of the report. The typical abstract is a paragraph of 150–200 words. But longer reports—say 20 or more pages—most likely would require additional paragraphs. We can't tell you exactly what the length of an abstract should be for longer reports, but a working estimate would be that it should not be more than 5 percent of the whole report. Thus a 40-page report would have an abstract of approximately two pages. (See Bibliographies and Literature Reviews, pages 105–108, for examples of summaries.)

Although the abstract is a compressed version of the report, you should not write it in a telegraphic style. Its words and sentences must be in good prose style.

Place the word *Abstract* at the top of the page, triple- or quadruple-space, and begin the abstract.

The abstract should look like Figure B-6, page 306.

MAIN PORTIONS OF THE REPORT

The main portions of your report follow the prefatory elements and consist of three main parts—the introduction, the body, and the ending.

The Introduction

The introduction attracts attention and presents a general idea of the topic of the report.

When readers turn to your report, they are likely to have a lot of things on their mind. What you have to do is get *your report* on their mind—quickly. No matter how much or how little they are expecting your report, no matter how much or how little motivated interest they have in reading your report, your readers are going to start looking for answers to several questions as they try to settle into your report. They'll want to know or be reminded why you are writing to them, why you are writing to them now, what you have to say, and how you are going to say it. And they'll want the answers to these questions before they read very far.

If you don't deliver the answers, they'll start getting restless and will soon find something to do besides read your report.

The English author C. S. Lewis put it another way:

I sometimes think that writing is like driving sheep down a road. If there is any gate to the left or right, the reader will certainly go into it.

To hold your readers' attention and prevent mental wandering, you must pave a road that's easy to follow, build an entrance that's unavoidable, and close the gates to the sides. These are the jobs of your introduction, the first main portion of your report.

The introduction may consist of a few paragraphs or perhaps several pages. When it's lengthy, you should use subheadings to indicate its subparts. Whether it's short or long, it should perform the following functions:

1. *Explain the subject.* Your readers need to know what they are going to read about. The title, letter of transmittal or preface, and abstract give them some information, but they might not provide adequate orientation. Often it is necessary to define the subject, explain some of the key terms used in your discussion, or give historical and other background information about the subject. Finally, you need to comment on the significance of the information. Work a bit on arousing your readers' interest. Why is your subject important? Why should your readers want to know about it? Of course, the more your readers want or need your report, the less you need do to arouse interest.

2. *Explain the purpose.* Although the purpose should be self-evident to you, make sure it's also evident to your readers. Your purpose might be to report on a study requested by your readers. If so, review the facts of the request or authorization: When did they make the request? How did they make it? Did somebody else make it? Such a review is especially important if there's no letter of transmittal. If the report is unsolicited, explain thoroughly the situation that led to the report. The value of the report and the objectives and purposes of your reporting should be clear to your readers.

Sometimes there's only a thin line between the purpose of a study that a report is about and the report itself. But we remind you that what is meant by *purpose* here is the purpose of the report, not the study. For example, the purpose of a study may be to pinpoint weaknesses in a machine's design. But the purpose of the report would be to explain the amount of deflection and the source of the stress causing a machine to vibrate too much, and to recommend what rate of speed and what kind of mounting brackets would solve the problem. That is, the purpose of the report is to present the results of the study.

3. *Explain the scope.* Always let your readers know the extent of your presentation or the limits of your study. In other words, explain just how much ground the report is covering. The statement of scope tells your readers what you see yourself responsible for reporting.

4. *Explain the plan and order of presentation.* Always preview the report for your readers. Tell them what the order of topics will be. This statement usually is the last function of the introduction and serves as a transition to the body of the report.

Almost every important or long report will need a formal introduction that fulfills these four requirements. For special circumstances you may need to discuss in detail the problem your report is designed to solve . . . you may need to state a hypothesis . . . you may need to review the literature relevant to the problem or hypothesis . . . you may need to explain the nature of the investigation—the sources and methods of collecting data . . . you may need to define important terms used in the report which you feel your readers will be unfamiliar with . . . and if the purpose of your report is to communicate your position on a set of issues, you may need to summarize your significant findings or recommendations.

In short, your introduction should include whatever is needed to prepare readers for the information they are about to receive. Don't be hasty in an introduction, but neither should you be long-winded. Get on with the main event as soon as possible. See Figure B-7 (page 307) for an example of an introduction to the student report entitled "Atomic Attack and the Nation's Water Supply."

The Body

The body, the longest section of your report, presents your detailed message. It takes no set organization, but its contents should be arranged in some logical, unified order. Regardless of the content and arrangement of your report, you must help readers to skim your report, to read it thoroughly, or to refer to specific parts of it by using the following formal elements—heads and subheads, graphics, and quotations.

1. Heads and subheads When your report is long enough and complex enough to need formal elements, you should separate the text into major divisions (similar to chapters in books), divide each major division into sections, and use heads and subheads as titles. The outline of your report is a good source for heads and subheads.

Probably no other scanning aid will help readers more than the liberal use of heads and subheads. To test this claim take any report, article, or

Atomic Attack and
the Nation's Water Supply

Submitted to
Dr. Robert A. Phelps
Professor of Environmental Science
Patterson Technical Institute

by
Joyce Upchurch
Sophomore
Environmental Science

November 29, 1977

Figure B-1 Title page.

1203 South Limestone
Acallah, FL 33110
November 29, 1977

Dr. Robert A. Phelps
Professor of Environmental Science
Patterson Technical Institute
Acallah, FL 33110

Dear Dr. Phelps:

The accompanying report titled <u>Atomic</u> <u>Attack</u> <u>and</u> <u>the</u> <u>Nation's</u> <u>Water</u> <u>Supply</u> is submitted as my major report for Biology 199: Environmental Biology.

The primary purpose of the report is to explain how fallout from a nuclear war would affect the nation's water supply. The major findings are that fallout will affect the nation's water supply, that the greatest immediate danger would come from suspended radioactivity, that the long-range danger would come from dissolved radioactivity, and that treatment plants would not remove much, if any, dissolved radioactivity.

I sincerely hope that this report will meet with your approval. I will be most happy to provide you with additional information should you desire it.

Respectfully yours,

Joyce Upchurch

Joyce Upchurch
Senior
Environmental Science

Figure B-2 Letter of transmittal.

<u>Preface</u>

This report presents the results of a study of the effects on the nation's water supply of fallout from a nuclear war. The major findings are that fallout will affect the nation's water supply, that the greatest immediate danger would come from suspended radioactivity, that the long-range danger would come from dissolved radioactivity, and that treatment plants would not remove much, if any, dissolved radioactivity.

This report was written for Dr. Robert A. Phelps as the final project in Biology 199: Environmental Biology.

ii

Figure B-3 Preface.

Table of Contents

iii

Figure B-4 Table of contents.

List of Figures and Tables

iv

Figure B-5   List of figures and tables page.

Abstract

Fallout from a nuclear war will affect the nation's water supply. The two types of radioactivity that will be a hazard to the supply of water are suspended and dissolved radioactivity. Suspended activity directly causes immediate problems and indirectly causes long-range problems. Dissolved activity, which presents long-range problems, cannot be removed by treatment plants. How water becomes radioactive and how fallout affects streams and rivers, reservoirs and treatment plants present the nation with problems as acute as civil defense shelter problems.

v

Figure B-6 Abstract page.

I. Introduction

Two days after a nuclear attack, 46 percent of the United States would be covered with fallout.[1] This was what a subcommittee of the Joint Congressional Committee on Atomic Energy heard in 1969, as the Office of Civil and Defense Mobilization explained what would have happened during a hypothetical attack on October 17, 1968. Of course, the exact amount of fallout the United States would receive as the result of a nuclear war could not be predicted. However, an attacking enemy would not take the precautions used in testing in order to minimize fallout. Thus there would be extensive fallout after a war, and it would affect almost everything and everyone in this country in some way.

Although many people would be killed in blast areas, in much of this country the greatest threat to life would come from radioactive fallout. Radiation can damage body tissue and even cause death. . . .

Since water is used for drinking, cooking, bathing, and for many industrial processes which require the presence of humans, the effects of a fallout on our nation's water supply ought to be considered. Most of the water used in this country comes from lakes, streams, and rivers, rather than from wells, so consideration will be given only to the effects of fallout on surface water. The increase or decrease of radioactivity in water after it has passed through a treatment plant will be considered primarily in conjunction with contamination of the treatment plant. Processes for removal of radioactivity from water will not be considered.

It is important to note the immediate effects of fallout, as well as long-range effects, because in many cases they differ. Conclusions cannot be reached concerning quantities of radioactivity in water, because the amount of fallout cannot be accurately predicted. From past studies, though, the nature and behavior of the radioactivity can be predicted.

Figure B-7 Sample introduction (two sentences have been omitted).

manual more than two or three pages long, remove the heading system, and see how suddenly the text appears tediously uninterrupted and the major topics disappear into the text.

For those who read your entire report the heading system will be a comforting reminder of their progress. For those who read only certain parts it provides easy reference to those parts they're looking for by giving key-topic identification at a glance. The heads and subheads should agree with the entries in the table of contents; in fact, the heading system is an "exploded" table of contents inserted at appropriate places throughout the text.

Although slight variations exist in the use of heads and subheads, their format is usually handled as shown and explained in Figure B-8.

You'll probably use the complete three-level heading system only in longer, more formal reports. Short, informal reports use only certain of these headings. For instance, for brief two- or three-page passages you may use only the sideheads.

In addition to making sure the levels of importance of your heads and subheads are clear from their positions, you should make sure the heads:

- Point to the text that follows and relate to each other grammatically.
- Are not followed immediately by a pronoun that refers to a word or phrase in them.
- Have written text between them, even if it's only an explanation of subdivisions to come.
- Have at least two lines of text between the last head on a page and the bottom of a page.

Remember that heads and subheads serve as excellent clues to content and arrangement of material. Think three times before you submit a report that doesn't have them.

2. Graphics We often think there is only one way to report information—through sentences and paragraphs. But tables (containing columns and rows of words, phrases, or, commonly, numbers) and figures (photographs, drawings, and charts) are frequently the best way to display certain kinds of information prominently. And finding the right way is your goal every time you report.

Certainly tables and figures should not be used unless they add to the understanding of your report. But if you've always relied solely on sentences and paragraphs to present your ideas in writing, you should stop to consider the use of tables and figures to present information. There is, of course, no substitute for prose in conveying most ideas. But there are times when you can depend too much upon prose, when prose reaches its limits of effectiveness. It all depends on the nature of the information to be

<u>CENTER HEAD</u>

    The center head introduces a major division of your report. Center it horizontally about one and a half inches below the top of the page. Capitalize all letters or capitalize the first letter of the first word and of all other important words. Underscore the head. If the center head is too long for one line, divide it into two or more lines, single-spaced, with the longest line at the top and each succeeding line shorter than the one preceding it. Unless the center head ends with a question mark or exclamation point, do not punctuate.

<u>Sidehead</u>

    The first subhead is the sidehead, which introduces a subdivision of a major division of your report. Begin at the left margin on a separate line, with double or triple space above and double space below. Capitalize the first letter of the first word and of all other important words. Underscore the head. Unless the sidehead ends with a question mark or exclamation point, do not punctuate.

    <u>Paragraph Head</u>. The second subhead is the paragraph head, which introduces a further subdivision of the major division of your report. Begin at the usual indentation point for new paragraphs. Capitalize the first letter of the first word and of all other important words. Underscore the head. Put a period after the head and start the first line of the paragraph two spaces after the period.

Figure B-8 Heads and subheads.

conveyed. The following information on using tables and figures will help you decide those times and how to formalize tables and figures.[1]

Tables. Tables are word-savers. They present simply and clearly large blocks of information without all the connecting devices needed in prose. Data on three insecticides is arranged in a formal table in Figure B-9. Notice that the headings on the top of the table all project *down* the table. Only the captions on the side project *across* the table.

Table 1. Insecticide Mixtures

Insecticide	Formulation	Amount per gallon of water	Concentration (percent)
Carboryl	50 W.P.*	6 ounces	2.5
Chlordane	45 E.C.**	1 cup	3
Dichlorvos	25 E.C.	2/3 cup	1

* Wettable powder
** Emulsifiable concentrate

Source: Nuisance Wasps and Bees. Agricultural Extension Service, University of Minnesota, 1970.

Figure B-9 Table.

Unless you take care in preparing tables, they can become the most confusing part of your report. The following general rules will help you set up tables:

- Whenever possible, set up a table so it can be typed on the page in normal fashion. Center it between the left and right margins.
- Whenever possible, make each ruled column or row the same width.
- Label each column and row to identify the data. If a column shows

[1]Various types of graphics used in mechanism description, process description, instructions, and analytical reports have already been discussed in Chapters 8, 9, 10, and 12.

amounts, state the units in which the amounts are given, using standard symbols and abbreviations to save space. Center a column heading above the column.

- If the space between columns is wide, use spaced dots or dashes as leaders (as in a table of contents).
- If columns are long, double-space after every fifth entry.
- If column entries are of unequal length, center the longest one and align the rest using the expressed or implied decimal points as a guide. If the table is a word- or phrase-table, align entries on an imaginary left margin in each column.
- If a particular column or row lacks data, use three periods or dashes in each space lacking data.
- If they improve legibility, use vertical lines to separate columns. See Figure B-10 for an example.

Table 7. Projected Population, Employment, and Dwelling Unit Characteristics

	Study area			Washington County			7-County metro area		
	population	employment	dwelling units	population	employment	dwelling units	population	employment	dwelling units
1960	27,960	5,209	7,385	52,431	8,640	13,716	1,523,956	607,032	451,974
1970	40,462	8,647	10,699	82,890	16,001	21,258	1,874,093	853,138	573,265
1980	60,600	15,700	18,558	118,800	29,200	34,765	2,230,100	1,106,600	702,629
1990	99,000	28,700	31,799	185,800	49,300	55,633	2,687,000	1,330,800	871,601
2000	144,100	54,400	48,263	267,500	90,300	83,981	3,176,300	1,610,250	1,029,985

Source : Metropolitan Council.

Figure B-10 Table using vertical lines to separate columns.

Figures. Like tables, figures are word savers. In addition they have high visual impact and help break up what would otherwise be pages of solid type.

Multiple-bar charts. (See Figure B-11.) These compare relationships and show trends. Many laymen find bar charts easier to understand than line charts. Each bar represents a quantity. The height or length of the bar indicates the amount of the quantity. It makes little difference whether the bars run horizontally or vertically, but horizontal bar charts are often used to report quantities of time, length, and distance; vertical bar charts to report heights, depths, etc.

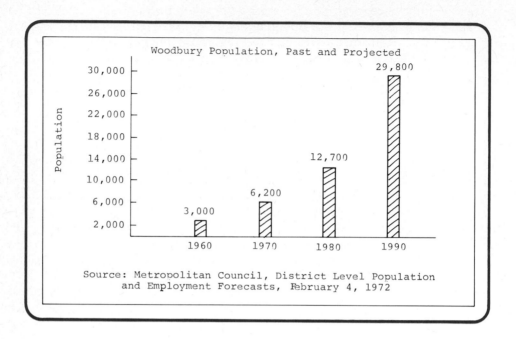

Figure B-11 Multiple-bar chart.

To make a multiple-bar chart:

- Determine whether horizontal or vertical orientation is appropriate for your data.
- Choose a scale for determining bar length (for instance, having one inch represent every 1,000 hours a machine has run).
- Measure off lengths of each bar.
- Draw the lines to make each bar. Make all bars the same width. Separate each bar an equal space.
- Shade the bars to make them show up.
- Label each bar (what it represents) and each scale (what the quantities and units of measure are). If desired, indicate the exact value at the end of each bar.
- If desired, rule a border around the chart.

Divided-bar charts. (See Figure B-12.) Consisting of one bar divided into segments, these show and compare percentages very well. The entire field of the bar represents 100 percent; each segment represents a portion of the 100 percent. They can be presented vertically or horizontally.

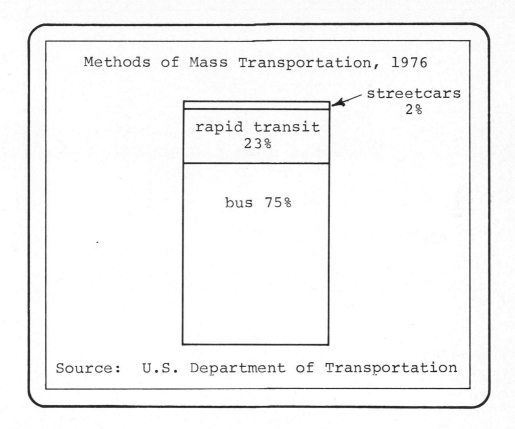

Methods of Mass Transportation, 1976

streetcars
2%

rapid transit
23%

bus 75%

Source: U.S. Department of Transportation

Figure B-12 Divided-bar chart.

To make a divided-bar chart:

- Choose a scale to determine percentages of overall length.
- Measure off segments of bar and draw lines to mark each segment. Start at one end and arrange segments from smallest to largest.
- Label each segment to identify item and percentage.
- If desired, rule a border around the chart.

Cosmographs. (See Figure B-13.) These show percentages well and are an interesting way to divide totals into their components.

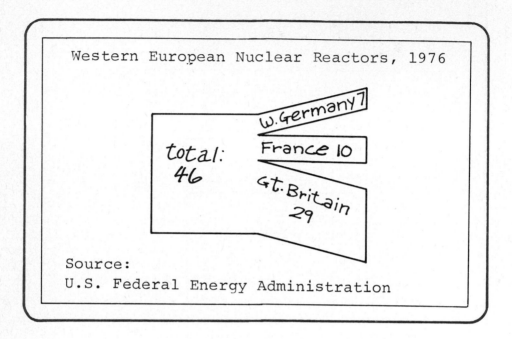

Western European Nuclear Reactors, 1976

total:
46

W. Germany 7

France 10

Gt. Britain
29

Source:
U.S. Federal Energy Administration

Figure B-13   Cosmograph.

Circle or pie charts. (See Figure B-14.) Like divided-bar charts, these show and compare percentages of a whole.

To make a circle chart:

- Draw the circle.
- Beginning at the 12 o'clock position and moving clockwise, slice the circle into appropriate-sized wedges.
- Make the slices in descending order.
- Group extremely small percentages (less than 2 percent) into one segment. The grouped segment may be labeled *miscellaneous* or *other* with the individual groups and percentages given in parenthesis or in a footnote.
- Label slices to identify items and percentages.

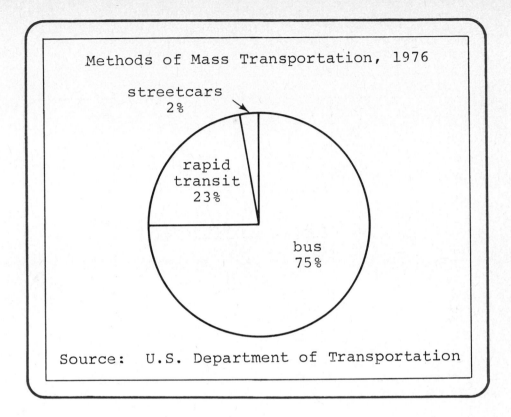

Methods of Mass Transportation, 1976

streetcars
2%

rapid
transit
23%

bus
75%

Source: U.S. Department of Transportation

Figure B-14   Circle chart.

Line charts. (See Figure B-15.) Like multiple-bar charts, these show comparisons between two or more quantities and show trends. Their curves help readers quickly grasp the results of comparative data. Since line charts are usually derived from plotting on graph paper during an investigation, you should trace the chart on a regular sheet of report paper without the original chart lines. Keep line charts simple, particularly if you do not have an audience skilled in reading them.

To make a line chart:

- Determine scale for variables.
- Rule horizontal and vertical scale lines.
- Mark off points for measurement, including interim "tic" marks.
- Label variables, units of measure, and so on.
- If desired, rule a border around the chart.

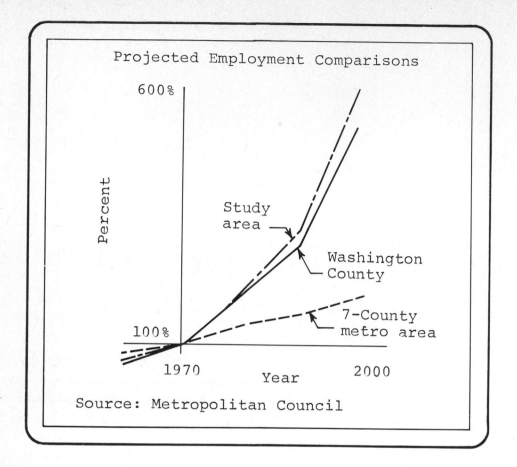

Figure B-15 Line chart.

Organizational charts. (See Figure B-16.) These resemble flow charts (see pages 144–145) but show static rather than moving relationships. They are used to show departmentalization, chains of command, and subordinate corporate levels by means of connected, labeled blocks. When completed, an organizational chart looks like a pyramid, with the top executive or office at the top.

To make an organizational chart:

- Determine the number of corporate levels you want to show.
- Draw geometrical figures large enough to hold names of units on each level.

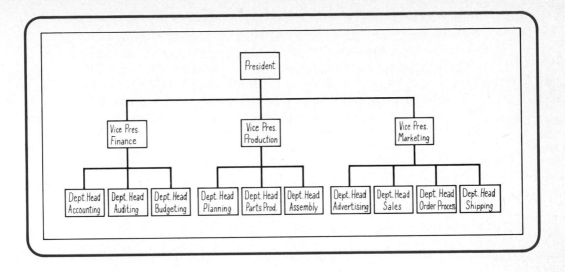

Figure B-16 Organizational chart.

- Label each geometrical figure.
- Draw lines to show chain of command. Use different types of lines to show other relationships (for instance, special supervision or authority relationships that differ from the formal hierarchical authority).
- If desired, rule a border around the chart.

Some report writers have problems using graphics. Here are four suggestions that will help you handle them. If you follow these suggestions, you'll do your bit in making your readers' task easier when they come to the graphics in your report.

1. Make your graphics large enough to be read easily. If possible, keep them of a size to fit sheets of paper with the same dimensions as your report. If you can fit them on a sheet with some text of your report, fine. Separate them from the text above and below them with adequate white space—triple space on a typed page should do it. Remember to maintain the one-inch margins.

When your graphics are too large to fit on a page with text, put them on a page by themselves immediately following or facing the page on which you analyze their contents. When they are too large to fit on a page, they may be folded or photographically reduced. The latter is preferable if the reduction doesn't make them too small to read without a magnifying glass.

2. Place your graphics where they will help readers most. Lists are part of the natural sequence of information in your reports, and their place-

ment is no problem. But graphics require your readers to read both them and the text, sometimes jumping back and forth from text to graphic. Failure to place them near the text they illustrate can cause readers to do a lot of flipping around through your report, rereading text and reexamining the graphic. Place the graphic at or very near your discussion of it.

3. Label everything clearly and carefully so your readers know exactly what they are looking at. If possible, arrange all lettering to be read from left to right. Identify figures by arabic numerals and descriptive titles, as in "Figure 1. The Ignition System." Identify tables by capital letters or capital roman numerals and descriptive titles, as in "Table A. Yield of Boneless Cooked Meat from Retail Pork Cuts." Number or letter graphics in the order in which you want them to appear in your report.

Label by name or symbol the parts of objects and components of diagrams that you want your readers to pay attention to. If you use letters to identify parts, identify the letters in an explanatory legend below the figure.

Label every column, row, axis, bar, and line in charts and tables.

If you borrow or adapt a graphic from other sources, give credit in parentheses following the figure number or table number or letter and descriptive title.

4. Introduce graphics before readers get to them. They are introduced or referred to by call-outs, which are references in the text of your report to direct readers to your graphics. They are referred to like this:

Figure 1 shows . . .	Table A shows . . .
. . . as shown in Figure 1 . . .	. . . as shown in Table A . . .
. . . (see Figure 1) . . .	. . . (see Table A) . . .
. . . (Figure 1) . . .	. . . (Table A) . . .

If the graphic is not on the same page as the call-out, include its location in the call-out, as in this example:

Recommended storage tanks (see Figure 2 on page 6) can be either buried or above ground.

Check to make sure that your graphics are numbered or lettered consecutively, that they appear in the order you want them to, and that they are referred to by call-outs.

3. Quotations   An important tactic that helps readers follow *your* writing is the skillful handling of quoted material in your reports. If you use quotations ineptly, you lose control of your report. It is important, therefore, to know when to quote and how to quote. Here are some conventions of quoting that will help you stay on top of quoted material and let you use it to support your views.

1. Avoid beginning or ending a report or a paragraph with quotations for two reasons. First, quotations in these positions produce a weak effect by

drawing the focus from your own writing. Because the beginning and end are the two most emphatic positions, you should use them for your own ideas and conclusions. Second, quotations at the beginning of a report or paragraph make it appear as though you're too indebted to the ideas of others and that *your* writing serves only to explain the quotation. The exception to these suggestions occurs when you want to use a quotation as an attention-getting device. Just remember to select quotations for the added authority they can give to *your* ideas.

2. Introduce quotations by acknowledging them with a general comment, such as "As one recent research study has found . . . " or with a specific reference, such as "Dr. Hiram Walton states . . . ."

3. All quotations must correspond exactly with the original wording, spelling, and interior punctuation. If you choose to omit words from a quoted passage, you must indicate the omitted words by using ellipsis points (three or four spaced periods). See Annex A, Writer's Guide, page 264. If you add a word or short phrase within a quotation, enclose the added words in brackets. Don't use parentheses because readers will assume the parenthetical statement exists in the original passage. See Annex A, Writer's Guide, page 258.

4. All quotations within text are enclosed inside quotation marks. A quotation within a quotation is enclosed in single quotation marks (typed by using the apostrophe). See Annex A, Writer's Guide page 282.

5. Single-space quotations longer than three typewritten lines, indenting and centering the quotations. Don't place quotation marks around single-spaced, indented quotations—they are unnecessary additional punctuation. See Annex A, Writer's Guide, page 281.

6. Document every quotation by footnote. Whenever you cite information from another source, include enough information about the source to enable your readers to locate the cited item. It has become a convention (and a convenience to readers!) to document by using footnotes (so-called because they often are gathered at the foot of the pages on which they appear) or endnotes (so-called because they frequently are gathered at the end of the report).

Like bibliography format, footnote format comes in many varieties. However, we suggest that you learn the format presented below, which is based on the form of *A Manual of Style*, 12th ed. (Chicago: University of Chicago Press, 1969).

Suggested footnote forms

● Book by single author:

[1] W. J. Patton, The Science and Practice of Welding (Englewood Cliffs, N.J.: Prentice– Hall, 1967), p. 80.

- Book by two or three authors:

[2]H. C. Morse and D. M. Cox, <u>Numerically-Controlled</u> <u>Machine</u> <u>Tools:</u> <u>The</u> <u>Breakthrough</u> <u>of</u> <u>Autofacturing</u> (Detroit: American Data Processing, 1965), pp. 91–93.

(The subtitle is always included. It is separated from the title by a colon.)

- Book by more than three authors:

[3]F. G. Abdellah, I. L. Beland, A. Martin, and R. V. Matheny, <u>Patient-Centered</u> <u>Approaches</u> <u>to</u> <u>Nursing</u> (New York: Macmillan, 1964), p. 216.

(The author entry can also read "F. G. Abdellah and others." Or "F. G. Abdellah et al.")

- Book with editor:

[4]O. H. Fidell, ed., <u>Ideas</u> <u>in</u> <u>Science</u> (New York: Washington Square Press, 1966), p. 84.

- Multivolume book, each volume having the same title:

[5]K. H. Moltracht, <u>Machine</u> <u>Shop</u> <u>Practices</u>, 2 vols. (New York: Industrial Press, 1971), 1:116.

- Multivolume book, each volume having a different title:

[6]W. Durant, <u>The</u> <u>Story</u> <u>of</u> <u>Civilization</u>, Vol. 1: <u>Our</u> <u>Oriental</u> <u>Heritage</u> (New York: Simon & Schuster, 1942), p. 274.

- Book in other than first edition:

[7]J. A. Nelson and G. M. Trout, <u>Judging</u> <u>Dairy</u> <u>Products</u>, 4th ed. (Milwaukee: Olson Publishing Co., 1964), p. 31.

- Essay or chapter from edited book:

[8]W. E. Smith, "Photographic Journalism" in <u>Photographers</u> <u>on</u> <u>Photography</u>, pp. 103–105. Ed.: Nathan Lyons (Englewood Cliffs, N.J.: Prentice-Hall, 1966), p. 103.

- Signed periodical article:

    [9]J. Fink, "Police in a Community—Improving a Deteriorated Image," The <u>Journal</u> <u>of</u> <u>Criminal</u> <u>Law</u>, <u>Criminology</u>, <u>and</u> <u>Police</u> <u>Science</u> 59 (December 1968): 624.

- Unsigned periodical article:

    [10]"A Plastic That Decays," <u>Time</u>, August 18, 1975, p. 63.

(Volume number may be omitted in citations of weekly periodicals. When a volume number is not given, the date is not put in parentheses and the page number is identified by "p." or "pp.," whichever is appropriate.)

- Signed newspaper article:

    [11]A. Claire, "Jam It Up with Blueberries," <u>The</u> <u>Lexington</u> <u>Herald</u>, August 28, 1975, p. 42.

- Unsigned newspaper article:

    [12]"Space Colonies Excite Conclave," <u>The</u> <u>Lexington</u> <u>Herald</u>, August 28, 1975, p. 56.

- Signed encyclopedia article:

    [13]<u>McGraw—Hill</u> <u>Encyclopedia</u> <u>of</u> <u>Science</u> <u>and</u> <u>Technology</u>, 1971 ed., s.v. "Doppler Effect," by G. H. Stroke.

(Articles in references arranged alphabetically don't need to be identified by volume or page. The abbreviation "s.v." or "S.v." is from the Latin *sub verbo* meaning "under the word or heading.")

- Unsigned encyclopedia article:

    [14]<u>Collier's</u> <u>Encyclopedia</u>, 1973 ed., s.v. "Poppy."

- Signed report:

    [15]R. M. Davis, <u>Effective</u> <u>Technical</u> <u>Communication:</u> <u>Copy</u> <u>Preparation</u> <u>and</u> <u>Reproduction—Motivation</u> (Wright—Patterson Air Force Base, Ohio: Air Force Institute of Technology [July 1974]), p. 24.

- Report by organization:

16UNESCO. <u>Bibliography of Publications Designed to Raise the Standard of Scientific Literature</u> (Paris: United Nations Educational, Scientific, and Cultural Organization, 1963), p. 10.

A footnote section at the end of the report proper would look like Figure B-17. The footnotes are numbered consecutively throughout your report with arabic numbers. The first footnote to a reference contains the complete information described in the examples above. For second and subsequent citations to the same reference, a variety of abbreviations are used.

"Ibid.," from the Latin *ibidem* meaning "in the same place," indicates that the source is identical to the one immediately before. Footnote 9 in Figure B-17 tells the reader that the source is the same as footnote 8. "Ibid., p. 188" (see footnote 2 in Figure B-17) means that the source is the same as the one before except that the page referred to is different.

When you cite an item again (but not in the immediately following footnote), the footnote need contain only the author's last name plus the new page references, as in the footnotes 5 and 16 in Figure B-17. However, if you have cited two or more publications by the same author, you'll have to include the title in footnotes to avoid confusion. Footnote 12 in Figure B-17 is an example.

The conclusion The last major part of your report proper is the conclusion. Like your introduction, it should emphasize the most important ideas in your report. So make your concluding section as strong as your introductory section. Some typical functions of formal end sections to the body of your report are (1) to summarize the major points of your report, (2) to state your conclusions, and (3) to state your recommendations.

1. *Summarize the major points.* Help your readers make sense of the mass of details presented in the body of your report by recalling the essential ideas covered. Just as the introduction offers readers a preview of the body, the conclusion offers readers a postview.

2. *State your conclusions.* When your report draws conclusions from the results you've observed and discussed, use the conclusion to list the logical implications of your findings. Sometimes the formal end section combines a summary of the major points and the conclusions reached. Such an ending is shown in Figure B-18.

3. *State your recommendations.* When recommendations are called for—that is, when your report fulfills an advisory function—they should be laid out in a series of parallel clauses, each separately paragraphed. Such a list of recommendations is shown in Figure B-19.

In a long end section the summary, conclusions, and recommendations could be three separate subsections.

There may also be times when you may want to provide up-front visibility for your conclusions and recommendations by placing them in the introduction. When you do, just use the principles discussed here.

SUPPLEMENTAL ELEMENTS

After the main portions of your report come the supplemental elements, which contain information related to your report that may be of interest to readers but that is not essential enough to interrupt your main line of discussion. You must decide what information can be placed in the supplemental elements to help reduce the length and complexity of the main body of the report. The following information might be appropriately placed in the supplemental elements rather than in the main portions of your report.

List of References or Bibliography

The list of references cited or the bibliography of materials used in writing your report may be treated either as a continuation of the main elements of your report (and thus placed immediately after the conclusion and footnote sections) or as a unit in the supplemental elements. The bibliography at the end of your report should be set up like Figure B-20. It may be arranged in alphabetical, chronological, or type-of-publication order.

Appendixes

A glossary or list of symbols to define unfamiliar terminology used frequently in your report may be placed in the introduction or the appendix. When the glossary or list of symbols is long and can be presented in list form, we recommend placing it in an appendix. The first part of a typical glossary is shown in Figure B-21. Copies of questionnaires, related correspondence, reports, and the texts of speeches or interviews, along with samples, exhibits, and all kinds of supplemental tables, figures, and case histories may be put in appendixes.

Footnotes

[1] G. Souice, "Pulling Power out of the Air" in Energy: Demand vs. Supply, pp. 182–194. Ed.: Nathan Lyons (Englewood Cliffs, N.J.: Prentice–Hall, 1966), p. 183.

[2] Ibid., p. 188.

[3] A. L. Hammond, "Artificial Tornadoes: A Novel Wind Energy Concept," Science, October 17, 1975, p. 257.

[4] McGraw–Hill Encyclopedia of Science and Technology, 1971 ed., s.v. "Energy Sources," by F. H. Rockett.

[5] Hammond, p. 257.

[6] W. Clark, Energy for Survival (Garden City, N.Y.: Doubleday Anchor Books, 1971), pp. 77–78.

[7] E. F. Lindsley, "Hydrogen Power: Storable and Renewable," Popular Science 206 (March 1975): 89.

[8] Lindsley, "Wind Power Without Batteries," Popular Science 207 (October 1975): 50.

[9] Ibid.

[10] Lindsley, "Robert Landing: He Rides on the Wind," Popular Science 206 (April 1975): 117.

[11] S. Walters, "100–Kilowatt Wind Turbine," Mechanical Engineering 98 (June 1976): 41.

[12] Lindsley, "Wind Power Without Batteries," p. 51.

[13] R. Stepler, "Eggbeater Windmill," Popular Science 206 (May 1975): 74–76.

[14] M. Seforza, "Harnessing a Tornado: Vortex Augmentor," Mechanical Engineering 97 (October 1975): 65.

[15] J. M. Fowler, Energy and the Environment (New York: McGraw–Hill, 1975), pp. 5–8.

[16] Clark, p. 20.

[17] J. C. Fisher, Energy Crisis in Perspective (New York: John Wiley, 1974), p. 116.

Figure B-17 Footnote page.

<u>Summary</u> <u>and</u> <u>Conclusions</u>

An attempt has been made in this report to inform the reader about the nature of radioactive fallout and how it is currently being handled by conventional measurement and removal methods with regard to surface water supplies.

1. Fallout will affect the nation's water supply. Although the quantities of radioactivity cannot be predicted, the nature of radioactivity can be predicted.

2. The greatest immediate danger would come from suspended activity. After an atomic attack radioactive material would tend to settle. Streams and rivers would scour sediment from their beds at times of flooding and high water. Later the sediment would be deposited downstream.

3. Dissolved radioactivity presents a long–range danger to water supply. Radioactive sediments would be leached from the bottoms of streams, rivers, and reservoirs.

4. Treatment plants would not remove much, if any, dissolved radioactivity. Radioactive filter sand can increase the radioactivity of treated water.

Figure B-18   Summary and conclusions.

VII. RECOMMENDATIONS

1. That the State launch a program for the restoration and preservation of the land grant records and other aged documents which are lodged in the office of the Secretary of State. A physical plant for this purpose could be equipped for no more than $25,000 and manned by two persons.

2. It would seem that, since the primary function of the Historical Society is the collection and preservation of information, documents, and relics pertaining to Kentucky history and since the society's personnel has been engaged in a substantial microfilming of historical data and is now annually accumulating approximately one million pages of records on film, the restoration shop should be the responsibility of, and located in, the Historical Society. Judgments must necessarily be made, and priorities set, on the historical worth of certain documents nominated for preservation.

3. That the Historical Society, in cooperation with the Secretary of State and the Finance Department, produce, in bound volumes, microfilmed copies of the land grant records for public use and that the originals be stored in a safe place.

4. That representatives of the office of the Secretary of State, the Library Department, and the Division of Archives and Records of the Finance Department should cooperate in the initiation of the program within the Historical Society so that all such agencies may be fully apprised of the worth of such a facility to their respective operations.

Figure B-19   List of recommendations. (Jack E. Royce, *The Preservation of Land Office Records.* Informa-ion Bulletin No. 89. Legislative Research Commission, Frankfort, Kentucky, January 1971, p. 18)

Bibliography

Clark, W. Energy for Survival. Garden City, N.Y.: Doubleday Anchor Books,
    1971.

Fisher, J. C. Energy Crisis in Perspective. New York: John Wiley, 1974.

Fowler, J. M. Energy and the Environment. New York: McGraw-Hill, 1975.

Hammond, A. L. "Artificial Tornadoes: A Novel Wind Energy Concept."
    Science, October 17, 1975, p. 257.

Lindsley, E. F. "Hydrogen Power: Storable and Renewable." Popular Science
    206 (March 1975): 88–90, 145.

-----. "Robert Landing: He Rides on the Wind." Popular Science 206 (April
    1975): 116–117.

-----. "Wind Power Without Batteries." Popular Science 207 (October 1975):
    50–52.

McGraw-Hill Encyclopedia of Science and Technology. 1971 ed. S.v. "Energy
    Sources," by F. H. Rockett.

Seforza, M. "Harnessing a Tornado: Vortex Augmentor." Mechanical
    Engineering 97 (October 1975): 65.

Souice, G. "Pulling Power out of the Air." In Energy: Demand vs. Supply,
    pp. 182–194. Ed.: Nathan Lyons. Englewood Cliffs, N.J.: Prentice-Hall,
    1966.

Stepler, R. "Eggbeater Windmill." Popular Science 206 (May 1975): 74–76.

Walters, S. "100-Kilowatt Wind Turbine." Mechanical Engineering 98 (June
    1976): 41.

Figure B-20 Bibliography.

Glossary

<u>acre-foot</u> – The amount of water required to cover one acre to a depth of one foot; equal to 43,560 cubic feet of water, or 326,000 gallons.

<u>adsorption</u> – Retention of an ion or molecule of variable size onto the surface of a molecule or molecular complex due to attractive physical chemical forces.

<u>aeration</u> – The bringing about of intimate contact between air and a liquid by spraying the liquid in the air or by agitation of the liquid to promote surface absorption of air.

> <u>step aeration</u> – A procedure for adding increments of sewage along the line of flow in the aeration tanks of an activated sludge plant. (C. F. Gould, U.S. Patent 2,337,384.)

<u>algae</u> – Primitive plants, one- or many-celled, usually aquatic and capable of elaborating their foodstuffs by photosynthesis.

<u>algicide</u> – Any substance that kills algae.

<u>average daily flow</u> – Average of all daily flow during at least one entire year (includes storm drainage).

<u>average dry weather flow</u> – Average daily flow comprised of domestic sewage, industrial waste, and ground water infiltration (no storm drainage).

<u>biochemical oxygen demand (BOD)</u> – The quantity of oxygen used in the biochemical oxidation of organic matter for five days at 20°C, usually expressed in parts per million.

<u>calcination/recalcination</u> – The process of regenerating lime from lime sludge after lime coagulation. Up to 70 percent of the lime can be recovered for reuse.

<u>chloramines</u> – Compounds of organic amines or inorganic ammonia with chlorine that are highly toxic to fish; their effect on man is unknown.

<u>chlorination</u> – The application of chlorine to disinfect the sewage.

<u>clarifier</u> – A tank or basin in which water, sewage, or other liquid containing settleable solids is retained for a sufficient time, and in which the velocity of flow is sufficiently low, to remove by gravity a part of the suspended matter. Usually, in sewage treatment, the retention period is short enough to avoid anaerobic decomposition. Also termed Settling or Subsidence Tank or Sedimentation.

<u>coagulation</u> – (1) The agglomeration of colloidal or finely divided suspended matter by the addition to the liquid of an appropriate chemical coagulant, by biological processes or by other means. (2) The process of adding a coagulant and the necessary reacting chemicals.

Figure B-21 Glossary. (The Conservation Foundation, *Water Quality, Training Institute,* Washington, D.C.: The Foundation, n.d. [c. 1974)].

coliform bacteria – A class of bacteria that live in the human intestines. They are always present in raw sewage. Chlorination usually kills them prior to discharge into waterways. Their presence provides positive evidence of pollution and the possible presence of pathogenic bacteria.

colloids – Finely divided solids that will not settle but may be removed by coagulation or biochemical action.

comminution – the process of screening sewage and cutting the screenings into particles sufficiently fine to pass through the screen openings.

denitrification – The reduction of nitrates in solution by biochemical action to nitrogen gas, which bubbles off the water into the air.

digester – A tank in which the solids resulting from the sedimentation of sewage are stored for the purpose of permitting anaerobic decomposition to the point of rendering the product nonputrescible and inoffensive. Erroneously termed digestor.

D.O./dissolved oxygen – The amount of oxygen dissolved in the water.

E.Coli (Escherichia Coli) – A species of genus Escherichia bacteria, normal inhabitant of the intestine of man and vertebrates. This species is classified among the coliform group. See coliform bacteria.

effluent – (1) A liquid that flows out of a containing space. (2) Sewage, water, or other liquid, partially or completely treated, or in its natural state, as the case may be, flowing out of a reservoir, basin, or treatment plant, or part thereof.

eutrophication – The enrichment of a body of water by the addition of nutrients. If it is a lake, it will gradually be filled in with organic matter that composts into land; this process is speeded up by pollutants, which lower the dissolved oxygen content, thereby inhibiting indigenous life. Sludges build up land masses on the edges and bottom of the lake.

groundwater – Water stored underground. The usual storage place is a zone or layer of sand, gravel, or other rock completely saturated with water that has seeped down from the surface.

Figure B-21 Glossary *(continued).*

ANNEX C
Library Research

People who don't know how to use a library properly suffer from two strangely different afflictions. They either don't realize the phenomenal amount of information available at their fingertips, or if they do, they are overpowered by it because they don't know how to find the information. Regardless of the affliction, the result is the same—inadequate data or information to get the job done.

But something happens to people who begin to learn their way around libraries. After finding the information they sought, they begin to regard libraries as a natural extension of their study or office.

The purpose of this annex is to identify basic reference sources available in most libraries and to give you some idea of the kind of information found in them. The more familiar you become with these sources, the easier it is for you to find the information you need. We have divided this annex into four sections:

- The first describes reference books—almanacs, yearbooks, atlases, biographical dictionaries, and encyclopedias.
- The second describes periodical indexes and guides to books.
- The third shows you how to locate the materials you need.
- The fourth explains how to take notes on your reading.

REFERENCE BOOKS

All libraries have a special reference section. The books in this section are collections of facts and statistics that you'll never read through, but will frequently consult. Constance Winchell's *Guide to Reference Books,* an annotated bibliography of about 7,500 reference books, is an excellent introduction to the whole field of reference books. It will be in your library's reference section or will be available from your reference librarian. In this section we will cover almanacs, atlases, yearbooks, biographical dictionaries, and encyclopedias. You can find the ones in your library by looking under the words *almanacs, atlases,* etc., in the card catalog.

Almanacs

If you think almanacs are books that tell you when to plant potatoes or go fishing, you haven't looked in a modern almanac lately. Almanacs contain enormous amounts of miscellaneous information, usually in the form of lists, charts, and tables. Most almanacs are published annually, so much of the information is associated with the events of the previous year. But a few contain historical information of a broader scope.

To give you an idea of the variety of information to be found in almanacs, we have listed below some of the information that can be found on every hundredth page of a typical almanac—*CBS News Almanac.* We'll start with page 51, because pages 1 through 50 review the previous year, as seen by CBS news correspondents.

- 51—Outline of United States history from the sixteenth century to the present
- 151—Annual salaries of U.S. government officials
- 251—Hospital costs per day, 1965–1972
- 351—Miscellaneous information about the state of Georgia (origin of name, motto, flag, seal, flower, officials, population, finances, economy, highways, birth and death rates, etc.)
- 451—Similar information about Miami and Memphis
- 551—Similar information about Ireland
- 651—Similar information about Southern Yemen
- 751—Part of index of U.S. colleges and universities, including name and location of institution, year established, enrollment, community setting, and tuition cost
- 851—List of art auction pieces bringing more than $40,000 per item, including artist's name, title of art, auction house or gallery that managed the transaction, and the sale price
- 951—Table of all-time leaders in various categories of National Football League statistics

But even this sampling doesn't illustrate the variety of factual information in the almanac. Here's a taste of more that's available:

- Distances between major U.S. cities
- Legal age for purchase of alcoholic beverages in U.S. and Canada
- The 50 leading stocks in market values (as of December 31, 1974)
- Minority populations of large U.S. cities
- Notable aircraft disasters since 1937
- Bestsellers of 1974–1975
- Sites and capacities of nuclear power reactors in the U.S.
- Nobel Prize winners, 1901 to present
- Olympic medalists, through 1972 games
- Average annual salaries of public school teachers in major U.S. cities

Such a listing may give you the impression that the information in almanacs is in random order. Actually, most almanacs are arranged by topics and have extensive indexes. We urge you to read the introductory pages of almanacs to learn the proper procedure to locate information.

Here are some good general almanacs that are likely to be in your library:

- *CBS News Almanac*
- *Economic Almanac*—covers information on business, labor, and government in U.S. and Canada.
- *Information Please Almanac, Atlas and Yearbook*
- *Reader's Digest Almanac and Yearbook*
- *World Almanac and Book of Facts*

Many other almanacs specializing in restricted subjects are also available. A good example is *Canadian Almanac and Directory*.

Yearbooks

Like almanacs, yearbooks are published annually and contain information about the previous year. They differ from almanacs in being restricted to selected topics indicated by their titles. Nearly every major professional organization publishes a yearbook. Listed below are some good yearbooks, with brief descriptions of the information they contain.

- *Commodity-Year Book*—covers basic commodities from alcohol to hogs to zinc. Sample articles are titled "Commodity Futures as a Hedge Against Inflation," "Analyzing Hogs and Pork Belly Price Trends," and "New Factors in Forecasting Cattle Futures Prices."
- *The Canada Year Book: The Official Statistical Annual of the Resources, History, Institutions, and Social and Economic Conditions of the Dominion*—published by the Canadian Bureau of Statistics, it re-

ports current information on government, population, scientific and industrial research, fisheries, transportation, banking, and other aspects of Canadian life.

- *Demographic Yearbook*—published by the statistical office, Department of Economic and Social Affairs, United Nations Organization. Each annual issue treats a special topic. The 1973 issue, for instance, concerned population census statistics—the third consecutive issue to feature the results of world population lists compiled during 1965–1973. There is tabular information on rates of population increase, life expectancy, birth rates, infant mortality, marriage and divorce rates, etc.
- *The International Year Book and Statemen's Who's Who*—provides information about world organizations; the government structures in the United Kingdom, United States, France, People's Republic of China, and the USSR; data on countries from Afghanistan to Zambia; biographical sketches of prominent persons.
- *The Municipal Year Book: An Authoritative Resume of Activities and Statistical Data of American Cities*—published by the International City Management Association, "provides local officials with information on questions and issues associated with local management. . . ."
- *Statesman's Year-Book: Statistical and Historical Annual of the States of the World*—contains information about countries and their governing bodies, and about world organizations like the United Nations Organization and the World Council of Churches.
- *Statistical Abstract of the United States*—prepared by the U.S. Bureau of Census, this book gives statistics on various industrial, social, political, economic, and cultural activities in the U.S. This book may be the most important data book of all for Americans. It includes data on every subject of public interest in the United States. In addition, it is a guide to other statistical publications.
- *Year Book of the United Nations*—records the significant activities of the United Nations: disarmament; peaceful uses of oceanbeds, outer space, and atomic energy; peace-keeping operations; strategies to encourage international trade and development; and activities related to international law.

Major encyclopedias also publish yearbooks as annual supplements to keep their material up to date.

Atlases

Atlases are compendiums of tables and maps that illustrate many of the same facts found in almanacs. Maps are the most valuable feature of an atlas. They present information on just about anything you'd ever need to look up—highway and railway routes, topography, climate, important places, population distribution, etc.

To give you a sampling of the information you can find in an atlas, we list some of the data you can find reported in maps at the front of the *Rand McNally Commercial Atlas and Marketing Guide,* an annual atlas that gives the latest information on the United States:

- zip codes
- telephone area codes
- college population
- major military installations
- retail sales distribution
- trading areas
- metropolitan areas
- manufacturing centers
- national forests
- and much more

If you want to find out whether Brazil is larger than Australia, how many people live in China, what the longest island is, what the smallest ocean is, or what type of government Luxembourg has, you can get the information from a world atlas. Major world atlases that are likely to be in your library are

- *Goode's World Atlas*—contains maps showing distribution of rainfall, urban resources, topography, and population; world maps, distribution maps, etc.
- *National Geographic Atlas of the World*—on oversized pages, this atlas provides on large-scale maps enormous amounts of detailed information about all countries.

If you look under the subject *Atlases* in your library's card catalog, you'll probably find three inches' worth of catalog cards on atlases of every description. You name it—continents, counties, diseases, hobbies—there's an atlas for it.

Biographical Dictionaries

Biographical dictionaries consist principally of brief, factual information about prominent persons. Some biographical dictionaries are arranged alphabetically by the subject's last name, some by field of achievement, and some by chronology. Some are general, and some are specific (there's even a book covering the great sinners of the past!). Some are restricted to persons already dead at the time of publication; others include both living and dead persons. Some of the titles follow:

About people past:

- *Dictionary of American Biography*
- *Dictionary of National Biography* (British)
- *Dictionary of Scientific Biography*
- *Who Was Who in America*

About people living:

- *American Men and Women of Science*
- *Current Biography*
- *Who's Who in America*
- *Who's Who* (British)
- *Who's Who in Finance and Industry*

About people both living and dead:

- *Asimov's Biographical Encyclopedia of Science and Technology*
- *Baker's Biographical Dictionary of Musicians*
- *Chamber's Biographical Dictionary*
- *Webster's Biographical Dictionary*
- *McGraw-Hill Encyclopedia of World Biography*

Two helpful indexes to biographical material are *Biography Index*, which lists biographical information in both periodicals and books, and *Biographical Dictionaries Master Index*, which indexes entries to over 725,000 persons that appear in 59 biographical dictionaries.

Encyclopedias

Atlases, almanacs, yearbooks, and biographical dictionaries aren't the only quick sources of information. Encyclopedias are also indispensable quick references. They provide information on various subjects and personalities.

Multiple-volume encyclopedias:

- *Collier's Encyclopedia*—strong in contemporary science and biography; excellent bibliographies and study guides in the index volume.
- *Encyclopaedia Britannica*—strong in scholarly treatments of art, history, politics, and the biological sciences; atlases in the index volume.
- *Encyclopedia Americana*—strong in science, technology, government, and business.
- *Encyclopedia of World Art*—preface states that coverage includes "architecture, sculpture, and painting, and every other man-made object

that, regardless of its purpose or technique, enters the field of esthetic judgment because of its form or decoration."

- *The International Encyclopedia of Social Sciences*—strong in anthropology, economics, history, political science, and sociology.
- *The Lincoln Library of Essential Information*—covers vast array of subjects: literature, history, geography, mathematics, all departments of science, economics, government. Entries are not arranged alphabetically but by topics.
- *McGraw-Hill Encyclopedia of Science and Technology*—strong in physical, natural, and applied sciences.
- *The Worldmark Encyclopedia of Nations*—according to its preface, a "practical guide to geographic, historical, political, social and economic status of nations."

Single-volume encyclopedias:

- *The Columbia Encyclopedia*—covers a wide range of material found in general reference works: arts, literature, geography, life and physical sciences, and social science.
- *Van Nostrand's Scientific Encyclopedia*—according to its preface, covers "the physical sciences, the earth sciences, the biological sciences, the medical sciences, the various fields of engineering, and the pure and applied mathematics and statistics."

PERIODICAL INDEXES AND GUIDES TO BOOKS

A good way to start your literature search is to look through the basic reference documents we've already mentioned, especially encyclopedias. They often have a list of references at the end of articles or have study guides and bibliographies on particular subjects in the index volume.

Next you should go to the various periodical indexes. For now, let's put off the card catalog as a primary research tool for identifying material, since its function is mainly to identify and locate holdings in a particular library. The time will come, though, when you'll want to use it as an index, too. What we want to do now is explain how to use indexes and to describe several important indexes and guides to books.

Periodical Indexes

Magazines and journals are called periodicals because they are issued at regular intervals—weekly, monthly, quarterly, semi-annually, or whatever. A periodical index is a reference that covers a given number of periodicals and gives the author, title, volume number, page numbers, and date of issue for items published in the periodicals covered by the index. The cover of the issues and the bound volumes of an index (see Figure C-1) indicate the time period covered.

JUNE 10, 1976

Vol. 76   No. 8

Includes indexing from April 21—May 20, 1976

READERS' GUIDE

to periodical literature

(UNABRIDGED)

An author subject index

to selected

general interest periodicals

of reference value in libraries.

THE H. W. WILSON COMPANY

Figure C-1 *Readers' Guide* cover. (*Readers' Guide to Periodical Literature;* copyright © 1976 by The H. W. Wilson Company; material reproduced by permission of the publisher)

Since you should use indexes in every library research project, find out where they're kept in the library and spend some time reading their prefatory material. At the front of every index are pages that explain how to use that particular index.

To find what periodicals are covered by a specific index, check the list at the front of the index. Each index covers its chosen field of periodicals (coverage is usually determined every few years by vote of index subscribers). Figure C-2 is the first page of the list of periodicals covered by *Readers' Guide to Periodical Literature,* one of the more valuable guides to popular and general literature in the United States.

To find out how an index abbreviates entries, check the explanation of abbreviations at the front of the index before the list of entries. The explanations from *Readers' Guide to Periodical Literature* show what such sections look like. The first page of the list of the abbreviated titles of periodicals indexed is shown in Figure C-3. The abbreviations used in the highly abbreviated and condensed form of index entries are shown in Figure C-4.

A portion of a sample page from *Readers' Guide to Periodical Literature* showing entries under the heading "HOUSES, Remodeled" is shown here. The third entry tells us that "Remodeling: Two Families Who Lived Through It—and What They Learned" is an illustrated article by D. R. Haupert that appeared in the October 1976 issue of *Better Homes and Gardens,* volume 54, on pages 104–111.

There are two kinds of indexes—general indexes, which cover many periodicals in a wide general field, and restricted subject indexes, which cover periodicals in a narrow subject field.

General Periodical Indexes

- *Readers' Guide to Periodical Literature* (1900–present) is an author-subject index of about 160 American periodicals of general interest. It

PERIODICALS INDEXED

All data as of latest issue received

Aging—$5.05. m (bi-m F-Mr, My-Je, Jl-Ag, N-D) Aging, Superintendent of Documents, U.S. Government Printing Office, Washington, D.C. 20402

America—$14. w (except Ja 3, and alternate Saturdays in Jl and Ag) America Press, 106 W 56th St, New York, N.Y. 10019

American Artist—$15. m American Artist, 1 Color Court, Marion, Ohio 43302

The American City. See The American City & County

The American City & County—$18. m Morgan-Grampian Publishing Co, Berkshire Common, Pittsfield, Mass. 01201

American Education—$13.50. m (bi-m Ja-F, Ag-S) American Education, Superintendent of Documents, U.S. Government Printing Office, Washington, D.C. 20402

American Forests—$8.50. m American Forestry Association, 1319 18th St, NW, Washington, D.C. 20036

*American Heritage—$24. bi-m American Heritage, 383 W Center St, Marion, Ohio 43302

The American Historical Review—$35. free to members of the American Historical Association. 5 times a yr (O, D, F, Ap, Je) American Historical Association, 400 A St, SE, Washington, D.C. 20003

American History Illustrated—$10. m (except Mr, S) The National Historical Society, Gettysburg, Pa. 17325

American Home—$5.94. m American Home, P.O. Box 4568, Des Moines, Ia. 50306

American Imago—$12. q Wayne State Univ. Press, 5980 Cass Ave, Detroit, Mich. 48202

American Libraries—available only to members. m (bi-m Jl-Ag) American Library Association, 50 E Huron St, Chicago, Ill. 60611

The American Scholar—$8. q United Chapters of Phi Beta Kappa, 1811 Q St, NW, Washington, D.C. 20009

The American West—$12. bi-m American West Pub. Co, 20380 Town Center Lane, Cupertino, Calif. 95014

Américas—$10. m (bi-m Je-Jl, N-D) General Secretariat of the Organization of American States, Washington, D.C. 20006

The Annals of the American Academy of Political and Social Science—$15. free to members. bi-m American Academy of Political and Social Science, 3937 Chestnut St, Philadelphia, Pa. 19104

Antiques—$24. m Straight Enterprises, Inc, 551 5th Ave, New York, N.Y. 10017

Architectural Record—$15. m (semi-m My, Ag, O) Architectural Record, P.O. Box 430, Hightstown, N.J. 08520

Art in America—$17.95. bi-m Art in America, 542 Pacific Ave, Marion, Ohio 43302

Art News—$18. m (q Je-Ag) Art News, P.O. Box 969, Farmingdale, N.Y. 11735

*The Atlantic—$13. m Atlantic, P.O. Box 1857, Greenwich, Conn. 06830

Audubon—$13. bi-m National Audubon Society, 950 3rd Ave, New York, N.Y. 10022

Aviation Week & Space Technology—$27. w Aviation Week, P.O. Box 430, Hightstown, N.J. 08520

*Better Homes and Gardens—$8. m Better Homes and Gardens, 1716 Locust St, Des Moines, Ia. 50336

BioScience—$32. m BioScience, 1401 Wilson Blvd, Arlington, Va. 22209

Bulletin of the Atomic Scientists—$15. m (S-Je) Bulletin of the Atomic Scientists, 1020-24 E 58th St, Chicago, Ill. 60637

Business Week—$21.50. w (except for one issue in Ja) Business Week, P.O. Box 506, Hightstown, N.J. 08520

Camping Magazine—$10. free to members of the American Camping Association. m (Ja-Je, bi-m S-D) Camping Magazine, Bradford Woods, Martinsville, Ind. 46151

Car and Driver—$7.98. m Car and Driver, P.O. Box 2770, Boulder, Colo. 80302

Ceramics Monthly—$8. m (S-Je) Ceramics Monthly, P.O. Box 12448, Columbus, Ohio 43212

*Changing Times—$9. m Changing Times, The Kiplinger Magazine, Editors Park, Md. 20782

Chemistry—$8. m (bi-m Ja-F, Jl-Ag) American Chemical Society, 1155 16th St, NW, Washington, D.C. 20036

The Christian Century—$12. w (bi-w the first 2 weeks in Ja and F, and from the 2nd week in Je through the 2nd week in S) Christian Century Foundation, 407 S Dearborn St, Chicago, Ill. 60605

Christianity Today—$15. (plus .40 for postage) fortn. Christianity Today, 1014 Washington Building, Washington, D.C. 20005

The Clearing House—$8.50. m (S-My) Heldref Publications, 4000 Albemarle St, N.W, Washington, D.C. 20016

Commentary—$20. m American Jewish Committee, 165 E 56th St, New York, N.Y. 10022

Commonweal—$17. bi-w Commonweal Pub. Co, Inc, 232 Madison Ave, New York, N.Y. 10016

Figure C-2 Periodical list. (*Readers' Guide to Periodical Literature;* copyright © 1976 by The H. W. Wilson Company; material reproduced by permission of the publisher)

ABBREVIATIONS OF PERIODICALS INDEXED

For full information, consult May 10, 1976 issue

Aging—Aging
Am Artist—American Artist
Am City & County—American City & County
Am Educ—American Education
Am For—American Forests
*Am Heritage—American Heritage
Am Hist Illus—American History Illustrated
Am Hist R—American Historical Review
Am Home—American Home
Am Imago—American Imago
Am Lib—American Libraries
Am Scholar—American Scholar
Am West—American West
America—America
American City. See American City & County
Américas—Américas
Ann Am Acad—Annals of the American Academy of Political and Social Science
Antiques—Antiques
Archit Rec—Architectural Record
Art in Am—Art in America
Art N—Art News
*Atlantic—Atlantic
Audubon—Audubon
Aviation W—Aviation Week & Space Technology

*Bet Hom & Gard—Better Homes and Gardens
BioScience—BioScience
Bull Atom Sci—Bulletin of the Atomic Scientists
Bus W—Business Week

Camp Mag—Camping Magazine
Car & Dr—Car and Driver
Ceram Mo—Ceramics Monthly
*Changing T—Changing Times
Chemistry—Chemistry
Chr Cent—Christian Century
Chr Today—Christianity Today
Clearing H—Clearing House
Commentary—Commentary
Commonweal—Commonweal
Cong Digest—Congressional Digest
Conservationist—Conservationist (Albany)
*Consumer Rep—Consumer Reports
*Consumers Res Mag—Consumers' Research Magazine
Craft Horiz—Craft Horizons
Cur Hist—Current History
Current—Current

Dance Mag—Dance Magazine
Dept State Bull—Department of State Bulletin
Design—Design
Duns R—Dun's Review

RG 6/10/76

*Ebony—Ebony
Educ Digest—Education Digest
Engl J—English Journal
Environment—Environment
Esquire—Esquire

Fam Health—Family Health incorporating Today's Health
*Farm J—Farm Journal
Field & S—Field & Stream
Film Q—Film Quarterly
Flying—Flying
Focus—Focus
*For Affairs—Foreign Affairs
Forbes—Forbes
*Fortune—Fortune

*Good H—Good Housekeeping

Harp Baz—Harper's Bazaar
*Harper—Harper's Magazine
Harvard Bus R—Harvard Business Review
*Hi Fi—High Fidelity and Musical America
Hobbies—Hobbies
*Holiday—Holiday
*Horizon—Horizon
Horn Bk—Horn Book Magazine
Horticulture—Horticulture
Hot Rod—Hot Rod
House & Gard—House & Garden incorporating Living for Young Homemakers
House B—House Beautiful

Int Wildlife—International Wildlife
Intellect—Intellect

*Ladies Home J—Ladies' Home Journal
Lib J—Library Journal
Liv Wildn—Living Wilderness

MH—MH
McCalls—McCall's
Mademoiselle—Mademoiselle
Mech Illus—Mechanix Illustrated
Mo Labor R—Monthly Labor Review
Mod Phot—Modern Photography
Motor B & S—Motor Boating & Sailing
Motor T—Motor Trend
Ms—Ms
*Mus Q—Musical Quarterly

N Y Times Mag—New York Times Magazine
*Nat Geog—National Geographic Magazine
Nat Parks & Con Mag—National Parks & Conservation Magazine

Figure C-3 List of periodical abbreviations. (*Readers' Guide to Periodical Literature;* copyright © 1976 by The H. W. Wilson Company; material reproduced by permission of the publisher)

ABBREVIATIONS

*	following name entry, a printer's device	Jr	junior
+	continued on later pages of same issue	jt auth	joint author
Abp	archbishop	ltd	limited
abr	abridged		
Ag	August	m	monthly
Ap	April	Mr	March
arch	architect	My	May
assn	association		
Aut	Autumn	N	November
ave	avenue	no	number
bart	baronet	O	October
bibl	bibliography		
bibl f	bibliographical foot-notes	por	portrait
bi-m	bimonthly	pseud	pseudonym
bi-w	biweekly	pt	part
bldg	building	pub	published, publisher, publishing
Bp	bishop		
co	company	q	quarterly
comp	compiled, compiler		
cond	condensed	rev	revised
cont	continued		
corp	corporation	S	September
		sec	section
D	December	semi-m	semimonthly
dept	department	soc	society
		Spr	Spring
ed	edited, edition, editor	sq	square
		Sr	senior
		st	street
F	February	Summ	Summer
		supp	supplement
Hon	Honorable	supt	superintendent
il	illustrated, illustration, illustrator	tr	translated, translation, translator
inc	incorporated		
introd	introduction, introductory	v	volume
		w	weekly
Ja	January	Wint	Winter
Je	June		
Jl	July	yr	year

For those unfamiliar with form of reference used in the entries, the following explanation is given.

Sample entry:
OIL well drilling
Striking it rich—oil in your own back yard.
J. M. Liston. il Pop Mech 145:84-5+ Ja '76

An illustrated article on the subject OIL well drilling entitled "Striking it rich—oil in your own back yard," by J. M. Liston, will be found in volume 145 of Popular Mechanics, pages 84-5 (continued on later pages of the same issue) the January 1976 number

Figure C-4 List of abbreviations. (*Readers' Guide to Periodical Literature;* copyright © 1976 by The H. W. Wilson Company; material reproduced by permission of the publisher)

covers such magazines as *American Heritage, Better Homes and Gardens, Esquire, Farm Journal, Hot Rod, Reader's Digest, Scientific American,* and *Sports Illustrated.*

- *Applied Science and Technology Index* (1958–present) is a subject index to articles in over 225 science, engineering, and industrial periodicals. It's concerned with material on aeronautics, automotives, chemistry, construction, electricity, engineering, geology, metallurgy, machining, physics, and other related subjects. It covers such magazines as *Journal of American Water Works Association, Coal Age, Fire Technology, Machine Design,* and *Welding Journal.*
- *Art Index* (1929–present) is an author-subject index to domestic and foreign art periodicals and museum bulletins. It's concerned with material on archeology, ceramics, engraving, graphic arts, landscaping, painting, sculpture, photography, industrial design, city planning, landscape design, and related subjects. It covers such periodicals as *The Art Journal, Ceramics Monthly, Landscape Architecture,* and *Sight and Sound, The International Film Quarterly.*
- *Biological and Agricultural Index* (1964–present) is a subject index that covers magazines from the biological sciences and magazines, bulletins, and books on agricultural science. It's concerned with material on agricultural chemistry, agricultural economics, agricultural engineering, animal husbandry, biochemistry, botany, conservation, food science, ecology, dairying, and other related subjects. It indexes such periodicals as *Agronomy Journal, Biochemical Journal, Biological Reviews, Crops and Soils, Developmental Biology, Journal of Forestry,* and *Western Horseman.*
- *The Business Periodicals Index* (1958–present) is a subject index to articles in approximately 115 English-language periodicals dealing with business, trade, finance, public administration, accounting, advertising, banking, and taxation. It covers such magazines as *Advertising Age, The Banker, Dun's Review, Harvard Business Review, Management Review,* and *Textile World.*
- *Education Index* (1929–present) is an author-subject index to material in some 200 periodicals, proceedings, yearbooks, bulletins, and monographs. It's concerned with material on all aspects of education, counseling and guidance, and psychology. It indexes such periodicals as *Agricultural Education Magazine, Business Education Forum, The Quarterly Journal of Speech,* and *The Vocational Guidance Quarterly.*
- *Engineering Index* (1906–present) is a subject-author index to over 1,500 technical, engineering, and scientific periodicals in 20 languages. It also indexes papers, reports, and proceedings issued by government bureaus, research institutes, industrial organizations, and professional societies. An especially helpful feature is the annotations of entries. It covers such periodicals as *Assembly Engineering, Journal of Safety Engineering, Ocean Engineering,* and *Water Well Journal.*

- *Humanities Index* (1974–present) is an author-subject index concerned with material on archeology, classical studies, folklore, history, languages and literature, political criticism, performing arts, philosophy, religion, and related subjects. It covers such periodicals as *American Literature, Dance Magazine, Film Journal,* and *Religious Studies*. A book review section follows the main body of index.
- *Industrial Arts Index* (1913–1957) is a subject index to articles in some 240 technical, engineering, science, business, and trade periodicals.
- *Public Affairs Information Service, Bulletin* (1915–present) is a subject index to government documents, reports, and articles from social science periodicals. It's concerned with material on public administration, international affairs, economics, and related subjects. It indexes such periodicals as *Business Economics, Journal of Police Science and Administration, Journal of Consumer Research,* and *Soviet Union*.
- *Social Sciences Index* (1974–present) is an author-subject index of 262 periodicals from the fields of anthropology, economics, environmental science, law and criminology, psychology, sociology, and related subjects. It covers such periodicals as *American Journal of Nursing, Bulletin on Narcotics, Community Development Journal, American Psychologist, Social Work,* and *Technology and Culture*. A book review section follows the main body of the index.

Restricted Subject Periodical Indexes

Restricted subject periodical indexes, usually sponsored by national professional organizations, attempt to complete the coverage of materials in special fields by indexing material from sources not covered by general periodical indexes. Most are quite new, but some have been around for over fifty years. Here are some typical ones.

- *Accountant's Index* (1920–present), published by the American Institute of Certified Public Accountants, is an author-subject-title index covering periodicals, pamphlets, and government documents relating to accounting, auditing, data processing, financial management, investments, taxation, and similar fields. It covers such magazines as *Abacus, Georgia CPA, Price Waterhouse Review,* and *Tax Counselor's Quarterly*.
- *Business Education Index* (1940–present), sponsored by Delta Pi Epsilon, National Honorary Graduate Fraternity in Business Education, is an author-subject index to 32 business education periodicals, including several state business education newsletters and bulletins. It also lists new books in the field. Among nationally circulated periodicals covered are *The Balance Sheet, Journal of Business Communication,* and *Today's Secretary*.
- *Cumulative Index to Nursing Literature* (1956–present), published by The Seventh Day Adventist Hospital Association, is an author-subject

index to nursing and related health sciences periodicals, such as *American Journal of Nursing, Children Today, Hospital Medicine,* and *Patient Care.*

- *The Environment Index* (1971–present), published by the Environmental Information Center, Inc., indexes thousands of citations from several hundred periodicals and books searched for significant environmental information.

In addition to the periodical indexes described in this section and the guides to books in the following section, you should know about another basic reference—*Ulrich's Periodical Directory,* an annual guide to American and foreign periodicals that classifies alphabetically by subject and title about 20,000 periodicals. A particularly useful entry in *Ulrich's* is the notations of indexes and abstracts in which periodicals are listed.

Guides to Books

In addition to general and restricted subject indexes to periodicals there are guides that serve the same purpose for books, pamphlets, and government documents.

- *Cumulative Book Index* (1928–present) lists English-language books published throughout the world. It does not cover government documents, most pamphlets, inexpensive paperbacks, editions limited to less than 500 copies, and other minor material. Entries are listed alphabetically by author, subject, and title. The main entry (author entry) gives the author, title, edition (if other than the first), pagination, price, publisher, and year of publication.
- *Scientific, Medical, and Technical Books,* 2nd ed., edited by R. R. Hawkins, is a subject index to important scientific, medical, and technical books published in the United States. Entries are arranged by fields of knowledge (chemistry, automotive engineering and repair, agriculture, etc.) and contain tables of contents and descriptive notes about the book. It describes about 8,000 books published from 1930 to 1956.
- *United States Government Publications: Monthly Catalog* (1895–present) has been published monthly ever since the office of the U.S. Superintendent of Documents was established. It indexes the publications of U.S. government agencies. Arranged by issuing agency, entries give author, title, publication data, price or availability status. Separate annual indexes arrange entries by subject, author, and title.
- *Vertical File Index* (1935–present) is a subject-title index to pamphlets, brochures, folders, leaflets, and some state and federal government documents. Often it provides short descriptive notes for entries.

Guides to Book Reviews

Should you want to learn more about a book before deciding to buy it or search for it, check the following guides to book reviews for evaluations of the book.

- *Book Review Digest* (1905–present) contains excerpts from reviews of books published or distributed in the United States. The reviews are restricted to those appearing within eighteen months following a book's publication, so it is therefore necessary to know the date of publication of the book. Entries are arranged alphabetically by the name of the author of the book. The review excerpts are arranged alphabetically by title of the periodical in which the review appeared. A subject and title index follows the author entry.
- *Book Review Index* (1965–present) lists thousands of review citations of thousands of books. The 1974 annual cumulation gives an idea of the enormous coverage of the *BRI:* approximately 76,400 reviews of approximately 35,400 books taken from 228 periodicals. The index is arranged alphabetically by author of the book reviewed.
- *Technical Book Review Index* (1917–present) is arranged alphabetically by author of the book reviewed. Entries include brief quotations from reviews.

LOCATING THE MATERIAL

After you know what material you want, you'll need to locate it. Some of the material is going to be in your library, but some isn't.

To find out whether your library has a particular periodical, check the card catalog or periodical list (a locally compiled list is usually kept in your library's periodical room). They will tell you what periodicals are in your library and exactly how extensive the holdings are—which volumes and issues are available.

If your library holds the periodical, find out where the recent unbound issues and the older bound issues are kept. Unbound issues are usually kept for a year, then the year's supply is bound and placed with the other bound volumes on the shelves. The recent unbound issues may be kept in the current periodicals reading room or some other place set aside especially for them, or they may be with the bound volumes on the shelves.

Many libraries have books, back issues of periodicals, and other material on microform instead of in their originally published form. If your library has microform material, find out where it is located and how it is arranged. Microform material is regarded as part of the library's holdings and will be included in the library's card catalog.

To find out whether your library has a particular book, check the card catalog. All cards in the catalog are filed alphabetically. A card will be alphabetized under three or more entries: (1) author (or editor), (2) title, and (3) subject(s). The card catalogs of some libraries are divided in two—the author-title catalog and the subject catalog. But in most small- and medium-sized libraries the author, title, and subject cards are filed together in one alphabetical sequence.

On the front of each drawer of the card catalog are guide letters or words. All cards beginning with words between these guide letters or words will be found in that drawer. Here are two examples:

NUCLEAR R—NURSERY   NURSES—NUTRITION

If you're working from a bibliography, you can simply look for the author's name. If you have only the title of the material, look it up. Even if you don't know the names of authors or titles of material on the subject you're investigating, you can use the card catalog as a subject index to see if the library has anything about that particular subject.

Although each library makes its own decisions on how to alphabetize its card catalog, the following principles are usually followed:

- *The, A, An* are ignored in alphabetizing. A book entitled *The Modern Technician* would be alphabetized in the *m*'s. But articles within an entry are important. A book entitled *Work for the Beginner* would follow *Work for a Man*.
- Foreign prefixes such as *de, von,* and *van* in names are usually ignored in alphabetizing.
- Names beginning with *Mc* and *Mac* are usually filed as if they were *Mc* and placed at the front of the *m*'s.
- Abbreviations like *Dr., Mr., St.,* and numbers like *19th* are filed as if they were spelled out. But *Mrs.* is usually filed as written.

Once you locate the catalog card, you'll find it contains much information. An author card is shown in Figure C-5.

1. The call number in the upper left corner of the card is what you need to find where the book is shelved.
2. The author line gives the full name of the author. It may also give the author's year of birth and, if dead, the year of death. The author of this book is the American Welding Society's Arc Welding and Arc Cutting Committee, so that name rather than that of a person is in the author line.
3. The complete title and publishing information of the book give you the bibliographical information you need to make a bibliography card or bibliography entry.
4. Notations on the special features of the book, including number of

pages, illustrations, and the height of the book (in centimeters), give you significant information about the physical aspects and contents of the book.

5. This line gives you other ways the book is cataloged in the library card catalog. But, more important, these words also are related key words you can look under in the card catalog to see whether there are other books on the subject.

6. These letters and numbers give the Library of Congress call number, the Dewey Decimal call number, and the Library of Congress catalog card order number. Below is the International Standard Book Number (ISBN). "MARC" means that the book is cataloged on Machine Readable Catalog tape. This information will be of little interest to you, but it is important to librarians.

7. The words indicate that this book is in the Library of Congress in Washington. The number is the date of this printing of the card. This information will be of no interest to you.

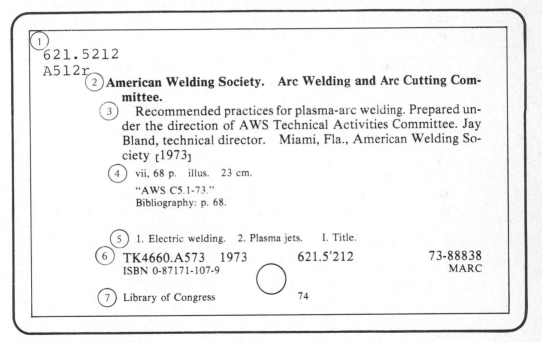

Figure C-5 Author card.

The title card (see Figure C-6) is identical to the author card except that the title of the book is typed above the author's name as well as appearing in its regular position.

The subject card (see Figure C-7) is identical to the author card except that the subject under which the card is filed is typed above the author's

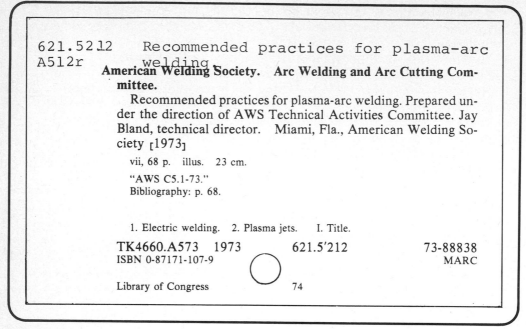

```
621.5212      Recommended practices for plasma-arc
A512r         welding
```
American Welding Society.   Arc Welding and Arc Cutting Committee.

Recommended practices for plasma-arc welding. Prepared under the direction of AWS Technical Activities Committee. Jay Bland, technical director.   Miami, Fla., American Welding Society [1973]

vii, 68 p.   illus.   23 cm.

"AWS C5.1-73."
Bibliography: p. 68.

1. Electric welding.   2. Plasma jets.   I. Title.

TK4660.A573   1973   621.5′212   73-88838

ISBN 0-87171-107-9   MARC

Library of Congress   74

Figure C-6   Title card.

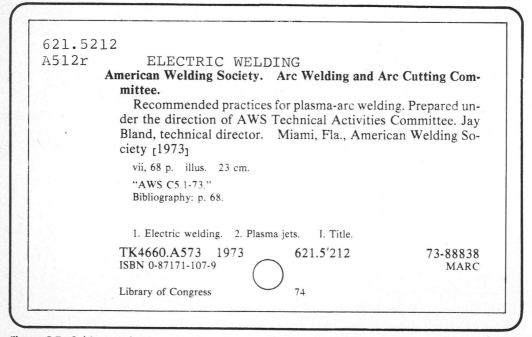

```
621.5212
A512r          ELECTRIC WELDING
```
American Welding Society.   Arc Welding and Arc Cutting Committee.

Recommended practices for plasma-arc welding. Prepared under the direction of AWS Technical Activities Committee. Jay Bland, technical director.   Miami, Fla., American Welding Society [1973]

vii, 68 p.   illus.   23 cm.

"AWS C5.1-73."
Bibliography: p. 68.

1. Electric welding.   2. Plasma jets.   I. Title.

TK4660.A573   1973   621.5′212   73-88838

ISBN 0-87171-107-9   MARC

Library of Congress   74

Figure C-7   Subject card.

name as well as appearing in its regular position. (This book has another subject card filed under "Plasma jets.")

In addition to author, title, and subject cards you should know about two important cross-reference cards when using the library card catalog as a subject index. The "see" card (as shown in Figure C-8) guides you from a subject heading not used in the system to those that are. For instance, if you're looking for subject cards on *Guns*, you'll find, as the "see" card in Figure C-8 shows, that *Firearms* and *Ordnance* are the subject headings for material on guns.

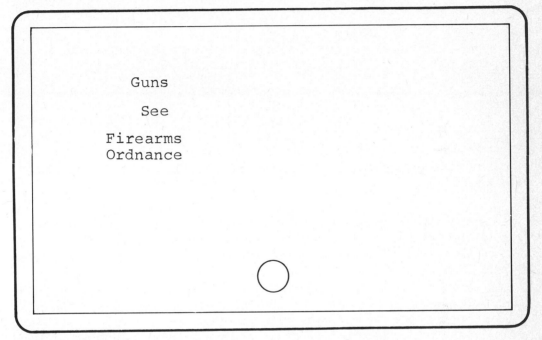

Figure C-8 "See" card.

The "see also" card (as shown in Figure C-9) guides you from a subject heading that is used to other closely related subject headings used.

When, with the help of the card catalog, you find the book you want, copy the call number. Then find out where books with that call number are located, go to the shelf and get the book. Be sure to copy the call number accurately and completely, because you won't be able to locate the book easily without the entire call number.

TAKING NOTES

The final step in library research is extracting information from the articles and books you've found. Careful note-taking is essential. After all, notes are the products of your work. Our memories are simply too short to hold

```
      Firearms

         See also

   Gunnery
   Ordnance
   Pistols


     also subdivision Firearms under armies and
   navies, e.g. U.S.Army--Firearms; U.S. Navy--
   Firearms.
```

Figure C-9 "See also" card.

the information we've found. So get a couple of packs of 3-by-5 and 4-by-6 cards and a pen so you can take notes as you read. Take your notes on these cards: They are easy to handle and rearrange and stand up better than pieces of paper.

When you compile a bibliography of potential source material, you'll make out bibliography cards. Fill out a separate card for each possible source. Usually 3-by-5 cards are adequate for this, and they'll be easy to tell from the 4-by-6 cards used to take notes on. As Figure C-10 shows, you can divide the bibliographical information for a book into three parts: (1) author or editor's name, (2) title of work, and (3) publishing information.

For a periodical you can divide the bibliographical information (Figure C-11) into four parts: (1) author's name, (2) title of article, (3) title of periodical, and (4) volume number, date, and page number.

When you take notes during your reading, you'll make out note cards. Usually 4-by-6 cards are better than 3-by-5 cards for this. Fill out a separate card for each note. As Figure C-12 shows, you should put three kinds of information on each card: (1) a brief descriptive heading at the top to help you with sorting and arranging note cards as you organize your material, (2) the note itself, and (3) the author and page or pages used at the bottom to identify the source of the note. If there's more than one work by one author or more than one author with the same last name, indicate title and author's initials as well as author's last name and pages.

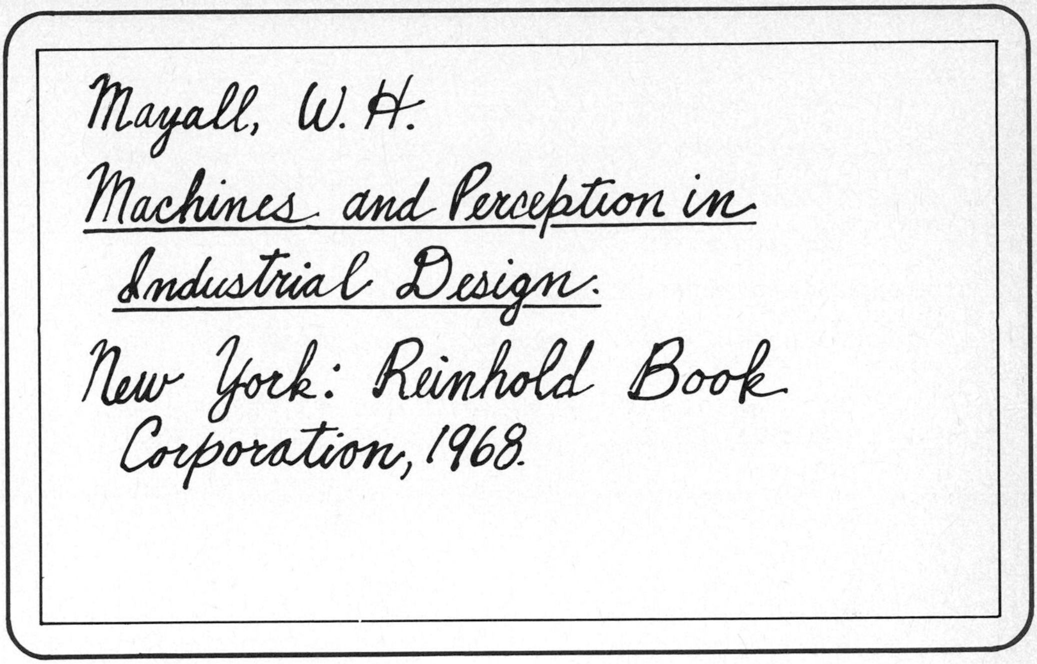

Mayall, W. H.
Machines and Perception in
Industrial Design.
New York: Reinhold Book
Corporation, 1968.

Figure C-10 Bibliography card for book.

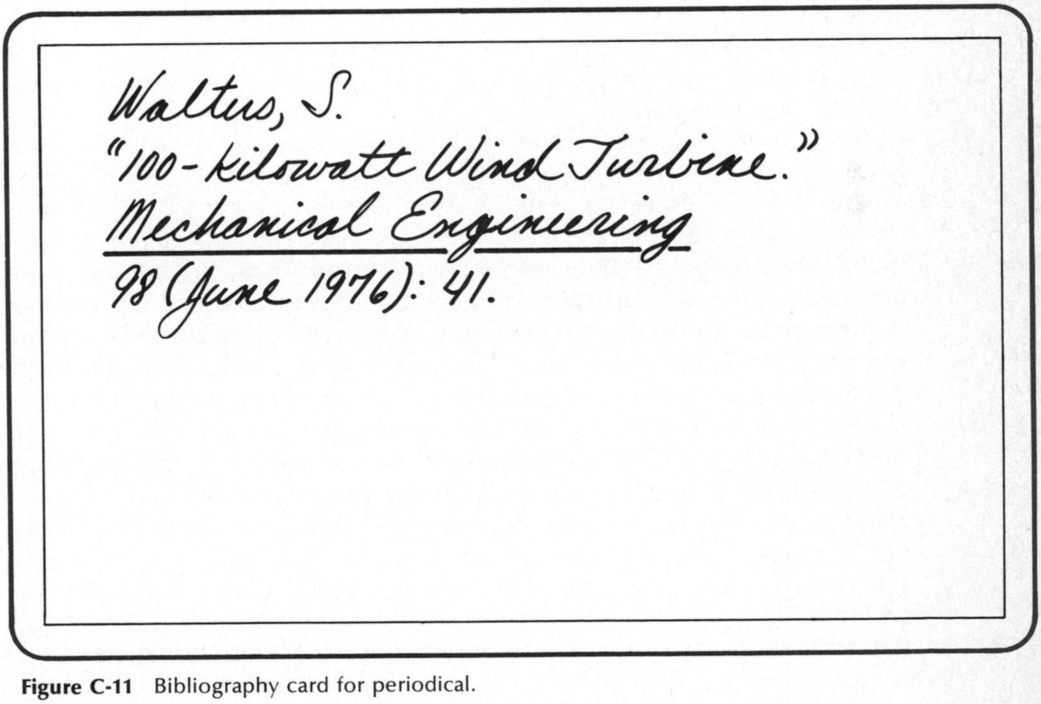

Walters, S.
"100-kilowatt Wind Turbine."
Mechanical Engineering
98 (June 1976): 41.

Figure C-11 Bibliography card for periodical.

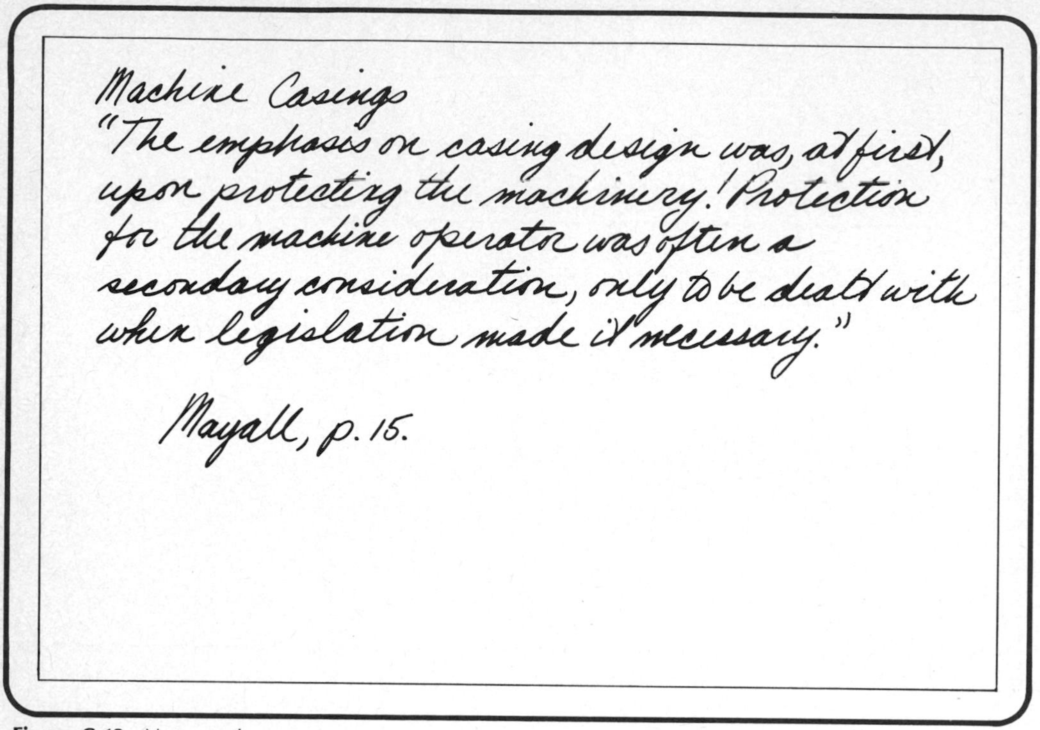

Machine Casings

"The emphasis on casing design was, at first, upon protecting the machinery! Protection for the machine operator was often a secondary consideration, only to be dealt with when legislation made it necessary."

Mayall, p. 15.

Figure C-12 Note card.

You should take three different kinds of notes—quotations, paraphrases, and summaries.

Quotations

Quotations are appropriate when you want to be sure not to misinterpret the author's opinions. They are fairly easy to do. Copy the passage word for word exactly as it's printed. Put quotation marks around the passage so there'll be no question in your mind later that the passage is a direct quotation. If you desire to omit part of the author's words, indicate the omitted part by ellipsis points (see Ellipsis Points entry in Writer's Guide, page 264). If you desire to insert some explanatory word or phrase of your own inside the quotation, indicate the insertion by putting it inside brackets (see Brackets entry in Writer's Guide, page 258). Figure C-13 shows an example of a clarifying statement inserted in brackets inside a quotation.

Paraphrases

Paraphrases are appropriate when you want to state facts taken from an author's writings. They require you to put the author's ideas in your own words, but they are also fairly easy to do. Just write *in your own words* what

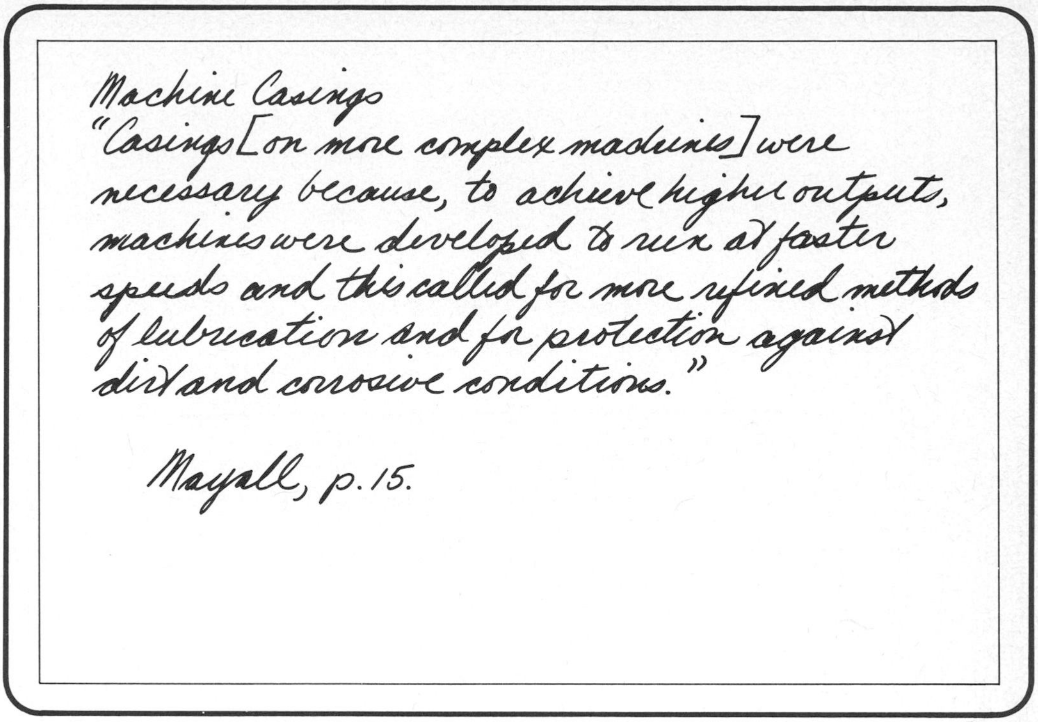

> *Machine Casings*
> "*Casings [on more complex machines] were necessary because, to achieve higher outputs, machines were developed to run at faster speeds and this called for more refined methods of lubrication and for protection against dirt and corrosive conditions.*"
>
> *Mayall, p. 15.*

Figure C-13 Quotation with bracketed statement.

the writer wrote in the original. Avoid merely substituting words. Try to rephrase the whole passage in your own expression.

Let's illustrate the paraphrasing of a passage. An original passage is shown in Figure C-14; a paraphrase in Figure C-15.

Notice two important features of this paraphrased note. First, the notetaker has rephrased the information of the original *to fit a particular need.* The original passage emphasizes the historical development of machines changing appearances as they become domesticated. The notetaker wants to retain only the idea that machines for the home are more esthetically shaped and ornamented than those for industry. Second, the notetaker has jotted a personal note below the paraphrased material as a reminder of examples as they must have popped into mind while reading and taking the note. This latter is an excellent practice to get into. If you don't write notes to yourself (bracket them to keep the notes separate from the paraphrased material), you run the risk of not being able to call back the ideas you had about a topic when you were working on it.

Summaries

Summaries consist of a few sentences in your own words to give the essence or major ideas of what you've read. Knowing how to paraphrase

Most early machines were built for working man, not for leisured man. If we compare them with, say, the architecture and furniture of the periods in which they were built, we can readily see one considerable difference. The machines lack the shapes and decorative devices which, in architecture and furniture, were applied to heighten visual appeal. But when some machines found their way into leisured environments they often acquired currently stylistic forms. Today some of us may find these forms faintly ludicrous, while others would regard them as appropriate on the grounds that any product must be related to its environment.

Figure C-14   Original passage. (W. H. Mayall, *Machines and Perception in Industrial Design;* © 1968 Litton Educational Publishing, Inc.; reprinted by permission of Van Nostrand Reinhold Company)

Influence of Environment on Machine Design
Although there may be little difference in operation and structure of a machine built for industry or the home, the machine built for the home is likely to become more esthetically shaped and ornamented.

[ex. sewing machines? lathes? food grinders? stoves?]

Mayall, p. 14.

Figure C-15   Paraphrase card.

also equips you to write summaries of longer passages—something you may want to do so you can jog your memory about research material or so you can provide your readers with a usable condensed version of a longer document. An original two-paragraph passage is shown in Figure C-16; a summary of the two paragraphs in Figure C-17.

As you can tell, the summary in this instance is similar to an extended paraphrase. When the original passage is lengthy, though, the summary

When we concentrate our attention on any particular object it is said to become "figural" while all surrounding features become "ground." Figure and ground effects are, of course, well understood in graphic design. Indeed much can be learned by studying graphic treatments to see how different features have been made figural according to the intentions of their designers. Perhaps the strongest cause for an object or a shape becoming figural depends upon whether it is regarded by the observer as meaning anything to him. In short we concentrate our attention upon what we want to see: which may be a fortunate tendency in some environments. Figural qualities also depend, however, upon the following additional factors:

degree of contrast between the perceived object and others, whether
   in terms of shape, tonal relationship or texture
relative sizes
degree of illumination

Generally speaking, a feature could be made figural if its shape and perhaps color and texture are made distinctly different from others in the visual scene. Larger relative size may help, and certainly the feature will be seen more clearly if the whole scene is well lit. All this may seem fairly obvious, but examine the dial gauge opposite. For the operator, the important features in this gauge are the scale and pointer together with an identification of what the gauge is measuring. Yet the most dominant element in the gauge is the central black circle surrounding the pointer mechanism. Almost certainly most observers will make this figural and so be distracted from what is really important. The modified gauge (below) shows how the scale and pointer have been made figural by making them more definite and by removing the black circle. The pointer, in particular, has been given greater significance by giving it a form more suited to its purpose; that is more meaning as a pointer. At the same time other distracting elements, such as the boundary lines about the scale markings, have been eliminated. We now have a gauge which is likely to be read more easily and probably more accurately.

Figure C-16 Original two-paragraph passage. (W. H. Mayall, *Machines and Perception in Industrial Design;* © 1968 Litton Educational Publishing, Inc.; reprinted by permission of Van Nostrand Reinhold Company)

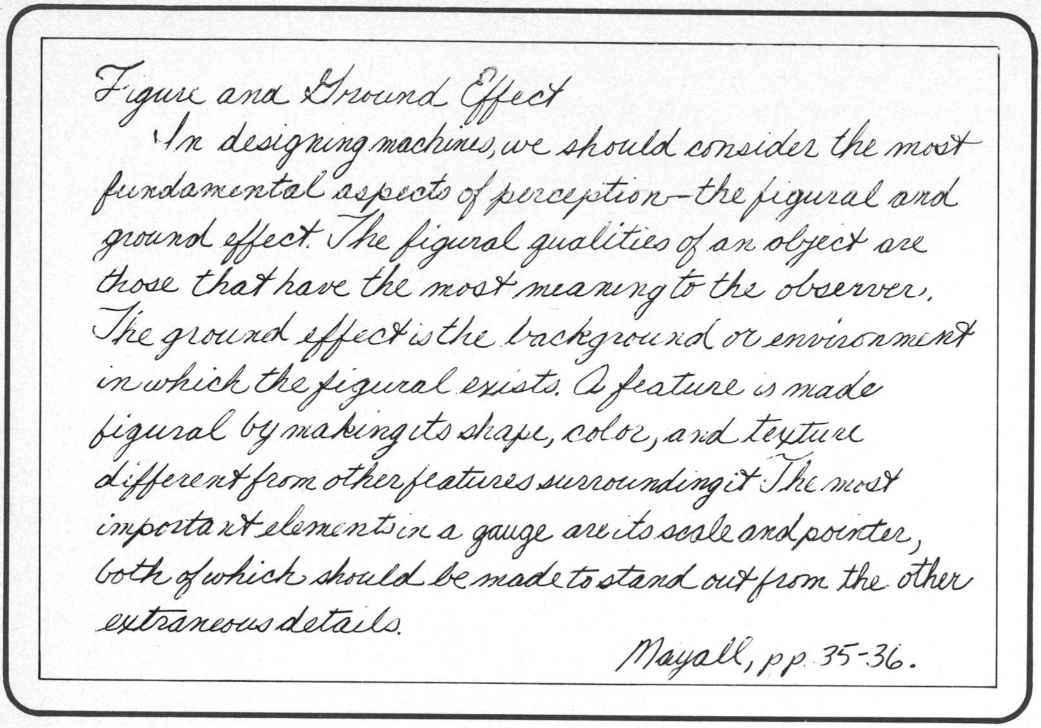

Figure and Ground Effect

In designing machines, we should consider the most fundamental aspects of perception—the figural and ground effect. The figural qualities of an object are those that have the most meaning to the observer. The ground effect is the background or environment in which the figural exists. A feature is made figural by making its shape, color, and texture different from other features surrounding it. The most important elements in a gauge are its scale and pointer, both of which should be made to stand out from the other extraneous details.

Mayall, pp. 35-36.

Figure C-17   Summary card.

becomes much shorter than a paraphrase, perhaps as short as one-fifth or less than the original. But the principle remains the same—get at the essential ideas, condense them, and put them in your own words.

Here are some tips on taking notes, regardless of whether they are in quotation, paraphrase, or summary form.

- Write down all the information you'll need , so you won't have to go back to the source.
- Write legibly so you can read your own handwriting. In paraphrasing or summarizing, don't use abbreviations and shorthand expressions that you won't understand later.
- Write one note to a card so you can rearrange them easily.
- Write on only one side of a card. If your note runs over to a second card, number the cards.
- Double-check to make sure you have included the page number(s) and author of the source the note comes from.

ANNEX D

Metric Conversion Tables

The metric system of measurement is used in virtually every country outside the United States and is increasingly used, especially in technical contexts, in the United States. In occupational research and writing it is often necessary, therefore, to be able to convert readily from the metric system to the U.S. system and vice versa. The following tables provide multipliers for converting both ways; the multipliers have been rounded to the third decimal place and thus yield an approximate equivalent.

Metric to U.S.			**U.S. to Metric**		
to convert from:	to:	multiply the metric unit by:	to convert from:	to:	multiply the U.S. unit by:
length					
kilometers (km)	miles	.621	miles	kilometers	1.609
meters (m)	yards	1.093	yards	meters	.914
meters	feet	3.280	feet	meters	.305
meters	inches	39.370	inches	meters	.025
centimeters (cm)	inches	.394	inches	centimeters	2.540
millimeters (mm)	inches	.039	inches	millimeters	25.400
area and volume					
square meters (m²)	square yards	1.196	square yards	square meters	.836
square meters	square feet	10.764	square feet	square meters	.093
square centimeters (cm²)	square inches	.155	square inches	square centimeters	6.451
cubic centimeters (cm³)	cubic inches	.061	cubic inches	cubic centimeters	16.387
liquid measure					
liters (L)	cubic inches	61.020	cubic inches	liters	.016
liters	cubic feet	.035	cubic feet	liters	28.339
liters	U.S. gallons*	.264	U.S. gallons*	liters	3.785
liters	U.S. quarts*	1.057	U.S. quarts*	liters	.946
milliliters (mL)	fluid ounces	.034	fluid ounces	milliliters	29.573
weight and mass					
kilograms (kg)	pounds	2.205	pounds	kilograms	.453
grams (g)	ounces	.035	ounces	grams	28.349
grams	grains	15.430	grains	grams	.065

*The British imperial gallon equals approximately 1.2 U.S. gallons or 4.54 liters. Similarly, the British imperial quart equals 1.2 U.S. quarts, and so on.

Selected Bibliography

The lists that follow are suggested for further reading on various areas of occupational writing. The lists, of course, do not include all the books devoted to a particular area of occupational writing, but they do include those books we think are particularly helpful to beginning occupational writers.

Business Letters and Reports

Adelstein, M. E. *Contemporary Business Writing.* New York: Random House, 1971.

Aurner, R. R., and M. P. Wolf. *Effective Communication in Business.* 5th ed. Cincinnati: South-Western, 1967.

Brown, L. *Effective Business Report Writing.* 3rd. ed. Englewood Cliffs, N.J.: Prentice-Hall, 1973.

Buckley, E. A. *How to Increase Sales with Letters.* New York: McGraw-Hill, 1961.

Caples, J. *Tested Advertising Methods.* New York: Harper & Row, 1947.

Flesch, R. *Rudolf Flesch on Business Communication.* New York: Barnes & Noble, 1974.

Himstreet, W. C., and W. M. Baty. *Business Communication.* 5th ed. San Francisco: Wadsworth, 1977.

Lesikar, R. V. *Report Writing for Business.* 3rd ed. Homewood, Ill.: Dow Jones–Irwin, 1969.

Lindauer, J. S. *Communicating in Business.* New York: Macmillan, 1974.

Norins, H. *The Compleat Copywriter.* New York: McGraw-Hill, 1966.

Sigband, N. B. *Communication for Management and Business.* 2nd ed. Glenview, Ill.: Scott, Foresman, 1976.

Schwab, V. O. *How to Write a Good Advertisement*. New York: Harper & Row, 1962.

Shurter, R. L. *Written Communication in Business*. 3rd ed. New York: McGraw-Hill, 1971.

Weisman, H. M. *Technical Correspondence*. New York: John Wiley, 1968.

Technical Writing

Effective Communication for Engineers. New York: McGraw-Hill, 1974.

Fear, D. E. *Technical Writing*. New York: Random House, 1973.

Houp, K., and T. Pearsall. *Reporting Technical Information*. 3rd ed. Beverly Hills, Calif.: Glencoe Press, 1977.

Jordan, S., J. M. Kleinman, and L. H. Shimberg, eds. *Handbook of Technical Writing Practices*. 2 vols. New York: Wiley-Interscience, 1971.

Mills, G., and J. Walter. *Technical Writing*. 4th ed. New York: Holt, Rinehart and Winston, 1978.

Mathes, J. C., and D. W. Stevenson. *Designing Technical Reports: Writing for Audiences in Organizations*. Indianapolis: Bobbs-Merrill, 1976.

Pauley, S. *Technical Report Writing Today*. Boston: Houghton Mifflin, 1973.

Pearsall, T. *Audience Analysis for Technical Writing*. Beverly Hills, Calif.: Glencoe Press, 1969.

Pickett, N. A., and A. A. Laster. *Technical English: Writing, Reading, and Speaking*. 2nd ed. San Francisco: Canfield Press, 1975.

Style and Usage

Brogan, J. L. *Clear Technical Writing*. New York: McGraw-Hill, 1973.

Brusaw, C. T., G. J. Alred, and W. E. Oliu. *Handbook of Technical Writing*. New York: St. Martin's Press, 1976.

Copperud, R. H. *A Dictionary of Usage and Style*. New York: Van Nostrand-Reinhold, 1970.

Flesch, R. *The ABC of Style—A Guide to Plain English*. New York: Harper & Row, 1964.

———. *The Art of Readable Writing*. New York: Collier Books, 1974.

Gunning, R. *The Technique of Clear Writing*. New York: McGraw-Hill, 1952.

MacLeish, A. *A Glossary of Grammar & Linguistics*. New York: Grosset & Dunlap, 1972.

A Manual of Style. 12th ed. Chicago: University of Chicago Press, 1969.

Newman, E. *Strictly Speaking*. Indianapolis: Bobbs-Merrill, 1974.

Perrin, P. G. *Writer's Guide and Index to English*. 5th ed. Chicago: Scott, Foresman, 1972.

Shaw, H. *Dictionary of Problem Words and Expressions*. New York: McGraw-Hill, 1975.

Strunk, W., and E. B. White. *The Elements of Style*. New York: Macmillan, 1972.

Business and Technical Speaking

Connolly, J. *Effective Technical Presentations*. St. Paul: 3M Business Press, 1968.

Howell, W. S., and E. G. Borman. *Presentational Speaking for Business and the Professions*. New York: Harper & Row, 1971.

Kindler, H. S. *Organizing the Technical Conference*. New York: Reinhold, 1960.

Mambert, W. A. *Presenting Technical Ideas: A Guide to Audience Communication.* New York: John Wiley, 1968.

Weiss, H., and J. B. McGrath, Jr. *Technically Speaking: Oral Communications for Engineers, Scientists, and Technical Personnel.* New York: McGraw-Hill, 1963.

Zelko, H. P., and F. E. X. Dance. *Business and Professional Speech Communication.* New York: Holt, Rinehart and Winston, 1965.

Graphics

Modley, R., and D. Lowenstein. *Pictographs and Graphs: How to Make and Use Them.* New York: Harper & Row, 1952.

Nelms, H. *Thinking with a Pencil.* New York: Barnes & Noble, 1964.

Pocket Pal: A Graphic Arts Production Handbook. 11th ed. New York: International Paper Company, 1974.

Index

Page numbers in italics refer to illustrations and examples.